PHILIP SCHUYLER AND THE AMERICAN REVOLUTION IN NEW YORK, 1733–1777

PHILIP SCHUYLER

and the

American Revolution in New York
1733–1777

by

Don R. Gerlach

UNIVERSITY OF NEBRASKA PRESS • LINCOLN
1964

Publishers on the Plains
UNP

The publication of this book was assisted by a grant from the Ford Foundation.

95049

MANUFACTURED IN THE UNITED STATES OF AMERICA

For the Memory of My Grandfather
Conrad Henry Gerlach
1873–1957

Table of Contents

List of Illustrations

List of Abbreviations

The following is a list of most frequently used abbreviations for sources cited in the footnotes:

British Public Record Office Papers

A.O.—Audit Office
C.O.—Colonial Office
S.P.—State Papers
T.—Treasury Papers
W.O.—War Office

NYHS................New-York Historical Society
NYPL................New York Public Library
NYSL ....New York State Library

Introduction

CONTEMPORARIES noted well the prominent position of General Philip Schuyler in early American society. Without having met him, the Duke de la Rochefoucauld-Liancourt indirectly learned in 1795 that Schuyler was a man of "much acuteness, and uncommon abilities." The general ranked among the "most considerable men in the United States." It was then common knowledge that because of their wealth and interests, the Schuylers and Rensselaers were families who merited high respect. Through intermarriage, the influence of the two houses was "altogether irresistible in the county." This royalist émigré, known for his philanthropy, model farming, and government service, wrote that the Schuylers were endowed with "more talents and knowledge," but that the Rensselaers possessed more riches, and money was "a powerful spring in the management of a state." [1] Talent and riches were an almost unbeatable combination—certainly the components of a powerful "interest."

Rochefoucauld-Liancourt had touched on significant points about Philip Schuyler—his personal talents, and the larger milieu—family influence and interest. How had he reached such a position? It could not be explained by birth and inheritance alone.

Another French nobleman and man of letters, the Marquis de Chastellux, who arrived in America as part of the French reinforcements under Rochambeau in 1780, perhaps offered an insight after a visit with the general in the winter of 1780–1781. "His fortune is very considerable," said the marquis; he predicted "it will become still more so, for he possesses an immense extent of territory, but deserves more credit from his talents and information than from his wealth." [2] As for talent and information, Schuyler was something of a son of the Enlightenment in the eyes of these French aristocrats. In 1782 the

[1] Joel Munsell (ed.), *The Annals of Albany* (10 vols.; Albany, 1850–1859), IV, 232–233. Hereafter cited as Munsell, *Annals*.

[2] Marquis de Chastellux, *Travels in North-America in the Years 1780, 1781, and 1782* (2 vols.; London, 1787), I, 375. Hereafter cited as Chastellux, *Travels*.

marquis flattered Schuyler further when he wrote the general that he hoped Americans would not look to the old maxims of the Greeks and Romans, but follow rather the wise counsels of Franklin, the Adamses —and the Schuylers! [3] The titled nobleman and the republican aristocrat doubtless understood each other admirably.

But what of all the years and labors behind such observations? What of Schuyler's labors to attain, maintain, and enhance the position the duke and the marquis described? What is the story of the most noteworthy scion of the Schuyler house? Is it not surprising that, if these assessments are accurate ones, Philip Schuyler has no biographer worthy of his importance?

This study is another step toward the completion of a needed biography of Philip Schuyler, for the second half of his life remains to be written. But more important, perhaps, an examination of this man offers a means by which the history of a particular era may be written with proper emphases on personal influences and on the importance of individuals. Schuyler's life cannot be told apart from the political history of New York province, for his significance lies in the very nature of eighteenth-century politics—in the power struggle of individuals and small groups of partisans. His story is, therefore, an approach to a better understanding of what the American Revolution was, at least in the colony of New York and with particular regard to one man's role in it.

An additional reason for investigating the life of Philip Schuyler (1733–1804) is the inadequate treatment hitherto accorded him. Schuyler has had two biographers, Benson J. Lossing and Bayard Tuckerman, in addition to one family genealogist, George W. Schuyler.[4] The genealogist evidently based much of his work on that of Lossing. Both Lossing and Tuckerman concentrated upon Schuyler's military career and his "times," leaving other, and perhaps more important, aspects of his life largely untouched. Neither examined his economic and political interests in detail or depth, nor did they really measure his relative merit within the whole framework of the late

    [3] Chastellux to Schuyler, Feb. 18, 1782. Index to the Schuyler Letters, I, 58. New York Public Library, Schuyler Papers.
    [4] Benson J. Lossing, *The Life and Times of Philip Schuyler* (2 vols.; New York, 1872). Hereafter cited as Lossing. Bayard Tuckerman, *Life of General Philip Schuyler, 1733–1804* (New York, 1903). Hereafter cited as Tuckerman. George W. Schuyler, *Colonial New York: Philip Schuyler and His Family* (2 vols.; New York, 1885). Hereafter cited as Schuyler, *Colonial New York*.

colonial period and the rise of New York State and the new republic. Lossing and Tuckerman did not appreciate the personal character of provincial politics as an explanation of the Revolution. Lossing's work is the more substantial, but like that by Tuckerman, it hardly meets modern standards of scholarship in footnoting, bibliography or, most important of all, balance. Both authors claimed access to the pertinent manuscripts; indeed, Lossing presents material from some sources which now appear to be missing from the manuscript collections, but neither took the trouble to offer documentation. And they made errors largely by trusting family legends or failing to examine all the scraps of evidence and by allowing their imaginations to explain things as though they had been documented. Their work generally suffers from a lack of proportion and from that malady shared by so many romantics given to fanciful imaginations—panegyric.

Philip Schuyler may have made his fame—to some of his contemporaries, notoriety—by military service in the War of Independence. But because he participated in other events and exerted influence in other matters, his political activities deserve fuller inquiry. It is also important to recognize that "The study of individual men reveals the complexity of motive in political behaviour which the broad study of political history tends to obliterate." [5] Hence, Schuyler's activities are interesting for the student of early American history because they explain the complex, personal nature of British and colonial politics— the personal impact of individuals on national life. Much of the evidence of the man's career must be gleaned from official, political records, especially the journals of the provincial assembly. And for that reason, too, his biography is largely political history.

It is evident that much of what Sir Lewis Namier described in his studies of England during the reign of George III is applicable to colonial politics. And the biographical technique which Namier used, when applied to colonial New York, is especially useful for exploring "a particular field of political or social history." [6] Often, as Namier said, "small men did things both infinitely smaller and infinitely greater than they knew." Another recent historian has emphasized the value of examining the activities of individuals; Esmond Wright remarks, "Revolutions, like other human phenomena, are caused by

[5] J. H. Plumb, "The Interaction of History and Biography," *The* (London) *Times Literary Supplement* (Jan. 6, 1956), p. xxi.
[6] *Ibid.*

decisions taken—or not taken—by individuals." [7] These doings cannot be discounted. What, after all, made a patriot, especially a conservative one? What specifically were the bases of Schuyler's prestige and "interest" that led the Second Continental Congress to select him as one of its four major-generals under Washington? How did a man of property and ambition get caught up in the Revolution which John Adams insisted took place in the minds and hearts of Americans before the clash of arms—a movement so fraught with dangers for men with heavy stakes in society?

This study is meant to narrate and explain Philip Schuyler's career up through the days of 1777 when the colony in whose economy and politics he was so involved framed its constitution as an independent and sovereign state. It is also a study of provincial politics and of one man who entered the "storms of public life," as he called them, rather late in the colonial era. It is a means whereby several theses about the American Revolution may be examined. Carl Becker has raised one point of controversy, and E. Wilder Spaulding has pointed to another. Becker maintained that two questions dominated the years 1765–1776 and determined party history in New York: "whether essential colonial rights should be maintained [and] . . . by whom and by what methods they should be maintained. The first was the question of home rule; the second was the question . . . of who should rule at home." [8] What can the life of Philip Schuyler show about this thesis, or about the suggestion of another scholar who commented on him more directly? Spaulding maintained that Schuyler, "always politically ambitious, fought the privileged group which neglected him." [9]

Can the American Revolution in New York have been largely a contest of rival groups, of Livingstons and De Lanceys, agrarians and mercantile interests, competing for favor and power—for the power to rule at home? Was the struggle one of the "lesser orders" against a privileged squirearchy, commonly called an aristocracy? Was Schuyler indeed neglected, and was he excluded from the privileged group or simply dissatisfied with what he shared? Certainly, Becker's question of who should rule at home did not involve a struggle for democracy

---

[7] L. B. Namier, *England in the Age of the American Revolution* (London, 1930), p. 149. Esmond Wright, *Fabric of Freedom, 1763–1800* (New York, 1961), p. 104.

[8] Carl Lotus Becker, *The History of Political Parties in the Province of New York, 1760–1776* (Madison, 1960), p. 22. Hereafter cited as Becker, *Political Parties.*

[9] E. Wilder Spaulding, *His Excellency George Clinton: Critic of the Constitution* (New York, 1938), p. 26. Hereafter cited as Spaulding, *George Clinton.*

as much as an intraclass wrangle among "aristocrats." And whereas Spaulding hit upon a key to the problem, Philip Schuyler was not totally neglected.

As a member of the ruling class, Schuyler is of special interest for what his life can tell us about the political history of his age. Although he was no democrat, he fought members of his own class for the varied privileges of power. Aristocratic as he was in temperament, breeding, and accomplishment, his family's origins had been humble. Indeed the entire New York aristocracy was a clique of parvenus. The first Schuylers in America were sons of an Amsterdam baker.[10] Subsequent generations acquired the aura of gentility by "ancient riches"—means accumulated by their forebears—and by building a tradition of social prominence, government service, and influence with the Indians. Schuyler was born near the top of the social pyramid of his day, but he was not content to rest at an inherited position. When, at the close of the Revolutionary War, the general described himself as a member of the "middling Class [of] Men of considerable property," he was being both accurate and modest.[11] However, he played an important, if at first reluctant, role in colonial politics and later, in the national era, in Federalist politics. His activities helped make possible the accomplishments of leaders even more renowned for their talents and achievements. Schuyler also represented the "inborn capacity" of the lower classes "for producing within themselves new elements . . . to rule them wisely." [12] And yet at the pinnacle of his position the squire of Saratoga was wary and critical of those "lower orders" from which his own family had gradually emerged.

Philip Schuyler deserves more attention than he has hitherto received because he was a member of the numerous class of relatively quiet but efficient men whose influence and labors are often relegated to obscurity, whose activities touched contemporary life at many points, and who made substantial contributions to the direction of larger affairs. He was a landowner, politician, speculator, financier, and general for a "rabble in arms," a canal promoter and humanitarian. He was an idealist as well as a hardheaded partisan, ambitious and proud to the point of vanity, but generous and hospitable, as

---

[10] John Ross Delafield, "An Armory of American Families of Dutch Descent," *New York Genealogical and Biographical Record,* LXIX (Jan., 1938), 20.

[11] Schuyler to —— (copy), Mar. 11, 1780. C.O. 5/1110:203–205.

[12] Gaetano Mosca, *The Ruling Class,* ed. Arthur Livingston, trans. Hannah D. Kahn (New York and London, 1939), p. 337.

polished as a frontier aristocrat in the age of Enlightenment could be, and as versatile, if not as accomplished, as many of his contemporaries of greater fame.

Following the nadir of his career, marked as it was by financial losses, military and political reverses, and serious questions of his loyalty to the patriot cause in 1777, Schuyler re-entered public life, notwithstanding his threat that he could no longer tolerate the vagaries of politics. Late in 1779, after a court-martial had acquitted him with the highest honor from charges of negligence in the loss of Fort Ticonderoga, he appeared in Congress as a delegate from New York. He was sent to Washington's headquarters to consult with the commander in chief on the state of the Southern Department. He attended Congress again in 1780, and was made chairman of a committee sent to confer with Washington on the reorganization of the staff departments and about devising a scheme for cooperating with the coming French reinforcements. The committee did not have the powers Washington thought the circumstances required. It did, however, manage to exert a measure of authority for raising supplies and recruiting an army. Washington testified both to Schuyler's energetic leadership and his committee's usefulness, but in August, Congress recalled the committee after it had irritated a good many of the members. Schuyler never set foot in the Congress again, although from his position in the New York Senate he advocated the augmentation of Congress's powers, and although he was named a delegate again in October, 1781.

When he entered the New York Senate in 1780, Schuyler became a strong champion of a national government more adequately endowed with centralized powers. Although there can be little doubt that his son-in-law, Alexander Hamilton, exerted no small influence on him in these matters, it is more probable that Schuyler became a Federalist because of his natural temperament and because his years of experience in the army, in Congress, and in state government during the critical decade of the 1780's showed him the weaknesses and dangers of a system of loose confederation.

During the 1780's, Philip Schuyler's political efforts were concentrated within New York. From his place in the state senate he continued to advocate a reformation of the Articles of Confederation—an endeavor that led him most naturally into the mainstream of nationalism and Federalist politics. Upon taking his seat in Congress in March, 1780, he had presented an act of the New York Legislature designed to "facilitate the completion of the Confederation"—a proposal by New York to cede its western lands for the support of the central government.[13] That autumn the New York Legislature sent him to a convention at Hartford which was called to consider ways of strengthening the powers of Congress. Schuyler firmly favored such steps, but the convention failed to give "vigor to the governing powers equal" to the current crisis.[14] It was in 1780, too, that Alexander Hamilton renewed a suggestion made earlier for a convention to frame a more effective instrument of national government.

Schuyler's involvement in state politics grew as the years passed. Governor George Clinton named him the state surveyor general in March, 1781. He served for three years. In 1783 he was a candidate for governor; he was once more badly beaten by Clinton as he had been in 1777. In 1783–1784, Schuyler served as a commissioner for the final settlement of New York's disputed boundary with Massachusetts, a post in which he had shown an interest as a colonist in 1764–1767. From 1785 to 1787 he also participated in negotiations for settling the New York–Pennsylvania boundary. His work as Indian commissioner for Congress and the state government was but another facet of a multi-sided career.

From his seat in the state senate Schuyler moved to the New York Council of Appointment in 1786 and 1788. This body shared the governor's appointive functions. After the Federalists came to power, the general served two annual terms in 1790 and 1794 on the council— then a partisan instrument for curbing the powers of an anti-Federalist governor. In 1787 he was named to the Board of Regents of the State University, and this post he held until his death in 1804. From the state senate, of which he was continuously a member from September, 1780, until May, 1784, and again from January, 1786, until July, 1789, he moved into the first United States Senate. And from January, 1792, until April, 1797, he once more enjoyed the status of a state senator.

A champion of the United States Constitution, Schuyler was Alexander Hamilton's most ardent supporter in the United States Senate, where he urged the adoption of his son-in-law's fiscal program for the infant republic. Using his experience from participating in the deliberations of Congress on the paper currency problem in 1779 and 1780, Schuyler contributed to the development of Hamilton's

[13] Alexander C. Flick (ed.), *History of the State of New York* (10 vols.; New York, 1933–1937), III, 310. Hereafter cited as Flick.

[14] Edgar A. Werner, *Civil List and Constitutional History of the Colony and State of New York* (Albany, 1884), p. 121. See also Flick, III, 316.

theories and plans for national finance and credit. However, the fact that the general's interest in these matters preceded his acquaintance-ship and then intimate relationship with Hamilton (who married Schuyler's daughter, Elizabeth, in December, 1780), does not neces-sarily mean that Hamilton had no similar interests, abilities, or in-dependent thoughts before his connection with his father-in-law.

The final decade of Schuyler's life was filled with a fourfold activ-ity: he was a politician, state senator, and partisan Federalist; he continued to play the roles of landlord, humanitarian, and canal pro-moter. His humanitarian activities centered on the reform of the state penal code and the construction of the New York prison with an eye to rehabilitation instead of mere punishment. Schuyler's leadership in the Western and Northern Inland Lock and Navigation Companies formed the basis of New York canal legislation and of the construction of an inland lock system that was the forerunner of the great Erie Canal. In all these endeavors, as well as in his participation in the New York Society for the Promotion of Agriculture, Arts and Manu-factures, Philip Schuyler acted as a real son of the Enlightenment.

Much remains to be studied and written of Philip Schuyler. Scholars have left his career after 1777 largely unexamined and unsung except in a most general and cursory way. He deserves closer scrutiny. His portrait still awaits completion. But when the last brush strokes are made, we shall see the picture of a life as much the revelation of an age as of Philip Schuyler himself.

Robert Livingston Schuyler once cited the need for a full-length biography of his illustrious kinsman—a work that would tell the whole story of family economy, provincial politics, wartime activities, per-sonal jealousies and intrigues, military insubordination, self-seeking, disregard for public welfare, revolutionary ardor and idealism, ill will between Yankee and Yorker, government weaknesses, Federalist maneuvers, Indian affairs and canal-building, a host of details and a multitude of varying interests. But he said such a biography was "not a work to be entered upon with a light heart by some budding Boswell or Plutarch in one of our universities, in search of the degree of doctor of philosophy in history." [15] That is precisely why this is but a part of such a biography—a biography which is an ap-proach to political history. It will, as Professor Schuyler said, require long immersion in historical sources as well as insight to complete the

[15] Robert Livingston Schuyler, "Philip Schuyler," *New York History*, XVIII (April, 1937), 131.

work. New York politics in the 1780's and in the Federalist era are not uncomplicated because they are so personal. Victor Paltsits, chief of the American History Division of the New York Public Library, once said he thought it would take ten years to write Schuyler's life, if one had nothing else to do! [16] Perhaps this explains why Schuyler has had no biographer worthy of him. The advice Shakespeare had for murderers will not do for Philip Schuyler's Boswell: "If it were done when 'tis done, then 'twere well/ It were done quickly." [17]

[16] *Ibid.*, p. 132.
[17] *Macbeth,* Act I, sc. 7, l. 1.

CHAPTER I

The Formative Years

-1-

"GENTILITY IS NOTHING BUT ANCIENT RICHES"
—George Herbert

PHILIP JOHN SCHUYLER was born in his father's house on the southeast corner of Pearl and State streets at Albany, New York, on November 10, 1733.[1] The household was still as Dutch as the gabled roof that covered it, for Albany was only as English as the garrison housed in the stockade half a mile up the street. Next door stood his grandfather's dwelling. The two houses faced the broad market street flanked by the Dutch and English churches—a fitting symbol of a life Schuyler lived in a society successively Dutch, English, and American. As was the custom of the day, Philip was christened with an ancestral name, although he later assumed two of them. Death had but shortly before deprived his parents of a son also given the name Philip, but John and Cornelia Schuyler were not daunted by the threat of high infant mortality, nor did they waver in their determination to have a male heir to bear the name of the progenitor of the Schuyler family in the new world. Sorrowed by the death of the earlier Philip, they were in this son to rear the greatest scion of their house. Although a younger son, he rose to the senior position by the death of four brothers. The day following his birth he was given the sacrament of baptism.[2]

[1] The date has been erroneously reported in a number of places as Nov. 11/22. The Old Style entry in the family Bible, now at the Schuyler mansion in Albany reads: "In het Jaar 1733 Den 10 Nove: is geboren onse Vyfde Soon Genamt Phillip." The New Style would be Nov. 21. As to the name "Philip John," the family Bible does not record a second name at the birth entry, but Schuyler's own marriage entry reads, "Ick, Philip Johannis Schuyler."

[2] Schuyler, *Colonial New York*, II, 242. The first son named Philip was baptized on Oct. 17, 1731, and "died young." See also the family Bible. Contrary to what Lossing, I, 26, says of his baptism on the day of his birth, which he gives as Nov. 20, is: *Year Book of the Holland Society of New York, 1906* (New York, 1908), p. 51: Baptismal

1

Prominent Dutch lineage—the prestige that can come only from long established family roots—was the base of young Schuyler's display of pride, an arrogancy not without a touch of vanity, but also the wellspring of ambition. And from all his known activities we can only deduce that it was ambition without reserve that drove him to raise the paternal name to its highest renown. For his enemies he gained little else but sharp notoriety. Schuyler was to find that his ancestry and rearing had their drawbacks as well as their advantages. To New Englanders they could be but special stigmas, for Yankees disliked and distrusted their Dutch neighbors in general and Philip Schuyler personally. In the New Hampshire Grants controversy, his breeding, his bearing, and his partisan interests were special objects for their scorn and vituperations.

But in New York the Schuylers' name was much hallowed by time, wealth, and service. The family had been almost systematically allied with other leading families of the province, who though once parvenus were soon established as a local squirearchy—commonly called an aristocracy—the Van Rensselaers, Livingstons, and Van Cortlandts. Philip's grandfather was mayor of Albany and also sat in the assembly. A great-uncle, Peter, had been given the first royal appointment as mayor, had sat in the governor's council, and even acted as governor between changes of administrations. All the Schuylers were active in Indian affairs. Philip's father and grandfather both served as Indian commissioners. Peter Schuyler earned such prominence in these dealings that he is said to have been offered a knighthood by Queen Anne when he presented several Mohawk chieftains at her court—a trip aimed at dramatizing the need for British action against the French in Canada. Not until Sir William Johnson became imperial superintendent of Indian affairs did the Schuylers have a real rival in this field. And they had buttressed their reputation with substantial holdings of real estate, the accepted way to wealth and position in an agrarian society.[3] Nor was their practical knowledge of winning social

---

"Records of the R. D. Church of Albany," 1725–1750, which gives Nov. 11 as the date of baptism and the family Bible which gives Nov. 10 as the date of birth. Both dates are of course Old Style. Old Style dates included in this study have not been converted to New Style.

[3] Ruth L. Higgins, *Expansion in New York* (Columbus, 1931), pp. 10, 22–26, 52–54, 58, 61. See also David Maldwyn Ellis, *Landlords and Farmers in the Hudson-Mohawk Region, 1790–1850* (Ithaca, 1946), p. 41; hereafter cited as Ellis, *Landlords and*

and political status anything but compatible with their attitude and activities in the operations of storehouse and countinghouse.

The Schuyler family was established in New Netherland about the year 1650, when two brothers emigrated from Amsterdam. Soon after their arrival, Philip Pietersen Schuyler firmly set in roots by marrying the daughter of the resident director of Rensselaerwyck, Brant Arentse Van Slechtenhorst. His brother, David Pietersen Schuyler, founded a lesser branch of the family. Philip Pietersen Schuyler (1628–1683) and Margaretta Van Slechtenhorst (1628–1711) promptly set about establishing the family in progeny and substance. They produced ten children, six sons and four daughters. Their ninth child was Johannes (1668–1747), the father of John, Jr., (1697–1741) and the grandfather of Major-General Philip John Schuyler (1733–1804).[4]

The Schuylers admirably demonstrated the ways of the provincial aristocracy: its modest beginnings and its pretensions to wealth, influence, and power. They, the Van Rensselaers, and the Van Cortlandts were "three of the greatest families in the province, whose influence—so harsh and yet so drowsy, so acquisitive and so backward—extended to every corner of it."[5] The ambition for place and power was an early characteristic of the Schuylers. When the Dutch church was built at Albany, the wealthier members of the congregation set armorial bearings in the windows. His unpretentious origins as the son of an Amsterdam baker did not prevent Philip Pietersen Schuyler from joining in the practice. His window was inscribed with his name

---

Farmers. For a discussion of the Schuylers in Indian affairs see Richmond P. Bond, *Queen Anne's American Kings* (Oxford, 1952), pp. 1–33. The account of the proffered knighthood is not well substantiated.

[4] The following sources contain records of the family's origins: George Rogers Howell, *The Origin and Meaning of English and Dutch Surnames of New York State Families* (Albany, 1894), pp. 5, 8; Cuyler Reynolds (ed.), *Hudson-Mohawk Genealogical and Family Memoirs* (4 vols.; New York, 1911), I, 28, *passim;* John Ross Delafield, "An Armory of American Families of Dutch Descent," *New York Genealogical and Biographical Record*, LXIX (Jan., 1938), 19–22; Edmund Burke O'Callaghan and Berthold Fernow (eds.), *Documents Relative to the Colonial History of the State of New York* (15 vols.; Albany, 1853–1887), IV, 406: hereafter cited as *Docs. Rel. Col. Hist. N.Y.;* Montgomery Schuyler, *The Patroons and Lords of Manors of the Hudson,* Order of Colonial Lords of Manors in America Publication No. 23 (New York, 1932), p. 12.

[5] George Dangerfield, *Chancellor Robert R. Livingston of New York, 1746–1813* (New York, 1960), p. 9. Hereafter cited as Dangerfield, *Livingston.*

and title, "Commissaris 1656," for the magistracy was his only real claim to prominence aside from being a well-to-do merchant with considerable capital or credit and great expectations.[6]

Philip Schuyler the Founder built a relatively modest landed estate. In fact, compared with some of the larger grants made in the colony, his holdings were trifling. Apparently his interests were almost wholly mercantile, not agrarian,[7] and these seemed appropriate enough for a son of the Netherlands. But his descendants combined these interests with greater zeal and expanded them generation by generation. At the same time each generation brought a relatively equal division of estates among the heirs, for the Schuylers, like many of their fellows, did not wholly espouse the English practices of entail and primogeniture or the strict family settlement. And as land was more easily available in the new world and also cheaper, it was not necessary to concentrate the holdings of the family to insure the maintenance or growth of its influence. Indeed, the constant subdivisions apparently encouraged each generation to rely on its own ambition and talents, thus breeding a kind of energy and acquisitiveness that prevailed even in Major-General Philip Schuyler.[8]

The second generation of Schuylers in America proceeded to establish a practice that followed quite naturally for years to come. They began the interlocking combination of family, economic, and agrarian interests that was the particular hallmark of eighteenth-century New York politics.[9] The system was based on common interest in wealth and on principle; it was further linked by ties of marriage. Other precedents were set: the large family, participation in business and public service, acquisition of land in piecemeal fashion rather than in single, large, undivided tracts, and the rather equalitarian division of estates [10] that prevented any one part of the Schuyler clan from

6 Schuyler, *Colonial New York*, I, 109–112.

7 "Abstracts of New York Land Grants, 1666–1764." C.O. 5/1134:1–3, 5, 14, 35. For a review of the land acquisitions of three generations of Schuylers, see Appendix B.

8 Charles Edward Ironside, *The Family in Colonial New York* (New York, 1942), p. 73; Schuyler, *Colonial New York*, I, 159, 162–166; Berthold Fernow (comp. & ed.), *Calendar of Wills on File and Recorded in the Offices of the Clerk of the Court of Appeals, of the County Clerk at Albany, and of the Secretary of State* (New York, 1896), p. 336.

9 Schuyler, *Colonial New York*, I, 185.

10 See, for example, *Collections of the New-York Historical Society for 1894* (New York, 1895), XXVII: Abstracts of Wills, III, 387. The large number of recorded wills testifies to the practice of New Yorkers avoiding the operation of entail and primo-

perpetuating a position as manorial lord at the expense of others. As property was subdivided, each generation was obliged to create its own lordly position, having a relatively limited base on which to build by reason of more moderate inheritances than primogeniture and entail would have permitted. And the junior branches of the family were to produce more energy and more ambition, a hardier kind of shoot from which Philip Schuyler, the general, was to inherit his vigor and will to succeed.

Captain Johannes Schuyler (1668–1747) of the clan's second generation in America vigorously participated in provincial politics and set about accumulating lands. It is certain that he outstripped both his father and son in both kinds of endeavor. Besides being mayor of Albany and a militia officer, he was an Indian commissioner, alderman, assemblyman, and deacon and elder in the Dutch church. He was an Indian trader and merchant.[11] He acquired a portion of the Saratoga Patent, which formed the nucleus of all his other speculative holdings and which was the central portion of his more famous grandson, Philip's, estate. His share in the Saratoga Patent amounted to more than 24,000 acres. He acquired 2,000 acres in the Schoharie valley, about 1,700 acres east of Schenectady, 1,000 acres on Tomlenack Creek, east of the Hudson, not to mention over 1,000 acres in Ulster County, over 1,000 acres on "Quasick Brook," and 2,000 acres north of the "Maquas" or Mohawk River.[12] The Saratoga lands were the heart of the estate, and it was there that he began to develop his holdings by erecting a sawmill and gristmill, laying out farms, and

---

geniture. Cf. Irving Mark, *Agrarian Conflicts in Colonial New York, 1711–1775* (New York, 1940), pp. 83–84, insists that equal division of estates was the exception rather than the rule.

[11] Edmund B. O'Callaghan (abstractor), *Calendar of New York Colonial Commissions, 1680–1770* (New York, 1929), pp. 10, 12, 16, 21, 23, 25; Cuyler Reynolds, *op. cit.,* I, 30; Schuyler, *Colonial New York,* II, 95–107, 223, 237; Edgar A. Werner, *Civil List and Constitutional History of the Colony and State of New York* (Albany, 1884), p. 307. Hereafter cited as Werner, *Civil List,* with the edition of 1884 or 1888 indicated in parentheses; Munsell, *Annals,* III, 2, 17, 22, 24, 36, 37 ff; Joel Munsell, *Collections on the History of Albany from its Discovery to the Present Time* (4 vols.; Albany, 1865–1871), I, 53–54, 59–60, 78: hereafter cited as Munsell, *Collections;* see also *Docs. Rel. Col. Hist. N.Y.,* V, 76, *passim,* for Indian dealings.

[12] C.O. 5/1134:51, 53, 55, 56, 61, 76, 87. See also *Calendar of N.Y. Colonial Manuscripts indorsed Land Papers in the Office of the Secretary of State of New York, 1643–1803* (Albany, 1864), pp. 122, 133, 193–194, 202, 217, 229–230. Cf. Schuyler, *Colonial New York,* II, 240–241.

exploiting the pine forests. It was the beginning of an economy his grandson Philip was to develop so extensively and so profitably.

John Schuyler, Jr., (1697–1741) was apparently propelled by the vigor of his father, for he followed the family commercial business, joined his senior on the Board of Indian Commissioners, served as an alderman in Albany, and endeavored to add a few thousand acres of land to the family holdings. Perhaps his most significant contribution to the family fortunes was his marriage to Cornelia Van Cortlandt, daughter and heiress of Stephen, first lord of the manor of Cortlandt. Few of his accomplishments in the Indian trade or otherwise are recorded; he assumed the life of a merchant in 1733, when he was a commissioner to furnish supplies to the forts at Oswego. Thomas Jones says of him only that he had "but little personal estate, embarked in trade in Albany, and sold provisions." [13]

– 2 –

"A CARELESS GOOD HUMORED YOUNG MAN"

OF PHILIP SCHUYLER's life from his birth until his second decade almost nothing is known. His father's death deprived him of male tutelage at an early age, and his rearing fell largely into the hands of two matrons, his mother and his aunt Margaretta, his father's sister. There is no record that the stripling was much influenced by his doughty grandfather. Doubtless the old man had something to say about the lad's upbringing, and certainly he stood as a living reminder of the success to which any Schuyler might aspire. For the son of a respectable family who would be thrown largely upon his own resources, a sound education was of the utmost importance.

The great Chancellor Kent, speaking from his recollections of Schuyler in his declining years, offered a clue about his training, his formal education, and his character formation. "The characteristic of

[13] Thomas Jones, *History of New York During the Revolutionary War,* ed. Edward Floyd De Lancey (2 vols.; New York, 1879), II, 315. Hereafter cited as Jones, *History of New York.* See also Schuyler, *Colonial New York,* II, 246–247; O'Callaghan, *Calendar of New York Colonial Commissions,* pp. 23, 25; *Docs. Rel. Col. Hist. N.Y.* makes no mention of John Schuyler, Jr. Even Anne Grant, *Memoirs of an American Lady* (2 vols.; New York, 1901) only mentions him in passing; hereafter cited as Anne Grant, *Memoirs.* Munsell, *Annals,* VIII, 39; X, 65, 85, 89, 93. For evidence of the Schuylers' business in supplying the troops and materials for fortifications see New York (state), *The Colonial Laws of New York From the Year 1664 to the Revolution* (5 vols.; Albany, 1894), II, 798, 908; III, 108, 804.

all his measures," said Kent, "was utility. They bore the stamp and unerring precision of practical science. There was nothing complicated in his character. It was chaste and severe simplicity; and take him for all in all, he was one of the wisest and most efficient men, both in military and civil life, that the state or the nation has produced. . . . His spirits were cheerful, his conversation most eminently instructive, his manners gentle and courteous, and his whole deportment tempered with grace and dignity." Even in his old age Schuyler's "faculties seemed to retain their unimpaired vigour and untiring activity; though he had evidently lost some of his constitutional ardour of temperament and vehemence of feeling." [14] Utility—practical science—simplicity—ardor—vehement feeling, stamped Philip Schuyler's character and behavior from the beginning.

There had been a school in Albany as early as 1650 when the founder of the Schuyler family established himself in Beverwyck, successively known as Fort Orange and Albany. In 1744 it had two hundred scholars.[15] Doubtless, young Philip Schuyler, then eleven, first used his hornbook here. But there was other schooling too. His home, dominated by his mother, was a secure one, and he was reared in a setting marked by frankness, sobriety, rectitude, and generosity. Cornelia Schuyler, it was said, was an indulgent mother but a firm disciplinarian. But a widow with five children had no light task if she soberly assumed the serious responsibility of both father and mother.[16]

Schuyler was almost eight when his father died. For seven years he was schooled at home. In his early teens he witnessed the dangers of a frontier exposed to Indian marauders, for the third of the great wars for empire between France and Britain caught the people of Albany between the two foes. Albany was a key to the Hudson valley, in certain danger from the French until the war effort was focused on the expedition against Louisbourg. Even then, the frontier did not escape the depredations of raiding parties which forayed within thirty miles of the Schuyler home. One of these raids was made against Saratoga,

[14] James Kent, "An Anniversary Discourse Delivered Before the New-York Historical Society, December 6, 1828" (New York, 1829), pp. 37, 39.

[15] Flick, III, 71.

[16] Lossing, I, 46–47. Although the Schuylers had eleven children, only five survived childhood. They were Gertrude, John, Philip, Cortlandt, and Stephen. John, the eldest surviving son, died in 1746, thus leaving Philip the senior except for his sister, Gertrude. Schuyler, *Colonial New York*, II, 242.

where the boy's uncle, whose Christian name he shared, was murdered late in November, 1745. Next year New York bestirred itself. Block-houses were erected and militia garrisons established north and west of Albany. In July, 1746, Governor Clinton himself went up to Albany to oversee preparations and assist in negotiations with the Indians. But no further hostilities of importance troubled the province, and early in 1748 a tenuous peace was signed at Aix-la-Chapelle.[17]

Philip Schuyler thus grew to manhood in an atmosphere tinged with the martial spirit, an ever-present uncertainty and danger that only an outpost of empire could know. However lightly it may have touched a mere lad, he could not escape it. And the thrill of danger did leave its mark. When he was not yet twenty Schuyler was anxious to be off to war as if it were but a youthful lark.[18] And yet his serious mind could not have failed to grasp the import of battle, although he had yet to discover how disagreeable military life could be. To learn that lesson he had to wait two decades, when in the midst of a war for independence he found that power and all its galling re-sponsibilities could be a bitter draught.

For all the attractions military life may have had for a lad, and for all the need for training in the arts of defense, Schuyler was not schooled for war. He had been given an education best befitting a merchant's son—training altogether appropriate for a Dutchman and a Schuyler. Had not his father, grandfather, and great-grandfather all been traders? Were not the sober realities of making a livelihood quite as weighty to the Dutch mind as the temptations of enhancing the family's status? Indeed, it was difficult to separate one from the other. And among these colonial squires there was no strong prejudice against trade. Hence, Philip Schuyler progressed from Albany's ele-mentary school to the hands of a Huguenot tutor at New Rochelle in impeccably conservative Westchester County. His education was a combination of practical training, academics, and tutelage in the social arts.

The Reverend Peter Stouppe, minister of the French Protestant church at New Rochelle, supplemented his income by tutoring young gentlemen from families of quality. New Rochelle was a natural center for talent and learning, for it had attracted versatile French and other religious refugees since 1695. The town was "famed for the polite manners of its citizens, and its French schools were patronized

---

17 Lossing, I, 49-61.
18 Schuyler to Abraham Ten Broeck, Sept. 21, 1753. Lossing, I, 68-70.

by New York families who wanted their children to learn not only the French language but polished behavior as well. In short, New Rochelle became fashionable and a resort of the socially prominent or the socially ambitious." [19] Prominence and ambition! The Schuylers had a measure of each quality. Here was the very place to heighten and direct a young man's "ardour of temperament and vehemence of feeling."

For two or three years (1748–1751) Philip Schuyler studied with the Reverend Mr. Stouppe and sat at Mrs. Stouppe's board. He learned French and devoured mathematics. He already knew both English and Dutch, for these were early subjects of instruction in primary school and at home.[20] Probably he was also versed in Latin. Somewhat later in life Schuyler learned German in order to read untranslated books on surveying.[21] Mathematics and the "exact sciences" were his favorite subjects. Surveying, navigation, accounting, natural history, husbandry, and "Newtonian philosophy" also interested him. He was to put them to extensive use in years to come. They were, in eighteenth-century parlance, eminently practical and useful.

Philip Schuyler did not enjoy the discipline of a college education. No facilities for such existed in New York until 1754, and by then he was rather old for beginning what other youngsters commenced before their late teens. Moreover, by 1754, Schuyler was caught up in the beginnings of the last of the great colonial wars for empire. Marriage soon followed, and then the making of a livelihood and creation of a larger place in the sun. Perhaps the schooling at New Rochelle was deemed adequate for a prospective wilderness merchant and nascent landlord. Schuyler might have gone to William and Mary, Yale, or even Harvard, although the Yankee environs of the latter were not altogether inviting to a Yorker. But he was directed neither at the

[19] Louis B. Wright, *The Cultural Life of the American Colonies, 1607–1763* (London, 1957), p. 56.

[20] Adolph B. Benson (ed.), *Peter Kalm's Travels In North America* (2 vols.; New York, 1937), II, 615. Schuyler's own entries in his Bible were written in "low" Dutch.

[21] Katharine Schuyler Baxter, *A Godchild of Washington* (New York, 1897), p. 437. "Reminiscences of My Father" by Catherine Van Rensselaer Schuyler, his youngest daughter. Schuyler's proficiency in mathematics and extensive use of it are evident in his activities as New York state surveyor, his service on several boundary commissions, and his calculations in finance and canal construction. See, for example, NYPL, Schuyler Papers Box 38: mathematical, scientific, and financial calculations, tables, and drawings. See also the books from his library, the Schuyler mansion, Albany, New York.

law nor the church. Nor was he intended for the scholarly professions or medicine. It is doubtful whether Schuyler or his family ever considered his going to college. It was not necessary for his career as his family conceived it.

From the supervision of the Reverend Mr. Stouppe, Schuyler probably passed to the purely practical exercises of the countinghouse and the training of excursions on the frontier.[22] Perhaps living at home and in the wilds was more healthful and more to his taste than the life he had experienced with the Stouppes at New Rochelle. It was said that Mrs. Stouppe served a meager diet; this and chinks in his bedroom walls that failed to keep out the winds and snow were doubtless the reasons why Schuyler fell ill with "rheumatic gout"— probably a form of rheumatism and pleurisy—the ailment that confined him to the house for the better part of a year. Moreover, the malady caused him such recurrent distress all through his life that it hampered his effectiveness as a general, damaged his reputation, and interfered with his active participation in politics and supervision of his property and other interests. During the Revolutionary War he was not always able to play an active role in the field, and this for a commander could only mean misfortune.[23]

Schuyler's ill health did not, however, completely deter him from youthful activities, for he still enjoyed the resiliency of youth. In the summer of 1751 he moved into wilderness training on the upper Mohawk, hunting and trading with the Indians. That too was most appropriate for a young man bred to the life of merchant and landlord, whose customers were Indians and whose market was Indian territory. At Albany it was common for sons of all classes to go off for a year on a trading expedition with the Indians, a kind of preparation for marriage and the establishment of a home.[24] In these circumstances Schuyler became a friend of the Six Nations, and as a friend, a powerful influence. Sometime in his youth, possibly before he was

[22] Schuyler, *Colonial New York*, II, 258–259.

[23] Schuyler's illness was also called "hereditary gout." See John M. Krout, "Philip Schuyler" in Allen Johnson, *et al.* (eds.), *Dictionary of American Biography* (20 vols.; New York, 1943), XVI, 477. Hereafter cited as *D.A.B.* See also Lossing, I, 65; Tuckerman, p. 34; Cuyler Reynolds, *op. cit.*, I, 33. In various of his letters of 1775 and 1776 to the president of Congress and others, Schuyler complained of bilious fever, violent rheumatic pains, violent lax and extreme sweatings at night, the ague, painful scorbutic eruptions, and of the debilitation of frequent bloodletting.

[24] Lossing, I, 66; Ironside, *The Family in Colonial N.Y.*, p. 39, citing Anne Grant, *Memoirs*, I, 184.

twenty, tradition has it that he assisted the Oneidas in nullifying a fraudulent sale of much of their land west of Utica. Supposedly, a few young braves under the influence of rum made the sale to some speculators without the consent of their elders. It was from this trans-action that Schuyler's name was adopted by these befriended tribes-men who thereby meant to honor him. So it was that full-blooded Oneidas named Schuyler were still visiting the town of Utica sixty years later.[25] During the War of Independence, Congress recognized Schuyler's influence with the Indians by naming him an Indian com-missioner, for the tribesmen called him "father."

Between school at New Rochelle, a kind of apprentice training in countinghouse, and on trading expeditions and the outbreak of the French and Indian War, Philip Schuyler showed no great promise or peculiarly forceful ambition. But appearances were deceiving. Perhaps this explains why his aunt Margaretta's influence is noteworthy. In her *Memoirs*, Anne Grant describes Schuyler's aunt Margaretta as an "American Lady" whose household of cultured ease was a social center of Albany. Admittedly, her home had none of the refinements of a handsomely appointed old country salon, but it was the best the Hudson valley then knew. And it was Aunt Schuyler who pointed out to her young nephew a mode of attaining wealth and power, just as she had advised his younger brother, Cortlandt, to procure a com-mission in the royal army. Schuyler may have been born and bred to position, but until the death of both his parents, he could not expect to own property or advance himself unless he acted on his own initia-tive. Thus it was that Schuyler, following the promptings of his aunt, was first to enter the employ of John Bradstreet, deputy quarter-master general for the British forces in the French and Indian War, and then turn to the development and expansion of his Saratoga estates once his mother passed from the scene. If the youth displayed no sign of energy and ambition, it was perhaps because he *"appeared merely a careless good humored young man,"* and because he was never "so little what he *seemed* with regard to ability, activity, and ambition, art, enterprise, and perseverance, all of which he possessed in an uncommon degree, though no man had less the *appearance* of these qualities." Schuyler was "easy, complying, and good humored,"

[25] Lossing, I, 66–67. When exactly this incident occurred is not clear. Lossing says Schuyler was "about twenty," which means 1753. Baxter, *A Godchild of Washington*, p. 432, says it was in 1751, but her reliability for dates is poor. The story is one of several that seem to be family tales without documentation of any sort.

and "the conversations, full of wisdom and sound policy, of which he had been a seemingly inattentive witness at the Flats [Aunt Schuyler's home], only slept in his recollection, to wake in full force when called forth by occasion." [26]

These were still carefree years. Not until 1755 were the serious aspects of war, the sobering duties of providing for a family, and the promptings of ambition to propel twenty-one-year-old Schuyler into energetic economic and political endeavors. He could still lounge in his aunt's home at the Flatts or in Albany, take time to enjoy the hunting and trading expeditions (for all their more serious import to the profit-minded merchant), and visit friends and relatives in New York City with an eye for the theater and the young ladies. But responsibilities were creeping up. They were perhaps signaled by the privilege of occupying his grandfather's pew in the boxlike Dutch church down the street from his home. When the old man expired, he had no living son who might inherit his place. The eldest grandson was then entitled to his senior's seat.[27]

A carefree young Schuyler is difficult to imagine because most of his life was so filled with enterprise and responsibility. Few descriptions of him remain. "He was . . . a tall youth, with a florid complexion, a benevolent cast of features, a fine, manly deportment, and distinguished for great kindness of manner." [28] Later representations of him suggest that he preserved these youthful qualities. Tall, erect, with a commanding presence, Philip Schuyler easily gained a reputation for arrogance and notoriety for an aristocratic temperament. His austere demeanor alone was enough to convey the impression, marked as it was by strong, chaste features, a rather long, sharp nose, and piercing eyes. Like his contemporary, Chancellor Robert R. Livingston, he "inherited a kind of self-consciousness, at once proud and sensitive, accepting respect as a matter of course but preternaturally quick to detect a slight or a sneer," [29] as if he could not differentiate between honor and vanity. George Washington gave the same impression, for no one could deport himself with more ostensible coolness than he. Schuyler was to find a firm bond of friendship with the Virginian. They were cast from similar molds. Still, Schuyler was also known for his "perfect command of temper, acuteness . . . and in the hour of

---

[26] Anne Grant, *Memoirs*, I, 280. See also II, 114. Italics added.
[27] Munsell, *Collections*, I, 59–60, 78, 80.
[28] Lossing, I, 66.
[29] Dangerfield, *Livingston*, p. 7.

social enjoyment, [he could] easily relaps[e] into all that careless frank hilarity and indolent good humor, which seems the peculiar privilege of the free and disencumbered mind, active and companionable. . . ." [30]

Late in his teens Schuyler amused himself with annual excursions down the Hudson to the pleasure-tempting city on Manhattan Island. His earliest extant piece of writing tells of one of those visits made in the autumn of 1753. In it he refers to a trip made the previous year. Writing to his friend Abraham Ten Broeck with that freedom and candor that mark intimate friendship, Schuyler recounted his doings and his observations. He reported how upon his arrival in New York he went immediately to the theater, for he had promised himself "before I left home that if the players should be here I should see them, for a player is a new thing under the sun in our good province." [31] Indeed it was. In July, 1753, one of the earliest professional companies of actors headed by Lewis Hallam, brother of the London actor-manager, had moved on to New York from Virginia, where he and his troupe had arrived a year earlier. When Hallam encountered opposition to the theater, he published a letter in the *New York Mercury* (July 2, 1753) appealing for public support. By September, when Schuyler wrote to Ten Broeck, resistance to the theater had passed, and Hallam had built a theater and was offering performances three times a week. To convince doubting Yorkers that the drama was not harmful, the players first performed Richard Steele's moralizing piece, *The Conscious Lovers*.[32]

"Phil.'s sweetheart went with us," Schuyler continued. "She is a handsome brunette from Barbadoes, has an eye like that of a Mohawk beauty, and appears to possess a good understanding." Schuyler had an eye for a girl, be she savage or civilized, but he was also interested in a woman who could think. With his companion he saw the "grand battery" and also paid his respects to Governor De Lancey, "whose lady," he said, "spent a week with us last spring." The De Lanceys

---

[30] Anne Grant, *Memoirs*, I, 281. Another contemporary has confirmed this picture of Schuyler by writing of him about twenty years later. *Voyages De M. Le Marquis De Chastellux Dans L'Amérique Septentrionale Dans les années 1780, 1781 & 1782* (2 vols.; Paris, 1786), I, 318, 345–346, says of Schuyler: "Il est assez communicatif, & il a raison de l'être; sa conversation est aimable & facile; il fait bien ce dont il parle, & parle bien de ce qu'il fait," and "le Général Schuyler est encore plus aimable quand il n'est pas avec sa femme, en quoi il ressemble à beaucoup de maris européens."

[31] Schuyler to Ten Broeck, Sept. 21, 1753. Lossing, I, 68–70.

[32] Louis B. Wright, *op. cit.*, p. 182.

and Schuylers were cousins. Following tea at five o'clock, the young men hurried to the theater for the six o'clock performance. There Schuyler saw Steele's *Conscious Lovers* and was amused by a "sprightly young man [who] played the violin and danced merrily."

But Schuyler indicated a more serious bent. He was "no better pleased" with the entertainment "than I should have been at the club, where, last year, I went with cousin Stephen, and heard many wise sayings which I hope profited me something." This was probably the Whig Club, newly founded by the Livingston interests, William Livingston, John Morin Scott, and William Smith, Jr.[33] That Schuyler should enjoy sober discourse there and not prefer the amusements of the theater instead was a minor but significant testimonial to an inclination. Little might he imagine that a decade and a half later he would be an active participant, not merely a spectator, in political debate. Little might he think of himself as a politician active in a movement of opposition to his cousins, the De Lanceys, or in interests which had given rise to the partisan club where the discourse he heard had prompted him to hope it had "profited me something."

On his trip to New York in 1753, Schuyler also planned a visit "into Jersey" to call on a kinsman, Colonel Peter Schuyler, who had visited Albany during King George's War.[34] The colonel, he thought, was a good soldier, "and as I believe we shall have war again with the French quite as soon as we could wish," young Schuyler expected the colonel would again lead his Jerseymen in the field. "I wish you and I . . . could go with him," he wrote his friend. "But I must say farewell, with love to Peggy, and sweet Kitty V. R. if you see her." [35] "Sweet Kitty V. R." was Catherine Van Rensselaer, a likely candidate for a wife—a spirited young woman endowed with intellectual powers that Schuyler admired. But the prospects for war proved more immediate than those for marriage.

[33] Dorothy Rita Dillon, *The New York Triumvirate* (New York, 1949), p. 95.

[34] Lossing, I, 69. Colonel Peter Schuyler was a grandson of Philip Pietersen Schuyler the Founder, whose son Arent established the Schuylers in New Jersey. See also Schuyler, *Colonial New York*, I, 185. The colonel was Philip Schuyler's cousin once removed, his grandfather Schuyler's nephew.

[35] Schuyler to Ten Broeck, Sept. 21, 1753. Lossing, I, 68–70.

– 3 –

IN THE KING'S SERVICE

THE HOSTILITIES which originated in the Ohio country in 1754 led to a European war and involved American colonists in a monumental struggle between Britain and France—the Great War for the Empire. A force of Virginia provincials headed by George Washington made a foray to the forks of the Ohio to warn off the French who were making good their claims to the territory. Washington was forced to fall back in the face of a larger French body. Because the Indians would be important as allies or enemies in the coming struggle, a colonial conference was called at Albany. Upon the advice of British authorities the colonies of New England, New York, Pennsylvania, and Maryland sent delegates to conclude a treaty with the wavering Iroquois. In late June and July the delegates at Albany also considered a plan of union. Unfortunately, none of the particularistic colonies adopted the plan for concerted action.

As an Albanian twenty-one-year-old Philip Schuyler should have been a witness to the conference held only a short distance down the street from his paternal home. But there is nothing extant to show his reactions; perhaps he was busy with other matters, or even off on some trading excursion.

New York also felt the first surges of French and Indian hostilities in 1754. Late in August an enemy party invaded the province, attacked settlers as far south as Hoosic, captured some Schaghticoke tribesmen and carried them off to Canada. Lieutenant Governor James De Lancey ordered the fort at Albany put in order and two hundred men from each regiment of militia to be ready to march on call. Although Albany suffered nothing from the invasion, it prompted the erection of a wall part way around the city in anticipation of future attacks.[36]

During 1755 there were still other military beginnings. It was the year of General Edward Braddock's defeat in the Pennsylvania backcountry. Governor William Shirley of Massachusetts replaced Braddock after his death in July, but Shirley postponed a campaign against Fort Niagara in the face of the arrival of French reinforcements which

[36] George W. Howell and Jonathan Tenney (eds.), *Bi-Centennial History of Albany: History of the County of Albany, N.Y., From 1609 to 1886* (New York, 1886), pp. 388–389.

had slipped through Admiral Edward Boscawen's sea blockade. However, several thousand New England militia and some British regulars under Colonel Robert Monckton and Colonel John Winslow seized Fort Beausejour at the northern reaches of the Bay of Fundy. By mid-year the British controlled the Bay of Fundy, and William Johnson began fortifications on Lake George in preparation for an expected French attack. Johnson assembled about 3,500 colonials and 400 Indians for the assault expected in September.

Philip Schuyler had expected hostilities at least as early as the autumn of 1753 when he told his friend "Brom" Ten Broeck of his belief that war with the French was as imminent as he could wish for. He hoped they might go to the field with his kinsman, Colonel Peter Schuyler of New Jersey. But within two years Schuyler made his martial debut in a somewhat different way. On May 3, 1755, the New York Legislature provided for raising eight companies of volunteers, and two days later Lieutenant Governor De Lancey commissioned young Schuyler to raise one of the volunteer units. Their task was to build fortifications north of Albany in cooperation with New England troops, all under the command of William Johnson. Proper inducements were offered—money and clothing for the men, and £100 to the company commander as well as eight shillings per day for his service. Schuyler had been "presented" to the lieutenant governor, who was his cousin, as a person able to raise such a company. When the men were mustered, Schuyler was to receive his commission.[37]

Schuyler raised his company, and on June 14 he was given his captain's commission to serve in Colonel William Cockcroft's regiment. Even now he began to display a certain anxiety that can only be explained as ambition and a jealous sense of propriety. After assembling his unit, he sent the lieutenant governor the muster roll with a request for the senior commission in the eight companies contemplated. Had he not raised his unit before all others? [38]

In July and August, 1755, Schuyler's troops were encamped at the Flatts, north of Albany. There he took part in preparations for the

[37] James De Lancey to Schuyler, May 5, 1755. NYPL, Schuyler Papers Box 42.
[38] Schuyler to De Lancey, June, 1755. E. B. O'Callaghan (ed.), *Calendar of Historical Manuscripts in the Office of the Secretary of State, Albany, N.Y.* (2 parts; Albany, 1865–1866), II, 638. Schuyler's commission is in NYHS, John W. Francis, "Old New York" (vols. of MSS; New York, 1865), XIII, 15. See also *Colls. N.Y. Hist. Soc. for 1891* (New York, 1892), XXIV, "Muster Rolls of New York Provincial Troops 1755–1764," 2, 4, 10–15.

imminent campaign to be launched in the lake country: the collection of carriages, shot, and other stores, all the accouterments of war. As a paymaster for his forces he had instructions from the lieutenant governor to pay officers from the date of their warrants and the enlisted men from the time of their enlistment.[39] On August 8, William Johnson moved his forces from Albany north to Fort Edward, high on the Hudson, and from there he pushed on to the south end of Lake George, where scouts brought news of the French already building a fort at Ticonderoga—the link between the waters of Lake George and Lake Champlain. Schuyler's company of course went along.

But Captain Schuyler was not to participate in the Lake George battle on September 8, in which Baron Dieskau's 1,400 French and Indians were routed and prisoners, among whom was Dieskau himself, taken. Rather, he was called from martial affairs to marital obligations; on September 7, 1755, he was married to his "sweet Kitty" Van Rensselaer.

This was not the last time a wedding interrupted Schuyler's military activities, but the nuptial call in 1755 was one of some urgency— and honor. It is no wonder that his role in the battle of Lake George is unrecorded as his biographers remark.[40] He simply was not there. In fact, Schuyler was probably back in Albany in late August or early September. A few days before the action at the lake the young captain "received an express to return to Albany in order (as it was given out) to marry a Miss Kitty Van Rensselaer, the daughter of Colonel John Van Rensselaer, of Claverack, on the east side of the river, below the city." Catherine was a young "lady then of great beauty, shape, and gentility," and was known by the name of "the Morning Star." "It was known when he left the Army that an action must commence, and that soon." [41] But propriety seemed to have the greater force than

39 O'Callaghan, *Calendar of Hist. MSS*, II, 639. See also *Colls. N.Y. Hist. Soc. for 1891* (New York, 1892), XXIV, 22.

40 Lossing, I, 124. Tuckerman, p. 53. Lossing says Schuyler was married on Sept. 17, 1755, and thereby suggests he was at the battle of Lake George on Sept. 8. But Schuyler's own inscription in his family Bible gives Sept. 7 as his wedding day, and counts his age as 21 years, 9 months, 17 days, which with the proper adjustment made from Old Style to New Style (as he would have had to do after 1752) coincides correctly with his birthday given in Old Style as Nov. 10, 1733.

41 Jones, *History of New York*, II, 316. For all his Tory sympathies and hostile insinuations against Schuyler, including those against the general's personal courage, Jones apparently reports the truth as to Schuyler's sudden marriage and his absence from the battle of Lake George. However, Jones also dates the marriage as Sept. 17

valor for the moment, and the call of a "lady of great beauty, shape, and gentility" who was in a family way proved more urgent than the summons to do battle against the enemy on Lake George.[42]

On September 4 the captain and his lady received their license to be married by posting a bond. The Dutch practice of licenses had been continued under the English government. The custom under Roman-Dutch law was for a couple to appear before a magistrate's court or ministers to petition for their marriage; the wedding was permissible after three Sundays or market days when the banns were published (in the court or church). But the granting of a marriage license by the governor and secretary of the province was a dispensation from the proclamation of banns, and it was a speedier method of marital preparations. Apparently the hastiness of the Schuylers' wedding did not permit the reading of the banns.[43] On Sunday, September 7, an Indian summer day brilliant with sunshine at Lake George, "Philip of the Pasture" and his "sweet Kitty," the "Morning Star," began almost half a century of married life in their native Albany. Schuyler made the proper notation in the family record begun by his father in a ponderous Dutch Bible: "In the year 1755 on the 7th of September did I Philip John Schuyler (being 21 years 9 months and 17 days old) enter the holy state of matrimony with Catherine Van Rensselaer (being 20 years 9 months and 27 days old). The Lord grant this marriage last long and in peace and to his honor." [44] The inscription ex-

instead of Sept. 7. Lossing and Tuckerman have manufactured their stories about his presence at the battle, have misread the marriage record, and quite deliberately or carelessly omitted any mention of the hasty wedding.

[42] Schuyler was married on Sept. 7, 1755. His first child, Engeltie or Angelica, was born on Feb. 20, 1756, as recorded in the family Bible now in the Albany mansion.

[43] *Names of Persons for whom Marriage Licences were issued by the Secretary of the Province of New York Previous to 1784* (Albany, 1860), p. 342. The petitioners for a governor's marriage license were required to give a penal bond of £500 that there was no "lawfull let or impediment of Pre-Contract, Affinity or Consanguinity, to hinder the parties being joined . . . and afterwards their living together as Man and Wife." *Ibid.*, pp. iii–iv. See also Ironside, *The Family in Colonial N.Y.*, p. 65, which says it was deemed plebeian to be married by the publication of banns. But it appears rather that the banns were not read for the Schuylers because of other reasons.

[44] Lossing, I, 118, cites weather conditions at Lake George. See Anne Grant, *Memoirs*, I, 280, for Schuyler's nickname, "Philip of the Pasture." The inscription in the family Bible reads: "In hett Jaar 1755 September den 7 en. ben Ick Philip Jo-hannis Schuyler (oude wesende 21 Jaer 9 Maende ende 17 dagen) in den Houwelycke Stadt Getreden mett Catharina Van Renselaer (oude zynde 20 Jaer 9 Maende Ende

presses something of Schuyler's character and admirable intentions, but it may be questioned whether he was able to live up to his invocation of a peaceful life to the glory of God. His political and military activities were hardly tranquil, and whether he glorified God by them is debatable. He scarcely contemplated a life of countless discomforts and irritations. Beset by the fires of ambition, assaulted by slander of his reputation which outraged his sense of honor and pricked his vanity, and plagued by the vexatious combination of personal ill health, the worries of responsible military positions, and political aspirations and disappointments, he did not possess a temperament that would enable him to bear all this with good grace. Chancellor Kent spoke of his "constitutional ardour of temperament and vehemence of feeling"—qualities that were much more dominant than tranquillity or an inclination to live quietly to the glory of the Almighty. But the Schuylers did enjoy a private life much more in keeping with the hope expressed in the marriage record.

Catherine Van Rensselaer (1734–1803) proved to be a loyal wife and good mother. She was very much the "lady of great beauty, shape, and gentility," that "Morning Star," she was described. Her dark and slender beauty is recorded in her portrait.[45] As she was a Van Rensselaer, the daughter of the Claverack branch of the patroon's family, great-great-granddaughter of Killian, the first patroon of Rensselaerwyck, her gentility could hardly be disputed. Determination and firmness of will were as dominant in her character as graciousness and the ability to put everyone at ease. Though there are no letters or other written testimony of her character and activities from her own hand, it is apparent from references made to her and from the quiet efficiency with which she ran her household that she met these qualifications, and more.

Catherine Schuyler's capability as a wife, mother, and the manager of an extensive household is marked by her charitable service as a

---

27 Dagen.) Den Heer witt geven dat Evy Langh to Same in vrede Ende tot Syn Eer maghe Leven." I am indebted to Professor Paul Schach for corroborating and correcting my translation. Cf. Lossing, I, 82.

[45] Portrait of Catherine Schuyler, NYHS Museum. Apparently the only evidence of her handwriting that exists is her signature on a document by which she and her husband gave the management of the Saratoga estate to their son John Bradstreet Schuyler in 1787. NYPL, Schuyler Papers. See also Harold Donaldson Eberlein, *The Manors and Historic Homes of the Hudson Valley* (Philadelphia & London, 1924), pp. 222–236.

nurse to enemy as well as friendly soldiers in the French and Indian War, her grace as hostess to countless distinguished guests, and even her determined defense of the family property from the British invaders of 1777. She made clothes for her husband's slaves and personally supervised other domestic chores: preserving, weaving, soap-making, candle-dipping, and dairying. Catherine may have been well born and gently bred, but she was also reared to good housewifery. The Van Rensselaer women were noted as good housekeepers.[46]

Most of all, Philip Schuyler's marriage meant that another link in the political-economic ties among the great families of the province had been forged. These informal interfamily relationships underlay the colony's political institutions. And Schuyler was to prove as active a participant in his father-in-law's interest as was Colonel John Van Rensselaer himself.

From the moment Schuyler was called to the altar, his active command of a company of volunteers fell by the board. But honeymoons were unknown to Schuyler's society, and he soon returned to his military duties. He remained with his company for but a brief period after his marriage, and by the end of the year his command passed to other hands. Retaining his captaincy, Schuyler turned to other, and perhaps more lucrative, work in the commissariat. At Fort Edward he took up the task of creating a depot of military stores. Much of his military life was centered in such labor, both in the Great War for the Empire and in the War of Independence.[47]

Sometime during the winter of 1755–1756, Schuyler formed a profitable connection that was to last for almost two decades, a friendship that brought him personal gain, involved him in political machinations, and in the end caused difficulties in the management of a large

46 Schuyler, *Colonial New York*, II, 253; Ironside, *The Family in Colonial N.Y.*, p. 25; Mary Gay Humphreys, *Catherine Schuyler* (New York, 1897), pp. 9, 35, 58, 92, 153–154, 234–235.

47 Ironside, *The Family in Colonial N.Y.*, p. 52; Schuyler, *Colonial New York*, II, 259; *Colls. N.Y. Hist. Soc. for 1891* (New York, 1892), XXIV, 36–39, 41–43, 46–47. The muster rolls of N.Y. provincial troops, 1755–1764, do not show Schuyler as a company commander after Dec. 2, 1755. See also *New York Historian Annual Report: Colonial Series* (2 vols.; New York, 1896–1898), I, 643, 668, 670, 723, 724–725, 734, 736, 777–779, 783, 785, 798, 800. Page 800 shows the last mention of Schuyler's company, and as following sources indicate the names and activities of officers and companies for 1756 without mention of Schuyler's, he could not have been with a company, but must have begun work with John Bradstreet. See also O'Callaghan, *Calendar of Hist. MSS*, II, 646, 647.

estate. It was his introduction to Colonel John Bradstreet, deputy quarter-master general for His Majesty's forces in New York.

John Bradstreet (1711?–1774) was something of an adventurer. He seems to have appeared first in America in Nova Scotia, where he may have been born or to which he was brought as a boy from England. Initially he was a trader. Next, at Boston, he became Governor William Shirley's adjutant, and because he was acquainted with Cape Breton Isle he was especially fitted for the campaign of 1745 against the French. He commanded provincial forces at Louisbourg, but he aspired to a higher post. He failed to buy a commission in the royal army, probably because he was unable to raise the required money. In 1746, Bradstreet was given the sinecure of the lieutenant governorship of St. John's, Newfoundland. When Shirley was named second in command in 1755, he put Bradstreet to work preparing an expedition to Niagara, one of the three attacks launched against the French. Braddock moved against Fort Duquesne, Johnson against Crown Point, and Shirley on Oswego. At first the French under Dieskau marched against Oswego, but they soon turned to Crown Point instead. Shirley remained determined to reinforce Oswego, however, and Bradstreet led a party to the fort on Lake Ontario and assumed command until Shirley arrived.[48]

When Bradstreet set out for Oswego, it was expected that much of Braddock's army could march up from the Pennsylvania back-country to reinforce the British forces on Lake Ontario or those of William Johnson at Crown Point. Perhaps the French could be driven out of the country at these two points.[49] Bradstreet demonstrated an energy that was typical both of himself and the young protégé he was yet to meet. But the forces he found at Oswego were much depleted by desertions. Wagons were scarce and hence the provisions short. Until these problems were remedied, there could be no action taken against Niagara.[50]

Meantime, William Johnson's troops defeated the French at the

48 Arthur Pound, *Native Stock* (New York, 1931), pp. 45–61. See also [John Bradstreet], *An Impartial Account of Lieut. Col. Bradstreet's Expedition to Fort Frontenac* (Toronto, 1940), pp. 1–3. Two forts were located near the mouth of the Oswego River where it empties into Lake Ontario. Fort Oswego stood on the west bank and Fort Ontario on the east bank.

49 William Shirley to Secretary of State Thomas Robinson, Sept. 19, 1755. C.O. 5/46:159–160.

50 Minutes of a council held at Oswego, Sept. 18, 1755. C.O. 5/46:177–184.

battle of Lake George, and Baron Dieskau, wounded, was sent south
to Albany. Schuyler, then in Albany and newly married, received the
French prisoners with some aplomb. His knowledge of French stood
him in good stead, and the hospitality offered by his bride and mother
won the gratitude of the Frenchman.[51] It was the first notable sign
of a hospitality Schuyler extended even to his enemies—a mark of
generosity and grace for which he was to become even better known.
One man would testify to it in the British House of Commons.[52]

The New York frontier was the main scene of military action in
1756. Philip Schuyler had come to the attention of John Bradstreet
the previous winter. Exactly how is not clear. But through his association with Bradstreet, Schuyler continued to participate in the war
effort. Doubtless the introduction of the two men was a combination
of social connections and the organizing ability Schuyler had demonstrated as a promising young officer. As a newly married man without a settled plan for supporting a family, Schuyler felt obliged to
make some unusual exertion. His uncle and aunt Schuyler, particularly the famed Margaretta, "not only advised him to accept an inferior employment [i.e., inferior to a regular command] in this business [the quarter-master general's], but recommended him to the
Brigadier Bradstreet, who had the power of disposing of such offices,"

51 Bernier to Schuyler, Oct. 5, 1755, cited in Lossing, I, 125–126. (This letter is not
now to be found among the Schuyler Papers.) Dieskau's aide-de-camp revealed how
much a stranger was moved to comment on the character of his young Albany host.
Your letter to the baron, wrote the aide, "has confirmed him in the good opinion of
you. . . ." Schuyler, at Fort Edward, had left his mother and wife to tend to the
prisoner's needs. "One can add nothing," said Bernier, "to the politeness of Madame,
your mother, and Madame, your wife. Every day there comes from them, to the
Baron, fruits and other rare sweets, which are of great service to him. He orders
me, on this subject, to express to you all that he owes to the attentions of these
ladies." And if the baron were restored to health and able to see General Johnson
again, "he will himself be the proclaimer of all the good words which should be
said of you, and which in justice he owes you, for the trouble and care that you have
had for him." See also Maj.-Gen. William Johnson to Maj.-Gen. William Shirley
(copy), Sept. 9, 1755. C.O. 5/46:227–231.

52 Lieutenant General John Burgoyne remarked in Commons on May 26, 1778, that
despite his destruction of Schuyler's property at Saratoga (which Burgoyne valued at
£10,000) Schuyler excused it as justifiable according to the principles and rules of
war. He then had Burgoyne escorted to Albany where he was quartered in the
Schuyler mansion, "a very elegant house," and where he was given "every . . .
possible demonstration of hospitality. . . ." The Parliamentary Register; or, History
of the Proceedings and Debates of the House of Commons: Series One (17 vols.;
London, 1802), VIII, 311–312.

daily increasing in importance. "They well knew that he possessed qualities which might not only render him a useful servant to the public, but clear his way to fortune and distinction."

Schuyler certainly needed to pay heed to the improvement of his fortunes, for already he had the beginnings of a family but no settled plan for supporting them. He might well have grown anxious with the arrival of his first child, Angelica, in February, 1756. And distinction was always something to cultivate and enlarge. Thus it was that Schuyler's "perfect command of temper, acuteness, and dispatch in business . . . made him a great acquisition" to Bradstreet, who soon recognizing these qualities, made him his secretary and deputy.[53] "Between the two men, as frequently between temperamental opposites, there grew deep confidence and affection." [54] Both men were energetic. Bradstreet became like a father to a man who had scant memories of a father's guidance.

In the spring and summer of 1756, Schuyler accompanied Bradstreet to Oswego with supplies for the garrison and helped clear the Oneida portage of enemy raiders. He shared these labors of his mentor, and in view of Bradstreet's later commendation of the youth's "zeal, punctuality & strict honesty," [55] we may assume that he was responsible for a share of the success and credit Bradstreet won as well. General Shirley, reporting on July 26, 1756, to Henry Fox, secretary of state, said of Bradstreet, "the transportation of the provisions and Stores this Spring to Oswego, (upon which the preservation of the place hath so much depended) is Chiefly owing to his indefatigable Activity, and Singular good Management in his Command." [56] Schuyler benefited from Bradstreet's favor as much as he suffered from his enemies' reproaches.

On their return from Oswego, Bradstreet's forces were attacked by a superior French contingent, "which they repulsed with loss." Schuyler courageously rescued a wounded Frenchman from abandonment. After he and Bradstreet had reached an island in the Oswego River with a group of eight men, they drove off a number of the enemy. Then before they could be cut off by the French, they retreated to

---

[53] Anne Grant, *Memoirs*, I, 281. See also Montgomery Schuyler, "The Schuyler Family," *The Order of Colonial Lords of Manors in America, Publication No. 16* (New York, 1926), p. 39.

[54] Pound, *Native Stock*, p. 68.

[55] Bradstreet to Schuyler, July 7, 1760. NYPL, Schuyler Papers Box 9.

[56] Shirley to Henry Fox, July 26, 1756. C.O. 5/46:585.

their boats. "The wounded Frenchman begged to be taken with them," but the boat was too small to accommodate him. Schuyler then swam the stream with the enemy soldier on his back and saw him to safety. During the Revolutionary War when Schuyler was in command of the Northern Department, the rescued Frenchman sought him out to thank him for saving his life.[57]

But Schuyler left the service in disgust over the developments of the year. The Earl of Loudoun, who replaced Shirley as commander, failed to move decisively against the enemy. Loudoun was much hindered by the unresponsiveness of colonial assemblies to his requests for troops, and despite the services of a sizable body of New York militia, he was obliged to dismiss the provincial levies and ordered the regulars into winter quarters as the season for active operations drew to a close. Meanwhile, the Marquis de Montcalm, who had succeeded to the French command in Canada, seized the offensive. In August, 1756, Montcalm took and destroyed forts Oswego and George. Schuyler, evidently impatient and dismayed that his labors to save Oswego should result in such defeat, resigned in disgust as the indecisive campaign ended.[58]

What exactly Schuyler did during the year or more he was separated from the fruitless military operations against the French is difficult to say. Perhaps he sold provisions to the defense establishment as once his father had. It appears that he became active in Albany city government, a step in keeping with the tradition of his father and grandfather. Albany was confronted by new problems created by the wartime conditions and the presence of militia and regular troops. Even before Schuyler left the service at the end of the 1756 campaign, he had procured a license to operate a ferry across the Hudson for a year (April 4, 1756, to April 4, 1757) on the condition that he pay a £5 fee if the military expedition continued. Otherwise he might operate the ferry for a mere £3. Ferrying troops and supplies was one way to make money.[59]

[57] Schuyler, *Colonial New York*, II, 259–260.

[58] His resignation may be inferred by the gap in the accounts he kept between 1756 and 1758. NYPL, Schuyler Papers Box 9, show amounts Schuyler received as pay for his services as director and manager under Bradstreet. His first year's pay was about £250. None is recorded for 1757. See also Flick, II, 236–237; III, 115, for Loudoun's activities, and also Stanley McCrory Pargellis, *Lord Loudoun in North America* (New Haven, 1933), pp. 171–186.

[59] Munsell, *Collections*, I, 100.

On September 29, 1756, the Albany City Council selected (by co-optation) Schuyler as one of the two assistants for the first ward. He took his oath of office on October 14 and attended the council regularly for a year. In September, 1757, he was again chosen an assistant, a position he retained during the year even after he returned to Bradstreet's commissariat service.[60]

The Albany council was confronted with the conduct of ordinary business: the appointment of firemasters, the payment of the bell-ringer, the repairing of the engine house and bridges, and the selection of a treasurer, marshal, and high constable. But the council also had to deal with wartime conditions; from a trade center the city became a military depot. In December, 1756, it set fines for the sale of liquor to soldiers at the request of Lord Howe, who complained of excessive drinking and abuses in the sale of rum to his troops. Intemperance and sales abuses weakened the men and rendered them unfit for duty. In January following, an ordinance was published to prevent accidents from unruly riding. No doubt the troops were the offenders. Later came the regulation of cartmen, of butchers' scales, and of the prices of meat and bread.[61]

Philip Schuyler, as his father and grandfather before him, held several appointive positions under the Crown government. Although they were relatively minor posts, they were a part of that wider recognition for which he began to strive even before his appointment as commissioner in the New York–Massachusetts boundary controversy in 1764 and his first election to the assembly in 1768. On January 10, 1757, when but a little more than twenty-three, Schuyler was made a commissioner of the excise imposed on foreign tea retailed in Albany. Under a *dedimus potestatum* made on January 5, 1758, and again on February 13, he and others were named to swear all officers appointed for Albany County. And on June 3, 1768, he was made commissioner for taking affidavits in the city and county of Albany.[62]

60 *Ibid.*, pp. 103–104, 108.

61 *Ibid.*, pp. 105–108, 111–112.

62 The New York Assembly named him a boundary commissioner on Oct. 20, 1764. *Report of the Regents of the University on the Boundaries of the State of New York* (Albany, 1884), II, 153. E. B. O'Callaghan (abstractor), *Calendar of New York Colonial Commissions, 1680–1770* (New York, 1929), pp. 47, 50, 71. See also *New York State Library Bulletin No. 58: March, 1902*, "Calendar of Council Minutes, 1668–1770" (Albany, 1902), pp. 432, 444. In view of the fact that these activities of Schuyler have never met the attention of other writers, especially his biographers, some question

During 1757 the war turned for the worse on the New York frontier. In June, Lord Loudoun, on orders from the secretary of state, William Pitt, assembled a large force at Halifax preparatory to an attack on Louisbourg. But the expedition did not materialize at this time. On learning of the arrival of a French fleet at Louisbourg, Loudoun abandoned his plans. By the time he returned to New York, Montcalm had seized Fort William Henry at the southern tip of Lake George. New York was thrown into panic and militia were rushed north. In November the French raided the German Flatts area of the upper Mohawk. The year of reverses was marked for Schuyler by the arrival of a new addition to his family, a daughter, Elizabeth, born in August.

Schuyler rejoined Bradstreet's department in 1758, probably because of the seriousness of the state of defenses and the opportunity to offer real service to the war effort as well as to himself. His family was growing; a third daughter, Margaretta, born in September meant another mouth to feed. Schuyler may have had the opportunity to sell timber to the forces, for Bradstreet was given charge of constructing batteaux for the transportation of troops, and he required lumber to build them.[63] At the same time the Schuylers' Saratoga estate had both timber and a sawmill.

Perhaps youthful and attractive Lord Howe had something to do with getting Schuyler to rejoin the service. George Augustus, Viscount Howe, was a frequent visitor at Aunt Schuyler's. As colonel of the 60th Regiment and battalion commander under Loudoun and as commander of the winter (1757–1758) expedition to Ticonderoga, Howe adopted vigorous measures for disciplining and acclimating the troops, requiring them to adapt to the realities of wilderness warfare in dress and tactics. Howe's vigor might easily have aroused Schuyler's enthusiasm once again. There is some evidence that the two men enjoyed more than a slight acquaintanceship. In August, 1757, Schuyler sent

---

might be raised as to whether or not the Philip Schuyler who held these posts and who sat on the Albany City Council is in fact the same Schuyler who is the subject of this study. There were other Philip Schuylers living at this time. (See Schuyler, *Colonial New York*, II, 150–151, 242, 306, 529, etc.) Although it is possible to confuse them with the Philip Schuyler under consideration here, it may be assumed that this is not the case, first because of their obscurity and the consistent record of activities of General Schuyler; second, because the general is referred to and referred to himself as Philip John or Philip J., and this designation clearly establishes his identity. Other Philip Schuylers are not referred to in this manner.

[63] Amherst to William Pitt, Feb. 14, 1758. W.O. 34/73:248; Abercromby's warrants to Bradstreet, 1758—payments for materials and artificers. W.O. 34/76:256–262.

Howe a bed for his use at Fort Edward. The young viscount asked for other favors from his Albany friend. This, their meetings at Aunt Schuyler's, their contacts through the Albany City Council and Schuyler's burial of the fallen nobleman, all testify to a relationship of more than a passing acquaintanceship or mere polite courtesies.[64]

Both Schuyler and Bradstreet served with Lord Howe in James Abercromby's expedition to the lakes in 1758. By then William Pitt had begun to revive the British efforts, but Abercromby's 12,000 men were repulsed by an inferior French force at Ticonderoga in July; the British commander's frontal attack was as disastrous as it was imprudent. Howe fell mortally wounded in a minor skirmish before the main engagement. His two brothers, Richard and William, were also to have a taste of warfare in the colonies, but unlike their elder brother they were not to enjoy the friendship of Philip Schuyler, who not twenty years later found himself on the opposite side from the Howes. Schuyler was not at Ticonderoga when Howe fell. He had remained at the head of Lake George to superintend the forwarding of equipment and supplies. It then became his sad responsibility to accompany Howe's remains to Albany, where they were buried in St. Peter's (Anglican) Church.[65]

After the defeat at Ticonderoga, Abercromby fell back to the foot of Lake George. There, Jeffrey Amherst succeeded him. Schuyler accompanied Bradstreet to Fort Frontenac on Lake Ontario. In August, Bradstreet forced the French to capitulate. Fort Frontenac had been a link in the French communications to the forks of the Ohio, and the victory there encouraged the French to abandon Fort Duquesne, which General John Forbes seized in November.[66] Amherst then made Bradstreet quarter-master general, and Schuyler served under him at Albany for the remainder of the war, collecting and forwarding supplies to the British forces to the north.

Other than these activities, Schuyler's doings are lost in the gaps in the record and in the larger conduct of the war. He continued in Bradstreet's service, handling supplies and large sums of money, buy-

[64] Lord Howe to Schuyler [Aug. 23, 1757]. NYPL, Emmett Collection, 8178. See also Anne Grant, *Memoirs, passim,* for a contemporary account of Lord Howe's activities in Albany.

[65] Munsell, *Collections,* II, 13. It is said that Schuyler placed Howe's body in his own family vault, but this seems unlikely as Schuyler was a member of the Dutch Reformed Church, and Howe was buried in St. Peter's (Anglican) Church. See also *Docs. Rel. Col. Hist. N.Y.,* X, 735.

[66] [John Bradstreet], *op. cit.,* pp. 1–3. See also Flick, II, 238–239.

ing lumber for building batteaux and drawing a handsome enough salary, £255 10s. in 1758, £242 18s. in 1759, and £255 10s. again in 1760.[67]

The year 1759 proved as disastrous for the French as 1757 had been for the British. Amherst took Ticonderoga and Crown Point, and James Wolfe captured Quebec. The end was soon in sight, but new problems and responsibilities awaited Philip Schuyler. Early in July, 1760, Bradstreet placed his private as well as public affairs in Schuyler's hands before following Amherst to Oswego. Schuyler was empowered to settle his friend's public accounts and private estate in the event of his death. The quarter-master general might fall in battle. There was another danger; he was also in ill health. "Your zeal, punctuality & strict honesty in his Majesty's Service, under my direction," said Bradstreet, were "sufficient proofs that I can[']t leave my public accounts & papers in a more faithful hand than in yours to be settled should any accident happen me this Campaign." Delivering all his accounts and vouchers to Schuyler, Bradstreet directed his trusted deputy to settle them in America or England in full confidence that he would "be properly rewarded, if settled in America by the Commander in Chief; if in England by the Administration." [68] Happily for Schuyler all went well for Bradstreet. Early the following year he sent his young protégé off on another venture, this time to England. The detail of Bradstreet's colossal and intricate accounts warranted personal explanation and attention. Schuyler thus went to England to offer detailed information and to see that they were settled systematically and as smoothly as possible.[69]

---

[67] NYPL, Schuyler Papers Box 9. In a letter to Henry Van Rensselaer, Mar. 17, 1759, Schuyler inquires about the provision of "Waggen Stuff" and urges him to saw enough boards for 100 wagons, doubtless used for the construction of batteaux for lake transportation, etc. NYHS, Misc. MSS (Schuyler).

[68] Bradstreet to Schuyler, July 7, 1760. NYPL, Schuyler Papers Box 9. See also Bradstreet to Schuyler, July 6, 1760. NYHS, Misc. MSS (Bradstreet).

[69] Pound, *Native Stock*, p. 68. A considerable tale has grown regarding the trip to England. Family legend has it that Schuyler took command of the packet boat on which he made the crossing when the captain died. (Baxter, *A Godchild of Washington*, p. 435, and repeated in Lossing, I, 181–182, and in Tuckerman, p. 66.) Another story offered is that of the packet boat on which Schuyler sailed meeting a dismantled slaver and of the rescue of its crew and wretched cargo. (Baxter, *op. cit.*, p. 435.) There have also been discrepancies in the account as to when Schuyler left New York and when he returned. (*Ibid.* See also John Richard Alden, *General Gage in America* [Baton Rouge, 1948], pp. 72–73, and Lossing, I, 184.) Baxter, *op. cit.*, p. 31, says also that Schuyler made two trips to England, one in 1754–1755 and another in 1761, but

– 4 –

"A STRANGER, A TRAVELLER"

IT WAS NO EASY undertaking to leave Albany in 1761 or to cross the Atlantic. Schuyler had a family and a wife four months pregnant to care for. His estate required attention as did the development of a prospective business. And there were plans for a new house to execute. A lengthy sea voyage was still fraught with dangers, not to mention added threats of privateers then vigilantly plying British waters.[70] But Schuyler went. Indeed, in the preceding October his ambition prompted him to offer Bradstreet his services in settling the quarter-master's accounts.[71] The trip offered a new experience and an opportunity to expand his interests and his knowledge and, of course, to win greater favor with Bradstreet, whose friendship was financially and politically valuable. The journey promised to be something of an equivalent to the grand tour made by gentlemen of means and distinction. It was appropriately adapted to the purposes of a provincial landowner, businessman, and ambitious frontier aristocrat on official government business.

First there were preparations to make. Schuyler went down to New York City in late January, 1761. There he procured bills of exchange drawn by Charles Apthorpe, merchant, on the London house of Trecothick, Apthorpe, and Tomlinson: £1,325 sterling for £2,451 New York currency. On February 16 he made out a power of attorney to Bradstreet, signed by the usual witnesses, in the presence of no less a figure than supreme court judge (and later chief justice) Daniel Horsmanden.[72] He had yet to procure passage on a vessel bound for

---

there is no evidence for the former, and it is very unlikely that Bradstreet even met Schuyler before the winter of 1755–1756. The true record may be ascertained from scraps of references in Schuyler's accounts and correspondence, the newspapers, and the packet boat log.

70 *The New-York Gazette* (Weyman), Mar. 16, 1761, reported the French had about 340 privateers in and about the English Channel, taking many English vessels.

71 John Bradstreet to Schuyler, Oct. 23, 1760. [Calendar of] the Colonel John Bradstreet Manuscripts in *Transactions and Collections of the American Antiquarian Society*, XI (Worcester, Mass., 1909), 65–66. Hereafter cited as Am. Antiq. Soc., *Trans. & Colls.*, XI. Bradstreet hoped William Pitt would remember his service in subjugating Canada and also expected Schuyler to recommend him for an appointment as commander of a regiment or as governor of New York.

72 The power of attorney (dated Feb. 16 and Mar. 7) and three bills of exchange (dated Feb. 28, 1761) for £400, £425, and £500; also "The Answer of Philip Schuyler

the mother country, a merchantman perhaps or a ship of war. Evidently, upon Bradstreet's recommendation General Jeffrey Amherst assisted him in finding an early passage.[73] A packet boat, the *General Wall*, offered the best prospects for a speedy crossing. Schuyler obtained a place for himself and a servant. They sailed on March 3. The voyage proved to be an unusual one.

Accompanied by HMS *Fay*, the *General Wall* weighed anchor in midmorning on March 3. The *Fay*, bound for Boston, soon left them, and for several days the packet made good speed with "fine fresh Gales." But on the eighteenth day out (Good Friday) the captain sighted trouble on his weatherbow to the westward—a privateer! The chase was on. The captain unfurled all sails, but after five hours' running, the Frenchman hoisted his colors and drew in to fire. When he ventured nearer, the captain returned the cannonade, but within an hour the privateer administered a broadside that raked the packet fore and aft. A running fight continued for several hours, during which the captain was mortally wounded by a shot through his left thigh. His boat was reduced to "a most shatterd condition." There was no prospect of withstanding the Frenchman's onslaught. The mails, including dispatches to the ministry from General Amherst, were thrown overboard, and the *Biscayen*, mounting twenty-four guns and 228 men, seized the *General Wall* for ransom. Captain Lutwidge (or Luteridge) agreed on the sum of £600, gave his captor two hostages and was obliged to disarm his packet. After transferring prisoners from the privateer, the *General Wall* "maide [sic] sail as well & as fast as posable [sic] we could get thing[s] in order." On March 22, Lutwidge died of his wound, but at midnight a sounding told the crew and a much relieved New Yorker that land was near. Lights from the Scilly Isles were reassuring on the twenty-third, and early the next day the battered ship made Land's End. That night it limped into Falmouth, and the mate hurried to report to the proper authorities.[74] Schuyler had but to collect his baggage and papers, unharmed

---

... to the bill of Complaint of John Evans . . . and Agatha his wife [1788]" in which Schuyler says he left Albany on or about Jan. 31, 1761, and embarked from New York on Mar. 3. NYPL, Schuyler Papers Box 10.

[73] Bradstreet to Amherst, Feb. 2, 1761. Am. Antiq. Soc., *Trans. & Colls.*, XI, 67.

[74] "Journal of the 10 Voyage of the General Wall Pacquet Boat to & From N.w York—By Tho. Robinson." C.O. 5/52:99–100. The story (in Lossing, I, 181–182) that Schuyler was chosen ship's captain after Lutwidge died because he was a good mathematician and navigator is fanciful. There is no such record in the ship's log. Moreover, Lutwidge did not die until the voyage was almost ended, and then it is reason-

by the privateer, except for a loss of £50 he paid as his share of the ransom (probably for the privateer's allowance for his keeping Bradstreet's accounts unmolested), and post overland to London.[75]

News of the eventful voyage traveled back to New York somewhat slower than the packet boat's crossing of twenty-one days. William Pitt quickly made arrangements to notify General Amherst of the lost dispatches in order that he might send copies and new information. A packet boat bearing the account left Falmouth on March 29.[76] On May 16, 1761, an "extraordinary" issue of *The New-York Gazette, or Weekly Post-Boy* reported the affair of the *General Wall,* but no mention was made of the passenger from New York who had managed to reach the mother country safely.[77] Schuyler himself wrote home to

---

able to assume that the next ranking member of the crew would take command. Although one mate was taken hostage by the privateer, it seems likely that there were other crew members qualified to take charge. It was Thomas Robinson who made the report to the postal authorities, not Schuyler, so it seems most unlikely that Schuyler had command of the boat. No other mention is made in official correspondence about the mishap, and Schuyler would probably have won mention had he assumed the direction of the vessel. See George Bell to the Postmaster General, Mar. 25, 1761, C.O. 5/52:95, and Robert Hampden to William Pitt, Mar. 27, 1761, C.O. 5/52:97. Hampden mentions a report of the *General Wall's* trip as given by "the Master," and Schuyler is not mentioned. Baxter, *A Godchild of Washington,* gives the reminiscences of Schuyler's youngest daughter, Catherine, who said her "account of the voyage was related to me by my father himself," but her account must be judged inaccurate inasmuch as she dates her father's trip in 1760, says he settled *his* accounts instead of Bradstreet's, that Captain Lutwidge died on the tenth day at sea when in fact he died on the twentieth day, and that her father brought the vessel safely to London when in fact it docked at Falmouth, the regular depot for mail boats. Her account adds more to the story. In a severe gale the *General Wall* was to have sighted a dismantled slaver with 200 Negroes in irons. The officers and crew were transferred to the packet, and the Negroes freed to make out the best they could on the abandoned ship. Again, the packet log carries no such account. The only element of truth in this tale is the resemblance it has to the transfer of officers and crew, held prisoner by the privateer, to the packet boat. Schuyler's daughter says further in her reminiscences that after the encounter with the slaver, the *General Wall* hailed a craft bound for the West Indies with a cargo of horses and told its captain the slaver's bearings in order that he might feed the Negroes horseflesh if he found their vessel. Finally, she says an English ship came to the rescue of the *General Wall.* This is false.

[75] Mr. La Fargue (captain of the privateer) to Schuyler, April 30, 1761. NYPL, Schuyler Papers Box 23.

[76] C.O. 5/52:101–110. See also copy of a letter from George Bell to Henry Potts, Mar. 30, 1761. C.O. 5/52:111.

[77] *The New-York Gazette, or Weekly Post-Boy,* May 16, 1761. See also *The New-York Gazette* (Weyman), May 18, 1761.

allay the anxiety of family and friends, and on May 15, William
Smith, Jr., dispatched a letter in reply. He had heard the report of
the unusual voyage the day before when the Falmouth packet arrived
in New York. Congratulating Schuyler on his escape and safe arrival
without the loss of his papers, Smith assured him his letters to Mrs.
Schuyler and Bradstreet had been forwarded, and then turned to an
inquiry about the "late Changes among the principal Offices." "Pray
let us know every Thing on your side that concerns us," he added.
"What sort of Folks have the Plantation Affairs in their Hands?" Mrs.
Smith gladly accepted his offers to procure some household furnishings, including seventeen yards of the best carpeting.[78] Thus the colonial visitor in the imperial capital might occupy himself with gathering a variety of things, from the highest political intelligence to the
material for adorning house and person.

Whatever Philip Schuyler saw and wrote from old England is no
longer part of the record. From March, 1761, until October, 1762, he
had ample opportunity to observe and accomplish a great deal. His
primary business was to settle Bradstreet's accounts. But these were
matters not quickly executed. The method of declaring accounts was
long and tedious. Copies had to be made in the Audit Office. From
thence they passed to the treasury to be declared and registered before
the Commissioners of the Treasury and Chancellor of the Exchequer.
Returned to the Audit Office for more clerical additions, they were
then sent to the office of the King's Remembrancer, from there to the
Lord Treasurer's Remembrancer, and finally to the Clerk of the Pipe.
Schuyler had fees and gratuities to pay all along the way. For gratuities to clerks he spent over £260; the auditor of the accounts received
over £470. Administrative methods devised in Elizabeth's reign [79]
were time-consuming and quite enough to try Schuyler's patience were
it not for other diversions in London and the countryside.

In May, shortly after his arrival in London, Schuyler received a plea
from the master of the privateer which had interrupted his voyage.
Monsieur La Fargue of the *Biscayen* had heard flattering words of
Schuyler from Peter Robinson, the mate taken hostage from the *Gen-*

[78] Smith to Schuyler, May 15, 1761. NYPL, Schuyler Papers Box 23.

[79] Account Book, 1756–1798, entry of Dec. 28, 1762. NYPL, Schuyler Papers. Box 9
contains a debit entry in Bradstreet's account with Schuyler (Dec. 28, 1762) to the
amount of £849 18s. 10d. in cash paid Thomas Farraine, auditor of accounts, for fees
and "sundry incidental" expenses. See also M. S. Giuseppi, *A Guide to the Manuscripts preserved in the Public Record Office* (2 vols.; London, 1923–1924), I, 118–119.

eral Wall. First apologizing that Schuyler should have paid £50 as a share of the packet boat's ransom (it was never his custom to exact so much from prisoners, he said), La Fargue asked Schuyler's kindness in procuring the exchange of three of his brothers who had been sent prisoners to Bristol.[80] Whether the New Yorker was able to effect such a release is not evident. But the gesture suggests that Schuyler was a gentleman of considerable presence, even at twenty-seven, that he inspired confidence, and that men who met him believed he had talents of persuasion and influence.

Schuyler's interests and business were sufficient to keep him well occupied between calls at the government offices. He must find proper bankers to handle his funds, buy furnishings for the new house being built at home, and run errands for fellow Yorkers like his friend William Smith, Jr.[81] For his own pleasure there were all the advantages of an imperial metropolis, the theater and clubs to attend and the whole of the English countryside to see. Through some gentlemen scientists Schuyler was introduced to a society of arts, and he struck up an acquaintanceship with Thomas Brand, a London surgeon, whose later correspondence reveals that the New Yorker was made a corresponding member of the society. These connections begun in London lasted several years, for Brand later relayed the compliments offered by friends in the city and told Schuyler that his proposal for a settlement at Detroit had been highly pleasing to them. They had readily approved it, but such a scheme had few prospects of success in the face of new imperial regulations such as the Royal Proclamation Line of 1763.[82]

It is not unlikely that Schuyler visited the English countryside and that he obtained ideas for planning his own house from the stately mansions he saw there. It is altogether probable that he also viewed the newly completed canal built by the Duke of Bridgewater, for Schuyler early developed an interest in canals, and his utilitarian mind was always ready to grasp some fresh innovation for possible

[80] La Fargue to Schuyler, April 30, 1761. NYPL, Schuyler Papers Box 23.

[81] Receipt May 2, 1761, by Pierpont and Campbell "in Cheapside near bow Church" for £925. Invoice of sundries sent from London to Col. Bradstreet totaling £625 13s. 1d. A long list includes glassware, chests, linen, dishes, candlesticks, silverware, shoes, buttons, locks, doorknobs, hinges, cups, sillabubs, decanters, globes, and figures for three chimney pieces. J. Campbell's signed receipt June 3, 1762, shows Schuyler spent over £900 while in England. NYPL, Schuyler Papers Box 2.

[82] Thomas Brand to Schuyler, Mar. 10, 1763. NYPL, Schuyler Papers Box 23.

use in his homeland.[83] His trip to Ireland has barely a record except for his own passing reference to it years later. Perhaps he ventured across the Irish Sea to visit his brother Cortlandt, who had purchased a commission in the royal army and served several years in Ireland on active duty before he resigned his position.[84]

In midyear, 1762, Schuyler was beginning to think of winding up affairs and going home. Preparing his personal accounts on May 31, he wrote, "If an Accident should happen to me my Executors will observe that all the before mentioned goods have been bought with bills for which I paid 85 per Cent Exchange at New York . . . and £5..5 Sterling Insurance besides freight & charges, that whoever has had any of them may pay at that rate to my heirs." After the encounter with the privateer he might well anticipate "an Accident." The accounts were detailed—sums for "taylors," a trunkmaker, barber, bookseller, razor maker, milliner, and shoemaker. His lodgings were itemized at over £90, his doctors' and apothecary's bills at £29. The "rheumatic gout" evidently followed him to London. He had purchased £700 worth of goods sent to America, properly insured, and they included almost everything imaginable from silver and gilt buckles and hats to a "Baggammon table," a case of drawing instruments, and a "spying glass," not to mention spurs, whips, and silk stockings. His losses on four lottery tickets he calculated at over £20.[85]

On May 24, 1762, "a state" of Bradstreet's accounts "having been approved and Allowed by Warrant of the Lords Commissioners of

[83] Benson J. Lossing, *History of American Industries and Arts* (Philadelphia, 1876), pp. 375–377. The Bridgewater canal linked the Worsley coal mines with Manchester.

[84] Schuyler's account of his presence in Ireland was made years later. Schuyler to Governor Trumbull, Nov. 10, 1775: "From Major Preston & the Officers of the 26th Regiment I have experienced the most polite & friendly attention, when I was a Stranger, a Traveller in Ireland." Letter Book, 1775–1776, p. 221, NYPL, Schuyler Papers. The exact time of Cortlandt Schuyler's sojourn in Ireland is not clear. Anne Grant, *Memoirs*, II, 45, 114, says he resigned his commission and suggests he came back to New York with his Irish wife and a family in 1764. A letter of John Cochran to Schuyler, April 2, 1766 (NYPL, Schuyler Papers Box 23) would indicate that Cortlandt did not purchase an army commission until 1766. Schuyler, *Colonial New York*, II, 256, 278, says Cortlandt was in Ireland from 1762 to 1764. Cortlandt gave Philip his power of attorney on July 20, 1762, which suggests his anticipated or actual departure from New York about this time. (*Index to the Public Records of the County of Albany, State of New York, 1630–1894: Grantees* [12 vols.; Albany, 1908–1911], X, 6492.)

[85] "Accounts, 1761 & 1762 in England." NYSL, Schuyler Papers.

His Majestys Treasury," Schuyler's mission was officially ended. Before he made his second and last Atlantic crossing he perhaps enjoyed a final round through London and the countryside. He had been paid well enough for his troubles and his pleasures. Aside from his salary he had profited from an invaluable experience. His expenses were reimbursed: £8 for carrying the vouchers from Albany to New York; £37 5s. 6d. for his and his manservant's passage from New York to Falmouth; a gratuity of £10 16s. to the officer of the French privateer for not carrying off Bradstreet's papers, and £10 for travel for Schuyler and his servant from Falmouth to London.[86] For his ordinary pay from December 25, 1760, to November 20, 1762, he received £487, and for his special services in settling the accounts in London (January 31, 1761, to November 20, 1762) he received another £593. At least he had earned more than he spent during the nineteen months abroad. Schuyler's connections with Bradstreet were indeed proving to be a "way to fortune and distinction." But they had only just begun.[87]

Schuyler's association with John Bradstreet raises the question as to the nature and extent of his profits, and to profiteering. In her *Memoirs,* Anne Grant says Bradstreet's "department was a very lucrative one, and enabled him first, greatly to enrich himself, and in process of time, his friend Philip Schuyler, who from his deputy, became, in a manner, his coadjutor."[88] It must be remembered that wartime profit-making, or for that matter, peacetime supply of His Majesty's troops, was hardly an opprobrious occupation. No stigma was attached to it. But for Schuyler there was relatively little on which he could directly profiteer. Before his trip to England and his mother's death, the development of his estate was only embryonic, despite ownership of his grandfather's gristmill and sawmill at Saratoga. There is no evidence that he sold much timber or grain from his lands. And until he came into his inheritance, his administration of the estate was for the benefit of other members of the family. Bradstreet's accounts show no details, only gross sums, many paid to par-

[86] John Bradstreet's Declared Account, 1756 to 1760. A.O. 335/1339:52–54.

[87] NYPL, Schuyler Papers Box 9. Schuyler's accounts as director and manager under Bradstreet show his salary for the following years: 1756, Schuyler and others, £368 11s. 11d.; 1757, nothing; 1758, £255 10s.; 1759, £242 18s.; 1760, £255 10s.; Dec. 25, 1760 to Nov. 20, 1762, £487 4s. (regular pay); Jan. 31, 1761 to Nov. 20, 1762 (for special service in settling accounts in London) £593 2s.; 1763 to April 9, 1764, £146; 1764–1765, £146; 1765–1766, £146; 1767–1768, £146.

[88] Anne Grant, *Memoirs,* II, 12.

ticular merchants by name. Schuyler's accounts reveal only minor sales of produce and the payments of his salary.[89]

In 1761, Schuyler did receive funds from Bradstreet in the form of loans, part of which were cancelled by Bradstreet's will in 1774. And in 1760, Schuyler had received an outright gift of £350 to buy a piece of land. Bradstreet made subsequent loans to Schuyler, most of which were repaid.[90] It is true that Schuyler benefited from his association with Bradstreet, but the most substantial part of any gains seems to have come *after* his return to Albany in 1762. He and Bradstreet continued their association, Schuyler developing his own estates, running errands for his aging friend, and joining in schemes for procuring more land. As for wartime peculations, none are in evidence. Schuyler was an agent who handled tens of thousands of pounds for the service.[91] He benefited from Bradstreet primarily from his loans and gifts and their joint speculation in land.

Although Schuyler employed idled troops in the development of his Saratoga property, this was in accordance with army regulations as long as the soldiers were paid for their services. But again, this hap-

[89] John Bradstreet's Declared Account, 1756 to 1760. A.O. 335/1339. Most of Schuyler's recorded acquisitions were salary payments. See footnote 87 *supra*. In 1762 he was paid (together with a Walter Hingham) £111 0s. 6d. for boards, £50 for rent of pasture lands (probably for livestock of the troops) and £256 5s. "for oars by Abraham Fonda on his account." NYPL, Schuyler Papers Box 9. Still, contemporaries believed Schuyler benefited handsomely from Bradstreet's connection. The Tory historian, Thomas Jones, hardly an unbiased writer, said that Bradstreet, extremely pleased with the "conversation" and "behavior" of young Mrs. Schuyler, appointed her husband deputy and by "this means, from moderate circumstances he became rich." (Jones, *History of New York*, II, 316.) Of Bradstreet, Professor John R. Alden has written that it "was notorious that he enriched himself at the expence of the crown" and that "Schuyler, his good friend . . . does not appear to have suffered from the connection." Although Schuyler was financially embarrassed before his London trip, his fortunes improved by virtue of the association. In 1766, General Thomas Gage questioned some of Schuyler's accounts with Bradstreet. Schuyler then proposed to visit Gage to prove the validity of his accounts, "but Gage refused to see him—this in spite of or perhaps because of the fact that Mrs. Gage and Schuyler were cousins." Alden, *General Gage*, p. 73.

[90] NYPL, Schuyler Papers Box 9. Bradstreet forgave Schuyler a debt of £3,454 18s. 3¾d. in his will. Schuyler's own statement to this effect is in "The Answer of Philip Schuyler . . . to John Evans . . . and Agatha his wife [1788]." NYPL, Schuyler Papers Box 10.

[91] Bradstreet's Account with Schuyler, 1756–1762, and Abstract of Monies received and credits given for the public service in the Quartermaster General's Department, 1756–1772, NYPL, Schuyler Papers Box 9. See also, for example, the copy of a letter, Abraham Mortier to Jeffrey Amherst, Oct. 2, 1760. T. 1/400:112.

pened largely after the London trip when Schuyler turned his full energies to the development of his estate, and there is no evidence to show that he was dishonest in such dealings.[92]

– 5 –

"THE PASTURES"

PHILIP SCHUYLER's Albany mansion became a social center well known for its comforts, quiet elegance, and the hospitality of its gracious owners. Writing in December, 1780, the Marquis de Chastellux testified to that: "A handsome house half way up the bank opposite the ferry, seems to attract attention, and to invite strangers to stop at General Schuyler's, who is the proprietor as well as architect. I had recommendations to him from all quarters. . . ." Upon the marquis' arrival, facilitated by Schuyler's dispatch of his sledge, he was conveyed "into a handsome saloon, near a good fire, with Mr. Schuyler, his wife and daughters." The nobleman also noted his pleasure with the agreeable companionship, the well-laid table and the excellent Madeira.[93] Ten years later another visitor, less distinguished perhaps than the marquis, had something else to add about the house. Writing for the London *Gentleman's Magazine,* he said:

While in Albany . . . we accepted an invitation from Gen. Schuyler . . . to spend a day with him at his fine residence near the city. We had heard much in praise of the delightful situation of the mansion and the enchanting views to be seen from it. But we never beheld a more enchanting picture than the broad and beautiful view that is seen from it. Its architecture, though not imposing, is yet attractive in its simple elegance. It is situated near the center of extensive grounds, sloping gradually towards the Hudson, whose bright waters, richly indented and beautifully curved shores are in full view, both from the north and the south. The grounds are laid out in all the elaborate art of French landscape gardening, with here and there parterres, some of which are nicely lawned. Beyond the western shores of the Hudson the Helderberg, precipitous and craggy, sweep in a majestic range, while still further in the distance are the blue peaks of the Catskills.[94]

[92] Anne Grant, *Memoirs,* II, 113–116. See also Alden, *General Gage,* p. 73. For a discussion of the postwar development of Saratoga, see Chapter II "Foundations of Interest and Influence," *infra.*

[93] Chastellux, *Travels,* I, 371, 374–375.

[94] L. B. Proctor, "Historic Memories of the Old Schuyler Mansion," (a pamphlet [Albany, 1888]), p. 4. This report taken from a London magazine was probably the first about the Schuyler mansion except for Chastellux's mention of it. In 1952 an-

It was a fine setting for a family seat. And Schuyler chose it quite evidently with an eye for beauty and an intent to impress. Construction was begun shortly after his departure for London in March, 1761.

During Schuyler's travels abroad much had been doing in Albany. The new house going up under Bradstreet's supervision progressed in good order, while Mrs. Schuyler prepared for another lying-in. The former developed satisfactorily enough, but the latter brought sorrow without the consolation an absent husband could not give. A set of twins, born on July 29, 1761, was probably too much for the Van Rensselaer constitution; the boy immediately died without baptism, and the other child, christened Cornelia after her paternal grandmother, did not survive infancy.[95]

Schuyler's house received its title from its master's youthful nickname, "Philip of the Pasture," and because it originally stood at the edge of the city's communal meadowland about a half mile south of Albany. The master had his first view of it as he hastily made his way up the Hudson from New York late in November, 1762. His anxiety to return to his family is suggested in a letter to John Bradstreet. "His sickness is a very good excuse for taking the shortest way home," wrote General Amherst.[96] Perhaps the sea voyage had been unsalubrious instead of salutary, or was it a recurrence of the "rheumatic gout," with "bilious fever" or a touch of homesickness? Arriving in New York on November 20, Schuyler wasted no time boarding a sloop bound for Albany. On a gentle slope of the western bank of the Hudson stood the house that was to be his lifelong haven. It must have

other London periodical devoted to showing stately homes of England and the United States included an article with illustrations of "the Pastures." See Helen Comstock, "The Schuyler Mansion, Albany, New York" in H. Granville Fell (ed.), *The Connoisseur Year Book, 1952* (London, 1952), pp. 100–104.

[95] The family Bible entry recording the birth of the twins reads: "s'morgens zyn geberen onse verden ende vyfden kinders den einen ein sone den andere ein docter, den sone stierf angedopt. den docter werde genaemt Cornelia . . . van den aenraende mantis is dit Rint over leeden den heer heift gegeven den heer heift genomen, heylije is de naeme des Heeren." See also Schuyler, *Colonial New York*, II, 243.

[96] Amherst to Bradstreet, Nov. 21, 1762, in Humphreys, *Catherine Schuyler*, p. 76. For the nickname and the name of the house, see Anne Grant, *Memoirs*, I, 280; cf. S. B. Malcom to Philip Jeremiah Schuyler, June 19, 1805: NYSL, Schuyler Papers. For the date of Schuyler's arrival in New York see "The Answer of Philip Schuyler . . . to the bill of complaint of John Evans . . . and Agatha his wife," which states he returned to New York "on or about the 20th day of November in the Year 1762." NYPL, Schuyler Papers Box 10.

been a reassuring sight to an ill and travel-weary voyager, even with the workmen still moving about the premises.

Plans for "the Pastures" were evidently laid even before Schuyler set out on his extended journeys in 1761, and it is not unlikely that the young owner submitted directions from the opposite side of the Atlantic after viewing the fine old houses of the mother country.[97] The style was rather new for Albany, still strongly Dutch in its ways and appearance, with its high-gabled buildings and well-swept stoops. But Schuyler was as decidedly English by adoption as he was Dutch by birth. The English influence was strong, and he first fell under its sway when royal troops marched in and out of Albany during the war. Eighteen months and more in England could not but make an impression on an eclectic mind such as his. "The Pastures" was built in the Georgian fashion, considerably more modest than a manor house, but spacious, comfortable, and impressive for its surroundings.

Contemporaries mistook John Bradstreet's role in supervising the erection of the mansion for ownership. But clearly Bradstreet built the house only in the capacity of an attorney, and Schuyler himself appears to have been the architect.[98]

"The Pastures" became a handsome home, a rather brilliant social center and visiting place for many distinguished guests, including Benjamin Franklin and Charles Carroll, John Burgoyne, who was held in genteel captivity there in 1777, Washington, Lafayette, Kosciusko, Steuben, Hamilton, and even Aaron Burr, who became one of Schuyler's bitterest enemies. Begun in May, 1761, the building was

[97] Pound, *Native Stock*, p. 68 says Mrs. Schuyler began the mansion on plans sent back by Schuyler after he had visited some English residences of distinction.

[98] Anne Grant, *Memoirs*, II, 50 n., says the house "was built by the wife of General Bradstreet. . . ." Thomas Jones, *History of New York*, II, 317, says Bradstreet built the house "and most gallantly made a present of it to Mrs. Schuyler." Jones also intimates that Bradstreet's relationship with Mrs. Schuyler was more intimate than Schuyler would have liked (II, 316). This is most improbable. Also a later writer, Frederic G. Mather, "The Schuyler House at Albany," Mrs. Martha J. Lamb (ed.), *Magazine of American History*, XII (July, 1884), 9, erroneously says Schuyler bought the house from the Bradstreet estate. See Schuyler's power of attorney to Bradstreet, NYPL, Schuyler Papers Box 10, and the "Extract from My Books August 25, 1788 [signed] Philip Schuyler," NYSL, Schuyler Papers, which refers specifically to "Capt. Schuyler's house." That Schuyler was the architect seems apparent from Chastellux, *Travels*, I, 371. See footnote 93 *supra*. Chastellux is creditable, for his information was acquired by direct conversation with Schuyler, and several otherwise undocumented stories about Schuyler are confirmed by the marquis.

neither quickly completed nor furnished. Indeed, when Schuyler first saw the house "only four apartments were finished, two on the first and two on the second floor . . . no other part of the house was floored except with unplaned boards . . . ," so Schuyler wrote his son-in-law, Alexander Hamilton, years later.[99]

Schuyler began to collect furnishings and minor accouterments abroad: "Crimson Flock" wallpaper (an imitation tapestry), hinges, locks, doorknobs, glassware, chests, candlesticks, decanters, figures for three chimney pieces, and sillabubs and cutlery. The boards, plank, and other lumber for the house came from Schuyler's mills and estate at Saratoga. Some of the workmen were his own slaves and servants. John Gaborial, master carpenter from Boston (who had built John Hancock's house), supervised the finer workmanship of the interior, including a finely turned staircase, and the massive door frames, the numerous window sashes and folding shutters. Some of Schuyler's own rough-hewn timber was made into door frames, sashes, shutters, and sills by craftsmen in New York City.[100] The brick was probably produced in nearby kilns.

Whatever Bradstreet spent on the house was done in his capacity as attorney, and Schuyler later settled with him for the £1,425 he expended. As late as 1767 the finishing touches had yet to be added. Through William Bayard, a New York merchant, Schuyler procured marble trim for the fireplaces from Philadelphia.[101]

There was in all the commotion of raising a new house and the settling of a home—the first of their own since the Schuylers married and set up housekeeping with his mother, Cornelia—a legal disturbance which threatened the composure of the young husband and father. Yet it was settled favorably enough. The Dutch Reformed Church of Albany brought an ejectment action against Philip Schuy-

[99] Anna K. Cunningham, *Schuyler Mansion a Critical Catalogue of the Furnishings & Decorations* (Albany, 1955), pp. 6, 8. For the time of the commencement of construction see NYPL, Schuyler Papers Box 10.

[100] *Ibid.* See also "Invoice of Sundries sent from London to Col. Bradstreet." NYPL, Schuyler Papers Box 2. The grand total of this lengthy list is £625 13s. 1d. See also "Extract from My Books August 25, 1788 [signed] Philip Schuyler" for Andrew Gautier's receipt for work done at New York for Captain Schuyler's house at Albany (the last payment was made April 4, 1764) and "A Compte of Mens Time in the Year 1762 Employed at Capt. Schuylers hous [sic] for Albany." NYSL, Schuyler Papers.

[101] Schuyler's account of the legal proceedings is in his "Answer . . . to . . . John Evans . . . and Agatha his wife [1788]." NYPL, Schuyler Papers Box 10. See also William Bayard to Schuyler, July 27, 1767. NYSL, Schuyler Papers.

ler because it claimed the land on which his house was being built. True to legal form the action dragged on for some years until late in September, 1765, when the parties arranged a compromise. Schuyler conveyed a tract he had bought from E. and P. Bogardus in exchange for his house lot. He also paid £275 to the church, for which he got another parcel of ground nearby. But the difficulty was still not completely resolved. A second controversy arose concerning a "41 Morgan & 400 rood tract," and this was not settled until February, 1776. The church then released claim to the 400-rood portion and Schuyler relinquished claim to the 41 morgens. In the first dispute John Bradstreet was still involved as Schuyler's attorney. He again proved to be a benefactor, for it was through Bradstreet that the pasture land south of Beaver Kill and west of the Hudson passed into Schuyler's possession.[102]

By 1767, Philip Schuyler ranked among the nine leading townsmen in Albany in the value of city property. His house had placed him in that position. Only seven others, numbering men like John De Peyster, Jacob and Henry Ten Eyck, Volkert Douw, and Harmen Gansvoort, ranked higher on the tax assessor's list.[103]

All in all, the provincial squire had made an auspicious beginning. His family roots gave him unquestioned position, but even that might

[102] NYPL, Schuyler Papers Box 10. See also the *Index to the Public Records of the County of Albany, State of New York, 1630–1894: Grantees* (12 vols.; Albany, 1908–1911), X, 6492. According to Marshall Harris, *Origin of the Land Tenure System in the United States* (Ames, Iowa, 1953), p. 211, a morgen of land was two acres.

[103] "Albany Tax Lists, 1766–1767." NYPL, Schuyler Papers Box 18. Schuyler's property was listed at £110. His fellows were listed on amounts ranging from £125 to £160. Some thirty years later Schuyler's position was considerably better. In all of Albany County only Stephen Van Rensselaer and James Duane had a real and personal estate valued more than Schuyler's. However, most of Schuyler's land lay north of Albany County. The three ranking property holders (in point of valuation) were: Van Rensselaer, $75,782.40 in real estate, $25,003 in personal property; James Duane, $19,680 in unoccupied lands, $12,050 in house and farm, $1,365 in personal property; Schuyler, $26,943 in house and lot, $5,348 in personal property. See "Assessment Roll of the real and Personal Estates [in Albany, Watervliet, Schenectady, Bethlehem, Colymans, Coxsackie, Princeton, Duanesburgh, Bern, Rensselaerville, and Freehold, 1799]," Albany Institute of History and Art. Schuyler's property at Saratoga was developed to such an extent that by 1777 his house, sawmills, storehouses, and outbuildings there were valued at an estimated £10,000 by General John Burgoyne, commander of the British invasionary forces, who burned them. *The Parliamentary Register; or, History of the Proceedings and Debates of the House of Commons: Series One*, VIII, 311.

be improved. His connections with Bradstreet opened the way to greater wealth and influence almost as much as his inherited land-holdings did. True to the fashion of his class and day he concentrated on the improvement of his estate, the expansion of lands and the fulfillment of an aspiration to rise to still greater wealth, still wider influence. For a decade he labored to buttress his position for the day when he might step into public affairs—another activity which he seems hardly to have contemplated or wished for before 1768. Despite the urgency of the political crisis of 1764–1766, there is no evidence that Philip Schuyler was troubled by anything but his attention to private interests. While one of the most serious of colonial-imperial disputes over taxation and Parliamentary sovereignty took shape, nothing appeared more important to the young landlord preoccupied with the projection of his Saratoga plantation than his personal affairs. The local, the particular, seemed dominant.

Peter (Quidor) Schuyler (1657–1724), first mayor of Albany, by Sir Godfrey
Kneller. From Albany City Hall.

Captain Johannes Schuyler (1668–1747) and his wife, Elizabeth Wendell (née Staats) ?–1737. Oil on canvas, attributed to John Watson.

The Protestant Dutch Church in Albany was built in 1715 and razed in 1806.

John Schuyler, Jr. (1697–1741) by an unidentified Hudson Valley artist. Oil on canvas, about 1725.

The Staats House, Albany, was built in 1667 at the corner of State and Pearl Streets. Birthplace of Philip Schuyler. From Gorham A. Worth, *Random Recollections of Albany, from 1800 to 1803* (3rd ed.; Albany, 1866), I, 27.

Philip Schuyler (1733–1804). Miniature by John Trumbull, Philadelphia, 1792.

Mrs. Philip Schuyler (1734–1803), née Catherine Van Rensselaer. Oil on canvas by Thomas McIlworth, about 1762–1767.

New York City about 1763, southwest view. Drawn by Captain Thomas Howdell; engraving by P. Canot.

New York City about 1763, southeast view. Drawn by Captain Thomas Howdell; engraving by P. Canot.

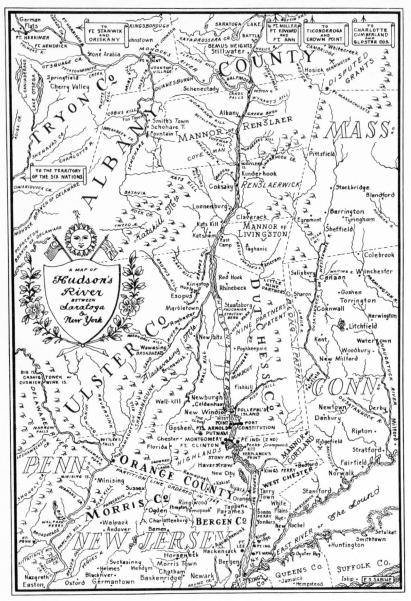

The Hudson River between New York and Saratoga by Ellen S. Sabine. From William H. W. Sabine (ed.), *Historical Memoirs from 12 July 1776 to 25 July 1778 of William Smith* (New York, 1958).

CHAPTER II

Foundations of Interest and Influence

– 1 –

THE COLONEL'S COLONY

IN A REPORT on New York in 1765, Lieutenant Governor Cadwallader Colden divided the population into four classes: the large landholders whose estates ranged from 100,000 to over one million acres; the gentlemen of the law; merchants; and, finally, the farmers and mechanics, forming the bulk of the populace, who were the "most useful and most Moral," but were "made dupes of the former." [1] According to Colden, Philip Schuyler belonged to the first category, but it is doubtful that he held even so much as 100,000 acres at the time. His holdings are difficult to determine, except in minimal terms, but Schuyler belonged to the landed aristocracy by reason of his interests, heritage, and ambition, if not by any exact measurement by Colden's standards.

Land lay at the center of Schuyler's many and dearest concerns, served as the basis of his wealth, the buttress of his position, the foundation of all his interests. In 1765 it was the hope of his future, for if he did not then have as many as 100,000 acres, his aspirations directed those endeavors by which he accumulated enough territory to rank as one of the great landed magnates of the day. Because the fires of Schuyler's wealth and position forged his conservative patriotism, an understanding of the foundations of his station is vital to our comprehension of his role in the Revolution in New York.

Despite the imperial crisis of 1764–1766, Schuyler remained preoccupied with private affairs—the security of his family's agrarian foundations. He was first a country squire, not a politician. Only reluctantly did he heed the urgings of an attorney and friend, William Smith, Jr., to divert his full energies from the development of his estates to the vagaries of provincial politics. In 1768, Smith was able to persuade him to stand for the assembly, if only for a short service. Within a few years, Smith assured him, he might be left in "full &

---

[1] Colden's report. C.O. 5/1098:45–46.

quiet Possession of [his] Wolves Foxes Snow Mills Fish & Lands at Saraghtoga." Meanwhile, Schuyler should give some attention to provincial affairs, not wholly at the expense of his landed enterprise, but as a means of promoting the agrarian interests in which so many others shared his squirely concern. Even in 1787, when Schuyler gave the management of his Saratoga plantation to his son, John Bradstreet, it was with sighs that only a man close to his property might utter: "I resign to your care and for your sole emolument," he said, "a place on which I have for a long series of Years bestowed much of my care and attention, and I confess I should part from it with many a severe pang did I not resign it to my Child." [2] This was the sentiment of a man who not only held land by inheritance, but also knew how laborious his efforts at acquiring an estate had been.

Late in the Revolutionary War, Schuyler described himself as a member of "the middling class" among men of considerable property.[3] It was an apt designation, considering that he was no manorial lord; but however great his holdings and interests, his ambitions and temperament made him more of a lord than a middler. Still, the Schuylers, unlike the Livingstons, Cosbys, Heathcotes, Van Rensselaers, Pells, Van Cortlandts, Philipses, and Morrises, held no manors. Perhaps the nearest any Schuyler came to so formal or legal a distinction was the occasion of Colonel Peter's visit to London where he was offered a baronetcy for his role in keeping the Indians detached from the French. But of the twenty-three manors erected under English rule in New York, all but two were granted before 1700.[4] And the Schuylers, especially the younger line from which Philip sprang, stood in no position for such an early distinction. All the manorial patents were granted to persons of great substance and importance in an effort to create a landed aristocracy devoted to the Crown and to the royal governors. The Schuylers as a family held sizable tracts. Individually, however, their possessions were not then substantial enough to warrant such a privilege.

[2] Schuyler to John Bradstreet Schuyler, Dec. 3, 1787. NYHS, Misc. MSS (Schuyler); see also Smith to Schuyler, Jan. 18, 1768. NYPL, Schuyler Papers Box 23.

[3] Schuyler to —— (copy), Mar. 11, 1780. C.O. 5/1110:203–205.

[4] Caleb Heathcote got Scarsdale Manor in 1701 and Killian Van Rensselaer II altered the patroonship to Rensselaerwyck Manor in 1704. *The Order of Colonial Lords of Manors in America Year Book No. 27* (New York, 1911–1936). See also Julius L. Goebel, Jr., "Some Legal and Political Aspects of the Manors in New York," *The Order of Colonial Lords of Manors in America, Publication No. 18* (Baltimore, 1928), pp. 8, 17–22.

If the Schuylers held no manor, they nevertheless ranked with the manorial class by marriage and common interest. And in view of the doubtful legal advantages of a manorial grant and because the substance of such a grant consisted of its more general social and political implications—of the holder's personal talents and wealth—it was not necessary to be a manor lord under the law in order to share the advantages of the position in fact. Manors, after all, were scarcely different from other estates except in name. They conveyed no title to the owner. They neither descended by strict feudal inheritance nor conferred any feudal obligations. They did not share the nature of medieval fiefs. Some of them did carry political privilege, but this was more substantial in matters of prestige than anything else—except for the Cortlandt, Livingston, and Rensselaer manors, which were given special representation in the colonial assembly.

Central to Philip Schuyler's estates was that portion of the Saratoga Patent (1684) which his grandfather Johannes had purchased from a son of one of the original grantees and passed on through his son John, Jr., Philip's father. In January, 1763, Schuyler acquired the nucleus of all his later holdings when his mother's estate was opened to settlement. This was a mere 1,875 acres of his father's share (6,650 acres) which was divided among Philip, his two brothers, Cortlandt and Stephen, and a sister, Gertrude. Contrary to the assertion of his two biographers that Schuyler waived his right under primogeniture in 1754 because of his generosity, is the last will and testament of his father, which was proved on May 11, 1743. This instrument provided that all lands and estates bequeathed to John Schuyler, Jr.'s, wife Cornelia, by her father, Stephen Van Cortlandt, were left to be used at her discretion. She was also to have the use of all her husband's property for the advancement and education of their children. Upon her death the children were to share the estate. It was not to be given to one son. Primogeniture was not operative unless a person died intestate, and both Schuyler's father and mother disposed of their property by will. Other than the 1,875 acres at Saratoga, Philip Schuyler's holdings when he began the independent activities of a landlord and speculator remain largely unspecified. His mother left him part of a farm in Cortlandt Manor. Other farms there were left to be divided among himself and his brothers and sister. He held an interest in the unpartitioned portion of the Saratoga Patent until surveyors made a division in 1769. From his uncle Philip, who died in 1748, he received "a piece of woodland" near present-day West Troy. All in all, Schuyler had only the beginnings of an estate that one day was measured not in thousands but in tens of thousands of acres.[5]

The difficulty of determining the exact or even approximate amount of land Philip Schuyler held at a particular time is scarcely more of a problem for the researcher than it was for Schuyler himself. In January, 1760, he wrote Colonel Henry Glen to ask him to "Inform the Bearer where the lands belonging to my father Lye in the patent [Schenectady] Called Glen's purchase." [6] It was the query of a young man awakened to the obligations of administering family holdings— to the labors of exploiting that which was his own, and to the ambition to accumulate still greater tracts of New York's unexploited wilderness.

Schuyler did not tarry for the settlement of his parents' estates to launch land schemes of his own. In September, 1760, he joined Oliver De Lancey, Peter Du Bois, Garret Abeel, and ninety-six others to petition for three tracts amounting to 200,000 acres. The first petition was for permission to take up vacant lands on both sides of the upper Mohawk, above the German Flatts between Cosby's Manor and the Oriskany Patent. The second was for an area above Fort Stanwix. In all, the two parcels amounted to approximately 100,000 acres. The third tract lay north of Saratoga on the east side of the Hudson. The petitioners requested a license to buy the land from the Indians.[7] Under the prevailing policy of limiting land grants to one or two thousand acres per grantee, the one hundred petitioners might acquire only 2,000 acres each—unless a few privately bought the interests of the others once the grant had passed through the official channels.

These early cooperative efforts came to nought. The lands were not

[5] "Certified Copies of Land Grants," and a "List of Divisions of the Saratoga Patent, Jan. 3, 1763." NYPL, Schuyler Papers Boxes 16, 21. See also *Colls. N.Y. Hist. Soc. for 1894* (New York, 1895), XXVII: Abstracts of Wills, III, 387; *Colls. N.Y. Hist. Soc. for 1897* (New York, 1898), XXX: Abstracts of Wills, VI, 205; "Field Book of the remainder of the lands undivided in the Saratoga Patent, Aug. 17, 1769," NYPL, Schuyler Papers Box 22; Schuyler, *Colonial New York*, I, 203, and II, 150, 242, 257; Copy of [uncle] Philip Schuyler's Will, June 28, 1748, in the Albany Institute of History and Art; for an example of the extent of Schuyler's later holdings, see Schuyler to William Constable, July 23, 1790, Albany Institute of History and Art. Marshall Harris, *op. cit.*, pp. 320–322, cites existing law of inheritance succession.

[6] Schuyler to Glen, Jan. 9, 1760. NYHS, Misc. MSS (Schuyler).

[7] *Calendar of N.Y. Colonial Manuscripts indorsed Land Papers in the Office of the Secretary of State of New York, 1643–1803* (Albany, 1864), pp. 293–294.

granted; nor could young Schuyler have been very cheered at the outcome of this first attempt to wring new holdings from the royal governor.[8] Nothing daunted, John Bradstreet endeavored to assist Schuyler and to add to his protégé's holdings in 1761 while he was still in England. On September 19, 1761, Daniel McCloud, Jacob Reeder, Benjamin Freeman, and seventeen others signed an agreement to turn over to Philip Schuyler the interests in 25,000 acres for which they were about to petition Lieutenant Governor Colden. Bradstreet arranged this scheme. The land lay east of the Hudson just north of the Saratoga Patent. This was probably within the very tract that the one hundred petitioners of September, 1760, had solicited but failed to acquire. Evidently this was meant to be an addition to Schuyler's Saratoga holdings and it was necessary to arrange for a corporate action in order to manage so large an acquisition. Doubtless the agreement the signers made to use their names in a petition while acting only in trust for Schuyler was a secret one. But it, too, came to nothing. The secrecy of the plans remains quite as enigmatic as their outcome.[9]

The extent of Schuyler's early land projects and the degree of success he had with these schemes are difficult to determine. Although these early petitions for lands were not approved, Schuyler, by his own statement in 1788, had made two land purchases before setting out on his London voyage. In December, 1760, he bought a parcel of land with a £350 gift John Bradstreet had made him. And in January,

[8] There is no evidence that Schuyler ever received such a grant or that he accumulated land in this manner. "Abstracts of New York Land Grants 1666–1764," C.O. 5/1134, shows no record of any acquisition by Schuyler, although contemporaries like George Clinton, Cadwallader Colden, Jr., Jeremiah Van Rensselaer, William and Philip Livingston, James Duane, and John Morin Scott managed to acquire grants from the governor. See also Chalmers MSS (4 vols., N.Y. History in NYPL), II, 76–77, "List of Patents and Warrants to survey lands granted in New York, Nov. 14, 1761–June 23, 1763 by Lt. Gov. Colden," and III, 10–11, "List of Grants of Land passed since the Death of Lieutenant Governor De Lancey by . . . Cadwallader Colden . . . March 27, 1761–Sept. 29, 1761." Schuyler, Colonial New York, II, 273–274, found "only one patent issued to him [Schuyler] personally" and that was in 1789 for a mere 45 acres on the outlet of Lake George.

[9] See footnote 8. The signed copy of the agreement is in NYPL, Schuyler Papers Box 16. Its preservation would suggest that it was kept as a means of protecting title to the grant and that the grant was in fact made. But there is no indication in the land grant records (including C.O. 5/1134) that the patent was issued to the twenty petitioners or that Schuyler got it.

1761, he made another land purchase near Albany with £1,000 Bradstreet had loaned him.[10] The record does not reveal what these acquisitions were, but the sums indicate that they were sizable tracts, and although the time of the purchases coincides with the September, 1760, petitions for land, the connection of the petitions with the avowed purchases remains a circumstantial one.

If Philip Schuyler contributed to the formation of colonial New York's landlord class, he was also the creature of the agrarian society in which he was reared. The family was still an important economic unit of society. It was the center of land speculation, leaseholding, clearing and planting, saw- and gristmilling, and even shipping and merchandizing. The rural landlord in New York often shipped his own and others' lumber, flour, grain, meat, cider, and iron ore to New York markets in his own vessels. He might act as a middleman for the sale of lead, powder, firearms, ironware, salt, cloth, and implements brought on the return trip. Philip Schuyler did all these things. His household was filled with servants—whites and slaves. His domain included leasehold tenants. His family was not merely a center of quiet gentility. It bustled with homely business. Even well-to-do women like Schuyler's wife made clothes for their slaves and supervised all the details of household production—soapmaking, candledipping, preserving, and weaving.[11]

Schuyler returned from England in November, 1762; with the conclusion of peace the following year, the energetic frontier aristocrat turned to the development of his estates. "Assiduously engaged in the management of his own private affairs, the operations of which were constantly increasing," [12] he was not long to be free from public service. From his grandfather he benefited from a patrimony of which his father had been deprived by an early death. His farm at Saratoga where Fish Creek empties into the Hudson, was already the site of saw- and gristmills his grandfather had erected. The farm was but a small portion of the nearly 2,000 acres that lay with it—the share Schuyler had drawn from the ancestral holdings in 1763. They needed only to be developed and exploited. He held interests elsewhere which, when taken with the Saratoga lands, probably amounted to

[10] "The Answer of Philip Schuyler of the City of Albany . . . to the bill of Complaint of John Evans . . . and Agatha his wife [1788]." NYPL, Schuyler Papers Box 10.

[11] Ironside, *The Family in Colonial N.Y.*, pp. 22, 24–25.

[12] Lossing, I, 196.

between ten and twenty thousand acres.[13] With Bradstreet, Philip Livingston and Governor Henry Moore, Schuyler made later additions to his holdings, largely speculative ventures in the Hudson and Mohawk valleys. His Saratoga estate, however, was the object of careful cultivation; there Schuyler planned to profit from its produce, not from its sale.

The landed magnate of Schuyler's generation might decide to leave his holdings idle, hoping to sell them later at a profit. Meantime, he would be obliged to defend his boundaries against interlopers. But if he chose to develop the holdings, he must run surveys, cut roads, build mills, and entice settlers. In this way the landlord would also function as a petty banker and capitalist. And if he chose to farm the land, he sometimes found keen competition among fellow landlords for acquiring tenants.

The improvements Schuyler began at Saratoga testify to his interests as a landlord just as his ventures elsewhere reflect his penchant for speculation. The way to increase the value of lands either for leasing or for sale was to erect the conveniences of settlement nearby and to encourage immigration. Schuyler dreamed of a colony, a manorial regime with himself, of course, as the local squire.

Following the mode of enterprise his Aunt Margaretta suggested, Schuyler profited from his connection with John Bradstreet during the war years. By 1763 his house at Albany, built "in the English taste, comparatively magnificent," was both his family headquarters

---

13 On the basis of the wills of Schuyler's grandfather, uncle, father and mother, and from what is known of the Schuyler holdings (see, for example, Schuyler, *Colonial New York*, II, 95–107, 240; C.O. 5/1134:51, 53, 56, 61, 76, 79, 83, 87, 88, 238, 240–241, 247–248; NYPL, Schuyler Papers Box 21; *Colls. N.Y. Hist. Soc. for 1895* (New York, 1896), XXVIII: Abstracts of Wills, IV, 134–136; *Colls. N.Y. Hist. Soc. for 1894* (New York, 1895), XXVII: Abstracts of Wills, III, 387; *Colls. N.Y. Hist. Soc. for 1897* (New York, 1898), XXX: Abstracts of Wills, VI, 205) we may estimate Philip Schuyler's holdings in 1763 to include the following: about 2,000 acres at Saratoga and the small improved farm of his uncle Philip with the mills; an interest in lands in the one-seventh share (approx. 24,000 acres) of the Saratoga Patent undivided until 1769; perhaps another 800 acres of miscellaneous lands from his grandfather; an unspecified amount of land in Cortlandt Manor from his mother; a share of about 2,000 acres of his father's personal accumulations; a share of his uncle Philip's personal accumulations (aside from inheritances). In Dec., 1760, and Jan., 1761, he purchased two undesignated pieces of land with a £350 gift and a £1,000 loan from John Bradstreet ("The Answer of Philip Schuyler . . . to the bill of Complaint of John Evans . . . and Agatha his wife [1788]." NYPL, Schuyler Papers Box 10). Schuyler also had his wife's interest in the Van Rensselaer estate of her father.

and the center "where he carried on the business of his department."[14] Schuyler continued his service to Bradstreet during the 1760's, disbursing military funds for him, and acting in general as his deputy in "the Public Service."[15] And at Saratoga, the scene of one of the world's most decisive battles (1777), Schuyler proceeded to build a colony.

The Saratoga establishment proved Philip Schuyler's political and economic genius. Wartime conditions enabled him to make use of a great number of workmen employed in public construction. During the slack seasons, when public business was interrupted, Schuyler seized the opportunity of hiring idled workers. He kept them in constant pay. He set workmen to construct "squares of buildings in the nature of barracks" which were to house "artisans and laborers of all kinds." His plan included "a nursery for the arts [and] the materials of a future colony, which he meant to plant out around him." Schuyler built a spacious and comfortable country house. His Negroes felled trees and managed several sawmills. The activity was doubly profitable. Rafts of deals and lumber floated downriver to New York brought a cash income. And at the same time land was cleared for his hired hands and tenants to cultivate.

In time the Saratoga estate grew in extent and value. Schuyler's "colony" was an "asylum for everyone who wanted bread and a home." Hundreds of people were employed in his mills, forests, and fields. In the winter months until freezing interrupted, the mill saws whined. When the water power failed, men could turn to logging. In the summer a "large and productive fishery" offered still other work. Schuyler provided his workmen with "lodging and firing," and paid them as well. He made the settlement a center for raising, dressing, and spinning flax into linen, "and as artisans were very scarce in the country, everyone sent linen to weave. . . ." Schuyler, it was said, could afford to pay his hands liberally, for he had abundant resources and "could afford to be the loser at first, to be amply repaid in the end." The author of the single contemporary account of his plantation thought it "inconceivable what dexterity, address, and deep policy were exhibited in the management of this new settlement; the

14 Anne Grant, *Memoirs,* II, 114.

15 "Abstract of Payments for the Public Service" shows Schuyler's salary as "director & manager in general" for Bradstreet, 1756–1772. NYPL, Schuyler Papers Box 9.

growth of which was repaid beyond belief." [16] By 1777, when the British laid waste to Saratoga, Schuyler's property consisted of "a very good dwellinghouse, exceeding large store-houses, great saw mills, and other out-buildings, to the value altogether of perhaps ten thousand pounds." [17] If the proprietor displayed such skill on private interests, what might he not contribute in political councils of the province? Here was the source of wealth and power which afterward enabled the New York squire to endure the losses he suffered in the Revolutionary War. Here were the foundations of his interest and influence in the politics of the province, and later the state, of New York.

To the mills at the Fish Kill falls at the Saratoga colony Schuyler added others, not only for lumber and grain, but also for flax.[18] He began his flax production in 1767. His tenants held leases which restricted such activity on their part, and encouraged only the productivity of the landlord's mills.[19]

Schuyler did not take his ease on the relatively small holdings he had inherited, but turned to other means of making his mark in the province. His personal ambitions and acquisitiveness led him to other activities of which the flaxmill was but one example of his energies. In 1762 he had toyed with a scheme for land speculation as far west as Detroit.[20] Like his attempts to procure royal land grants in 1760, his proposal for promoting a settlement west of Lake Erie fell by the way. Perhaps he overreached himself. The scheme certainly ran athwart the Royal Proclamation Line of 1763, and this prevented it from becoming anything more than a passing thought. Detroit was

[16] Anne Grant, *Memoirs*, II, 114–116. Cf. "Philip Schuyler's Daybook, 1764–1770," NYHS. There seems to be no evidence as to how liberal Schuyler was in paying wages, but the daybook for the Saratoga estate substantiates Anne Grant's general observations.

[17] Testimony of Lt. Gen. John Burgoyne to the House of Commons, May 26, 1778. *The Parliamentary Register; or, History of the Proceedings and Debates of the House of Commons: Series One*, VIII, 311.

[18] Mention of these mills is made in: "Philip Schuyler's Saratoga Daybook, 1764–1770," pp. 177, 180, NYHS; Johannes Schuyler's will (Feb. 29, 1741/42), *Colls. N.Y. Hist. Soc. for 1895* (New York, 1896), XXVIII: Abstracts of Wills, IV, 134–135; William Smith, Jr., to Schuyler, Jan. 18, 1768: NYPL, Schuyler Papers Box 23; Lewis A. Leonard, *Life of Charles Carroll of Carrollton* (New York, 1918), p. 284; Tuckerman, p. 73.

[19] Copies of leases (indentures). NYPL, Schuyler Papers Boxes 16, 21.

[20] Thomas Brand to Schuyler, Mar. 10, 1763. NYPL, Schuyler Papers Box 23.

also rather distant from his Hudson and Mohawk valley holdings, but the settlement project was nonetheless a revelation of his ideas for undertakings closer to home.

The Detroit scheme passed. Schuyler turned his thoughts to encouraging immigrants to settle on his lands already in hand. This means of development had more promising prospects. Schuyler's energies must have risen to fever pitch and his zeal must have overflowed to produce a report in 1764 that he was promoting settlement by immigrants even to the point of detaining them in his own bailiwick. *The New-York Gazette* carried an item to explain:

It being generally reported that Capt. Philip Schuyler, of Albany, had unfairly detained the Rev. Doctor Clark and his Society at Stillwater, on their Passage to the New Settlement; this is to inform the Public, that, from the Copy of a letter which I have lately seen, and the Occurrence of other Circumstances, I believe this Report to be false, their delaying there so long being the Effect of a previous Application to this Gentleman for that Purpose.[21]

Clark had led a group of immigrants up the Hudson, and Schuyler evidently dealt with them about possible settlement on his lands. But it was a competitor, James Duane, who persuaded Dr. Clark to locate his Scots on lands east of the Hudson and north of Batten Kill (near present-day Salem, New York).[22]

As late as October, 1773, immigrants were moving up the Hudson with a view to settlement. In July that year William Smith, Jr., wrote Schuyler that the streets of New York were full of Scottish immigrants. Schuyler had mentioned wanting a blacksmith and a weaver, and Smith directed some of the newcomers to offer their services to the Saratoga magnate. A year later Schuyler was introduced to two Scots who were looking for a place to settle for themselves and others. His familiarity with the countryside and ownership of extensive acres made him a person to whom immigrants were encouraged to apply. One has only to look at a list of Schuyler's tenants to see how at least partially successful he was in attracting Scottish immigrants; the list includes McBrides, Stuarts, Scotts, Andersons, and McCarthys.[23]

[21] *The New-York Gazette, or Weekly Post-Boy,* Nov. 29, 1764.

[22] Edward P. Alexander, *A Revolutionary Conservative: James Duane of New York* (New York, 1938), p. 72.

[23] *The New-York Journal; or, the General Advertiser* (Holt), Oct. 28, 1773. Smith to Schuyler, July 19, 1773, and Samuel Loudon to Schuyler, July 22, 1774. NYPL, Schuyler Papers Box 24. For the tenants see indentures of leases in NYPL, Schuyler Papers Boxes 16, 21, 22, and the Account Book, 1769–1805.

Schuyler also attended to the well-being of his tenants and to the well-rounded facilities for life in his "colony." His attention ranged to soliciting a minister and a bell for the church erected there—a marked improvement over the time (1755) when a preacher was obliged to use the spacious barn at the Flatts, another portion of Schuyler property, for religious assemblies. In recommending a Scottish Presbyterian divine to Schuyler in November, 1771, William Smith, Jr., reminded him that the cleric might not only prove useful to his boys as a tutor, but could also promote immigration from North Britain. Schuyler's brother-in-law, Dr. John Cochran from New Jersey, also made recommendations; he offered to refer a doctor who was interested in settling near Saratoga to Schuyler's consideration.[24] Schuyler's attention to all these advantages did indeed show "deep policy" and the lengths to which a calculating promoter might go in the management of his settlement.

Account books may appear as dry as the dust they accumulate, but Philip Schuyler's Saratoga daybook reveals much of its proprietor's lively energies, ambitions, and how he made part of his fortune. The book indicates that his talents and initiative created his position rather more than the easy and limited accumulations of inheritance, and that Schuyler had an eye for the growing greatness of his country —a fact that partially explains why he joined the patriot cause rather than that of the loyalists.

The Schuyler economy was of course rooted in the land. It was one of leaseholding, timber and sawmilling, tar-making and gristmilling, with storekeeping, fishing and flaxmilling thrown in for good measure. Such a diversified economy was quite unexceptional for the day. Even merchants were not so much the followers of an occupation as they were pursuers of varied economic activities. In their own way landlords were merchants too.

Schuyler kept a store at Saratoga, for the convenience of his tenants as well as for the benefit of his own purse. His overseer managed its business. Here he sold staples of all types. The tenants might pay in cash or kind (hay, grain, and timber cleared from their leaseholds). Schuyler sold rum at twice and more what he paid for it. But the cost of transport up the river on his own schooner and in wagons overland

[24] Munsell, *Collections*, II, 375. See also Schuyler to Philip Van Rensselaer, Nov. 18, 1774, in Baxter, *A Godchild of Washington*, p. 189; Smith to Schuyler, Nov. 9, 1771: NYPL, Schuyler Papers Box 23; Cochran to Schuyler, Feb. 19, 1772: NYPL, Schuyler Papers Box 24.

was worth something, and his tenants could not expect him to sell at cost. He did not make a heavy profit on all items, however. "Woolen chack" bought at three shillings a yard sold for only three shillings six pence or four shillings.[25]

The profits from the Saratoga store are difficult to determine before 1767, for although the accounts indicate Schuyler's sales, they do not record what the items cost him. In 1765 his business was largely in grain and lumber. His charge for sawing logs was £6 per hundred. The items he sold to his customers were drygoods, blankets, nails, grain, and knives, but not much rum or molasses. In 1766 he began to increase the sale of rum.[26] Table I, while incomplete, illustrates the approximate rate at which Schuyler profited by his retail of food-stuffs and drygoods. It must be remembered, however, that these figures do not take into account the cost of transporting the supplies to Saratoga, whether in his own schooner, or in river craft and wagons belonging to others. Still, it appears that his income was substantial. Whether by profits from the store, or by good will and the services he provided through it, Schuyler stood to benefit by the attraction it lent to prospective tenants and by the value it thereby added to his property. And the store accounts record only a fraction of his dealings —a business that ranged from farm rents to lumber sales, land speculation and fishing, from continuing labors with the deputy quartermaster general's department to the charges of milling services established along the northern tributaries of the Hudson.

By 1772, Colonel Schuyler's far-reaching merchant activities were important enough to discourage certain people from even contemplating a competitive establishment. It was about this time that William Duer became one of the colonel's friends. In 1768, Duer came to New York from Antigua to arrange for a regular and constant supply of lumber for the plantations of Antigua and Dominica. Schuyler aided Duer in settling at Fort Miller, north of Saratoga, where he erected sawmills of his own. Schuyler provided both advice and some of the means whereby the West Indian could establish himself. But when a certain O'Hara proposed to build a store in the vicinity, Duer's overseer, R. Snell, warned him off by telling him that "in a Short time there would be a large store set up at Saratoga to sell for Cash, and one here [Fort Miller] to sell on Credit and that the 2 stores would

25 Schuyler's Saratoga Daybook, 1764–1770, pp. 75, 85, 328, 332–334. NYHS.

26 Ibid., pp. 17, 26, 34, 38, 40, 43–44, 47, etc. Cf. The New-York Gazette, or Weekly Post-Boy, Jan. 30, July 3, Dec. 4, 1766, for current New York prices of various commodities.

TABLE I *

Prices Current in N.Y. City	Prices Schuyler Paid for Goods	Prices Schuyler Received for Goods
1767		
Rum (gal.) 2s. 7d.	2s. 6d.–3s.	5s.–6s.
Sugar (lb.) 1s. 1d.–1s. 3d.	(no listing)	1s.
Tea (lb.) 5s. 6d.–6s. 2d.	7s.	8s. 6d.
Molasses (gal.) 1s. 8d.–1s. 10d.	2s.	4s. 6d.
Salt (bu.?) 3s. 3d.	1s. 9d.–5s.	1s.–8s.
Blankets (ea.) (no listing)	10s.	15s.
Nails (lb.) (no listing)	9d.	1s.
Hats (ea.) (no listing)	3s. 6d.	£1 1s.
1768		
Rum (gal.) 2s. 6d.–2s. 7d.	4s.	5s.–6s.
Sugar (lb.) 1s.–13d.	6d.	1s.
Tea (lb.) 4s. 3d.–5s. 6d.	6s.–7s.	8s.–8s. 6d.
Molasses (gal.) 1s. 8d.–2s. 2d.	3s. 6d.	4s. 6d.–5s.
Salt (bu.?) 2s. 3d.–3s. 3d.	3s.–4s. (per skiple)	6s. (per skiple)
Blankets (ea.) (no listing)	10s.	15s.
Tobacco (lb.) (no listing)	9d.	1s.
Strouds (yd.) (no listing)	8s.	12s.–13s.
Chack (yd.) (no listing)	3s.	4s.–4s. 6d.
1769		
Rum (gal.) 2s. 6d.	(no listing)	6s.
Sugar (lb.) 1s.	9d.	1s.
Tea (lb.) 4s. 3d.	(no listing)	8s.
Molasses (gal.) 2s. 2d.	(no listing)	(no listing)
Salt (bu.?) 2s. 3d.	5s.	8s.
Linen (yd.) (no listing)	2s. 6d.	2s. 8d.
Chack (yd.) (no listing)	3s.	4s.
"Read Cloth" (yd.) (no listing)	8s.	10s.
Corn (skiple) (no listing)	1s. 6d.–2s. 6d.	3s.

* The figures for this table were obtained from two sources: (a) Schuyler's Saratoga Daybook, 1764–1770. NYHS. (b) the following issues of the *New-York Gazette, or Weekly Post-Boy* give current price listings; Feb. 5, July 2, Dec. 10, 1767; Feb. 4, Sept. 12, Dec. 19, 1768; Jan. 30, 1769. Some of the items (cloth, blankets, nails, hats, tobacco) had no listing in the newspaper, but Schuyler's purchases and sales of them are recorded. Where there are gaps in the record, this has been indicated by the words, "no listing." The years 1767, 1768, and 1769 have been selected simply because the account books are most complete for these years and most sketchy for others.

be supported by Two of the Principal Gentlemen in the County. [H]e immediately apprehended that it was Mr Duer and Mr Schuyler, and said that if he was sure of that, he would not stay there in opposition to Coll. Schuyler." But probably no such store was in fact contemplated, for Snell told Duer that as O'Hara would likely "make Inquiry into that matter" and as Duer would see Schuyler in New York, he ought "to talk to him on that head, so that he may give no Satisfaction to any Inquiry that may be made." [27] All would be well if the parties involved agreed to a common position and then held to it. The development of an interest sometimes meant the exclusion of unwelcome rivals, however small they might be.

The colonel's storekeeping was but a minor enterprise when compared to sawmilling and fishing. Charles Carroll reported from his visit with Schuyler in April, 1776, that from his two sawmills at Saratoga he disposed of great quantities of plank in the neighborhood and at Albany. But these were not the only outlets. Schuyler sent timber as far down the Hudson as New York City, where he had an arrangement first with James Abeel and then with John and Gerard De Peyster, merchants, for the sale of white and pitch pine boards and plank at predetermined prices.[28] The lumber was sent down river by sloop or schooner; only unseasoned stuff could be floated in rafts.

Apparently Schuyler did not always receive as much cash from his lumber business as he could have wished. His agreement with the De Peysters provided that the merchants be allowed interest for whatever sums they might advance him until such time as he should "be Again in Cash." Nor was the lumber always quickly disposed of at the prices Schuyler wanted. In October, 1774, he must have felt the pinch of the purse, for he wrote the De Peysters, instructing them to sell the boards and plank they held at the best price they could get, notwithstanding any restrictions to the contrary in their articles of agreement. There was, however, no indication that the sawmills would cease operating. The next month Schuyler asked for five dozen millsaw files, and several barrels of nails, necessaries for continued operations.[29]

[27] R. Snell to Duer, Jan. 26, 1772. NYHS, Duer Papers. For further evidence of Schuyler's merchandizing see "Ledger, 1774–1796." NYPL, Schuyler Papers.

[28] Leonard, *Life of Charles Carroll*, p. 284; "Articles of Agreement, Philip Schuyler and Gerard De Peyster, Mar. 16, 1772." NYHS, Misc. MSS (Schuyler).

[29] *Ibid*. See also Schuyler to John and Gerard De Peyster, Oct. 3, 1774. NYHS, Misc. MSS (Schuyler); Schuyler to Philip Van Rensselaer, Nov. 18, 1774, in Baxter, *A Godchild of Washington*, p. 189.

Even in the winter months Schuyler's overseer at Saratoga was kept busy with the lumbering work. If the mills could not saw, at least the hands could cut and draw a supply of logs in preparation for the spring freshets. There were also repairs to make when ice broke the floodgates of the millrace. An overseer was plainly necessary, both to tend the constant stream of business and to keep an eye out for trespassers. Moreover, his value was even greater when the landlord was indisposed by ill health as Colonel Schuyler often was.[30]

Throughout his lumber dealings in the 1760's and early 1770's Schuyler was faced with difficulties created by subordinates. Using his mills or selling him timber, they were often unable to settle their accounts promptly. Stanton Tefft was a case in point. Tefft ran a sawmill at Batten Kill. Unable to pay his debts in cash, he was obliged to beg Schuyler's patience and promised to pay the money he owed, with interest if necessary. Otherwise he could only pay in kind, in boards and plank which were on hand or which could be sawed from stocks of timber. Relations between the two men became so strained that in September, 1771, Tefft wrote a plaintive missive, expressing his obligation for Schuyler's forbearance, and literally begged for mercy. Schuyler finally decided to take the boards in payment, though he preferred the cash. Tefft was still rather pressed to deliver payment, even in kind.[31]

Further difficulties for Schuyler arose with James Abeel of New York. Abeel handled the colonel's lumber sales before he switched his business to the De Peysters in 1772. Abeel had begun his agency for Schuyler in 1764, and hundreds of pounds worth of boards and plank passed through his warehouse from the Saratoga mills. Yet Abeel fell behind in his remittances, evidently because of bad debts by those who had purchased Schuyler's lumber and who could not, or would not, pay for it. As of November, 1771, Abeel owed Schuyler almost £350, including about £100 in bad debts. The matter hung on for several months. By March, 1772, when Schuyler rode down to New York for the assembly session, Abeel had managed to whittle down the balance due the colonel to about £130. He then asked Schuyler to take security for the remainder, and promised to pay interest from the preceding June and to pay all this by May 1 following. The matter was resolved in another way, but not without the colonel threat-

30 Philip Lansingh to Schuyler, Dec. 27, 1771. NYPL, Schuyler Papers Box 23; Lansingh to Schuyler, Jan. 2, 1772, and John Cochran to Schuyler, Feb. 19, 1772. NYPL, Schuyler Papers Box 24.
31 Tefft to Schuyler, Sept. 10, Dec. 17, 1771. NYPL, Schuyler Papers Box 1.

ening recourse to the law. Abeel would pay in rum, iron, and other goods, and with an order on a Mr. B. Van Allen for whatever he had "in hands of" Abeel. More than this Abeel said he could not do for the time. He vowed he must take the consequences of any legal action that Schuyler might decide to institute. But if he were arrested, he warned the colonel, it would not only be distressing to Abeel, but would also be "doing Yourself no good." Schuyler abruptly terminated his arrangement with Abeel after eight years and transferred his business to the firm of John and Gerard De Peyster.[32]

Another of Philip Schuyler's enterprises—fishing—extended from his Hudson River bailiwick as far as the West Indies. The colonel began this venture shortly after his return from England, evidently with high hopes of success. Herring were plentiful in the upper Hudson, and the West Indies as well as the valley farmers were likely customers. "I am glad your fishery is like to turn out well," wrote John Cochran, "& will be glad of a sample whenever you please." The fishery did indeed show promise. From Kingston, Jamaica, Philip Livingston reported in May, 1764, that Schuyler's first shipment of herring had arrived, and he promised to "put them of[f] to your most Advantage, both for your Sake, and also out of regard to my native Country, that a beneficial Branch of Commerce may be added to the trade of our Province." This was the year the New York Society for Promoting the Arts, Agriculture and Economy was founded, and Schuyler entered into the spirit of the society whose aims were to diversify the local economy; fishing was a part of the program. The trade Schuyler opened in fish lasted through the decade, but it was not always as profitable as the beginnings had promised. In November, 1770, he received only twelve shillings per barrel for herring sold at Antigua; his 1764 shipment to Philip Livingston had brought thirty-one shillings three pence per barrel.[33]

Little evidence remains to prove that Schuyler's enterprises extended to a very sizable commerce in an extract from his lumber business—

[32] "James Abeel in Account Current with Philip Schuyler," NYPL, Schuyler Papers Box 1; Abeel to Schuyler, Mar. 17, 1772, NYPL, Schuyler Papers Box 24; "Articles of Agreement, Philip Schuyler and Gerard De Peyster, Mar. 16, 1772," NYHS, Misc. MSS (Schuyler).

[33] Cochran to Schuyler, July 5, 1763; Livingston to Schuyler, May 7, June 16, 1764. NYPL, Schuyler Papers Box 23. See also Munsell, *Annals*, I, 258, for an account of the sales of the sloop *Olive Branch* in voyage to the West Indies from New York . . . Nov. 3, 1770.

pitch. But he seems to have sold some tar.[34] Perhaps it was a venture planned like the fishery, but which, like the scheme for settling the Detroit country, did not materialize. At least no accounts or other correspondence remain to show that tar was an important sales item, or that Schuyler produced naval stores aside from timber.

For the transportation of supplies to Saratoga and the conveyance of his produce to market Schuyler relied mainly on the most natural highway available—the Hudson River. His operations were extensive enough to warrant the possession of a number of river craft. Schuyler's river transport began in 1761, when he was still in England. John Bradstreet built him a schooner, appropriately christened *The Saratoga*, in preparation for the young landlord's return when he turned his attention and efforts to the exploitation of his lands and the erection of a multi-sided interest. How many other such craft the colonel built or acquired is difficult to say. It is likely that he had several small vessels (sloops) besides the schooner, and that these busily plied up and down the Hudson as his business grew.[35] All in all the vessel was a profitable and comfortable investment for a river valley landlord to have. In 1765 one of Schuyler's kinsmen, Thomas Livingston, the New York merchant, attempted to buy a share in it and to enter a partnership in which "Couzin Schyel" was to procure lumber at Albany cheaply and ship it down river, while Livingston proposed to retail it to the advantage of both.[36]

If storekeeping, lumbering, and fishing were important enterprises

34 John Cochran to Schuyler, July 20, 1764. NYPL, Schuyler Papers Box 23.

35 For a discussion of the number and nature of the river craft cf. Schuyler, *Colonial New York*, II, 258; Bradstreet's Account with Schuyler: "1761 By your Charge for building the Schooner Saratoga for me [£]600_____" NYPL, Schuyler Papers Box 9; Lossing, I, 196, 221; Humphreys, *Catherine Schuyler*, p. 84; C. E. Gregg, "General Philip Schuyler and the Schuyler Mansion," *The Dutch Settlers Society of Albany, Yearbook* (Albany, 1949–1951), XXV–XXVI, 13; Baxter, *A Godchild of Washington*, p. 227. There is no evidence that any of Schuyler's vessels were engaged in trade beyond New York City. They were limited to river commerce. *The New-York Gazette, or Weekly Post-Boy*'s listing of Custom House Entries; Inward, Outward & Cleared for Departure for 1761–1762, 1764–1773, show no mention of the *Saratoga* or any other vessels Schuyler is said to have owned. Nor is there any indication in "Naval Office Lists from Janry 5, 1755 to Janry 5, 1765," C.O. 5/1228, that Schuyler's vessels cleared the port of New York. Other Schuylers, the Livingstons, and Waltons had vessels so registered, but not Philip Schuyler.

36 Thomas Livingston to Schuyler, Mar. 5, 1765. NYPL, Schuyler Papers Box 23. For other uses of the schooner see "Invoice of Sundries shipped on the Schooner 'Saratoga,' June 1, 1763." NYPL, Schuyler Papers Box 1.

for the celebrated scion of the Schuyler family, his land revenues were even more basic to his prosperity. Philip Schuyler was primarily a landlord. His other activities merely supplemented his essential concern for the improved values and production of the lands he inherited and those with which he speculated. Commercial interests rounded out the agrarian magnate's domain, made his "interest" more complete, more comprehensive.

Those who have questioned Schuyler's methods of accumulating a fortune have not carefully investigated his activities or documented them, either for the years before 1775 or for those that followed.[37] Even the basic element of his family economy, the use of lands, has been only intimated and passed over with merely suggestive generalizations. The details of his enterprise consisted of collecting leasehold rents, buying and selling speculatively, making loans, accepting mortgages and encouraging immigration and settlement.

On the eve of the American Revolution, Schuyler extended his agrarian interests to the realm of finance, acted as a petty banker in the advancement of personal loans through bonds and mortgages. He was constantly acquiring personal notes. It would appear that he began these dealings as early as 1765, with the encouragement of John Bradstreet, who also offered him support more substantial than mere advice. In 1765 he took a mortgage on half of "Great Barn's Island" (opposite Hell Gate) in the East River for a £1,600 loan to Mary Behenna. That same year he signed an indenture with Thomas and Catherine Livingston of New York by which they mortgaged Livingston's share in the Saratoga Patent for £352. In 1766, Schuyler held bonds from William Bayard for over £2,000, and in 1768 he took a note from his brother-in-law, John Cochran, for £1,400.[38]

Not all Schuyler's notes were mortgages nor did all involve such sizable sums. Two of his tenants, Levy Croker and Anthony Saunders, signed a note (July 4, 1771) for £500, and Schuyler took a bond and mortgage from a certain Bridget Potter in May, 1773, for little

[37] See, for example, Schuyler, *Colonial New York*, II, 255–257; Alden, *General Gage*, p. 73.

[38] Robert A. East, *Business Enterprise in the American Revolutionary Era* (New York, 1938), p. 22. See also, for example, the indenture, Dec. 18, 1772, of Philip Schuyler and William Bailey, NYPL, Schuyler Papers Box 16; the Mary Behenna indenture, May 8, 1765, NYPL, Schuyler Papers Box 20; the Thomas Livingston indenture, May 2, 1765, NYSL; the Cochran note, April 30, 1768, NYPL, Schuyler Papers Box 42. See also "Philip Schuyler's Account Current with Beverly Robinson, 1765–1769," NYPL, Schuyler Papers Box 2.

more than £107. Other persons borrowed still lesser sums ranging between £4 and £24, while some ran as high as £75.[39]

Bonds and mortgages were no inconsiderable part of Schuyler's financial dealings, but his leases of farms were much more extensive. In the long run, they were more profitable in that they brought returns in produce and increased land values and in penalties by way of the "quarter sale." Schuyler granted leaseholds for terms of three lives, reserving a fourth or, more commonly, a tenth of all produce as a rent. Upon the death of the surviving lessee or upon the lessees' voluntary withdrawal, the tenants surrendered their farms to the landlord, who could then re-lease them. The "quarter sale" was the payment of one-third, one-fourth, or one-tenth of the sale price to the landlord whenever a tenant decided to dispose of his interest by selling it to another tenant. Schuyler told Charles Carroll, delegate to Congress, in the spring of 1776, that the "most advantageous way of leasing lands" was to require on "every transmutation of property, from one tenant to another, a quarter part of what the land sells for. . . ." In the "course of a few years, from the frequent transmutations of tenants, the alienation fines would exceed the purchase of the fee-simple, though sold at a high valuation." [40]

It does not appear, however, that Schuyler was more interested in exploiting the quarter sale than in clearing and tilling the soil. It is more evident that he encouraged agricultural production more than he was willing to rely upon transmutation fees for an income; they were lucrative but not necessarily regular. The colonel's leases usually included a reservation of all rights to any mines and to mill sites, timber and water. Only rarely did he allow tenants to erect a sawmill, and then the provisions were severe. In July, 1771, for example, when he granted such permission to Levy Croker and Anthony Saunders for a mill on Moses Creek, he limited it to a ten-year period and demanded sixty-seven good logs fit for sawing as a fee each year. At the end of ten years the mill and dam were to be turned over to Schuyler as his private property.[41]

Not all of Schuyler's lease provisions were illiberal, however. He usually arranged for the tenant to hold his land free of rent for about

[39] Ledger, 1774–1796, and Account Book, 1769–1805. NYPL, Schuyler Papers. See also Box 42 for various notes.

[40] Leonard, *Life of Charles Carroll*, pp. 282, 284. See also Alexander, *James Duane*, p. 66.

[41] Indenture with Croker and Saunders. NYPL, Schuyler Papers Box 42.

the first five years or so as an incentive to clearance and development. But once the rent commenced, a tenant might be dispossesed if he was more than forty days delinquent in his payments. The other advantage the tenant almost invariably had was an option to buy his farm if ever it were put up for sale. Some leases stipulated a flat annual rental, while others provided an acreage rent. Some specified that the tenant pay a percentage of the produce and all taxes and quitrents. Schuyler's conveyances varied but little. Some were made in fee simple with reservations of perpetual rents. Others were given for three lives. Included were provisions for at least one day's work or "riding" per year—a feudal vestige of service to a lord—for mill tolls and the right of distraint.[42]

Philip Schuyler's "good understanding improved by reflection and study," his "active turn" and fondness for husbandry, together with his shrewd business acumen combined to produce "a most beautiful and most valuable estate," to the mind of one observer.[43] It was at Saratoga that Schuyler's genius in politics and economics had full scope, and it was there that he exercised those talents which prepared him for larger public affairs. The man showed scarcely less ability in provincial politics, but that performance clearly sprang from his personal interest and from his experiences as a country squire.

– 2 –

SCHUYLERS, VAN CORTLANDTS, LIVINGSTONS, AND VAN RENSSELAERS

IF PHILIP SCHUYLER occupied himself primarily with the many facets of a growing private domain, he was never too preoccupied to concern himself with the estates and business of kinsmen and fellow landlords. For several years he administered his parents' estate; the last acre and shilling were not divided until 1789. The Livingstons

---

[42] David M. Ellis, James A. Frost, Harold C. Syrett, Harry J. Carman, *A Short History of New York State* (Ithaca, 1957), p. 159. See also Ellis, *Landlords and Farmers*, pp. 41–42, 47–48, for a discussion of Schuyler's leases. For copies of the leases see NYPL, Schuyler Papers Boxes 16, 21, 22, and also the Account Book, 1769–1805. It might also be observed that Schuyler's lease terms were lenient enough so that his tenants caused no disturbances nor complained of grievances such as those occasioned on the Van Rensselaer, Livingston, Van Cortlandt, and Philipse estates where discontent broke into open rebellion. But the Schuyler lands were not plagued with Indian claims or boundary disputes. Mark, *Agrarian Conflicts*, pp. 73, 131–163, 204.

[43] Leonard, *Life of Charles Carroll*, p. 284.

recognized his talents, and their involvement in the Saratoga Patent made Schuyler a likely coadjutor for their affairs. His father-in-law, Colonel John Van Rensselaer, was beset by problems that Schuyler found were to his own interest to help resolve, especially since Mrs. Schuyler would one day share in her father's holdings. Finally, there was the ubiquitous John Bradstreet, with whom to concert schemes for extending landholdings. Schuyler's relationship with him was so intimate that he became the person best qualified to administer Bradstreet's estate after the old man died. But Bradstreet's affairs were to bring him long years of vexation.

Cornelia Van Cortlandt Schuyler was a woman of some business acumen, and she was obliged to use her talent for over twenty years. Widowed in 1741 when Schuyler was only eight, with five children to rear, she conducted the business which fell to her, both from her husband and his father, who left the family with the lands on which a still greater influence could be built. She also had her own share in the Cortlandt Manor lands to supervise. When she died in 1762, it fell to Philip, the eldest surviving son, to execute her will and manage the division of the lands, although his mother had designated all her surviving children (Philip, Cortlandt, Stephen, and Gertrude) as executors.

In January, 1763, Schuyler's brothers and sister agreed to a division of the paternal lands at Saratoga. Some of the territory, however, remained unsurveyed, and hence, unpartitioned until 1769.[44] For these years Philip acted as guardian of the inheritance. His establishment on the upper Hudson enabled him to care for the property close at hand, a fact to which the letters of his brother-in-law, John Cochran, attest. Dr. Cochran married Schuyler's widowed sister, Gertrude, in 1760, and when Cornelia died, Cochran, of course, took up his wife's interests in the estate. From New Brunswick, New Jersey, the Cochrans were obliged to rely on Schuyler's proximity to the lands and on his judgment for their administration. They did so in the firm knowledge that his advice was sound. Even for his nephew, Peter (Gertrude's son by her first marriage), Schuyler had special concern. Cornelia had left funds to be administered for her grandchildren's benefit, and Schuyler both tended them for his nephew and became involved in Peter's rebellious behavior. John Cochran frequently corresponded

44 The division of lands made in January, 1763, in NYPL, Schuyler Papers Box 21. See also the field book of the Saratoga survey and partition in 1769. NYPL, Schuyler Papers Box 22.

with his brother-in-law about these family difficulties and about both the Schuyler and Van Cortlandt lands. In 1766 he suggested the business would only be complicated by the passage of time, and if accidents happened, their affairs would become more troublesome. Schuyler first proposed to sell thirteen of the Cortlandt Manor farms, but his delays suggested that he deemed it better to wait for more auspicious times, and in 1768 he finally advertised the sale.[45]

Even with a disposal of the Cortlandt Manor business Schuyler remained well occupied with managing the undivided Saratoga lands. Cochran, for example, continued to entrust him with his holdings there in hopes Schuyler might profitably dispose of them for him. In 1769 the unsurveyed portion of the Saratoga Patent was partitioned, thus clearing the way for an orderly, more accurate, division among the heirs and a correct disposal of the lots for those who wished to sell. Still Schuyler was not freed of responsibilities or importunities. In July, 1770, Cochran asked him to inquire into reports that New Englanders were cutting timber on his lands. Such trespassing, he said, should not be left unpunished. As Schuyler was well occupied with his own affairs, Cochran suggested that he hire someone to see to Cochran's business. Although Schuyler's administration of his mother's estate did not end until 1789, when he paid out the last small share of its earnings, most of it was settled by 1774.[46] One burden disposed of, however, meant freedom to take up others.

The Livingstons doubtless made a good choice when they selected Philip Schuyler for the position of estate-adviser extraordinary. Their kinship, their common social position and economic interests, and their share in the Saratoga Patent were reasons enough for this, but they also recognized Schuyler's talents and energy. Schuyler, too, benefited from his connection with them. When the heirs of Robert Liv-

---

45 Cochran to Schuyler, July 5, 1763; Jan. 12, Feb. 16, July 20, Oct. 16, Nov. 5, Nov. 30, 1764; Jan. 28, Feb. 29, April 3, Aug. 7, Sept. 15, Dec. 16, 1765; Feb. 6, April 2, July 3, Aug. 6, 1766; Jan. 31, June 9, Aug. 23, Oct. 20, Nov. 30, 1767. NYPL, Schuyler Papers Box 23. See also copy of a land sale announcement, Nov. 20–21, [1766], NYPL, Schuyler Papers Box 19. *The New-York Journal, or the General Advertiser* (John Holt), April 14, 1768, carried an announcement of a sale of ten of the Cortlandt Manor farms.

46 "Cornelia Schuyler's Estate in Account Current with Philip Schuyler, 1760–1789." NYPL, Schuyler Papers Box 10. The account shows sums realized from various lands sold, and from rents from Cortlandt Manor farms. Between 1763 and 1774 the estate brought in £6,363 15s. 10d. and from 1774 to 1789 only £800 more. See also Cochran to Schuyler, Dec. 24, 1769, and July 15, 1770. NYPL, Schuyler Papers Box 23.

ingston (nephew of the first lord of Livingston Manor) divided his lands, Schuyler made sizable additions to his own property from their holdings. Livingston's wife, Margaret, was the eldest daughter of Colonel Peter Schuyler, Philip Schuyler's great-uncle. She had been given her father's three-fourteenths share of the Saratoga Patent. In 1768 the Livingston heirs divided this inheritance, and Schuyler purchased nearly 8,000 acres of it.[47]

But even before this the Livingstons singled out Schuyler to execute commissions for them. Robert J. Livingston wrote him in July, 1767, saying his grandmother wanted Schuyler to rent some pasture land for £9 per annum or whatever he could get for it. In April, 1768, William Smith, Jr., Elizabeth Livingston, Robert J. and Peter R. Livingston sought Schuyler's opinion as to the value of a 340-acre lot in the Saratoga Patent. They had a prospective buyer, and wondered if they should take £425 cash or £500 in a four-year term: "the Bargain rests intirely on your saying it shall or shall not be so," they told him. A few weeks later Smith and the Livingstons, joined this time by Robert R. Livingston, decided to sell four-fifths of the "Dovegat Farm" in the Saratoga Patent for £1,700. This was evidently one of the two four-thousand-acre parcels Schuyler acquired from the family in 1768. Still waiting for John Livingston's decision to sell his shares, they informed Schuyler that if he agreed in time, one deed would suffice for all of them. Until then, Schuyler was to give them an accurate description of the farms in order that the deeds might be properly drawn, and then he was to enter into proper securities for payment when the deeds should be delivered to him.[48]

John Livingston did not release his share in the Saratoga Patent, but he asked Schuyler as a holder of a major interest there to handle affairs for him in his absence. In 1771 he gave Schuyler the power of attorney to sell or lease any part of the lands and to receive rents as they fell due. These dealings were the occasion of one of Schuyler's displays of generosity. Responding to an offer Schuyler made, James

---

[47] Schuyler, *Colonial New York*, II, 257. A three-fourteenths share of the Saratoga Patent was about 36,000 acres. See also William Smith, Jr., to Schuyler, Jan. 18, 1768; Robert R. Livingston to Schuyler, Feb. 1, 1768; Smith to Schuyler, May 30, 1768, all in NYPL, Schuyler Papers Box 23.

[48] Robert J. Livingston to Schuyler, July 25, 1767; William Smith, Jr., *et al.*, to Schuyler, April 12, 1768. NYPL, Schuyler Papers Box 23. See also William Smith, Jr., *et al.*, to Schuyler, April 21, 1768, and Smith to Schuyler, May 30, 1768, NYSL (Schuyler), about Schuyler's payment to the Livingstons. Finally, see Schuyler, *Colonial New York*, II, 257.

Livingston wrote from Montreal, "The Farm you have lately purchased & which you are so kind as to let my Father [John Livingston]
have a part in . . . is out of his Power to accept, money being a very
scarce Article here & he having already more Land than he knows
what to do with." Schuyler was empowered to divide the farm at
Dovegat, and his offers of accommodation at Saratoga were readily
accepted by the elder Livingston.[49] A Livingston may have had more
land than he knew what to do with, but Schuyler as yet knew no such
satisfaction.

Robert Livingston, Jr., third lord of the manor, was another of his
clan who did not sell his share in the Saratoga Patent to Schuyler in
1768 when his other kinsmen disposed of theirs. But he too relied on
Schuyler as a fellow landlord to keep a watchful eye on his property
during his absence. Schuyler reported mischief by tenants in May,
1772, during prevailing unrest in the Hampshire Grants. Livingston
assured him, "I shall not Suffer any of my Tenants to cutt trees . . .
to prevent the free co[u]rse of the Water but to make it an article in
their leases to keep it Clean." When Schuyler asked about making an
exchange of land in the patent, Livingston told him he could not
arrange it, as he had willed the land to his children. In fairness he
thought he must speak to them of the matter.[50]

When in June, 1772, "Granny Livingston" as William Smith, Jr.,
said, "flew to the Stars," Schuyler was called in to help Smith execute
her estate. Smith wrote him that the devisees of their grandmother
Livingston wanted to sell the lands and divide the proceeds, and that
he was agreeable to joining Schuyler to execute the will. But Smith
would not consent to be sole executor. Schuyler had valuable knowledge of their affairs without which a settlement could not be easily
made. Thus, other details were added to the Hudson magnate's business affairs. And they were not disposed of quickly or easily. The following year another of the numerous Livingston clan, Susannah, in-
quired of Schuyler if he had sold her land; would he do so if he had
not made the sale as he was supposed to; if he could not, would he
collect the rents due?[51]

On the very eve of Lexington and Concord, Philip Schuyler was

[49] Robert R. Livingston to Schuyler, Feb. 1, 1768; James Livingston to Schuyler,
July 6, Aug. 11, 1771. NYPL, Schuyler Papers Box 23.
[50] Robert Livingston, Jr., to Schuyler, June 5, 1772. NYPL, Schuyler Papers Box 24.
[51] Smith to Schuyler, June 17, Nov. 9, 1772; Susannah Livingston to Schuyler, July
12, 1773. NYPL, Schuyler Papers Box 24.

acting for the estate of still another of the Livingstons, this time for Thomas, the New York City merchant, who also had a share in the Saratoga Patent. Schuyler proposed to sell four parcels of land in lots of 306, 322, 327, and 835 acres. The sale announced by Schuyler would begin on April 20 at the Merchants' Coffee House in New York.[52] But other things were afoot. After several years during which they had been so intimate in their common business as also in politics, the war abruptly interrupted the colonel's dealings with the Livingstons.

In 1776 when Philip Schuyler was faced by the machinations of New England politicians in Congress, who were anxious to replace him with their own candidate to command the Northern Department, he wrote a letter to Samuel Chase and Charles Carroll, assuring them he would send supplies north to the army—"Provided," he said, "I am not before that Shot for High Treason to my Country with which I have been charged by a set of most infamous Scoundrels as ever existed, with whom I have had a long landed Controversy as an Agent to Colo: Rensselaer, & who would fain ruin my Reputation if they Could."[53] *A long landed controversy as Rensselaer's agent.* Little might he imagine when he took up his father-in-law's interests that personal hatreds and suspicions of long standing were in the making. And if these matters affected his reputation beyond New York, they also were a vital part of the political role that he played in the latter days of the colonial era. Van Rensselaer's "long landed Controversy" ran concurrently with Schuyler's involvements in his mother's estate, the Livingstons' Saratoga interests and his service in the provincial assembly where his position proved advantageous for the settlement of Van Rensselaer's difficulties. Together with his personal business they called for great attention and perseverance. Entanglement in the Rensselaer troubles meant Schuyler was caught up in the violence of tenant riots, a boundary dispute with the Livingstons, the Hampshire Grants controversy, and the difficulties of dealing with the governor and his council. The Grants dispute was related to the New York–Massachusetts boundary controversy, and the colonel also played a role in this as boundary commissioner. The boundary question touched the Van Rensselaer lands which lay just west of both Massachusetts and New Hampshire. The situation was complicated. But it did not particularly daunt young Schuyler, who was always a par-

---

[52] *The New-York Gazette; and the Weekly Mercury,* April 17, 1775.
[53] Schuyler to Chase and Carroll, May 31, 1776. NYPL, Schuyler Papers, Letter Book 1776, p. 196.

tisan and seldom one to shrink from committing himself to a cause. However, he later found reason to regret these involvements when sectional animosities blazed hotly against him as the Yorker who had defied the will of contentious Yankee squatters and intruders.

John Van Rensselaer headed the lesser branch of the patroonal family, if indeed his numerous descendants can be called lesser in view of the other branch's fewer numbers (but greater wealth). The difference between the offshoots of the first patroon's younger son (Jeremiah) might better be indicated by the terms "upper" and "lower" manors. John Van Rensselaer owned Claverack, the lower manor, about thirty miles downriver from Albany. He was the son of Hendrick, who was a younger brother of the fourth patroon, Killian. The two brothers shared the family estate after it passed to their father's (Jeremiah) line because his nephew, the third patroon, died without issue. Killian as elder brother followed in the succession of patroons who held the upper manor, and his brother Hendrick founded the Claverack branch, or lower manor which John Van Rensselaer inherited. The Claverack estate contained some 62,000 acres, and when these handsome holdings passed to his hands, John also inherited considerable pains—troubles he shared with his able and interested son-in-law, Philip Schuyler.[54] Like his great-great-grandfather Van Slechtenhorst, who managed the affairs of the first patroon of Rensselaerwyck, Schuyler helped his father-in-law, himself a descendant of the patroon, with his widely flung property interests.

Schuyler's "agency" to Van Rensselaer appears to have developed at the same time the Hampshire Grants controversy materialized. The governor of New Hampshire, Benning Wentworth, helped provoke the troubles by granting lands to men who moved into territory Van Rensselaer claimed as his own. Squatters from western Massachusetts also intruded on his holdings.

In a wider sense the dispute arose over the old sea-to-sea grants and the subsequent conveyance of New Netherland to the Duke of York. The duke's patent in 1664 set the eastern boundary of New York at the western shore of the Connecticut River. In 1725 and 1731 surveys were made which established the New York–Connecticut boundary at a line parallel to the Hudson River and twenty miles east of it. After the establishment of New Hampshire, its authorities asked that its western boundary be a northward extension of the New York–

[54] Schuyler, *Colonial New York*, I, 222–225, 232–233, 235–236.

Connecticut line. Assuming this to be the case, Governor Wentworth began issuing patents for lands west of the Connecticut River as early as 1749. New York authorities objected. Massachusetts also maintained that New Hampshire's boundary was confined to the Connecticut River. In April, 1750, Governor George Clinton of New York asserted his colony's claims to all the land west of the Connecticut River. The Great War for the Empire interrupted this dispute, but Lieutenant Governor Colden revived Clinton's claims in 1763. The following year the king in council set the eastern boundary of New York at the western bank of the Connecticut River. And when New York authorities attempted to void all of Wentworth's patents and to survey and sell lands already in the hands of settlers, the people of the Grants rose in protest. They would neither leave, nor repurchase their holdings from the government of New York.

When New York began to reassert its jurisidiction over the area, its government stipulated that New Englanders occupying lands as of May 25, 1765, might have their holdings surveyed and prove their ownership. Otherwise they would forfeit possession. But the Yankees refused to make the trip to Albany to give their proofs. The ministry in 1767 ordered a stay in any further New York grants in the disputed area, and this suspension lasted until 1773. In 1773 the Board of Trade decided on a new policy. Grants made by Massachusetts before 1740 and by New York before 1749 were allowed to stand, provided the settlers claiming them actually occupied their lands. Grants made by New York or New Hampshire since 1749 were to be considered valid, but where patents overlapped, wastelands might be awarded as compensation to the most recent patentees. Finally, all other lands were to be regranted at £5 sterling per hundred acres plus the usual quitrents. New Yorkers disliked the ministry's ruling because they were interested in speculation. Yankees disliked New York's jurisdiction. Governor Tryon decided to explain the difficulties to the London government in person. In his absence, Lieutenant Governor Colden aggravated matters by making grants in the face of royal instructions to the contrary.[55]

Settlers in the disputed area not only threatened the Van Rensselaer holdings, but also menaced that part of the Saratoga Patent

[55] Mark, *Agrarian Conflicts*, pp. 164–199, gives a comprehensive survey of the dispute down to 1791 when Vermont was admitted to the Union. See also Dillon, *The New York Triumvirate*, pp. 173–175.

which lay east of the upper reaches of the Hudson. As Schuyler held an interest there as well as in his father-in-law's lands, it is not difficult to understand why he adopted Van Rensselaer's cause as his own. It was very much to his interest to do so.

Schuyler's involvement in the land controversies was complicated in another way. On October 20, 1764, the New York Assembly named him one of its commissioners to settle the boundary with Massachusetts. He served until 1767, and again after the Revolutionary War, but the controversy remained unsolved until 1788.[56] As a champion of New York's claims and protector of the Van Rensselaer interests threatened by Massachusetts squatters, he added animosity to the suspicion and mistrust with which Yankees had tended to view all Yorkers since the days of Dutch rule in New York. When a new boundary commission was named in 1767, Schuyler was not included. He was then too enmeshed in Van Rensselaer's private interests against Massachusetts squatters to be suitable to serve in an impartial way on the commission—too partisan for an appointment to square with informal canons of propriety.

The years 1751–1766 were unsettled ones for tenants on Livingston and Rensselaer manors. Nursing discontentment with conditions of their tenures and rents, and with grievances of dispossession and ejectment suits, they first broke into rebellion in Livingston Manor in 1765. They raided the lord's ironworks and in general abused the Livingston property. The tenants were armed with Indian claims to the manor lands and were abetted by Massachusetts speculators. In 1766 the rioting spread south of the manor to the Van Cortlandt holdings and northward into Rensselaer's lands. The discontent had mushroomed into a "Great Rebellion." The militia was called out. The courts dealt severely with the leaders, among whom was William Prendergast, who was saved from the hangman's noose only by the governor's pardon. So bitter were the Livingston tenants that in 1768 they rejected Judge Robert R. Livingston's candidacy for the Dutchess County assembly seat. And when the Van Rensselaers and Livingstons turned patriot in the Revolution, their tenants joined the loyalist cause. It is also interesting to note that men like John Morin Scott and William Smith, Jr., who encouraged the Sons of Liberty in the

---

[56] *Report of the Regents of the University on the Boundaries of the State of New York* (2 vols.; Albany, 1884), II, 153, 156, 182–184, 189, 191, 194, 205, 210, 216.

Stamp Act riots of 1765, were also active in the judicial suppression of the tenants and the protection of property rights in 1766.[57]

Needless to say, Philip Schuyler espoused the landlords' cause. The riots were all the more disturbing, following as they did the Stamp Act uproar in New York in 1765 and in Albany early in 1766. Schuyler had a part in the growing discontentment among his father-in-law's tenants, for as his agent he corresponded with William Smith, Jr., on legal proceedings for ejecting those tenants who were delinquent in their rents and who were taking advantage of Indian claims to Rensselaer's lands to purchase title to them from the tribesmen.[58]

Following the waves of Stamp Act turbulence, a mob that had ranged for months in the eastern part of Rensselaer Manor shifted its movements in mid-June to Livingston Manor. When Harmanus Schuyler, sheriff of Albany County, led a posse of over a hundred men to disperse the rioters on June 26, he was encountered by about sixty disgruntled farmers who not only shot off his hat and wig, but also killed a militiaman and wounded seven others. Three of the rioters were shot down. The government took action. The council and assembly approved of a requisition of regular troops to assist civil officers in quelling the riots. The regulars were called in from Albany. The anti-rent agitators were routed, their leaders seized, and a special commission for the trial of the rioters was sent to the northern counties. Members of the council, the attorney general, and lawyers accompanied Chief Justice Horsmanden north for the proceedings.[59] Even the governor went up to Albany, hoping his presence might mollify the disgruntled.

The rioting was but the counterpart to other, and perhaps more serious, worries which confronted John Van Rensselaer and Philip Schuyler. The rebels submitted to their landlords, moved back into Massachusetts and Connecticut, or turned north to the Hampshire Grants, there to cause more trouble. The rioters were suppressed. But

[57] Mark, *Agrarian Conflicts*, p. 131. See also Ellis, *et al.*, *A Short History of New York State*, p. 77; Dillon, *The New York Triumvirate*, pp. 98, 166–167, 170; Clarence Edwin Carter (comp. & ed.), *The Correspondence of General Thomas Gage with the Secretaries of State, 1763–1775* (2 vols.; New Haven, 1931–1933), I, 95, 99.

[58] William Smith, Jr., to Schuyler, April 15, 1765. NYPL, Schuyler Papers Box 9. See also Mark, *Agrarian Conflicts*, p. 135.

[59] *The New-York Gazette, or Weekly Post-Boy*, July 3, 31, Aug. 21, Sept. 4, 11, Oct. 9, 1766. See also Mark, *Agrarian Conflicts*, pp. 143–150.

the tenant farmers had struck a damaging blow when they, too, questioned the validity of Van Rensselaer's title to his holdings. Certain retired army officers who were interested in procuring lands in return for their years in the military had begun to petition the governor for grants within the bounds of Claverack. They were emboldened by the tenant uproar.

William Smith, Jr., ever watchful where the interests of the Livingstons or Van Rensselaers were concerned, warned Schuyler in February, 1767, of a new menace based on the petitions for land grants within Claverack. A rumor had been whispered about that "Orders were given to prosecute Mr Renselaer for an Intrusion on the Lands at Claverack as the Kings Soil. You may imagine that my Friendship to him," wrote Smith, "would not suppos[e] me to leave this account untraced." Smith called on the governor, who satisfied him that no such order had been given. He could not determine who was responsible for the rumor except for a "Letter written by an officer" to an unknown person "signifying that such an order would be sent by this Packet." Smith drew Governor Moore out and learned that he had a letter from Lord Shelburne, the secretary of state, regarding the unsettled Massachusetts boundary. Shelburne urged Moore to see that there were no more outbursts like those of 1766. Moore and Governor Bernard of Massachusetts were to have boundary commissioners named to settle the line.[60]

Sir Henry Moore had taken the landlords' side in the dispute, had resisted the Indian claims to Van Rensselaer's title, and had taken a position against the pretensions of the squatters. Moreover, he wrote an explanation to Lord Shelburne, which was "very full and clear and not without salt," according to William Smith, Jr. Said Smith, it

represents Mr. Renselaer's tenderness to the Tenants and Freebooters who are set down on his Lands, throws the blame where it ought to be, excuses himself for sending Regulars into the County, alledges [sic] that the settlers are altogether unjustifiable in their Conduct, that they have abused good Nature and forbearance, apologizes for the sheriff, shews that this Province has done everything it could to force a settlement of Limits, sharply recriminates upon the Bostonians and in the End promises to go into the Measure his Lordship recommends that our New England Foes may be forced to a Decision.[61]

[60] *Ibid.*, pp. 156–158. See also Smith to Schuyler, Feb. 23, 1767. NYPL, Schuyler Papers Box 23.
[61] *Ibid.*

Early in 1767 the land fever produced new threats to John Van Rensselaer's property, and the colonel was obliged to petition the governor and council not to grant lands to which he held title and claim. Petitioners for land carried their case to the courts, maintaining that Van Rensselaer's title was invalid because it had been acquired without proper extinguishment of the Indians' title. Their importunities had gone as far as the Privy Council, and it was this action which produced the legal suits. Philip Schuyler even proposed to appeal his father-in-law's case to the king in council and posted a bond for the procedure, but the land issue remained a vital one within the governor's council in New York, and it does not appear that an appeal was ever prosecuted. Moreover, the governor's council faced the difficulty of confirming an old grant to Van Rensselaer without breaking the 1767 instructions from the ministry not to issue new patents pending a settlement of the Hampshire Grants controversy. And as the ministry made no decision on the Grants until 1773, Van Rensselaer's claims could not be fully settled until such action was taken. The business was further complicated by Governor Moore's death and by the succession of Lieutenant Governor Colden, the Earl of Dunmore, and finally William Tryon to the executive chair. As Van Rensselaer's agent, Schuyler was obliged to explain the controversy first to Dunmore and then to Tryon and to solicit their aid.[62]

Schuyler's implication in provincial politics had added significance, then, by virtue of his connection with his father-in-law and with William Smith, Jr., who sat in the governor's council. His position in the assembly and in the minority faction there was affected by the Van Rensselaer land dispute, and also proved to be an important element in its settlement. The dispute pointed up the dominance of agrarian interests in Schuyler's political activity and in assembly factionalism.[63]

[62] The following sources reveal the remaining evidence of the rather intricate problem: William Smith, Jr., to Schuyler, Mar. 21, 1767; Feb. 11, 1769; June 8, 1771, NYPL, Schuyler Papers Box 23. See also *The New-York Gazette, or Weekly Post-Boy*, Nov. 7, 1768; W. L. Grant and James Munro (eds.), *Acts of the Privy Council of England: Colonial Series* (6 vols.; London, 1908–1912), IV, 699–701; V, 358, 597; and E. B. O'Callaghan (ed.), *Calendar of Historical Manuscripts in the Office of the Secretary of State, Albany, N.Y.* (2 vols.; Albany, 1865–1866), II, 777.

[63] For the details of the Van Rensselaer land troubles and Schuyler's dealings with the governor see William H. W. Sabine (ed.), *Historical Memoirs from 16 March 1763 to 9 July 1776 of William Smith* (New York, 1956), pp. 128–129, 133–134, 137–138, 146,

– 3 –

ADDING SUBSTANCE TO AN INTEREST

IF PHILIP SCHUYLER's entanglements with the estates of his parents, the Saratoga holdings of the Livingstons, and the interests of his father-in-law present a complicated story, his connection with Colonel John Bradstreet was deeper, broader, and more enduring than all the others put together. The tangled web of their relationships is a series of cross-connecting schemes for acquiring land and patronage, the business of military supply, the rivalry of landed interests, and the interactions of royal officials, personal connections, and family life.

Schuyler's connection with Bradstreet began in the winter of 1755–1756 and terminated with the old soldier's death in September, 1774. It opened with their common efforts in the quarter-master general's department and expanded in many directions: Schuyler's trip to England as Bradstreet's deputy in 1761–1762, Bradstreet's endeavors to procure land for his absent protégé, his supervision of the erection of Schuyler's Albany mansion, and the construction of the schooner, *Saratoga*. The energetic Albanian continued to be linked with Bradstreet's military ventures after 1763. Bradstreet lived with the Schuylers; he loaned them money and made gifts to the youthful landlord. Together they launched speculative land ventures that outlasted a decade. The intimacy of their relationship became evident when Schuyler's son, born in September, 1763, was christened John Bradstreet. After the infant died the following August, the Schuylers named a second son, born in the year of the Stamp Act, in honor of their friend and benefactor. The old man was pleased enough with the gesture to make his namesake one of his heirs.

When Bradstreet set out on his expedition to Detroit against the Indians in 1764, he left behind him to tend his affairs as able and reliable a man as he had been fortunate to know. Schuyler was well enough occupied with his mills and Saratoga lands to preclude an

---

179. Hereafter cited as Sabine, *Smith Memoirs,* I. A second volume of the memoirs is as follows: *Historical Memoirs from 12 July 1776 to 25 July 1778 of William Smith* (New York, 1958), hereafter cited as Sabine, *Smith Memoirs,* II. See also Smith to Schuyler, Nov. 27, 1772; July 5, 1773; Mar. 22, 1774; June 1, 1775, NYPL, Schuyler Papers Box 24. And see William Tryon to Schuyler, May 25, 1772, in NYHS, John W. Francis, "Old New York" (New York, 1865), XIII, 17; Schuyler to Peter Van Schaack, July 7, 1774, in NYHS, Misc. MSS (Schuyler); *The New-York Gazette, or Weekly Post-Boy,* Aug. 3, 1772; Assembly Journals, Feb. 5, 1773, in C.O. 5/1201.

adventurous foray against Pontiac with his old friend. But he was not too busy to continue an agency for Bradstreet similar to the one he was developing with his father-in-law, John Van Rensselaer. In June, 1764, Bradstreet turned over to Schuyler's care everything that pertained to the deputy quarter-master general's department. He also instructed him to collect all public debts against any return and to inform General Thomas Gage in New York of his appointment.[64]

Schuyler's agency under Bradstreet as a deputy quarter-master general continued for a decade after the Great War for the Empire. If he was able to turn his position into a profitable source of income, it is impossible to determine the exact extent to which he managed it. But as he was developing his lands at the very time he was Bradstreet's deputy, it is not difficult to surmise the connections. He may have sold grain and timber to the military establishment. But what is more evident is his taking the opportunity to hire seasonably unemployed men from the military. While public business was interrupted, Schuyler employed workmen to construct barracks for artisans and laborers of various kinds at Saratoga "not only as a nursery for the arts which he meant to encourage, but as the materials of a future colony, which he meant to plant out around him." [65]

[64] Bradstreet to Schuyler, June 2, 1764. NYPL, Schuyler Papers Box 9. Schuyler to Gage, June 14, 1764. William L. Clements Library, Gage Papers.

[65] Anne Grant, *Memoirs*, II, 114–115. See also Thomas Man to Schuyler, April 15, 1767. NYPL, Schuyler Papers Box 23 (for evidence of Schuyler's service under Bradstreet). Abraham Mortier to Sir William Johnson, Jan. 19, 1765, in Division of Archives and History, University of the State of New York, *The Papers of Sir William Johnson* (12 vols.; Albany, 1921–1957), IV, 638. Hereafter cited as *Sir William Johnson Papers*. And see "Abstract of Payments for the Public Service," NYPL, Schuyler Papers Box 9, for evidence of the sizable sums Schuyler handled and the substantial salary he drew for himself. Schuyler's diligent attention to the deputy quarter-master general's business is revealed by his correspondence with General Gage: Schuyler to Gage, June 14, 18, 24, 30; July 7, 23, 24; Aug. 5, 1764; June 16, 1766. Copies of letters, Gage to Schuyler, June 24, July 15, 30, Aug. 6, Sept. 30, Oct. 14, 27, 1764. William L. Clements Library, Gage Papers. The Gage Papers also include "Mr. Schuyler's Abstract of the Public Expences in the year 1765 in the Albany Department," but this gives no indication that he sold any stores, provisions, firewood, forage, or other such items listed; and it does not appear that Schuyler made any sales to the army, or if he did, there is no evidence of how much. For other evidence of Schuyler's work with Bradstreet, see John Bradstreet to Sir Jeffrey Amherst, Sept. 14, 1760; Bradstreet to Schuyler, Oct. 23, 1760; Gen. Thomas Gage to Bradstreet, June 30, 1766; L. Fd. Caryre to Schuyler, July 4, 1766; Bradstreet to Gage, Sept. 15, 1766; Oct. 25, 1766; Nov. 14, 1767. Am. Antiq. Soc., *Trans. & Colls.*, XI, 65–66, 88–89, 92.

Schuyler benefited both directly and indirectly from Bradstreet's process of self-enrichment. Together they plunged into every possible activity for advancing their interest, be it the quest for patronage or seizing lands. Bradstreet's role is not always completely clear, if we are to judge by the remaining evidence of his activities, but it is un-clouded enough to see that he was always in the background of Schuy-ler's schemes. Anxious to prevent intrusions upon land to which his father-in-law laid claim, Schuyler was not above making an attempt on other lands whose titles were shaky because of arrears in quitrents. In this he had Bradstreet's full, however secret, backing. The prevail-ing system of settlement, of land grants, and the whole spirit of pro-vincial politics prompted, if indeed they did not directly foster, this sort of calculated aggrandizement.

The frontier policy of colonial New York was ridden with weak-nesses: large grants were not conducive to rapid settlement and im-provement; the patroon and manorial system forced some colonists into a distasteful way of life and drove many of them elsewhere; and careless marking of boundaries resulted in complaints from Indians and whites alike.[66] The granting of patents embracing enormous es-tates may have been the most conspicuous feature of the land policy in the province between 1665 and 1750.[67] But even before Philip Schuyler stepped on the scene, grants were smaller. Governors Love-lace (1708–1709) and Hunter (1710–1719) had orders to limit them to one or two thousand acres per patentee. Hence, the practice of cor-porate petitioning for sizable grants such as the Schoharie Patent of 1714 by which five New Yorkers procured 10,000 acres, but a limit of 2,000 each.

Such restrictions prompted ambitious or aspiring landlords to be constantly active in acquiring smaller holdings in order that they might piece together large domains. It was no longer possible for them to be satisfied with one or two major acquisitions. The more ventures they planned, the greater their activity and anxiety, and the larger the prospects for dissatisfaction and disappointment. More-over, the limitations of grants to 2,000 acres per patentee encouraged evasionary tactics. Joint patentees in a corporate venture could always withdraw after the patent was issued and sell their interests

[66] Laura Adella Hatfield, "The Frontier Policy of New York to 1776" (M.A. thesis, University of Chicago, 1916), pp. 4–6.

[67] Ruth L. Higgins, *Expansion in New York* (Columbus, 1931), p. 22.

to one or a few of their fellows.[68] Philip Schuyler was something of a victim as well as an agent of this system.

The procedure for procuring a land grant was time-consuming. The patentee had first to extinguish any Indian title. For this he needed a license from the governor to purchase a tract. Then he must deal with the Indians. In 1763 private persons were forbidden to buy lands directly from the Indians; that must be done by the governor and Indian superintendent. Provided this was successful, the governor must be petitioned for a survey. The provision for surveying was not always well observed, but Cadwallader Colden as surveyor general was interested in accurate surveys to describe the boundaries with greater precision. Finally the governor and council must approve the grant and issue a warrant to the attorney general, who drafted the patents.[69]

In view of the lengthy procedure, the increasingly antiquated policy, and the decrease in available lands, it is not surprising that Schuyler and Bradstreet found it easier to purchase lands than to attempt to procure entirely new patents. They were victims of an old land policy, and they could only deal with it by adopting modified methods of acquisition, by procuring lands by a variety of purchases when they could not directly acquire patents.

In 1760, Schuyler joined ninety-nine other ambitious speculators in a petition for several tracts along the upper Mohawk and the eastern side of the Hudson. The stakes were 200,000 acres, only 2,000 per patentee unless some of the partners agreed to hand over their shares once the patent was issued. The effort came to nought.[70]

Again in 1761, Bradstreet attempted to procure for Schuyler 25,000 acres east of the Hudson and north of the Saratoga Patent by arranging, in his absence, for twenty petitioners to join a corporate request

[68] Flick, III, 156. See also the agreement signed by twenty petitioners for land (Sept. 19, 1761), who proposed to acquire 25,000 acres by acting in trust for Philip Schuyler. NYPL, Schuyler Papers Box 16.

[69] Higgins, *Expansion in New York*, pp. 29–30, 103–104. See also Flick, III, 154–155.

[70] *Calendar of New York Colonial Manuscripts indorsed Land Papers in the Office of the Secretary of State of New York, 1643–1803* (Albany, 1864), pp. 293–294. "Abstracts of New York Land Grants, 1666–1764," C.O. 5/1134, does not record the venture, so it must have failed. NYPL, Chalmers Manuscripts (4 vols.), II, 76–77, "Lists of Patents and Warrants to survey lands granted in New York Nov. 14, 1761—June 23, 1763 by Lt. Gov. Colden," and III, 10–11, "Lists of Grants of Land passed since the Death of Lieutenant Governor De Lancey by . . . Cadwallader Colden . . . March 27, 1761—Sept. 29, 1761."

to the governor. The petitioners signed an agreement whereby they attested their projected action was a trust for Schuyler. By it they promised to convey title to the anticipated grant to Schuyler on demand. This scheme also failed to materialize. But about the same time Schuyler managed to buy what he could not procure by government grants. In 1760, Bradstreet made him a gift of £350, and in December he made a purchase with it. Again in January, 1761, Bradstreet loaned him another £1,000, with which he bought a tract near Albany.[71] From then on what he could not accumulate through inheritance, he relied largely on his purse and credit to procure. Even so he learned that there were obstacles which money sometimes could not remove.

Between 1761 and 1768, Schuyler and Bradstreet apparently were engrossed mostly with business other than land speculation. But by 1768 they resumed their purchasing penchant with some vigor, nor did they hesitate to apply for grants through the royal establishment. In 1768, Schuyler also entered the New York Assembly, a position from which he might well have imagined he could pursue his agrarian interests with greater effectiveness and ease. But before he ventured this, he carefully courted the favor of the royal governor, Sir Henry Moore, and added a new title to his name, that of colonel.

New York provincial politics was a potpourri of many influences, and the local aristocracy, while holding a commanding position, did not rely solely on principle to guide them, nor was their position due only to "the strength of family ties, their economic power as landlords, or an excessively restricted franchise." Men moved into and out of the governor's "interest" as he granted them favors, not wholly because of political conviction or principle.[72] Philip Schuyler is a good example of this kind of maneuvering. Completely at ease in dealing with a governor for lands, he was ready to pay favors as well as to court them; he was not always on the governor's side in the assembly.

[71] See footnote 68 *supra*. See also *Index to the Public Records of the County of Albany, State of New York, 1630–1894* (Albany; Grantees: 12 vols., 1908–1911; Grantors: 14 vols., 1902–1907; *Lis pendens:* 4 vols., 1915–1917; Mortgagers: 6 vols., 1913–1914) which show no record of a purchase in 1760–1761. Schuyler spoke of his purchases years later in a general way. See "The Answer of Philip Schuyler . . . to the bill of Complaint of John Evans . . . and Agatha his wife [1788]." NYPL, Schuyler Papers Box 10.

[72] Milton M. Klein, "Democracy and Politics in Colonial New York," *New York History,* XL (July, 1959), 221, 240.

Philip Schuyler began his political climb during the administration of Sir Henry Moore (1765–1769). During that time Moore commissioned him a colonel, and together they dealt in speculative schemes. For his part, Moore courted the popular party of the moment and avoided Lieutenant Governor Cadwallader Colden as only a man could who wanted none of his predecessor's odium attached to himself.[73] For three years Moore refused, for example, to request the assembly to vote Colden compensation for damages he had incurred in the Stamp Act riots. Nor did he vigorously press prerogative. Although Moore wanted a part in the assembly's selection of an agent, he did not prevent it from choosing one by unilateral action. Moore's inclinations toward the popular position led him to dissolve the assembly in January, 1768—earlier than required by the septennial act —in order to please the Livingston faction and help them in their election bid for more power. One of the faction members, Philip Livingston, Jr., son of Peter Van Brugh Livingston, was Moore's secretary.[74]

Exactly when or how Schuyler was introduced to Governor Moore is not clear. But the new governor made a trip to the Mohawk country late in the summer of 1766, and if he did not know the young Albanian before the excursion, he could not escape a meeting then, for Schuyler was prominent as a landlord and a commissioner for the New York–Massachusetts boundary settlement. The governor could hardly have avoided meeting him. Moore's purpose in journeying north was to tour the province and arrange the Quebec boundary with Governor Guy Carleton.

At Albany the governor made his headquarters with the Schuylers. What could be more suitable for entertaining such a prominent guest, his wife and daughter than the new mansion Schuyler had but recently erected? Moore was impressed by such genteel display so near the frontier. And he was quick to offer his thanks for Schuyler's courtesies and to remark politely that he would think it long until he had the pleasure of seeing his host in New York where he might reciprocate the hospitality. Moore's trip to Sir William Johnson's, "attended

[73] John F. Burns, *Controversies Between Royal Governors and Their Assemblies in the North American Colonies* (Boston, 1923), pp. 357–369. Hereafter cited as Burns, *Controversies*. The odium was the result of Colden's role in the Stamp Act riots, his struggle with the assembly to raise New York's supply quotas, and his advocacy of judicial tenure at pleasure instead of on terms of good behavior.

[74] Jones, *History of New York*, I, 19.

by several Gentlemen" of Albany, Schuyler included, was designed to arrange a purchase from the Oneida Indians. It was successful. Johnson bought 200,000 acres for the Crown, a tract which Sir Henry intended to share with General Thomas Gage and others, including Philip Schuyler, Lord Holland and a number of Johnson's friends.[75]

The Mohawk River land purchase arranged in the late summer of 1766 caused Schuyler no little trouble. The governor had designs which led to adjustments in Schuyler's expectations, but these eventually put the governor in his debt. To Moore's invitation to visit him in New York, Schuyler gladly responded. It was an opportunity to develop his interest with Sir Henry. Early in December he called at the province house to reopen his talks with the governor. Schuyler found there were difficulties about the Mohawk purchase. One of the Waltons, an influential merchant family, had a claim for land, and what this would do to the division of the 200,000 acres was uncertain. The governor began to find out. Later that month he wrote Schuyler and Sir William Johnson to ask if any part of the purchase could be spared by the other proprietors, not for the Waltons, but for enlarging Lord Holland's tract. Quick to see a means of ingratiating himself with Governor Moore to even greater advantage, Schuyler offered to surrender his share in the Mohawk tract, thus alleviating Moore's difficulties with other importunate speculators. It was not an easy thing to do in the midst of the current "Land fever contagion." [76] But Moore was grateful. If anything could be done about other lands (of which they had first talked) that might be to Schuyler's advantage, Moore vowed he would be very glad to take the earliest opportunity of returning the compliment Schuyler had paid him on this occasion.[77]

[75] For accounts of Moore's movements see *The New-York Gazette, or Weekly Post-Boy*, Oct. 9, 16, 1766. See also Moore to Schuyler, Oct. 13, 1766, and Feb. 2, 1767: NYPL, Schuyler Papers Box 23; Humphreys, *Catherine Schuyler*, pp. 92–93. For evidence of the land scheme see *Sir William Johnson Papers*, V, 266–268; Alden, *General Gage*, p. 71; see also *Catalogue of Maps and Surveys, in the Offices of the Secretary of State, State Engineer and Surveyor, and Comptroller, and the New York State Library* (rev. ed.; Albany, 1859), p. 326, for the "Map of a tract of 17,000 acres surveyed for Thomas Gage, Peter Hasenclever, Philip Schuyler, John French, Peter Lewis, *et al.*, Oct., 1766."

[76] William Smith, Jr., to Schuyler, Mar. 21, 1767. NYPL, Schuyler Papers Box 23. Smith mentions "the Land fever contagion now prevalent."

[77] For Schuyler's dealings with Moore, see Lossing, I, 216; Moore to Schuyler, Dec. 29, 1766, Feb. 2, 1767. NYPL, Schuyler Papers Box 23.

Schuyler could hope, then, to profit after all. Moore's obligation to him was an almost invaluable debt on which Schuyler might collect later to even greater advantage. At a time when he was anxious about his father-in-law's lands, Schuyler could claim the governor's indulgence in that matter. Rumor had it that the Crown would prosecute John Van Rensselaer for intrusion on the "Kings Soil." But the governor proved a champion of Van Rensselaer's position.[78]

Never content to concentrate on but a single enterprise at once, Schuyler laid other plans and exerted other influences. He hoped to buy still another parcel of land, the Hallenbeck Patent, but his friend and attorney, William Smith, Jr., warned him not to count on this too strongly. It was not certain that the tract could be had. At the same time, Schuyler's influence with the governor did not go unrecognized by others. Gerret Van Sante, Jr., a fellow Albanian, asked him to approach Sir Henry about an addition to a 3,000-acre grant. Van Sante was willing to offer £25, "but this matter I must leave to your discretion whether it can be safely done," he wrote. "You'll excuse my Importunity in this Matter, as I don't know any person who can so effectually serve me." [79]

If Sir Henry Moore could not make the way altogether smooth for Schuyler's territorial ambitions, he could offer him other sops by way of compensation and reassurance. Schuyler thus extended his interests from real estate to patronage. There were militia appointments in the offing in 1767. In May, Schuyler received good news. His Mohawk purchase was to be settled, and by way of remuneration for his loss of half the original one-fifth share intended for him, he was to have a militia colonel's commission. Something less than half a share might not be as handsome an acquisition as the whole, but there were other compensations; the governor was in his debt. And Moore promised the commission for Schuyler's regiment would "be made out as soon as I receive the names of your Officers." His own commission as a colonel was issued in August [80]—a title he bore with the distinction valued by many provincial leaders.

Governor Moore intended to call on Schuyler in Albany in 1767, but was obliged to delay the visit until the following spring because

[78] William Smith, Jr., to Schuyler, Feb. 23, 1767. NYPL, Schuyler Papers Box 23.

[79] Van Sante to Schuyler, April 5, 1767; see also Smith to Schuyler, Mar. 21, 1767. NYPL, Schuyler Papers Box 23.

[80] The commission, Aug. 20, 1767. NYPL, Schuyler Papers Box 42. See also Moore to Schuyler, Mar. 22, May 18, 1767. NYPL, Schuyler Papers Box 23.

his family kept him at the seashore. The governor, however, remained solicitous for Schuyler's affairs, and suggested if John Bradstreet had any papers that required presentation that he send them down. The assembly was to meet in mid-November, and Schuyler himself went down with Bradstreet's accounts.[81] He was in New York City again in December when talk centered on the impending elections to follow the assembly's dissolution. William Smith, Jr., began to urge him to consider "setting up" for an assembly seat.

Land speculation remained the important topic of Schuyler's correspondence with Governor Moore in 1768. In February, following a survey, Moore submitted a proposed division of the 1766 Mohawk purchase for Schuyler's approval. Schuyler's share had been whittled down to 12,000 acres, while the other half of it was added to the governor's portion as a suitable tract for Lord Holland. But the governor desired his "opinion of the Lands lately purchased at Schoharie; I am partly concern'd in them," he said, "but as the Tract is inconsiderable I believe that I shall dispose of my Share, if it could be done to advantage." As with the Mohawk purchase of 1766–1767, Schuyler quickly offered to sacrifice some of his interest in the Schoharie lands, evidently to augment Moore's advantage there, but the governor insisted he could not think of depriving him of so valuable a purchase. The recent partition of the 1766 purchase, said Moore, made Schuyler's newer (Schoharie) lands valuable by reason of their proximity to the river. Moore would, however, be grateful for a lesser favor; if Schuyler would recommend him, the governor promised to hire a Cornelius Pummins as postilion. The colonel had discharged Pummins to the services of a Mr. Dobbs of New York.[82]

Later in February, 1768, Governor Moore changed his mind about Schuyler's land offer. He decided to accept it, hoping he had not made any agreements to prevent this new favor. To keep Schuyler from thinking him fickle, Moore told him that petitions for the land before the council were obstructed by a caveat entered by the Waltons. The Waltons had received permission to buy them in 1762, and now they

---

[81] Moore to Schuyler, Nov. 1, 1767; see also John Cochran to Schuyler, Nov. 30, 1767. NYPL, Schuyler Papers Box 23. Bradstreet to Gen. Thomas Gage, Nov. 14, 1767. Am. Antiq. Soc., *Trans. & Colls.*, XI, 92. Bradstreet wished to present accounts for paying troops he had raised in 1764, and indicated if Gage consented, letters given to Schuyler would be placed before the assembly and that Schuyler would give any assistance the general desired.

[82] Moore to Schuyler, Feb. 1, 22, 1768. NYPL, Schuyler Papers Box 23.

did not propose to relinquish their rights. Moore said the only way to procure the Schoharie tract was to grant some of the land to the Waltons. He vowed he would not have asked Schuyler for this favor except that the Albanian's letter was couched in such strong terms as to lead the governor to imagine his projects were intended elsewhere. Schuyler, he hoped, would not be disappointed by this sudden acceptance. And said Moore, "[I] can assure that it will be an addition to the many obligations which you & your family have conferr'd on [me]." Many obligations indeed. Schuyler met Moore's latest request. Here were the grounds for influence—an obligation owed by the governor. Two weeks later Moore expressed his indebtedness even more clearly: he would be happy to show how much he was obliged "not only for this last mark of your regard for me, but for many others I have experienced, & I hope you'l command any services in my power." [83] What a happy prospect for a newly elected assemblyman! Schuyler might indeed have occasion to draw upon the governor's services and this reservoir of good will. Had Moore lived, the colonel may not have had as many difficulties with his father-in-law's disputed land title.

Other land schemes went apace during 1768. Governor Moore paid Schuyler a visit in Albany in May, when he went up to see Sir William Johnson about settling a boundary with the Iroquois at the Treaty of Fort Stanwix.[84] Doubtless he congratulated the colonel on his recent election to the assembly.

The policy of pushing the Indians westward that culminated in the Treaty of Fort Stanwix in 1768 opened the way for John Bradstreet to lay plans for further speculations. Schuyler was his assistant in these projects. Both men had a special connection with the governor, and Schuyler was now an assemblyman to whom Sir Henry had promised his services. Bradstreet expected the colonel to use his position and presence in New York to good advantage. George Croghan, the Indian agent and trader, dealt for Bradstreet with the Indians for lands at Auquagha. Having paid half the purchase money, he sent surveyors to lay out his bounds. In the meantime, Bradstreet told Schuyler to "please to let the Governor into this affair & take his directions how I must proceed if the Lands will do." Croghan was to show Schuyler still another Indian purchase his friend proposed to

[83] Moore to Schuyler, Feb. 28, Mar. 14, 1768. NYPL, Schuyler Papers Box 23.
[84] Moore to Schuyler, May 16, 1768. NYPL, Schuyler Papers Box 23. See also *The New-York Gazette, or Weekly Post-Boy*, May 30, 1768.

make. Perhaps the colonel could make inquiries about its possibilities. Bradstreet was also fishing for a promotion, and he told Schuyler, "If any Representation goes home from your Quarter, it would be a good Oppertunity [sic] to do me Service by a Mention of my former Services." This he hoped Schuyler would "manage if you can as from yourself." But Bradstreet was hoping against all likelihood of becoming quarter-master general. General Thomas Gage was scarcely an enthusiastic friend, and Bradstreet knew this when he wrote facetiously of Gage's "good intentions towards me." Bradstreet had long been a thorn in Gage's side.[85]

Schuyler's fuller involvement in provincial government circles in the winter of 1768–1769 when he took his seat in the assembly gave Bradstreet a new advantage in soliciting an appointment from London. Governor Moore remained friendly with the two Albany colleagues, despite Schuyler's role in the formulation of the assembly's resolutions (against the Restraining Act, the Townshend duties, and for the right to correspond with other colonies) which had obliged Moore to dissolve the house. In January, 1769, the governor laid plans for a visit to Sir William Johnson and for a call on Bradstreet and Schuyler in their own bailiwick.[86] In February they had a fresh opportunity to consult together and to strengthen their connections. Moore's dissolution of the assembly in January was followed by further elections, and Schuyler was returned to his seat.

Much of Philip Schuyler's and John Bradstreet's influence, their success and hopes was pinned on Sir Henry Moore, and they cultivated the favor of the old man as assiduously as they dealt with him for lands. But Moore died in September, 1769, and with him passed much of their hope for the immediate future. It was difficult, if not impossible, to develop such a connection with Lieutenant Governor Colden, who served in the interim (1769–1770), or with the Earl of Dunmore, whose tenure as governor was a brief one (1770–1771). William Tryon offered fresh prospects and possibilities.

[85] Bradstreet to Schuyler, Nov. 15, 17, 1768. NYPL, Schuyler Papers Box 9. See also Alden, *General Gage*, pp. 72–73. Notwithstanding Bradstreet's ultimate promotion (May, 1772) to a major-generalship, he wished further recognition for his services and believed that he was being "hardly used" because other officers were promoted over him and because he was the only general officer without a regiment. Bradstreet to [William Petty, Earl of Shelburne?], May 10, 1773. Am. Antiq. Soc., *Trans. & Colls.*, XI, 95–96.

[86] Moore to Schuyler, Jan. 30, 1769. NYPL, Schuyler Papers Box 23. See also *The New-York Gazette, or Weekly Post-Boy*, Feb. 20, 1769.

The changes in administration were awkward both for Schuyler's agency in the Van Rensselaer land dispute before the New York Council and for his own prospects for land speculation. He was obliged to explain the Van Rensselaer case to two new governors. One of his cohorts, Philip Livingston, Jr., who had been Moore's personal secretary, confided to Schuyler his fear that with Moore's death they would lose the Mohawk River lands they wanted and on which they had spent good money for the surveys. Livingston reported that Moore had written the ministry about various applications for lands after the cession at Fort Stanwix. But no grants could be made until the royal pleasure was known. When Moore urged the government to set low terms for land grants as a means of encouraging settlement, and asked for a speedy decision lest he be obliged to make grants first to persons holding a mandamus from the Crown, he was put off. Moore was told that the Board of Trade had the matter under advisement. But he was anxious to please all parties, and hoped that he might make grants either to petitioners like Schuyler and Livingston or to those persons who held mandamuses before the Indian cession was made. This, Livingston told the colonel, would permit Jeffrey Amherst and others to enjoy a preference over everyone else. A certain Coxe had located on the tract Schuyler and Livingston wanted. Livingston feared he would make good his claim "if not prevented by" Schuyler. He suggested that Schuyler persuade the surveyor to give him the return he had made. The colonel should keep all the papers, for they had paid for the work and could properly claim it as their own. If this were done, Livingston surmised, no other survey could be made or returned by any other person in the course of the winter. And without a survey a mandamus could not be used against them. Instead, they might arrange to procure a mandamus of their own, and trust that a decision from London would permit them to go ahead with their acquisition. This stratagem apparently met with no more success than several petitions for land that John Bradstreet made between Moore's death and the arrival of Governor William Tryon.[87]

87 Philip Livingston, Jr., to Schuyler, Oct. 8, 1769. NYPL, Schuyler Papers Box 23. See also Ellis, *Landlords and Farmers*, p. 49, which mentions a "Coxe Patent" that was evidently passed over Livingston's and Schuyler's interests. For Bradstreet's actions see *Calendar of N.Y. Colo. MSS indorsed Land Papers*, pp. 500–501, 508, 522, 524–525, 698. See also Grant and Munro, *Acts of the Privy Council of England: Colonial Series*, VI, 538, and Robert R. Livingston to Robert Livingston, Mar. 24, 1771, in NYHS, Robert R. Livingston Collection.

By deliberation or coincidence, Schuyler's preparations for entering the provincial assembly had been quite thorough. His education had been broadened by war service and a journey to the imperial capital. His friend, John Bradstreet, offered him the advantages of counsel, loans, and gifts. His inheritance had been enlarged by other acquisitions. The Saratoga plantation thrived under his hand, and his agrarian foundation had been buttressed with a multi-sided economy: farming, lumbering, milling, fishing, river-shipping, and storekeeping. He had established both a country seat and a comfortable town mansion. And his connections involved him in the affairs of the Livingstons and Van Rensselaers: inheritances, tenant riots, land claims, and boundary disputes. His association with Governor Moore brought him new lands, a colonelcy in the provincial militia, and influence. But Colonel Schuyler, magnate and politician, was to learn that the strength of his position would not always assure him of an effective share of power in the New York Assembly.

CHAPTER III

Outline of a Political Heritage

ANY CONSIDERATION of Philip Schuyler's activities in the New York colonial assembly, any understanding of how his conservative patriotism was forged, demands not only a review of his wealth and position, but also a survey of the state of New York politics at the time he emerged from the scene of his agrarian labors and entered the arena of partisan politics. The colonel stepped on the political stage just as the dispute over Parliamentary authority was reaching crisis proportions—just as New Yorkers were finding greater appeal in the use of extralegal action. He was reluctant to enter the assembly because private business held stronger attractions than did imperial issues. His estates and enterprises demanded extensive attention. They may have seemed more demanding because they were more immediate than the issues of an imperial quarrel. But in another sense Schuyler found that his family interest could not be separated from provincial affairs, nor was his business and social position wholly independent of political activities. They were all meshed together. He was obliged to enter the "storms of public life," as once he described them, because politics, whether partisan or statesmanlike, afforded an important means of protecting and advancing personal interest. Most agrarian aristocrats shared this obligation. At the same time, he found that newer, more radical methods were loosening the familiar bonds of land and family. Appeals to the mass population and the use of popular demonstrations were altering the aristocratic system of which he was a part. And elements outside the assembly threatened more and more to wrest the leadership from the hands of cautious, privileged men within the house. Thinking to advance their own welfare, assembly partisans experimented with manipulation of the outsiders, only to find the game was more dangerous than playing among themselves.

87

– 1 –

THE AGRARIAN SETTING

THE POLITICAL CLIMATE of New York was a peculiar one. Basically conservative and quiescent, provincial society in the decade, 1760–1770, was jarred by radical elements of discord. Conditions in New York were the product of long development marked by wars of empire and a general absence of vigorous British interference in local affairs. The relative freedom which the colonies enjoyed during the years typified by Walpole's "salutary neglect" and non-interference proved a definite encouragement to the decay of royal power and of prerogative, and eventually provided, therefore, a challenge to imperial authority and Parliamentary supremacy. Even the war years which brought renewed exertions on both sides of the Atlantic did not greatly alter the colonists' basic inclination to be left alone—to benefit from as much non-interference from the mother country as possible. The longer they experienced the lack of restraint or the freedom from close imperial regulation, the more the colonists desired to perpetuate and even to advance this condition. Their inclinations were no less strong for want of legal justification. They were rooted deeply in the social and economic structure of the colony. An understanding of Philip Schuyler's position demands a review of the components of that structure.

New York was primarily an agrarian province. During the decade her population remained small, climbing from about 100,000 to around 168,000. In 1765 the province ranked as one of the smaller colonies. Massachusetts, Connecticut, Pennsylvania, Virginia, and the Carolinas each had a larger population. By far the largest portion of her people were scattered in rural areas along the Hudson River and the Mohawk valley. Albany, the largest of all the counties in territory and population, was likewise primarily rural. The county seat contained only a small fraction of the district's 42,700 people.[1] Large

---

[1] Evarts B. Greene and Virginia D. Harrington, *American Population Before the Federal Census of 1790* (New York, 1932), pp. 6, 102–103. See also Governor Tryon's report on New York, C.O. 5/1105:552–571. In comparing figures given by Greene and Harrington for 1771 and 1790 (pp. 103–105) one may estimate that the city of Albany probably had a population of about 1,500 in 1771 as compared with 3,498 in 1790. Albany County population rose from 42,706 in 1771 to 75,921 in 1790. The county population in 1756 was 17,424.

landholding discouraged growth in both population and settlement.

Farmers were the most numerous class of laborers in colonial New York, and landlords, though fewer, were no great encouragement to free farmers. Despite their interest in enhancing property values, the landlords did not often sell their lands, but ran their estates on the principles of leaseholding and tenantry. Still, it must not be forgotten that for all the large manors and other vast holdings, New York was primarily an area of small- to moderate-sized farms.[2] Holders of these farms, whether tenant or owner, were not without significance or influence.

New York agrarian interests were both aristocratic and quasi-feudal. They were aristocratic because the landlords enjoyed certain privileges. Some of the manors had been given the advantage of representation in the assembly and could be veritable pocket boroughs of the lords of the manors. Agrarian magnates enjoyed access to office, in a franchise based largely on property holding and in the prestige and practical advantages of their wealth. Because some held estates in several counties it is not difficult to see why they considered plural voting a vital part of the political structure. Because elections were conducted *viva voce* a landlord could stand at the polling place as a silent but clear reminder that tenants were expected to adhere to his influence and interest. But tenants did not always follow their landlord's desires, nor did the *viva voce* method invariably afford certain means of controlling elections.

It was their potential wealth that made the landlords aristocrats— aristocrats by speculation. They had ample means to provide for their comfort and for a measure of ostentation. But the value of their property lay primarily in hope for the future—expectations of rising values and increased developments. Extravagant land grants of royal governors had also helped to make New York aristocratic. The granting of patents to enormous estates was the most conspicuous feature of land policy in the province from 1665 to 1750. These estates and the alliance of proprietors by marriage and interest encouraged a widespread, overwhelming pride of place. Vanity was but the reflection of something more substantial, yet it in turn lent added weight to the sounder pretensions to power. A landed estate was more than a source of potential wealth, or an object of speculation. It was of course the emblem of status.

2 Flick, II, 285.

The conditions of land tenure in New York were fundamentally quasi-feudal. The inhabitants and owners alike were governed by aristocratic principles. New York manorial life bore several features of the feudal past, but inasmuch as the old set of feudal relationships was gone, the remnants can be called only quasi-feudal. These were the quitrent, manorial courts, and fee-farming. Quitrents to the Crown were a reminder of the old lord-vassal relationship. They were small, but payments were often in arrears. Manor lords were given the right to hold a court leet and a court baron. Thus they had power to dispense justice in local criminal matters and to settle disputes of tenure, boundaries, and tenants' relationships. No evidence exists, however, to indicate that courts leet were ever active. Fee-farming with payment of rent in kind was still another, perhaps more practical, suggestion of a feudal past. Tenants held their farms for two or three lives, or in fee simple "for ever" with the stipulation of a fixed rent. The tenant not only paid his rent in kind, but was often obliged to serve his landlord by several days annual service, mainly "riding" with horses or oxen. Moreover, the landlord monopolized saw- and gristmilling and reserved mining rights. He might eject his tenants if they failed to meet their obligations, and if they should sell their farms, he shared a percentage of the sale. This was the hated "quarter sale." [3]

Landholding was thus aristocratic and monopolistic. The large patents ranged from 100,000 to 300,000 acres. An enormous one like the Hardenburgh Patent (1708) contained upward of one million acres. At first the English governors had been cautious in making grants. Andros (1674–1683), for example, required definite surveys and carefully fixed quitrents. For a time after the Glorious Revolution new governors, especially Fletcher and Cornbury, made more extravagant grants, partly to enrich themselves by the fees. But the Board of Trade pushed through reforms which restricted patentees to one or two thousand acres each. By 1750 the practice of single enormous patents had given way to more limited but numerous ones. By then, too, many of the great grants in the eastern and southern reaches of the province, as well as unappropriated lands, were threatened by claims of New Hampshire, Massachusetts, and New Jersey. And the two systems of landholding of New England and New York proved troublesome to Yorkers when Yankee farmers, accustomed to small free farms, re-

3 Dangerfield, *Livingston,* pp. 14–15.

fused to accept a tenant's position, and threatened to take lands claimed by the privileged holders. Boundary issues rose to plague both colonists and the imperial government. These disputes continued throughout the Revolutionary era.

Agrarian New York also benefited from a lively commerce in which she found outlets for her agricultural produce. Her trade was small compared with that of other colonies, however. Except for some iron produced largely on Livingston Manor, most of New York's produce was agricultural. Flax and wool weaving formed a part of limited local industry. Beaver hats were made for the local market. The chief exports were flour and grain, timber, beef, pork, furs, and skins. Flour headed the list, but by midcentury New York's reputation for fine flour was being ruined by unprincipled traders who mixed it with Indian corn. The regulation of the quality of flour thus came before the New York Assembly. Also the profitable fur trade was falling off in the face of the disappearing beaver and the diversion of the Indian trade to Canada and Pennsylvania.[4]

New York enjoyed a steady but slow economic growth in the eighteenth century—in population, expanding farm lands, and in towns and trade. Between 1750 and 1770 the main population growth was centered in the Hudson and Mohawk valleys. The years 1760–1765 were largely prosperous ones, but with the passing of wartime conditions which had boosted the economy, a general recession set in and ran coincidentally with the Revolutionary movement. It is difficult to determine how much this was the result of the colonial-imperial clash,[5] but the discontented might easily use the fact of its existence, however incomplete their information and erroneous their logic, as an argument against prerogative, imperial power, and the authority of Parliament. When trade was dull, however momentarily, ports unemployed, and currency short, it was always easy to blame the Sugar Act of 1764 for hampering West Indian trade, or the Currency Act for restricting the circulating medium and, hence, the general prosperity.[6]

---

[4] Lawrence Henry Gipson, *The British Empire Before the American Revolution: Provincial Characteristics and Sectional Tendencies in the Era Preceding the American Crisis* (10 vols.; Caldwell, Idaho, and New York, 1936–1961), III, 122–124. Hereafter cited as Gipson, *The British Empire*.

[5] Flick, II, 264–265.

[6] Insofar as agriculture was concerned, William S. Sachs, "Agricultural Conditions in the Northern Colonies Before the Revolution," *Journal of Economic History*,

New York's trade lay mainly with England, but the West Indies and other colonies also offered her markets. Between 1747 and 1765 direct trade with the mother country was in great imbalance. The province imported far more than it exported. Exports to Britain, for example, totaled over £42,000 in 1750, but imports totaled over five times that amount. Between 1760 and 1770, New York's imports remained on the average about six times greater than her exports to Britain except for one year (1769) when the balance was only £1,000 greater for imports than exports. The same disparity persisted. Between 1770 and 1774, New York's exports averaged almost £81,000 per year and her imports over £440,000. The province was obliged to pay for this imbalance in money earned from intercolonial exchange, and from the intercourse with southern Europe and the West Indies. Thus New York benefited from a broad economic complex, for while one part of her trade was in great imbalance, there were other compensations which provided a kind of equilibrium. Part of the losses in the unfavorable trade balance were made up through cash imported by new immigrants, the earnings of New York shipping, and sums spent by the British government for defense in the province.[7]

Provincial economic life was not specialized. New York merchants followed not so much a single occupation as a diversified economic activity—including landholding. Landlords, likewise, did not restrict themselves to farming or speculation, but entered the commercial field by the sale of lumber and flour from their mills and grain from their fields, by the use of river boats for their own transportation and the

---

XIII (Summer, 1953), 274–290, shows that, as 90 per cent of the population of the northern colonies made their livings from agriculture, the years 1763–1775 were fairly prosperous for this large group which had agricultural incomes. Sachs also indicates that complaints of hard times came largely from urban groups. Farmers were not portrayed as suffering from economic hardships. Even the New York tenant riots of 1765–1766 were not evidence of a depressed agricultural economy, but rather a reaction against tenure provisions of the landholding system. And after 1769 merchants also benefited from improved business conditions until late 1772 or early 1773. When colonists complained of hard times, they were arguing against British legislation (e.g., the Sugar Act and the Stamp Act), hoping for its modification according to what they imagined or believed were their best interests.

[7] Flick, II, 266–267, 334. Cf. Becker, *Political Parties*, pp. 68–69, which cites David Macpherson, *Annals of Commerce* (4 vols.; London, 1805), III, 475, 476, 486, 495, 508. Governor Tryon's report on the province in 1774 gives his estimate of the annual value of exports to foreign countries at an average of £150,000 sterling and foreign imports he estimated at £100,000 sterling. C.O. 5/1105:549.

sale of manufactured goods and staples to their tenants. Hence, "it is questionable whether any clear distinction can be drawn between the mercantile and landed aristocracy . . . [for] there was scarcely a family in provincial New York which, in at least one of its branches, was not engaged in commerce." [8] Landlords also diversified their basic landed economy.

– 2 –

ASSEMBLY ASCENDANCY

IN MANY RESPECTS the province of New York bore a remarkable resemblance to the mother country—her society, agrarian-commercial economy, and her basic political principles and institutions. In spite of her Dutch origins and lingering Dutch customs, New York was governed according to basically English tenets. She was a microcosm, but not an exact duplicate. Yet for all these similarities the province evinced certain tendencies and embraced local interests which made it possible for it to diverge from the mainstream of empire just as other colonies did.

Whatever similarities there were between the colony of New York and Great Britain, the differences that existed were also important. The governor's council, for example, did not wholly correspond to the House of Lords. Peers did not serve at royal pleasure as did the councilors. The royal governor did not function *in* the legislature quite the same way the king functioned *in* Parliament. In Britain the king's veto had fallen into disuse, but the royal veto, exercised by the governor or by the king in Privy Council, was a "living reality in New York." [9]

The hallmarks of New York political society were an unwritten constitution, devotion to legal procedure and orderly due process, and adherence to principles and forms of mixed government—that nice balance of monarchical, aristocratic, and democratic elements. There was also the solid belief in the ideals of liberty and property. But the principles on which the province operated proved ultimately to be conflicting ones. Local interpretations and local ambitions more and more became centers of controversy and dissatisfaction. It was recog-

[8] Flick, II, 365, 371.

[9] Ross J. S. Hoffman, *Edmund Burke, New York Agent with his letters to the New York Assembly and intimate correspondence with Charles O'Hara, 1761–1776* (Philadelphia, 1956), p. 77.

nized that landed proprietors were entitled to share the business of government. Those who owned a stake in the country—those of credit and reputation—had an unmistakable right to govern it. This was the belief of Englishmen at home and in the colonies. But the activities of factions within the government of New York added an irritant, and the battle for place was quite as partisan, if not more so, in an outpost of empire as it was at the imperial capital. It was, however, a battle which sometimes made imperial policy difficult to administer. Moreover, it was not so much a conflict between lesser classes and the agrarian-mercantile aristocracy as it was a struggle within the governing class itself—a struggle which spilled over into the wider contest about imperial authority.

New York followed the general lines of English theory on the legislative power vested in a tripartite corporation of executive, legislative council, and assembly. The governor corresponded to the king. The council resembled the House of Lords, and inasmuch as it was an advisory body it also resembled the Privy Council. The assembly could be likened to the House of Commons. However, local political developments shifted the power from a locus of the proprietor's and monarch's governor to the assembly. By the middle of the eighteenth century the assembly had won a lever that threatened the exercise of royal prerogative and that, in a special way, bade fair to upset the traditionally mixed powers of government.[10] But within the assembly still another situation unfolded. Two major parties or factions emerged, based on a curious combination of family, commercial, and agrarian interests, as well as principle. These factions, much like those in British politics, were motivated largely by the desire to rule, to hold power or to wrest it from a rival's hands. The American Revolution in New York may be explained in part by this shift of power.

From the governors' active exercise of royal prerogative to the assembly's opposition and its victory in winning a predominant position for directing local affairs, the shifting balance was subject to modifications by factions within the governing class and the assembly, and by a revival of prerogative—this time the authority of Parliament asserted through the Crown establishment. In order to understand Philip

10 A comprehensive outline of the divisions and various officials of provincial government, and a discussion of the tendency toward legislative encroachment on various executive powers (such as that of appointment) are given by Rex Maurice Naylor, "The Royal Prerogative in New York, 1691–1775," *The Quarterly Journal of the New York State Historical Association*, V (July, 1924), 237, *passim*.

Schuyler's role in New York politics we must consider briefly the way in which the assembly won its position of advantage over the governor, for this struggle for ascendancy formed the framework of the factional wrangling within the assembly. The factors of family and faction within the assembly likewise were vital to Schuyler's political career, and, finally, we must look to the imperial program of the early 1760's as an assertion of Parliamentary authority which began to clash with local ambitions and interests. In its last stages the course of the Revolution took an extralegal turn which culminated in open rebellion and war. Finally, turning full circle, New Yorkers moved back to the conservatism of established or traditional government, damming the radical current that had borne them away from the first British Empire.

The central fact in the political history of New York before 1765 was the contest between the governors and the assembly. It has not been determined how much, if at all, factionalism may explain this development, but some such partisan divisions are evident before midcentury. "The contest was doubtless inevitable, for the governor and the assembly represented different interests and opposing principles," the former the British government, the latter the colony.[11] One of the conditions which made possible the Revolution in New York was the degree of legislative freedom enjoyed by the province and encouraged by conditions rising from the Great War for the Empire.[12] Wartime circumstances merely added impetus to a process in operation long before hostilities opened. As early as 1691 the assembly limited the governor's salary to a two-year appropriation. From that time it proceeded to curb the governor at every opportunity. In 1694 it began to audit expenditures, and when the receiver general's accounts were not opened for them, the assembly complained vigorously. The struggle to procure an accounting for funds expended led the assembly to name its own treasurer. In 1704 the government of Queen Anne permitted New York to do this only after the province had raised extraordinary supplies not a part of the standing revenue. But even this was a toe hold for subsequent encroachments. The personal clash with governors Sloughter, Fletcher, Cornbury, and Lovelace "aroused and strengthened in the Assembly the conviction that the representatives must be very vigilant in defending their rights." When Governor Hunter requested a permanent settlement for the

11 Becker, *Political Parties*, p. 5.
12 Flick, III, 173.

support of the government, the assembly answered by voting only an annual appropriation and demanded that the receiver general report to them as well as to the governor and the council. As early as 1711 he had insisted the assembly was stretching its claims beyond its legal powers, but in 1715, Hunter was forced to yield. Within four decades the assembly made itself virtually the complete power in local government.[13] Yet it was but the vehicle of power for parties or factions.

There were other points of dispute between governor and assembly over who was to wield a supremacy. If New Yorkers believed in mixed government—in a proper balance of the aristocratic, monarchical, and democratic elements—it was also evident that some coveted places of greater advantage over other individuals or institutions of which such government was comprised. The assembly wanted a voice in the erection of an equity court and opposed the governor's attempt to establish himself as head of a court of chancery. It disliked and opposed the governor's prolongation of the life of an assembly by prorogation, and petitioned for frequent elections. During William Cosby's administration the house objected to the governor seating himself on the council whenever it sat as the upper house of the legislature. It also refused to allow the governor's council to amend money bills.[14] Despite the shadowy differentiation that seemed to prevail in England about the executive, judicial, and legislative authority of the king, and in spite of New Yorkers' inclination for mixed government, their actions suggested an alteration of this principle and practice, for the assembly's quarrels with the governor implied the establishment of clearer distinctions among the three branches of government.

With Governor Clarke (1736–1743) the assembly quarreled about requests for long-term appropriations, and showed its displeasure with

[13] Burns, *Controversies,* pp. 304, 310–311. See also Flick, III, 175. The assembly made several major advances during 1696–1739. In voting specific instead of general appropriations it deprived the governor and council of any discretion in issuing warrants. It appointed commissioners of accounts. It lodged funds with a treasurer named by itself, and empowered him alone to make payments. The assembly constantly challenged the council's right to amend money bills. It made the receiver general responsible to the legislature for his disposal of funds, and after 1714, lodged no money with him for the support of government; hence, he was limited to collecting quitrents and administering the imperial trade system. In 1739 the assembly arranged to pay officials by name and specific amount, and if the governor refused to make appointments desired by the house, he ran the risk that it would grant no salaries. Naylor, "The Royal Prerogative in New York, 1691–1775," pp. 240–241.
[14] Burns, *Controversies,* pp. 314, 317–318.

his demands by cutting his salary. And during the administration of George Clinton (1743–1753) the assembly so effectively clipped gubernatorial powers that the office of governor was left almost a cipher.[15]

George Clinton was a military man. He was neither patient, sagacious, nor diplomatic. In one of New York's most disturbed administrations he alternated between extremes of aggressiveness and conciliation. The assembly took advantage of these fluctuations to advance its position at the expense of the governor, chipping away at his powers during Clinton's conciliatory moods. Although his instructions were to regain the control of money matters lost by his predecessor, Clinton followed the advice of James De Lancey and yielded to the assembly's every demand. Thus, the assembly won a pronounced ascendancy. It restricted its appropriations to one year. From 1748 to 1750, Clinton refused to sign appropriation bills under this condition, but in 1750 he relented under pressing need for funds. He no longer insisted on five-year appropriations and on the granting of supplies "in general." Instead, he accepted an act of 1744, providing for specific, itemized appropriations. The assembly paid salaries to individuals named by its legislation, not to the offices which they held. Thus it won a power over appointments. When Clinton attempted to procure a fixed support bill, the assembly vowed it would not "pass any bill for raising money . . . and leave it to be disposed of at the will and pleasure of a Governor." The assembly was permitted to name committees to purchase and distribute munitions, to raise, supply, and pay provincial troops, to name officers and build fortifications. Furthermore, it appointed its own London agent. In 1748, when it named Robert Charles, the assembly dismissed the old agent, but Clinton approved the new officer inasmuch as he agreed to providing Charles a salary in the government supply bill. Clinton also gave judges their commissions for good behavior. This established a point of later contention, when with the death of George II the commissions fell vacant and Lieutenant Governor Colden insisted on renewing them on terms of royal pleasure.

By 1748 the assembly had made itself virtually the real power in government through control of the purse and of appointment of subordinate officials. Yet for all their successes Clinton's administration left Yorkers dissatisfied with Britain's administrative methods, "more estranged in their allegiance, and more strongly intrenched in their

[15] *Ibid.*, pp. 322–345.

control of both Governor and government." Apparently, the dissatisfaction and estrangement were the aftereffects of battle, and despite
the successes, the prospects that the ministry would take action to
remedy the "subversion" of the government were not comforting to
those who were "practically dictating their own policies" in New
York.[16]

Even Lieutenant Governor James De Lancey who had opposed
Governor Clinton lost his popularity because he became identified
with prerogative. Once De Lancey won an appointment from Clinton
as chief justice on terms of good behavior, not pleasure, he proceeded
to attack the governor's position. But when De Lancey became acting-
governor and tried to compromise his leadership of the anti-preroga-
tive faction with the instructions he received to restore the prerogative, he lost his popularity. The assembly still refused to make more
than an annual grant, and in 1754 it even withheld supplies, arguing
that the province had not been actually invaded by the French and
that no emergency existed to warrant an appropriation. If members
of the assembly preferred a greater measure of control of local affairs,
they chose a strange way to assert the preference and to prove their
ability to govern wisely and well. The failure to vote funds for their
own defense and thus to escape the possible administration of affairs
from London suggested a dangerous irresponsibility. And assembly
domination could mean ineffective government—delays in fundrais-
ing, halting attempts to deal with problems of regulating the trade
and other relations with the Indians—a condition which suggested to
imperial authorities the necessity of greater supervision from the hub
of the empire. Between 1757 and 1760, however, De Lancey had little
friction with the assembly. Wartime demands diverted some attention
and energy from the conflict between legislature and executive.[17]

During the administration of Charles Hardy (1755–1757), the assembly also refused the governor's demands for a permanent revenue,
insisted on annual appropriations and reluctantly voted a troop levy.
Moreover, Hardy was instructed by the Board of Trade not to press
for a permanent revenue for the time being. The war required as
much cooperation and as little friction as possible. Still, the assembly
won the advantage during the war on both issues of salaries and spe-

16 *Ibid.*, pp. 345–346. See also pp. 327, 343; and Gipson, *The British Empire*, III,
127–128, 131; and Flick, III, 175, *passim*.
17 Burns, *Controversies*, pp. 346–353.

cific appropriations. It steadily refused to make either permanent or long-term appropriations.[18]

Cadwallader Colden's administration (1760–1765) was but another stage in the running battle between governor and assembly. Colden, a convinced prerogative man, sought permanent salaries for officials, and he maintained that judges be appointed for pleasure. In attempting to establish its own control over the judiciary, the assembly was raising the question of imperial as against local authority, for Colden had orders from the Privy Council to appoint judges at pleasure. The assembly apparently did not appreciate the home government's concern for the independence of the judiciary and preferred to establish a degree of control over it rather than permit what they assumed was an external influence on the local courts. Colden tried bargaining for permanent salaries for the judges in exchange for granting tenure during good behavior. When the assembly received the overture, the council refused to permit it. Everyone remained disgruntled, and the judges, having accepted their commissions during pleasure, went without salaries. Colden despaired of escaping the assembly's influence. In his report on the state of the province in 1765 he wrote that the assembly had established the practice of making only annual grants and then of passing them only at the close of each session so as to use them for bargaining. Colden proposed a remedy: "The Parliament laying internal taxes in the Colonies, and paying all the officers of Government, as it is suggested they may intend to do, will destroy the great and undue influence which the Assembly has gained over the Administration." This Colden hoped might be done. He also knew that it was "cheifly [sic] for this Reason that the popular Leaders so violently oppose the Act for laying a Stamp Duty." [19]

With both Colden and Sir Henry Moore (1765–1769) the assembly insisted on maintaining what it had come to consider as ancient rights against imperial authority and what by virtue of the 1688 settlement had become Parliamentary sovereignty. Moore courted the popular faction and avoided Colden as much as possible in order to escape the opprobrium attached to his lieutenant. For three years Moore even refused to ask the assembly to vote Colden reimbursement for damages he had incurred during the Stamp Act riots. When Colden anonymously published a defense of his conduct, the assembly voted

18 *Ibid.*, pp. 353–355. See also Flick, II, 241.
19 Colden's report on New York, Dec. 6, 1765. C.O. 5/1098:49.

that the pamphlet adversely reflected on the honor, justice, and dignity of the legislature as well as the courts.[20]

Aside from the apparent strains between the governor and assembly, the Great War for the Empire revealed certain defects in imperial power. For colonies refusing to appropriate much needed funds there seemed no remedy. Inasmuch as the New York Assembly succeeded in setting limits on the use of its appropriations, the war may be said to have been a direct impetus for the Revolution, for such limitations endangered the imperial system and challenged Parliamentary sovereignty. Moreover, merchants violating imperial laws of commerce, and trading with the enemy went unpunished. And the problem of Indian relations—the peace of the frontier for which the war had in part been fought—raised local opposition to schemes for a royal defense establishment in the colonies. New York politics in the 1760's consisted of a double dichotomy—two political entities, imperial government on the one hand and provincial government on the other, struggling for a *modus operandi,* and two factions struggling for power within a single, broadly composed ruling class. This complicated the existing structure of local power which had shifted largely from Crown and governor to the assembly, especially as the assembly in turn became the battleground of factions fighting an almost purely partisan battle for influence, place, and patronage. Indeed, this may have been the key to the long struggle between the assembly and governor. Having won such a position of power over the royal governor, the assembly might well afford the luxury of partisanship. But factionalism also meant that the provincial position with respect to stronger imperial administration and the exercise of Parliamentary sovereignty was weakened.

– 3 –

FAMILIES AND FACTIONS

WITHIN THE New York Assembly there were few men but aristocrats. It was an exclusive gathering of merchant princes, landlords, and their spokesmen. In gradually winning its battle for dominance with the governor, the assembly turned more and more to its own intrafactional struggles. The contest was one among peers, although some enjoyed more power and influence than others. As such, it mir-

[20] Burns, *Controversies,* pp. 366–367.

rored a wider struggle carried on outside its halls. The bases of this factional strife were varied. Religion, commerce, landed interests, and pure lust for place all made it a very heated conflict. Although the principals engaged in diversified economic activities, the tensions followed two main lines—the agrarian and the mercantile.

Lieutenant Governor Colden outlined the classes of New York in four categories. These, too, indicated how the agrarian mercantile division was made. First there were the large landowners who held from 100,000 to over one million acres. Next came the gentlemen of the law, and merchants. Finally, there were the farmers and mechanics. The lawyers and landholders were allies. They used the press in much the same fashion the pulpit was used against popery.[21] The merchants and city-dwelling mechanics formed another combination.

New York was a "land where all aristocrats were parvenus, and where there was the closest tactical connection between aristocracy and success." [22] Often the aristocrats were men whose family origins were relatively humble. Certainly, this was true of Philip Schuyler. Family connection in this aristocracy was important, but it was not the only factor in forming parties or factions. Even adherence to principle could be accompanied by a penchant for factionalism. "Kinship took but second place to 'interest.' " [23] And "the fact that families split on many occasions shows other forces to have been powerful" determinants of political alignment.[24] Indeed, at first there seem to have been no parties, only centers of influence—the governor and the assembly. But once the assembly was assured of its domination, the power struggle quite clearly took a new turn. The landlords and merchants became centers of influence, the nuclei of factions, at almost the same time the assembly was increasing its position at the expense of the governor. It was important not only to control the governor, but also to direct the assembly, for factions might achieve their ends by controlling the assembly and through it they could wield influence with the governor by supporting or embarrassing him as circumstances dictated. Because the interests and issues were so varied between 1765 and 1769 a distinct party alignment hardly existed. Yet provincial society had all the markings of such alignments, and we

21 Colden's report on New York, Dec. 6, 1765. C.O. 5/1098:45–48.
22 Dangerfield, *Livingston*, p. 10.
23 Klein, "Democracy and Politics in Colonial New York," p. 238.
24 Flick, III, 151.

must consider the way in which they operated before 1768, when Philip Schuyler joined the political fray.

Local social and economic conditions determined factionalism. The bases of this factionalism included the alliance of great families who held wealth, the franchise, and the means of expressing their aims in the circles of government as well as the prestige to influence tenants' votes. Family alliances tended to form around two primary centers, the De Lanceys and the Livingstons. But the fact that they took their names from persons or particular leaders must not mislead us into thinking that the factions were wholly family arrangements or that other factors were not important in bringing about the alignments. What held these groups together was not so much the ties of blood or even those of marriage, but other, more practical interests—the lust for place. Principle, too, on occasion played a part in determining alignments.

The Livingston group, called the "popular," "Whig," "country," or "Presbyterian" party, shared a "general distaste for taxes on property, fear of Parliament, an appetite for office and patronage, and a suspicion of the lower orders." It feared riots, whether against a stamp act or against landlords. It was really no less aristocratic than the De Lanceys. But it differed from them in its fundamental agrarian interests and in its anxiety to enjoy as much privilege as they. The De Lanceys, termed the "court" party because they tended to dominate appointive offices and to fill the inner circle of royal government, were more oriented toward mercantile pursuits, and were more disposed to obey British authorities than the Livingstons. Moreover, the De Lanceys were Episcopalians and the Livingstons were largely nonconformists, Presbyterians, or members of the Dutch Reformed Church. In a day when the Anglican Church was associated with established government and when colonists constantly feared the possible imposition of an episcopate in America, religious differences were vital.[25] Historically, Anglicanism was linked with royal power;

[25] Dangerfield, *Livingston*, p. 39. See also p. 22. Charles H. Levermore, "The Whigs of Colonial New York," *American Historical Review*, I (Jan. 1896), 239, says the animosity of Episcopalians and Presbyterians was "the most potent political force in the colony." He characterizes the Livingstons as "aristocratic Whigs, equally ambitious to clip the pinions of ambitious royalty and to curb the insolence of the unlettered mob." P. 245. However, Levermore failed to indicate what might have been the overriding concern of the Livingstons—clipping the wings of their peers who enjoyed place and favor when the Livingstons did not.

dissent was the ally of republicanism or any opposition to the pre-rogative.

Lawyers, too, found their way into the party division. At times suspected of radicalism, of inciting the Stamp Act riots, they became a privileged class by virtue of a connection with the landlords. Gentle-men of the law rose to wealth through litigations of the landowners, who were obliged to use complicated legal actions to deal with trouble-some tenants or neighbors who questioned boundaries. In 1765, Cad-wallader Colden complained to the secretary of state that the lawyers were inimical to the royal interests and that their power was increas-ing because they deprecated royal authority and endeavored to en-large the "popular" side of government.[26] This seemed particularly dangerous to men who were convinced of the values of a mixed gov-ernment in which the "monarchical, aristocratical, and democratical" —or popular—elements were properly balanced.

Both the De Lanceys and Livingstons considered themselves Whigs —adherents to principle. In this way they reflected a condition in Eng-land, where the Whigs had long been entrenched in power and had divided into several factions vying for place. Both the New York groups generally opposed royal prerogative, but the Livingstons were more decidedly vigorous in this than the De Lanceys, perhaps because they did not share as much proximity to the inner circle of royal gov-ernment. Both maintained a common objective—control of the assem-bly. By this means they intended to win appointments. The Whig label tended to become meaningless, however, except for emotional electioneering or appeals for the support of the general populace. In much the same way that party names lost their original significance in England after the acceptance of the Protestant Hanoverian suc-cession, the Whig label in New York was largely a convenience adopted whenever it might prove useful. Once the De Lancey "Whigs" secured place, they were less critical of the power they had opposed when the Livingstons had the ascendancy. Indeed, the De Lanceys could then support prerogative just as the Livingstons could, if given the proper opportunity. Both groups also proved they could cater to radical elements, "if this was the best way to exploit the unpopular-ity" of their opponents and regain control of the assembly. Although the governor made most selections for office, the assembly controlled salaries, named its own treasurer, and wielded influence with the

26 Colden to Halifax, Feb. 22, 1765. C.O. 5/1097:302.

agent in London through a committee of correspondence. The house was also the vantage point from which the dominant faction could legislate and petition to its own best advantage and interest. "To parties whose intellectual existence was largely predicated upon their views on direct taxation, and whose physical existence depended upon office and patronage, control of this body was a matter of the first importance." [27]

The appearance of the two factions resulted from a long and complicated development: the running battle between the governor and assembly, and the local aristocracy's movement into and out of the governor's interest as he granted them favors or denied them. As much as New York politics were involved with family ties and the economic power of the landlords, and despite the semi-feudal nature of their bases, the factions were not primarily groupings of medieval or feudal relationships. At times devotion to policy, principle, and conviction could be as strong as lust for patronage.

Personal and family connections shifted perceptibly before 1760–1770 when the two factions finally emerged with fairly well-drawn lines. The origins of the De Lancey-Livingston feud are obscured in the depths of New York's history. But "what was involved was essentially a clash between Land and Trade." [28] Even this explanation offers difficulties because both families had secondary economic interests. Although agrarian, the Livingstons were also merchants; the manor was the site of an iron foundry, too. And the De Lanceys, though primarily merchants, also had interests in landholding and speculation.

Originally the feud was neither wholly private nor personal, but largely political and economic. During Governor Burnet's administration (1720–1728), Robert Livingston ("the Founder") was secretary for Indian affairs. Principle as well as personal advantage determined his interest in curbing the Albany-Montreal fur trade. The Albany trade was directly contrary to Britain's desire to divert the Indians from their French allegiance. As long as Albanians sold better quality goods to Frenchmen for retail to the Indians, the tribesmen could not be induced to come into the British orbit. English goods sold directly to the Indians would, however, undercut the French. Livingston sent his own agents to deal directly with the Indians. Hence, he opposed

27 Dangerfield, *Livingston*, pp. 41–42. For a good brief description of the Livingstons and the De Lanceys, see Hoffman, *Edmund Burke*, pp. 86–99.
28 Dangerfield, *Livingston*, p. 21.

the Albany trade as contrary to the British policy of diverting the trade from the French—principle—and as inimical to his own private profits—personal advantage.

While other retailers and Mohawk valley land speculators rallied to his position, opposition to Livingston rose around the leadership of Stephen De Lancey, Peter Schuyler, Adolph Philipse, and other New York and Albany merchants who valued their profitable trade with the French at Montreal above adherence to British policy. At first the Livingston group won the contest. Trade between Albany and Montreal was prohibited. But the order was widely evaded. The government then taxed the northern trade more heavily than it did Livingston's western trade. When the De Lanceys finally seized the assembly, they ousted Livingston from the speakership and procured a royal disallowance of the law barring trade with Canada.

Family ties did not so much clarify these lines of political divergence as they obscured them. The issue was not the power of personal connections alone; it was a real economic and political one.[29] Both Stephen De Lancey and Peter Schuyler were related to Livingston; De Lancey was his nephew and Schuyler his brother-in-law. But these connections made no difference in the larger issues at stake. If they had, we might expect Philip Schuyler, Peter's great-nephew, to have joined the De Lanceys, for they were cousins. The mothers of Lieutenant Governor James De Lancey and Philip Schuyler, Anne and Cornelia Van Cortlandt, were sisters. However, Philip Schuyler was also related to the Livingstons, but this connection was less one of blood than of marriage. In one respect it was looser than blood kinship. Schuyler's ties with the Livingstons, as with other members of the group which bore their name, were primarily common agrarian interests and the mutual concern for gaining power. And these were stronger even than blood bonds.

Further family shifts took place in the second-generation Livingstons and De Lanceys. Philip Livingston proved unenthusiastic about his father's trade program and was generally friendly with the De Lanceys. When he broke with them, it was because Governor Cosby challenged existing land titles and thus threatened his fortune. Hence, he moved out of the governor's interest. Burnet served his father's

---

[29] Klein, "Democracy and Politics in Colonial New York," pp. 224–225. Note also Leonard Labaree, *Conservatism in Early American History* (Ithaca, 1959), pp. 1–31. Labaree also indicates that the "identity of interest and attitude" within the ruling families of colonial America was "more important than ties of blood." P. 23.

interest in the Indian trade, but Cosby threatened the Livingston estate by resurrecting old land titles and demanding payment of quit-rents. Philip Livingston himself remarked, "We change Sides as Serves our Interest best." [30] For twenty years the Livingstons fluctuated. But when Governor Clinton opposed Philip for defrauding the Indians and trading with the enemy during King George's War, Livingston rejoined the De Lanceys to oppose him. When the De Lanceys won control of the assembly and the lieutenant governor of that name refused to act on behalf of Livingston against Massachusetts boundary claims, and when De Lancey was slow to ask Parliament to defer the passage of the Iron Act so as to enable Livingston to expand his iron-works, the Livingstons again deserted the De Lanceys. Nor was it sur-prising that "in 1755, when the Livingston ironworks were overrun by the antirent insurgents, James De Lancey's offer of assistance should have been so feeble, so grudging, so late, and so much re-sented." [31]

Another division of the agrarian mercantile interests became appar-ent in 1758 when the Livingstons defeated the De Lanceys. William Livingston's accusation "that the De Lanceys and their adherents had been very lukewarm about driving the French from North America in the early stages of the French and Indian War" was responsible for this turn. "This was, in effect, a revival of the old landlord-merchant dispute, in which the landlords were for a strong policy against the French regardless of expense, and the merchants were for a weak and frugal one." Thus, interest often connected people who were entire strangers and separated those who had the strongest family ties.[32]

Perhaps the strength of the two factions appears extremely personal because they took their names from leading men within their ranks. But the day came during Philip Schuyler's assembly career when he, not a Livingston, provided the leadership of the opposition faction. New York politics were not merely "feudal," informal or personal, however, nor were they even determined by intermarriage. Nor did the power of the factions depend on any strong aristocratic control of the electoral machinery or limitation of the franchise.[33]

[30] Klein, "Democracy and Politics in Colonial New York," pp. 225–227.

[31] Dangerfield, *Livingston*, p. 22.

[32] *Ibid.*, p. 23. See also Klein, "Democracy and Politics in Colonial New York," pp. 227–228.

[33] Cf. Becker, *Political Parties*, pp. 10–15, and Klein, "Democracy and Politics in Colonial New York."

The political dependence of tenants upon their landlords is difficult to document. Their economic dependence was not as burdensome as has been imagined, for terms of leases were often quite generous. The tenant was not obliged to begin payments of his rent for an initial period of settlement, a period that ran from a few months to as long as nine years. Their rents were nominal, and non-payment was not always promptly followed by eviction. Farmers also had a good measure of self-government, for they chose their constables, assessors, and collectors; they were a power with which to be reckoned in assembly elections. If the landlords were so certain of controlling their tenants' votes, one wonders why they bothered to try to buy them. Perhaps Sir Lewis Namier's observation about British politics is applicable: he who can bully has no need to bribe.[34] In a real sense bribery of various kinds was evidence of the virility of the prevailing political system—of its deeper sense and usefulness. As for *viva voce* polling, the tenants apparently did not consider it as oppressive or undemocratic. Nor is there evidence that the proprietors regarded the verbal poll as essential to their political control. Farmer riots concerned land titles, rents, security of tenure, and personal obligations—not political democracy. And when in 1769 the assembly voted on the institution of a secret ballot, the Livingstons—the landed interests—favored the measure, while the De Lanceys objected, maintaining that secrecy was merely a means whereby crafty lawyers might influence the voters and corrupt the electoral process.[35]

When the aristocratic landlords exerted an influence in local elections, it was because of their prestige, not merely their coercion, and because of the illiteracy and indifference among many who had the franchise but did not exercise it. The franchise in New York was not as severely restricted as we are sometimes led to believe.[36] Even the

34 L. B. Namier, *England in the Age of the American Revolution* (London, 1930), pp. 4–5. ". . . no one bribes where he can bully."

35 Klein, "Democracy and Politics in Colonial New York," pp. 229, 231. See also NYPL, Schuyler Papers Box 21, for lease terms. New York Assembly Journals, Dec. 22, 1769, and Jan. 9, 1770, indicate who favored the secret ballot. The number included the landed Livingston interests like Van Cortlandt, Ten Eyck, Ten Broeck, and Schuyler. The vote was 13 to 12 against adoption. The De Lanceys won; they included merchants James De Lancey, Walton, Kissam, Rapalje, Jauncey, and Cruger.

36 Cf. Klein, "Democracy and Politics in Colonial New York," p. 232, and Becker, *Political Parties,* pp. 10–13. Becker says that over half the male population over twenty-one had no political privilege. Klein has shown that the franchise was not limited to freeholders, and that there were many freemen—men who found it easy to purchase the freedom of the cities of New York and Albany at nominal fees. Even

economic bond between landlord and tenant was never so strong as to be taken for granted—as the elections of 1768 and 1769 especially showed. There is a patent difference between men who had the vote and used it and those who had but did not choose to exercise the franchise.[37]

The lines of the political factions in New York were apparently drawn after 1760. Thomas Jones, an eyewitness, insisted that before 1750, New York passed its happiest days—free from parties, animosities, and discord. In 1752, however, the Presbyterians and lawyers founded a Whig club led by William Livingston, the younger William Smith, and John Morin Scott. They objected to taxes for the support of Episcopal churches as provided by law and to any Anglican episcopate or Anglican regulations devised for the newly formed King's College (1754). After the Great War for the Empire they opposed the imperial program set forth by the Grenville ministry and subsequent administrations. In this they were much more consistent than the De Lanceys. But the De Lanceys gained control of the assembly, and much of New York's conservative reaction to ministerial measures was due to their direction of the legislature. A political magazine issued in 1780 said of the factions in the Revolutionary movement that "the Livingstons waited to see what side the De Lanceys would take, and when [they] . . . attached themselves to the government, the Livingstons instantly joined the other party." [38] If this

those too poor to purchase their freedom could procure it gratis. Freemanship was a device to open the polls to all classes. See also Flick, II, 311. Virtually all white adult males could vote. The 1699 law limited the vote to all freeholders over twenty-one who held lands or tenements worth £40 and free of all encumbrances (Albany and New York City freemen excepted), but the law of 1701 defined a freeholder as any person holding land for his or his wife's lifetime, mortgages notwithstanding. Thus, all tenants on Livingston and Van Rensselaer manors undoubtedly qualified. And tenants of Westchester County manors were also regarded as powerful (Klein, pp. 233–235). Klein's investigation indicates that all white adult males in New York City and probably Albany had the vote as did at least 65 per cent of them in rural counties (pp. 236–237). It was in Albany and New York that one-third of the adult males of the province lived. He estimates that about 75 per cent of the colony's adult white males had the franchise.

[37] Flick, II, 383. By 1775, Cadwallader Colden believed that the freeholders of Livingston and Rensselaer manors were numerous enough to control Albany County elections. Colden to Dartmouth, April 4, 1775. C.O. 5/1106:316–317. For a further discussion of the connection between land tenure and the franchise, see Appendix C, *infra*.

[38] Jones, *History of New York*, I, 1–15; II, 560.

seems an oversimplification, it is nonetheless a revelation of a basic condition, a fundamental antagonism.

Yorkers did not quite accept factionalism or partisan politics as an honorable pursuit, and yet they persisted in behavior of which they did not wholly approve. The tenor of the views found in the provincial newspapers as well as in private correspondence suggests a certain distaste for partisanship. Both sides accused the other of this disagreeable activity, yet both practiced it quite vigorously, perhaps dismayed only in finding obstacles to their game. Men of the revolutionary generation conceived of parties as selfish interest groups. Their ideal of politics appears to have involved *"ex tempore* majorities and minorities formed by the issue of the moment and undistorted by pre-existing organization not related to the instant issue."[39]

Americans have used pressure and partisan politics continuously and vigorously but have despised the men engaged in the game of carrying out the demands of the political community.[40] And eighteenth-century New Yorkers did not desist from partisanship despite their avowed aversion to it. Holt's *New-York Journal* (April 26, 1770) agreed with Thomas Jones that there was no party grouping before 1760, but observed the new inflammation in the body politic in the decade following. The *Journal's* editorialist, "Americanus," supposed that it began with the Livingstons' domination of the assembly from 1761 to 1768. Having lost dominance in both council and assembly in 1768–1770, they were mortified as only a "haughty, proud, overbearing, sycophantic and mean-spirited" family could be. The hostility they raised had, it was charged, altered the peaceful ideal of royal government. But the De Lanceys' victory in seizing control did not mean that their faction was consistently loyal to the establishment or that it always upheld the ideal. Like the late Lieutenant Governor James De Lancey, who was torn between his initial leadership of the assembly interest against Governor Clinton and his instructions to restore prerogative and a proper balance between executive and legislative branches, the faction that bore De Lancey's name courted the radical elements which opposed the Townshend Acts. They did this in order to win support for the election contest of 1768. Indeed, the De Lanceys hid their oligarchy behind a mask of democracy. A popu-

[39] Cecelia Kenyon, "Republicanism and Radicalism in the American Revolution: An Old-Fashioned Interpretation," *The William and Mary Quarterly: Third Series,* XIX (April, 1962), 156.

[40] *Ibid.,* p. 178.

lar gesture thus swept the Livingston faction from control.[41] The De Lanceys' tactics of the moment were purely diversionary, however, for although they at times sought to embarrass the governor in order to dominate him, they persisted in their general identification with the interests of prerogative and the mercantile community. But they faced a trend that proved quite beyond their power to resist or control.

– 4 –

LOCAL REACTION TO IMPERIAL MEASURES

WHEN PHILIP SCHUYLER made his debut in the New York Assembly, the factional struggle in which he became engaged was about to take a new turn. The development of extralegal methods to resist both imperial policy and the faction in power commenced in 1765 with the Stamp Act Congress, which only professed a "due subordination" to Parliament but did not so much as formally or explicitly acknowledge Parliament's right to regulate trade. The issuance of the Massachusetts Circular Letter of February, 1768, was another step in the extralegal movement. The assembly of the Bay Colony denounced the Townshend Acts as violating the principle of no taxation without representation, reasserted the impossibility of representing America in Parliament, attacked any move by the Crown to make governors and judges independent of the assemblies, and solicited proposals for united action against the measures. In 1768 the Massachusetts General Court refused to be prorogued, met in extralegal session, and insisted both on the right to issue such a circular and the right to refuse rescinding it. By considering the letter, the New York Assembly was drawn more decisively into the political whirlpool that was stirred by successive stages of development of imperial administrative measures and of local factional struggles. These measures did not comprise a policy inasmuch as they had no long-range goals, nor were they carefully planned as parts of a comprehensive program. The government in London simply acted by expediency, fitting each new measure to an immediate situation with as much good sense as possible. Its decisions were neither precipitous nor ill considered, but

[41] Becker, *Political Parties*, p. 60. Levermore, "The Whigs of Colonial New York," p. 248, remarks about the De Lanceys' masquerade.

rather the fruit of careful investigation and deliberation. Each measure was designed to meet a particular problem.[42]

Parliament's legal authority to legislate for the colonies cannot be denied, however much the colonists may have contested it. The Crown had the legal authority to veto colonial laws. The royal governors had like authority within local self-government. And the facts of the historical development of Parliamentary authority—of the 1688–1689 settlement—meant that the colonial argument denying Parliamentary authority as encroachments on colonial establishments originating with the Crown ignored the political realities of the times quite as much as it ignored the Coronation Oath Act. England was legally correct in imposing navigation laws as well as other regulations within the empire. Whatever the logic of the colonists' rationale for their acquisition and advancement of power, they were legally on shaky ground. They demonstrated that men are inclined to act quite as much from fears of what might happen and from what they imagine to be the circumstances as they are motivated by an awareness of the true state of affairs.[43] Colonials who did not know that the empire neither destroyed nor hampered their trade and economic well-being, who did not know that neither king nor ministry were unfeeling tyrants, may nonetheless have preferred to follow a course that could scarcely have led them anywhere but to total independence. This they may have followed as unconsciously as a few calculating radicals specifically aimed at independence. And even with a large measure of self-government, many of the colonists pursued a course that suggested they wanted still more. Composed of members of the aristocratic gov-

[42] Jack M. Sosin, *Whitehall and the Wilderness* (Lincoln, Nebr., 1961), p. x, *passim*.

[43] For example, the colonists feared that the Sugar Act would drain specie from the provinces, prohibit trade with the West Indies, and force New Yorkers to develop home manufacturing because they would not be able to buy goods from Britain. But British goods were cheaper, there were few skilled workers in the colonies for manufacturing, and the Sugar Act (and the Stamp Act too) provided that the revenue collected would be spent in the provinces for supplies and services. There would be no drain of specie. Further, trade with the West Indies was not damaged, for the duty did not increase the wholesale price of molasses. Jessie Stoddart, "Home Rule and the Development of the American Revolution [in] New York, 1760–1775" (M.A. thesis, University of Nebraska, 1961), pp. 80–83. Colonists could also argue about hard times and voice fears that imperial legislation would worsen them. But such apprehensive assertions were aimed at producing modification of certain acts of Parliament. Sachs, "Agricultural Conditions in the Northern Colonies Before the Revolution," p. 287.

erning class, the New York Assembly illustrated how easily even a self-governed people can fall into difficulties over disagreements resulting from the jealousy of some of their leaders over power and the privileges of others. Therefore, when we examine Philip Schuyler's role in the Revolution in New York, we must do it with an eye not only to the colonists' relations with the imperial authority, but also with attention to their dealings with one another.

Both imperial measures and local ambitions made for a tangled situation in New York between 1761 and 1768. Even governors on occasion resisted imperial directives for the sake of personal and local interests. There was, for example, the old ruling against large land grants. By persistently making these grants, governors aimed at enriching themselves with fees from the patents, believing all the while that they were creating a proper subordination among the agrarian aristocrats, who were expected to allow themselves to be bound to the governor's interest. No such subordination inevitably followed. In fact, the creation of manorial holdings encouraged tenant riots, clearly disturbing the system of hierarchy and subordination, and many proprietors turned against the governor and all that he stood for, and eventually became patriots, not loyalists. Their large holdings actually prompted a kind of spirit of independence that ran counter to the spirit of subordination and prerogative. Cadwallader Colden, writing to the secretary of state in September, 1763, pointed out another problem connected with land grants. He had been instructed to annul irregular and unconditional grants, but complained that the lawyers were well skilled in chicanery to prevent this. "This requires Judges of ability & skill in the Law to restrain" the landlords, he said. But such judges were not easily found in New York. Moreover, the judges in the province were not disinterested, "for the distinguished families, in so small a country as this, are so united by intermarriage & otherwise, that in few cases [could] a cause of any consequence" be brought before a judge supposedly "intirely disinterested, or free from connections with those interested. . . ."[44] This was but one example of how the measures of imperial government, well considered as they were, ran counter to local aspirations and wishes, and did not square with the realities of provincial politics in any fashion conducive to lasting contentment.

The dichotomy of royal-parliamentary prerogative and New York

[44] Colden to Egremont, Sept. 14, 1763. C.O. 5/1097:35–36.

Assembly factionalism took a number of forms. There was, for example, the issue of the tenure of judges. On the death of George II,
judges' commissions lapsed. When they were renewed, they were
issued for pleasure instead of on the earlier terms of good behavior.
Lieutenant Governor Colden offered to commission the judges as
formerly, provided the Livingston-dominated assembly would grant
them permanent salaries and thereby insure their independence. This
the assembly refused. The governor's council refused to approve any
commissions issued on terms of good behavior. At first the judges declined to act, but they were persuaded to accept their offices for
pleasure when salaries were provided from the royal quitrents. Consequently the legislature did not vote them salaries. But this was not
all. The tenure controversy was compounded by the patronage problem. The death of Chief Justice De Lancey created a vacancy on the
supreme court. The opening signaled a scramble for office. Instead of
preferring a local judge for the promotion, Colden gave the post to
Benjamin Pratt of Boston. Justices Horsmanden and Chambers resigned in protest. They later relented. Both the assembly and council
disliked Pratt's appointment. Because of this the assembly refused
salaries for the judges until they should be given tenure on good behavior, and it passed resolutions against the judges for accepting
office on other terms. Pratt's death produced another scramble in 1763,
and this time the elder William Smith lost an opportunity for advancement. Daniel Horsmanden became chief justice, and the Smiths,
father and son, promptly turned with greater displeasure against the
governor's interest. The younger Smith was already a member of the
Livingston faction. His father, however, remained on the bench.[45]

In 1762 the Livingston assembly struck another blow at Lieutenant
Governor Colden and the principle of prerogative. When it discovered that Colden had tempted John Pownall, clerk of the Board of
Trade, with the agency for New York in return for his promotion to
lieutenant governor,[46] the assembly declared that no governor should
ever again be allowed to interfere in appointing an agent. According
to imperial requirements, the agent was to be chosen by a legislative
act, not by the resolution of the assembly which required no approval

45 Sabine, *Smith Memoirs*, I, 4. See also Dillon, *The New York Triumvirate*, pp.
57–60; Burns, *Controversies*, pp. 358, 361; Jones, *History of New York*, I, 223–231;
Colden's report on New York, Dec. 6, 1765, C.O. 5/1098:49–50.

46 *Colls. N.Y. Hist. Soc. for 1876* (New York, 1877), IX: Colden Letter Books, I, 38,
80, 85, 107. See also Burns, *Controversies*, p. 364 n.

by council and governor. This new resolution helped sharpen the differences between assembly factions and between the assembly and governor, province and empire.

The boundary claims of New York and Massachusetts afforded still another point of discord; this, however, lay largely between New York and the imperial government because the matter was taken up by the Privy Council. The Livingston agrarian interest, however, was also much concerned about protecting their lands, many of which fell into the disputed territory. The delays in a resolution of the problem and a pronouncement from the ministry could only increase the dissatisfaction of New Yorkers in general and the Livingstonians in particular. Because their land interests were very much akin to those of other landlords, the agrarian faction became even more disturbed by the manner in which they were treated.[47]

Following the Great War for the Empire the assembly factions turned their attention from the king and his governors to the growing menace of Parliament. The Livingstons were early critics of this new menace, and during 1761–1768 "they instituted a series of mild reforms, designed to ease the fiscal burden of poor men." [48] Britons, too, were bending under the financial burdens of defending the colonies—colonies which had not altogether satisfactorily shared the cost. Parliament's measures for relieving these cares and compelling the colonies to bear a greater share of the load met with increasing opposition in New York and elsewhere. The New York Assembly was caught between two currents, one of Parliamentary power and one of radical resistance to that power. It attempted to steer between them.

---

[47] Dillon, *The New York Triumvirate*, pp. 170, 174–175. See also Colden's Proclamation, Dec. 28, 1763, C.O. 5/1098:635–637; and Shelburne to Moore, April 11, 1767. C.O. 5/1098:477–479. An Order in Council of July, 1764, set the Connecticut River as New York's eastern boundary. It confirmed Lieutenant Governor Colden's 1763 Proclamation. Yankee squatters still refused to take title to their claims from the New York government. An order in 1767, halting further grants of land in disputed territory until 1773, only irritated Yorker landlords and speculators who wanted an early and decisive ruling on their behalf. Landlords remained unsatisfied with the ministry's order that the governor molest no one in quiet possession of grants who could produce valid deeds under the New Hampshire seal; they insisted that these men were squatters on their lands. When the Board of Trade ruled in 1773 on the validity of land titles and the territory available for purchase, New Yorkers had little cause to rejoice. They did not wish to pay £5 sterling per one hundred acres or the usual quitrents, but preferred to speculate without such fees. Mark, *Agrarian Conflicts*, pp. 168–186.

[48] Dangerfield, *Livingston*, p. 24. Robert R. Livingston argued against a land tax.

But in 1768 the De Lanceys made use of the position by an oblique reference to the Livingstons' failure to steer the course, and the Livingston majority was reduced to a minority. The victory resulted in making the assembly more and more conservative. The Livingston leadership was gradually replaced by those outside the house who protested even more radically, and the De Lanceys became more staunchly the ally of the imperial cause. They chose to obey Parliament as a means of controlling the threats of radicals who were challenging their power. "The De Lanceys went with Parliament and disappeared," just as imperial power disappeared from America. But the Livingstons and other less aristocratic dissenters sided with the Revolution, then devoted all "their energies to rescuing it from what they conceived to be itself." [49]

New York's interests were, theoretically, those of the British government, but "in fact the assembly looked at the empire from the local point of view," and "used its position to exact tremendous concessions in the practice of local self-government." During the 1760's the factions which made up the assembly used it for similar purposes. Earlier, the assembly had won a certain superiority in government through its power over appropriations. It had also won control of the judiciary indirectly through an organized legal profession and the ties of family and interest. "But the assembly could not deal so effectively with parliamentary measures as it had dealt with the measures of the governor." [50] This was very largely due to the inability of factions to deal successfully with a more united, larger, and hence stronger, imperial government. To do so required stronger unity than one faction could produce merely by winning temporary dominance over another —or even stronger unity than an institution like a colonial legislature could muster against the power of Parliament. The factions were deprived of any advantage of unity because of the very nature of their quarrels, although as a center of influence the assembly had once had a marked advantage over the governors. Thus, New York's interests found themselves more at the mercy of ministerial measures devised to finance and govern a widened empire. Only when the entire colony refused to recognize it could New York effectively resist a law of Parliament. When the assembly was split into parties, its ineffectiveness gave way to the machinations of extralegal committees and congresses. These bodies took up the work a faction-ridden assembly performed

[49] *Ibid.*
[50] Becker, *Political Parties,* pp. 6, 21.

with difficulty—the assertion of colonial rights and privileges. The atomization of power among the rival assembly's groups and the more radical elements outside the house eventually produced a resolution to the problem of Parliamentary authority. The solution was to escape it and to declare independence.

The New York interests did, however, deal successfully with imperial measures up to a point. Although they were able time after time—occasionally by cooperating with other colonies—to persuade the ministry to alter its measures by concessions, they proved they could not ultimately resist Parliamentary authority short of rebellion and independence. At one point New York's concession to the Mutiny Act (when the assembly voted supplies after first refusing exact compliance with the law) appeared to be a tacit recognition of Parliamentary sovereignty in return for its permission to issue paper currency. But if the issue was no longer a vital one for the assembly factions, it was used later by the less conservative elements outside the house, who forced the reconsideration of the issue. Indeed, as a corporate body, the assembly had decided to submit to Parliament, but the power struggle shifted out-of-doors to extralegal bodies. Taken in its larger context, the assembly's gesture seems little more than a practical and temporary *quid pro quo;* thus the philosophic or theoretical issue of Parliamentary supremacy was not resolved once and for all, although the practical politics of the thing seemed settled.

The difficulties of the assembly factions in dealing with imperial government and Parliamentary authority are visible in several notable cases before 1768, when Philip Schuyler entered the debates as an assemblyman. These were the Currency Act (1764), the Mutiny Act and the Stamp Act (1765), and the Townshend Acts (1767).

For the Sugar or Revenue Act of 1764, New Yorkers had little protest. The assembly endorsed a formal memorial drawn by a number of merchants to the Board of Trade and ordered the agent, Robert Charles, to oppose the Sugar Act while it was still under consideration. The great landlords dominating the assembly feared Parliament might lay a tax on land, and their objection to the Sugar Act—framed as a broad theoretical statement of the natural rights of mankind to be free from all taxes except those levied by themselves or their representatives—was aimed at avoiding a danger which *seemed* to threaten them [51]—a danger which was more imagined than imminent. No vio-

[51] Randolph G. Adams, *Political Ideas of the American Revolution* (3rd ed.; New York, 1958), p. 16.

lence accompanied the protests. The Sugar Act revised an early piece of legislation (1733) by reducing duties on syrups, molasses, and sugar imported from non-British to British colonies; prohibiting the import of foreign-made rum; and laying new duties on indigo, coffee, wine, and silks. Moreover, the whole system of customs administration was tightened; customs officials were given greater authority, and the powers of the vice-admiralty courts were enlarged. The act to finance the defense of the colonies was the first measure for raising a revenue as contrasted to regulating trade only. But it was the Stamp Act which raised the furor. Perhaps this detracted from objections that might otherwise have emerged against the Sugar Act. This too was a revenue measure which struck the more vocal segments of the colonial population.

Raising revenue from stamped paper prompted a tumult because it appeared especially onerous to the colonists; as in the Sugar Act, no money save silver was to be accepted in payment of these taxes. Moreover, the Currency Act of 1764 provided a safeguard to these provisions by regulating the emission of colonial bills of credit as legal tender in the colonies. And the Restraining Act of 1767, limiting assembly legislation until New York provided fully for the support of the royal troops, seemed to threaten legislative independence.[52] Although the violence that followed the Stamp Act was aimed primarily at the stamps, the opposition was indirectly leveled against the other revenue and currency measures that buttressed the Stamp Act.

The factions in the New York Assembly displayed no marked division on the measure, although the Livingstons took the lead in the opposition. They and William Smith, Jr., raised objections based largely on the fears of a burden of internal taxes. The assembly offered a hurried protest to the plans for a stamp tax—a protest so hasty and ill-framed, "too warm assuming and tedious" in fact, that the New York agent, Robert Charles, refused to present it to the ministry as manifestly offensive.[53] The remonstrance denied Parliament's right to tax the colonies for raising a revenue. But neither New York nor any other province came forward with an alternative method of raising a revenue as George Grenville, First Lord of the Treasury and Chancellor of the Exchequer, had invited them to do. And after a year's delay the proposed stamp tax passed into law.

[52] Becker, *Political Parties*, pp. 25, 57. See also Flick, III, 185–188.
[53] Sabine, *Smith Memoirs*, I, 23–24; Edward P. Lilly, *The Colonial Agents of New York and New Jersey* (Washington, 1936), p. 131 n.

The Livingstons, who had won control of the assembly in 1761, named a committee to correspond with both the New York agent in London and with other assemblies about the Stamp Act, the Currency Act, and the measures tightening imperial regulation of trade. This committee also named delegates to the Stamp Act Congress suggested by Massachusetts, and the Congress in turn declared the act unconstitutional. But because the stamps were to be sold before any reply from London could reach the colonies regarding their protests, some other means of resistance seemed necessary. Even if it were united, the assembly could not thwart Parliament as it once had the governor. The division of the assembly into factions made it appear even weaker, and the immediate direction of resistance passed from the hands of the assembly.

Although the De Lanceys and Livingstons did not divide sharply on the initial question of resisting the Stamp Act, the development of violence in the demonstrations against it helped draw party lines between radicals and conservatives. Fundamentally, both factions were conservative. It remained to be seen which was the more conservative and which could better cater to the radical element of the population.

The destruction of property in the Stamp Act riots suddenly produced the realization that a movement directed merely against the British government might grow into a larger threat to the local governing class. The doctrine of self-government was "a two-edged sword that cut into the foundations of class privilege within the colony as well as into the foundations of royal authority without." [54] At this point the Livingstons decided to call a halt to the violence. Robert R. Livingston offered the mayor of New York his services in bringing an end to the demonstrations. The merchant interests, promoted by the De Lanceys, had settled on a quieter means of protest—non-importation of British goods until the Stamp Act should be repealed. The Livingstons, less cautious than their rivals, had permitted themselves to be drawn into a movement which they soon realized they could not easily control—a threat by the lower classes, which committed the violence, to the ruling class's interest in property, order, and the maintenance of their own position of leadership.

The Livingston interest headed by Judge Robert attempted to warn the populace of the dangers of mobocracy and arranged a means of averting further violence. This was the surrender of the stamps to the

[54] Becker, *Political Parties*, p. 32.

city officials. In a sense, the two assembly factions were momentarily driven together by their common fears of a more radical third element. The Livingston faction found that the radicals led by John Lamb, Isaac Sears, and John Morin Scott threatened their interests and position more than the De Lanceys did. The radicals outside the house in time replaced the Livingston faction's leadership in opposing the more conservative De Lanceys and the authority of Parliament. Meantime, the two-faction arrangement persisted.

De Lanceys and Livingstons united, too, to control a mass meeting called for resisting the Stamp Act—whether by riots or the conduct of business in quiet violation of the law. By this means a relatively mild set of resolves was formulated. They provided that internal taxes were unconstitutional, that no tax be laid except by the assembly, and that jury trial without appeal be preserved. The radicals framed their own expressions more vigorously, denouncing "encroachments" and urging a "legislative sanction" against the stamps which was to withhold salaries from officers who complied with the Stamp Act.[55] Thus far the assembly factions remained relatively united in their common conservatism, and the whole province was determined to resist the Stamp Act.

The arrival of more stamps on January 7, 1766, prompted the formal organization of the Sons of Liberty and their determined effort to resist vigorously any compliance with the law. *The New-York Gazette,* reporting the organization, asked, "If the Parliament . . . has a Right to controul and make Laws for the Colonies (in consequence of the supposed Subordination) on *some* Occasions, why not all?" The meeting "appeared to be unanimous in a determined Opposition to the Stamp Act" and resolved to "go to the last Extremity" to prevent the act from being enforced. Those who delivered or received any stamps would "incur the highest Resentment of this Society, and be branded with everlasting Infamy." But as long as the stamps were quietly sequestered in city hall and as long as the "better sort" of the populace avoided the tumultuous activities of the Sons of Liberty, the sons could not hope to win much of a position of leadership. Even the arrival of a new shipment of stamps was quietly dealt with on the night of January 8/9. A number of armed men boarded Captain Haviland's brigantine, the *Polly,* seized ten boxes of stamps and took them up river to the shipyards, where they burned

[55] *Ibid.,* pp. 38–39, 49.

them in a bonfire. "When the whole was entirely consumed, they all quietly dispersed, without doing any Mischief, or even alarming the City." [56]

The Sons of Liberty did, however, commence the system of committees of correspondence.[57] Their *raison d'être* was not that they were needed to nullify the Stamp Act, for almost every class opposed it. But the sons were formed because of a difference of opinion as to the proper method of resistance. Thus, they helped draw a distinction between radical and conservative elements in the province, and eventually even between the two generally conservative assembly factions.

The repeal of the Stamp Act in March, 1766, brought a momentary resolution of the question of how to resist Parliamentary authority. The colonists did not closely heed the Declaratory Act, else they might not have rejoiced so much at the repeal of the stamp tax. Parliament still asserted its authority to legislate for the colonies in all cases whatsoever. Fresh disputes arose over New York's method of dealing with the Mutiny Act of 1765, and the Townshend Acts furnished opportunity for still another contest.

In May, 1765, Parliament extended the British Mutiny Act to the colonies, thereby establishing billeting regulations and calling on the assemblies to vote incidental supplies to the troops stationed to defend them. In December, the New York Assembly framed a set of resolves,

---

[56] *The New-York Gazette, or the Weekly Post-Boy,* Jan. 9, 1766.

[57] Relatively little is known about the Sons of Liberty, especially as to their numbers and names. Men known as leaders of this segment of the populace apparently left few personal papers to reveal much about their membership and organization. John Lamb was a wine merchant. Isaac Sears, the son of a Yankee fish peddler, was commander or part owner of a merchantman or privateer and also was a "small" merchant. Alexander MacDougal, the son of a Scottish immigrant and milkman, had a similar career; following the call of the sea, he captained two privateers and finally became a merchant. *D.A.B.,* X, 555–556; XII, 21–22; XVI, 539. Roger James Champagne, "The Sons of Liberty and the Aristocracy in New York Politics, 1765–1790," (Ph.D. dissertation, University of Wisconsin, 1960), indicates that the records give only a fleeting glimpse of the careers of Sears, Lamb, and MacDougal. Champagne also shows that the aristocrats created the Sons of Liberty, and that Sears, Lamb, and MacDougal were a major force in shaping events after 1773. The two assembly factions used imperial issues for local political purposes, and also used the sons in much the same way. Because of their defeat in 1769 the Livingstons associated with the more radical element in order to prepare for an election battle early in 1776, and this explains much of the partisan factionalism between 1769 and 1775. See also Champagne's, "New York and the Intolerable Acts, 1774," *The New-York Historical Quarterly,* XLV (April, 1961).

stating that it was unnecessary to provide barracks because there were already more than enough of these in New York and Albany. Any expenses for the supply and transport of troops should be considered *after* they were incurred. When royal forces were quartered in barracks belonging to the king, the assembly maintained, they were furnished with their necessaries without any expense to the countries in which they were quartered. But in July, 1766, the assembly partly complied with the requirements by providing supplies, omitting, however, salt, vinegar, beer, and cider on the grounds that such items were not provided even in the mother country. (Their action coincided, revealingly, with tenant riots for which the assemblymen willingly endorsed the use of troops for quelling disorders.) Moreover, the assembly provided that the supplies be dispensed through the mayors and corporation officials of New York and Albany instead of by officials named by the governor as specified by Parliamentary statute. Such a deliberate rebuff to Parliamentary authority and royal prerogative could not be permitted, and Parliament retaliated by a Restraining Act. The Privy Council disallowed the New York provision bill in April, 1767, on grounds that it did not meet the requirements of the Mutiny Act. The Restraining Act denied further legislation by the New York Assembly until such time as it complied fully with the Parliamentary statute.[58]

The ministry had other reasons for displeasure with New York. Provincial merchants had petitioned for relief from the navigation acts, despite the repeal of the Stamp Act and modification of the Revenue Act of 1764, and this seemed scarcely a gesture of gratitude. The assembly had voted relief to the sufferers from stamp act riots reluctantly, but refused any for Lieutenant Governor Colden. And illegal trade with Holland not only persisted, but increased.[59]

To deal with these problems Parliament passed three acts during the winter of 1767. By the first, the supervision of colonial customs was to be placed in the hands of commissioners residing in the colonies. The Townshend revenue act laid duties on tea, lead, glass, paper, and painters' colors, the revenue to be used to pay the salaries of judges and other colonial officials when necessary, and writs of assistance might be issued from supreme courts in each colony to enforce

[58] Nicholas Varga, "The New York Restraining Act: Its Passage and Some Effects, 1766–1768," *New York History*, XXXVII (July, 1956), 237. See also Assembly Journals, Dec. 13, 1765, for the resolves on the Mutiny Act.

[59] Becker, *Political Parties*, pp. 54–56.

the act. The third act suspended the legislative privileges of the New York Assembly until "provision shall have been made for furnishing the King's troops with all the necessaries required by law." The Restraining Act was to become effective October 1, the Townshend duties on November 20, 1767.[60]

What alarmed New Yorkers was not so much the Townshend duties but their connection with the Mutiny and Restraining acts. Taken together they gave the appearance to the colonists of total suppression of legislative autonomy. The act suspending the assembly was legal, but in the eyes of many colonists, especially the radicals, the historic development of the provinces "had reduced this legal principle . . . to the status merely of a historical curiosity." Many of the colonial leaders in 1767 would not have admitted its validity. Conservative John Dickinson of Pennsylvania, for example, thought New York had been punished "in a manner pernicious to American freedom, and justly alarming to all the colonies"; he insisted that the Mutiny Act imposed a tax and that "repeal of the Stamp Act could have no significance if other parliamentary taxes could be forced upon the Americans in this fashion." [61] But for a time New York seemed indifferent to these measures, and before the Restraining Act went into effect, the assembly reversed itself and complied fully, if indirectly, with the Mutiny Act. The ministry then suspended the Restraining Act. In June, 1767, the assembly voted £3,000 from which the commander in chief could purchase required articles. But it did not otherwise make an explicit provision for supplies formerly denied the troops. In this, it was tacitly acknowledging Parliamentary supremacy, and yet was saving face, so it appeared, by refusing to be explicit in providing the supplies it once denied the troops. The manner of compliance suggested that the tacit recognition of Parliament's authority was not wholly unqualified nor was it given altogether ungrudgingly. In addition to the £3,000 voted the commander in chief, the assembly displayed further pliability by appropriating £1,500 more for the troops. In its address to the governor the assembly vowed that "sure we are that this House could never be justly accused of too much Parsimony . . . All Requisitions from the Crown have ever been answer'd with ready and liberal Grants." [62] But how much was "too much Parsimony," and how "ready and liberal" had the assembly been in the

60 7 George III, chaps. 41, 46, 59.
61 Flick, III, 202.
62 Assembly Journals, June 3, 1767. C.O. 5/1218.

past? The ministry approved these gestures, and the Restraining Act never operated to disallow provincial legislation.

If the New York Assembly made adjustments to Parliamentary authority, Parliament also granted its own concessions to the colonies. Aside from the repeal of the Stamp Act, Parliament lowered the duties under the Sugar Act of 1764. But it also insisted on its supremacy in the Declaratory Act in 1766—its right to legislate for the colonies in all cases whatsoever—and its retention of the use of the revenues from the Sugar Act for purposes of colonial defense. Yet for all the practical compromise, Britain and her colonies remained fundamentally divided on principle. The former insisted on maintaining the doctrine of Parliamentary sovereignty, the latter that of "no taxation without actual representation." The quarrel might again easily arise, given the appropriate circumstances.

There was good reason behind the quiescence in New York and its assembly factions. The Townshend duties roused no particular opposition as they did among Boston merchants who formed a non-importation association. The New York Sons of Liberty showed no inclination to act until the time drew nigh for the appearance of the customs commissioners in Boston. New Yorkers read John Dickinson's "Letters from a Farmer in Pennsylvania" in the *New-York Mercury* in the winter of 1767–1768, but these criticisms of the Townshend duties seemed to have roused no particular enthusiasm for the moment. The reaction, when it came, was much delayed. What had prompted the New York Assembly to comply with the Mutiny Act was its hope for permission to issue paper currency—a measure it had no right to expect from the ministry if the colony proved recalcitrant in supporting His Majesty's government in other matters. In this the Livingstons, who had refused initially to vote appropriations (except for billets) until *after* the other expenses of the troops were incurred, changed their position in order to encourage the ministry to permit the issuance of paper currency. Perhaps they also remembered that royal troops could be a boon, for as landlords they had called on the military to quash tenant riots in 1766. New York merchants wanted a relaxation of the restraint on paper currency too; they also petitioned that restrictions against trade with French colonial ports be raised. In order to procure these favors it seemed expedient to submit to the Mutiny Act to show their good will. Perhaps Parliament would reciprocate further.[63]

63 Varga, "The New York Restraining Act . . . ," pp. 239, 251.

Thus far the Livingston-dominated assembly showed no marked disagreements with the De Lancey faction. Both were conservative. Both joined in conciliatory action directed against a common center—Parliament. There were only the suggestions of sharp divergence to follow, for however much mutually conservative interests tended to unite the factions when they faced a common enemy, their essential partisan nature would not permit anything but the most temporary lull in their relations with one another. It was one thing to join hands in the assembly to resist Parliament; it was another matter to decide the issues of patronage and to struggle for dominant position within the assembly.

The election of 1768, prompted by a septennial act, "reflected two main tendencies; the rising importance of the mercantile [De Lancey] interest, and the reaction of the conservative classes from the violence of the stamp act period." [64] After this time, the two old factions were more sharply divided, but less on the issue of "home rule" than on the question of who should rule at home. It was at this juncture that Philip Schuyler first entered the faction-ridden political arena. With the disappearance of members of the Livingston family from the assembly, Schuyler assumed much of the opposition leadership against the De Lanceys. Any personal or private aspects of the old family feud were eventually lost in the broader considerations of political interest, and the tangle of movements mixed with partisanship and principle.

– 5 –

"PASTURE ENOUGH FOR THE BEASTS"
—LORD CHESTERFIELD TO SAMUEL DAYROLLES, NOVEMBER 16, 1753

GIVEN HIS WEALTH, his accumulative talents, and his penchant for increasing the family's standing, given his involvement in the aristocratic interests of allied families and of individuals bent on winning place and riches, what measure of power in his society had Philip Schuyler a right to expect? If, as has been suggested, Schuyler was such a "landed aristocrat," [65] why did he not become a loyal adherent of the governor's interest and the loyalist cause in the American Revo-

---

[64] Becker, *Political Parties*, p. 59.
[65] Ellis, *et al., A Short History of New York State*, p. 119.

lution? Indeed, why did any "aristocrat" turn "patriot"? We shall better be able to answer these questions after examining Philip Schuyler's activities in the last provincial assembly, but we may consider here several aspects of the wider framework of his successes and disappointments.

Philip Schuyler believed that government should be in the hands of men of wealth and of long-established families. There can be no doubt that as a Federalist in later years he believed in the rightful exercise of power by the rich, the well-born, and the able. Even before the War of Independence he cherished these convictions and subscribed to the basic tenet of privilege. No one questioned his talents, however much they might chafe at his ambition and stern pride, or how much they might castigate his "bullying, overbearing manner." All his experience before entering the assembly suggested an alliance with established power.

Until he appeared in the New York Assembly in 1768, Philip Schuyler had every reason to expect a share in the direction of provincial affairs—a sizable share commensurate with his enlarging position. He had begun to develop and expand a large estate, and it was accepted principle that those who owned the country had a stake in its governance. He had won the attention and favor of the governor, Sir Henry Moore, who was willing to have him join in speculative ventures in the Mohawk country. Although Moore asked him to sacrifice a share of his allotment in one land purchase, he thereby laid himself under further obligation to Schuyler, promised to recompense him with lands elsewhere, if possible, and commissioned him a colonel in the New York militia. The colonelcy was also an acknowledgement of his influence—and of his interests on the upper Hudson. His regimental district comprised lands on which unruly tenants or pretentious intruders could be disciplined if ever they made disturbances like those that had culminated in the "Great Rebellion" of 1766. The colonelcy of a militia regiment meant power to recommend appointments and to keep order against disturbances from the Hampshire Grants people. And when Schuyler's father-in-law, John Van Rensselaer, was threatened by Yankee squatters, it was Governor Moore who had sided with the landlord's interests. Schuyler had served creditably in the Great War for the Empire and held several minor posts in local government. He might well regard them as the beginnings of bigger and better things.

For a time after Governor Moore died, Schuyler was cut adrift in the uncertain currents of the interim between administrations. But when Governor William Tryon arrived in the province, Schuyler promptly solicited his favor. It was doubtless sharpened ambition and annoyance that prompted Henry Van Schaack to complain to Sir William Johnson in July, 1772, that Schuyler was busily attentive in "getting things established [with Governor Tryon] as [he] had them in Sr Harrys time." [66] What more pointed testimonial could there be to Schuyler's position during one administration and his concern for regaining or reasserting it in another? In the assembly Schuyler found he was no longer the man of prime power that he was in his own bailiwick as landlord and colonel. Assembly politics were complex, and Schuyler knew enough about them before plunging in to acknowledge the possibility of losing himself in the political labyrinth. The uncertain fluctuations of interest between governor and factions did not allow him to attain power quietly nor permit him to enjoy it in much tranquillity.

Before he was commissioned colonel, Schuyler showed no great concern for the patronage of the government. But from the moment he recommended others for commissions in his regiment, his appetite for the dispensation and share in other political appointments sharpened. Before 1767 he served as a boundary commissioner for the settlement of the New York–Massachusetts line. When the assembly appointed him to this post in 1764, it recognized his talents for mathematics and surveying, but more, it acknowledged his interest in the disputed territory—an interest founded in his personal agrarian enterprises and in his marriage alliance which prompted concern for the title of his father-in-law's lands. In 1767, however, Schuyler was replaced on the boundary commission; he could only count then on the position of William Smith, Jr., to keep a watchful eye on interests east of the Hudson.

One student of the times has written that Schuyler, "always politically ambitious, fought the privileged group which neglected him," and that the royal governors blundered in overlooking the possibility of attaching him to their cause by favors and attention. A contemporary, Timothy Dwight, said of Schuyler and George Clinton that it was chiefly owing to them that New York made early and decided

[66] Van Schaack to Sir William Johnson, July 27, 1772. *Sir William Johnson Papers*, VIII, 549–550. For the way in which Schuyler "got things established in Sir Harry's time," see Chapter II, *supra*.

resistance to British measures. "Perhaps only the pugnacious Schuyler was more consistent in his detestation of everything that emanated from the De Lancey party." [67] How much truth is there to the motive ascribed here? We shall measure its accuracy when considering the last sessions of the provincial assembly, but we have already seen that royal governors did not neglect Schuyler—certainly not during 1760–1770, when he remained primarily occupied with private business. If he was neglected then or later, it was not the neglect of total indifference nor was it because the governor's and the De Lanceyites' political horizon ended at the northern border of Westchester. Schuyler benefited from his connections with Sir Henry Moore and from a later governor, William Tryon, both of whom had interests in the north. But as he was politically ambitious, an understandable counterpart to his economic interests, he may not have been satisfied with the amount of favor or advantage he did manage to curry with the chief executive. When he joined the assembly, he found that the enjoyment of power was not so much a gift to be granted by the governor as it was a prize to be wrested from the opposing faction of his peers, and we shall see that he acted with a certain "independency of spirit" in dealing with both the governor and the assembly politicians.

As for the motivation of Schuyler's leadership in resistance to British measures, we must look both for a personal interest and for a broader, more general, philosophic climate. It is no easy task to measure a man's character and intentions when so little remains of his expressions of sentiments and purpose. His writings are mainly idealistic. It may be a mistake to assume that, because of this, Schuyler was wholly an idealistic champion of liberty and "home rule." Neither will the fact that his position is described in such terms permit us to judge him as a primarily selfish, much less an avaricious, colonial whose eye was fastened always and only on his account books or land records. The practical reasons for his behavior must be sought in the context of his assembly activities, and even these are surrounded by certain intimations of idealism. Idealism, after all, involves mundane goals, and idealism both forms and is formed by practical politics. It is probably as much a matter of unconscious rationalization as it is of carefully studied aims for the future, or of unachievably lofty standards for which men strive in an effort to improve both their conduct and their circumstances.

[67] Spaulding, *George Clinton*, p. 26.

In private and public life Schuyler was guided by a determination to preserve and uphold traditional standards of family, rank, and order. There was little in his career that was not in harmony with the actions of other intelligent and realistic men of property. Like them, he yielded to compromise and expediency. And in doing so, he demonstrated that eighteenth-century American conservatism was not a matter of refusing change altogether, but of accepting and directing it to accomplish what conservatives considered to be a nice balance between the ideal and the possible. Being thus temperamentally inclined, the Saratoga squire could "never stay long in any company of radicals. He could never quite forget that he was a landed aristocrat who, in Albany at least, belonged to the ruling class." [68]

Schuyler's conservatism was in large measure a state of mind, a condition of temperament. It was based on his position as a man of property and good connections. It is questionable whether he ever formed any clear-cut or comprehensive political philosophy, but his actions and predilections had those qualities which nonetheless are usually associated with conservative temper: caution, respectability, solidity, a deep concern for good order and for property interests because liberty did not exist without property. Schuyler's sense of dignity, his stability, and perseverance pointed to a devotion to steady but unexcited progress. He was a man attentive to duty, methodical and calculating in the use of talents and the execution of plans, opposed to hasty, uncontrolled change, devoted to accepted social form, and suspicious of the abilities or influence of the great number of people so revealingly styled the "lesser orders." Doubtless, this suspicion was based on a somber view of human nature—on doubt that men were able to accomplish quickly any fundamental changes of society that might be characterized as lasting or meritorious. He was a patriot insofar as he was willing to cast his lot for his native land rather than for royal government and the empire. Yet he evinced no disposition to scrap the solid, fundamental institutions of the mother country which had taken root in New York and which had grown to

[68] *Ibid.*, p. 35. Conservatism is difficult to define because there is no general agreement about the precise meaning of the word. However, Schuyler's life suggests the validity of calling him a conservative if that term is referred to as "an attitude, position, tendency, or policy involving or favoring preservation or continuation of some element or elements in the existing situation," without identifying the term "exclusively with any of those elements." Kenyon, "Republicanism and Radicalism in the American Revolution: An Old-Fashioned Interpretation," pp. 157–163.

meet its peculiar circumstances. And, quite clearly, he showed no interest in relinquishing the direction of society or the state to parvenus.

Any latent inclinations toward complete political independence in the American colonies are difficult to discern or to document with precision. Yet they seem to underlie the disputes surrounding idealistic questions of "home rule" and more earthy, even selfish, struggles among factions over who was to have the power to rule at home. Perhaps only a few men consciously developed a philosophy of independence. But the grounds for a widespread acceptance of this philosophy remained even after the practical imperial adjustments of 1764–1770, when compromises on taxation, the Mutiny Act, paper currency, and the Restraining Act appeared to have resolved animosity and contention. Those grounds in New York were local partisan politics, combined with recurrent appeals to a principle—no taxation without actual representation. Practical compromise quieted the principle, but partisan politics might resurrect it. In view of the subsequent outbursts over Parliamentary supremacy, the compromises seem not at all to have solved the basic contest of right and power. And Philip Schuyler stepped into the political arena, the product as much as the producer, of the larger current that momentarily swept him away from conservatism to a moderately radical point of view on both the home rule issue and the local partisan quarrel between factions. His occupation with land and farm produce gave him a measure of independence greater than many of the people of his day enjoyed—made him free to turn from complete concentration on private business to participate in the politics on which his well-being in a wider sense depended. Thus he knew how inextricably bound together his liberty and property were. A man of "independency of spirit," backed by substantial wealth, may act with a good deal more freedom than one who does not enjoy these advantages. He may, indeed, be as free to oppose an established order as much as he may be expected to support it.

A man born in an age of sporadic controversy, in the ebb and flow of factional politics within a province such as New York and of heightened clashes between local, ambitious interests and royal-imperial authority, could hardly be expected to be shocked after having witnessed these realities as a participant instead of as a mere observer. But once seated in the assembly, Philip Schuyler may have looked upon affairs with a new perceptiveness. Caught up in the factional whirl he had viewed earlier somewhat from afar, he probably worked out a philosophy based on considerations of the realities of those struggles and of the private and public advantages or disadvantages of the wider imperial system. Because he was an intelligent and talented man, we would be justified in thinking that he did this. Schuyler doubtless saw certain fundamental difficulties in the royal administration of local interests, in spite of all his successes with the imperial government, his land acquisitions and colonel's commission, and his influence with governors and other royal officials. And these difficulties influenced his choice to transfer his opposition to a faction to the resistance of a wider authority with which that faction became more and more identified. The government's land-grant policy, for example, and the evolving structure of landholding obliged him to seek acquisitions by purchase from original patentees or the Indians, either directly, through sheriffs' sales for the arrears in quitrents, or indirectly, by cooperative ventures with other speculators. Sometimes he was thwarted or threatened by these conditions, or his share was cut below what he first expected. Disputes in which he was involved, whether the wider Hampshire Grants controversy or the more immediate claims against his father-in-law's land titles always meant lengthy delays while a distant ministry was consulted for a ruling. This, combined with the opposition from members of a rival faction whose interests clashed with Schuyler's, meant that the colonel could identify the antagonisms of local partisans with royal-imperial authority. By the time the Revolutionary War broke, Schuyler had reached that position from which he saw his mixed agrarian interests were more immediately identified with local control, less vitally with those of a commercial empire. Faced with an ultimate decision, he said, like the Prophet Joshua, that he and his house would serve their country.[69] It was an excellent rationalization of localism and particularism.

As a landed gentleman Schuyler was a member of the Livingston faction, which was probably bound less by family connection than by strong agrarian interests and a desire to win the power wrested from them by the De Lancey faction, a group made up primarily of courtly, commercial, and urban gentlemen. No precise distinction can be made between mercantile and agrarian aristocrats of the time. Schuyler himself had both agricultural and commercial interests. Merchants and agrarians were not divided exclusively along occupational lines; each group had a certain interest and involvement in the other. Still, there was a perceptible difference between them. The elections of

[69] Lossing, I, 307.

1768, for example, showed that the Hudson valley counties, primarily agrarian, were defeated by the strength of the southern counties, where the more pronounced mercantile interests held sway. In these elections the De Lanceys won an ascendancy over the Livingstons which they then increased in 1769. Except for Dutchess County, the Livingstons made a clean sweep of the Hudson valley north of West-chester.[70] It may be granted that had the Livingstons attracted the support of the merchant interest in which even some of them were involved, the agrarian-commercial division would not be an accurate portrayal. But the facts speak otherwise. Notwithstanding Schuyler's varied interests in commerce and speculation, he remained fundamentally an agrarian. Thus he stands forth as an advocate of a rural, upcountry group whose interests were multiple, but whose single-minded aim was to seek its own advantage both in imperial policy and in the closer combat for control of local affairs with the mercantile-minded De Lanceys.

In a day when Americans were profoundly concerned with religious topics and more subject to the influences of the frontier than today, there were other reasons why Schuyler led a Whiggish faction—the voices of dissent and protest in New York. He was a member of the Dutch Reformed Church, a likely ally for the Livingstonian Presbyterians, and an opponent of any established church. The De Lanceys were quite the opposite. And when issues of support of one religious group over another arose, as they did in the Revolutionary era, the intensity of religious motivation was anything but inconsequential. Vital issues arose concerning obligatory support of a state church, the religious foundations of King's College (which in turn involved the chartering power of the assembly), and despite the few grounds for it, there was an ever recurrent fear that an Anglican episcopate might be established in America. A dissenters' broadside issued in January, 1769, voiced the anxiety that "that curse of curses an American Bishop" with all his spiritual courts and great power might be introduced.[71] Dissenters shuddered at the thought of ecclesiastical courts and pressures. Schuyler's role in the religious controversy centered primarily in his interest in freeing New Yorkers from compulsory sup-

[70] Spaulding, *George Clinton*, p. 22.

[71] "Reasons For the present glorious combination of the dissenters in this city, against the further encroachments and strategems of the episcopalians, from a brief recollection of what the latter have already done, to exalt their own party on the ruins of every other religious persuasion amongst us." [1769], NYPL.

port of an established church and in granting them an opportunity to endow their own religious bodies.

Although these religious topics formed a vital part of political thought, there were other, more natural, foundations to Philip Schuyler's political position. Schuyler had a catholic temperament that reflected the influences of the frontier on whose borders he lived. He was no leveler as were many products of the wilderness, for he represented a certain stage of development in frontier life and a certain class which precluded his advocacy of anything like the modern concept of democracy. Egalitarianism had no attractions for this aristocrat, except as it applied to his own peers. Active as the frontier leaven was, it had little to do with Schuyler's inclinations except as it paralleled the man's natural, or classical, strains of jealousy and ambition and his convictions that an urban merchant or lawyer, a De Lancey aristocrat, was in fact no better qualified to govern New York than was an agrarian like himself. In this way the leveling influence of the frontier, though scarcely a determining factor in Schuyler's political temperament, reflected his peculiar resistance to the pretensions of others who he felt were no more than his peers and who were engrossing an undue share of power and place. Here was no question of a lesser breed challenging the position of their betters as was true of radical resistance to the local power elite. Instead, the issue was one of members of the same class resisting and coveting the peculiar position won by their fellows.[72] And with a limited number of places to fill through the favors of the royal government, the power controversy was not so much a question of deliberate neglect of influential and ambitious members of the governing class as it may have been simply that there was not pasture enough to feed the beasts.

[72] The local struggles for power in the province are also reflected by conditions in Albany. During the 1760's a group of British newcomers turned many inhabitants of Dutch descent against them by their efforts to dominate city politics. The Albany Dutch found themselves divided between leaders who held royal appointments (such as Mayor Abraham C. Cuyler and city-county Clerk Stephen De Lancey) and those who were members of the common council—a difference in the measure of power and prestige of each. The divergence carried through the Revolutionary War years and into the struggle for ratification of the United States Constitution. The Dutch patriots' feelings were not aimed against Englishmen in general, but against individuals who made themselves unwelcome. It is reasonable to deduce a connection between this sentiment and an ultimate choice of loyalty to the American cause. Alice P. Kenney, "The Albany Dutch: Loyalists and Patriots," *New York History*, XLII (Oct., 1961), 331–350.

Led step by step in what almost appears a relentless, predetermined pattern of resistance, Philip Schuyler joined other members of the local ruling class in the Revolutionary movement. They were reluctant rebels, and because of their fundamental loyalties to empire and generally conservative attitudes, they undoubtedly were responsible in a large measure for halting the Revolution decisively short of violence or terrorism or of extreme "democratical" practices. Schuyler was never quite comfortable among men of more liberal and leveling inclinations, like George Clinton or Samuel Adams. His swing into the current known as Federalism or nationalism, notwithstanding his earlier patriotic and non-Tory behavior, proved that his primary nature was on the side of tradition, established power, and the rule of a few. Because of his Revolutionary aberration, Schuyler's behavior must be viewed as a forced and momentary departure from fundamentals, followed by a return to conservatism. Certainly his behavior in the New York Assembly points to this conclusion.

If Schuyler's acquisition of influence as an assemblyman included a challenge to established authority, it was also true that it depended to some degree on working with the men in power and on using the existing political structure. In order to win a place for himself and to advocate the cause of an agrarian faction with diversified interests, he resisted the De Lanceys, opposed the empire notwithstanding his protestations of loyalty to it, and finally joined the rebellion. Even before independence was won he was concerned in checking any further political swing to the left. Although not responsible for a direct share in its formation and promulgation, Schuyler was an advocate of the New York state constitution of 1777—a frame of mixed government whose essence was privilege and stability, whose outlines were those of the old province's elitist system. His next major work was to help achieve on a national level what New York had managed to erect within her own bounds—a system of controls for a society threatened by radical men and liberal ideology. As a Yorker and as an American, Schuyler won influence such as he had never had as a colonist. It was not the active sort of influence maintained by continuous public officeholding, although he did occupy positions of public trust. Schuyler's weight was that of a man with a heavy stake in society—a gentleman who was largely quiet, sporadically energetic, but who, on the whole, constantly and steadily applied his influence and interest. He had wanted to serve his country in 1775, but the issue by then was whether "country" meant the empire or America and New York. He was closer to the latter than to the former, and he chose it as only a man can choose that which is most familiar to him—that by which he is most likely to realize his own best hopes. Like his friend the younger William Smith, who played the political game with Schuyler in provincial days, he was patriotically enthusiastic for the future greatness of America. But whereas Smith's opposition to Parliament's claim to tax the colonies did not lead him to break with the Crown or empire, Schuyler proved more willing to sever the old ties and to transfer his connection from the empire to a rising nation.[73] An examination of Schuyler's activities in the colonial assembly shows how his conservative patriotism was forged from the basis of his wealth and position and how the partisanship of provincial factions underlay his position in the American Revolution.

[73] Sabine, *Smith Memoirs,* I, vii.

CHAPTER IV

The Initiation to Assembly Politics

PARTISAN QUARRELS could not have been wholly unfamiliar to Philip Schuyler before he actually entered the mainstream of provincial politics. Such disputes had long been present in New York. During the very month Schuyler was born, reports of a controversy appeared in John Peter Zenger's newly founded *New-York Weekly Journal*. The news recorded the bickering of the 1733 elections in which the opposition to Governor William Cosby made an issue of his removing Chief Justice Lewis Morris and appointing James De Lancey to the high court in his stead. Morris had disallowed Cosby's claim to half the salary of the acting governor—a demand based on Cosby's beginning his governorship before actually arriving in New York. Zenger's paper was an opposition organ for men like Morris, James Alexander, who had been expelled from the governor's council, and barrister William Smith, Sr.

In 1768, Schuyler opened a stormy political career with election to "the Legislature," as he later put it, "of the State In which I drew the breath of life and for which I have suffered so much merely because I Sacrificed my own feelings In Its favor. . . ." [1] The inference of a political birth seems as evident as the reference to his birthplace. The Restraining and Mutiny acts with which the New York Assembly had complied in order to bargain for fewer restrictions on paper currency, and the particulars of the Townshend Acts of 1767 afforded no great issues for the provincial elections of 1768.[2] The De Lancey faction did, however, use the assembly's compliance with the Mutiny Act as a partisan weapon, but not as a point of serious philosophical contention nor as an issue to debate the wider questions of home rule and resistance to imperial administration. The assembly session preceding the election gave only the slightest clues to the action that followed its dissolution. It was then that the contest at the polls clearly revealed the struggle for power between factions—and very little else.

[1] Schuyler to Robert R. Livingston, Mar. 5, 1778. NYHS, Robert R. Livingston Collection.
[2] Becker, *Political Parties*, pp. 58–59.

The contrast between the session preceding Schuyler's election and the first assembly in which he sat was remarkable on the point of disturbance. The legislative session of November 17, 1767–February 6, 1768, was notably quiet. The assembly was largely occupied with the reports of the commissioners on the Massachusetts boundary controversy.[3] This, together with routine business and the further compliance with requests for troop supplies, kept it largely from controversial partisan heats. In its reply to the governor's address the assembly voiced concern that the Restraining Act suggested that it had fallen under Parliamentary displeasure. However, the members vowed that their zeal for the king inclined them to bear the burden rather than to disturb the peace. And in addition to the £3,000 voted in the earlier session (May 27–June 6, 1767), the assembly appropriated £1,500 for regular annual troop supply.[4] The most excitement generated occurred when the house considered Cadwallader Colden's anonymous pamphlet defending his conduct in the Stamp Act crisis, when he had wanted to receive the stamps and execute the law. The assembly voted the pamphlet a reflection on the honor, justice, and dignity of the house as well as of the council and judges, and a committee was appointed to detect the authors and publishers. The committee summoned John Holt, publisher of *The New-York Journal*, for questioning. Following its investigations, which failed to detect Colden as the author, the house proclaimed that the pamphlet tended to destroy the people's confidence in the government and rendered it odious at a time when respect for authority was vital to peace and good order. Governor Moore was asked to prosecute the author should his identity be discovered.[5]

The assembly proved agreeable and cooperative in voting salaries to the governor, judges, and other royal officials. Contrary to instructions, however, it refused to grant the money in the king's name, phrasing it instead in the name of the province, and directing the treasurer to give his bond to the speaker of the house instead of to the king. Only the slightest sign of friction between land and trade interests, the Livingstons and the De Lanceys, was evident. The assembly passed a liquor excise over the objections of the New York City members, despite their contention that it was unfair that the city and county

[3] Assembly Journals, Nov. 25, 1767; Jan. 29, Feb. 3, 5, 1768. C.O. 5/1218.
[4] Assembly Journals, Nov. 23, 1767; see also entries for Nov. 27, Dec. 1, 1767. C.O. 5/1218.
[5] Assembly Journals, Dec. 23, 1767; Jan. 8, Feb. 6, 1768. C.O. 5/1218.

of New York should pay more of these taxes than other parts of the province.[6]

– 1 –

"NO LAWYERS, NO PRESBYTERIANS!"

ON FEBRUARY 6, 1768, Governor Moore dissolved the assembly in accordance with the septennial act. Four days later he issued writs for an election, the returns for which were to be made by March 22. The campaign which followed suggested that the vital issue was not yet one of "home rule" but rather the question of who was to win power to rule at home. The De Lanceys did capitalize, however, on the wider issue of local self-government by suggesting that the Livingston-dominated assembly had neglected New York's interests and had not sufficiently asserted the rights of the colony in so lavishly granting money for the king's troops. Suggestive as they were of discontent with imperial administration, these accusations signified more substantially the philosophical justification or explanation of what was primarily a factional struggle and a clash of local interests.

Of Philip Schuyler's political activities before the election of 1768 almost nothing is known. As the entire province had been opposed to the Stamp Act, it is not unlikely that he joined others to oppose the tax. It does not appear, however, that he was in any sense an enrolled member of the Sons of Liberty, although he may have associated with a number of them at Albany.[7]

Philip Schuyler was too circumspect, too reluctant to risk damaging his standing with the governor, and too much in character as a landed aristocrat to join in the rampagings of so disorderly a group as the Sons of Liberty, however much he may have shared their hos-

[6] Assembly Journals, Dec. 28, 30, 1767. C.O. 5/1218. See also Colden to Hillsborough, April 25, 1768. C.O. 5/1137:179.

[7] Lossing, I, 215. See also Colden to Conway, Feb. 21, 1766. C.O. 5/1098:95–98; *The New-York Gazette, or Weekly Post-Boy*, Jan. 23, 1766; *The New-York Mercury*, Jan. 27, 1766. Lossing's assertion that Schuyler associated with the Albany Sons of Liberty is undocumented. Beverly McAnear, "The Albany Stamp Act Riots," *The William and Mary Quarterly*, Third Series, IV (Oct., 1947), 486–498, gives no indication that Schuyler was involved in the local fray. It appears that he was neither at home when the Sons of Liberty visited his house (seeking Henry Van Schaack, who was rumored to want a post as stamp tax collector), nor with the group assembled at a local tavern for purposes of intimidating men suspected of harboring ambitions to be stamp officers—a group whose members were specifically named by Henry Van Schaack.

tility to the Stamp Act. There were other means of associating with their cause without bearing their stigma. In May, 1766, when news of the repeal of the detested measure reached New York, Schuyler apparently was in the city. He reportedly feasted with the Sons of Liberty at Howard's tavern, and joined them at Trinity Church to hear a congratulatory address.[8] But he would do no more than that. Doubtless he was far more satisfied with the toasts drunk to the king and to the perpetual union of Britain and her colonies than with riotous destruction of property, forceful intimidation of citizens, and the roaming of the rabble. Moreover, in 1766, Schuyler's attention remained focused on his estates and on the possibilities of acquiring more land with the cooperation of Sir Henry Moore. Until the elections of 1768 he confined himself to the responsibilities of his new commission as colonel of a militia regiment and to the plans for developing his estates.

There were several reasons why Schuyler's debut on the political stage was a tardy one. When assembly elections were held in 1761, he was in England on business for John Bradstreet. It was not likely that he could be elected *in absentia*. Moreover, the opportunity to "set up" for an assembly seat depended upon the decision of one of the incumbents to relinquish his place. Then, too, Schuyler's private interests remained predominant. For a man not yet thirty, a person of his status could be expected to show first concern for the conduct of family business. Public affairs were secondary and seemed important only insofar as participation in them added considerable advantage to the individual's private interests.

Schuyler was in New York City in December, 1767, when the old assembly was still sitting. Shortly before Christmas, when the New York Society for Promoting the Arts, Agriculture and Economy held its monthly meeting, Schuyler was on hand to tell of one of his recent accomplishments. "Philip P. [*sic*] Schuyler, Esq; being present," read the report of the society, "informed them that he had erected a Flax-Mill at Saragtora [*sic*] in the Year 1767, and delivered to the Society a Calculation of the Difference of the Work done by the Mill and by Hand in the same Time: whereupon they adjudged a Medal to Mr. Schuyler, and returned to him their Thanks for executing so useful a Design in the Province."[9] While in New York the colonel listened

[8] Lossing, I, 215–216.
[9] *The New-York Journal, or the General Advertiser* (John Holt), Jan. 14, 1768. See also Schuyler's Saratoga Daybook, 1764–1770, p. 177 (NYHS) for mention of the "fulling Mill."

to the counsels of his friend, the attorney William Smith, Jr., who urged him to prepare for the impending dissolution of the assembly and the elections to follow. Smith felt it was time his friend considered the responsibilities and advantages of an assembly seat. It was fitting that Schuyler join the patrician club in the active direction of local affairs. The agrarian interests needed his support against the De Lanceys, who were expected to make a rigorous fight to seize the assembly from the Livingstons. At the same time the Livingstons were endangered by their own loss of popularity.

The Livingstons' strength was concentrated among the great landed families, but they had "tended to court the radicals and were . . . in some sort of alliance with Governor Moore." Peter Van Brugh Livingston's son, Philip, was the governor's secretary. Another Philip Livingston, the New York City merchant, was speaker of the assembly; his brother William was influential in managing the more radical supporters of the faction. Representing Livingston Manor was Peter R. Livingston, son of the third lord and nephew to William and Philip. And a cousin of Philip and William, Judge Robert R. Livingston, was one of the most powerful figures in the colony. The judge also sat for Dutchess County (1759–1768), and was feared by Lieutenant Governor Colden because he was not only a judge but a landed magnate with a large political following.[10]

The De Lanceys, on the other hand, were "more representative of the mercantile interest," more identified with the Church of England (though Judge Livingston was himself an Episcopalian), and more cautious as a whole in resisting the power of Crown and Parliament. Although their strength was concentrated in New York City, they had been less inclined than their rivals to court the radicals of the area—a disposition from which they were now to waver. The De Lanceys found their connection with Lieutenant Governor Colden, whose daughter had married Peter De Lancey, the Westchester assemblyman and brother of the late lieutenant governor and chief justice, James De Lancey. Another brother, Oliver, was a member of the council. In 1768 the leadership in the assembly fell to Captain James De Lancey, the lieutenant governor's eldest son and heir.[11]

Happily for Philip Schuyler, the upper Hudson area was not rent

---

[10] Hoffman, *Edmund Burke*, p. 86. Hoffman identifies Philip Livingston, the governor's secretary, as the son of Philip Livingston the merchant. Edwin Brockholst Livingston, *The Livingstons of Livingston Manor* (New York, 1910), pp. 8, 179, indicates that the governor's secretary was the son of Peter Van Brugh Livingston.

[11] Hoffman, *Edmund Burke*, p. 87.

with the troubles facing his Livingston allies in the vicinity of New York City. The Livingston interests suffered a marked disadvantage in fighting the election contest of 1768. The lawyers who were a part of the faction were suspected by property owners of having staged the Stamp Act riots; nor did the mercantile interests feel they could represent them well, and the church interest disliked them for their identification with dissent and non-conformity. Even the Sons of Liberty turned against the lawyers, charging them with basely deserting their cause by opposing the plans to conduct business without stamps.[12] The Livingston agrarians suffered from their connection with the legal profession, and thereby lost their majority in the assembly. This connection was such that, to those suspicious of the lawyers' interests in the affairs of landed proprietors, even the prosecution of tenant rioters in 1766–1767 now produced an unfavorable aspect.

Although Philip Schuyler had little difficulty in winning an assembly seat, the election of 1768 was a bitterly fought contest. The De Lancey faction had rather languished before 1768, but they displayed new vigor when they won a striking victory in New York City, where the main election battle was fought. Noticeable in the contest were the rising importance of the mercantile interest and the recoil of certain propertied men from the Stamp Act violence. The rising mercantile-church interest raised the cry of "No lawyers, no Presbyterians!" Their radical allies produced their own vituperation, reflected by a broadside which though printed was not published for the election. Even before the election writs were issued, this broadside was prepared for the purpose of giving "A Few Observations on the Conduct of the General Assembly," in which a certain "Philanthropos" issued a warning against "artful, designing and ambitious men . . . grasping at power, solely to aggrandize themselves and their families, without any view to the public interest. . . ."[13] He meant, of course, the Livingston agrarians who had held the assembly. While enjoying control, they refused to permit the laying of any tax burden on land,

12 Becker, *Political Parties*, pp. 59–60.

13 "A Few Observations on the Conduct of the General Assembly of New-York, for some years past, addressed to the Freemen and Freeholders of the City and Province. [signed] Philanthropos." (New York, Feb. 9, 1768), NYPL. Mark, *Agrarian Conflicts*, p. 213, indicates it was printed but not published. Its composition, however, reveals the tenor of the campaign. See also Colden to Hillsborough, April 25, 1768. C.O. 5/1137:175–182. Colden's letter reveals the partisan tactics. For example, he complained that "The Faction in Opposition to the Authority of Parliament, lay great Stress on my having become obnoxious to the People. . . ." He commented on the

but saw rather that the colony's revenue was raised by excises on trade. Only recently, during the last session of the assembly, the New York City members had protested the unfairness of a liquor excise, but the agrarians had carried their measure over the few objections.

One scholar has said that we may infer, although there is no direct evidence, that the radicals were displeased with the assembly's grant of troop supply.[14] Yet there is evidence enough. In July, 1766, the assembly had resolved to pay any extraordinary expenses not otherwise provided *after* the royal troops arrived in the province. This action Philanthropos insisted was a "most extraordinary and stupid resolve . . . a lasting monument of their folly and wickedness. . . ." Citing the action of the assembly in voting additional troop supply again in 1767, he pronounced the body guilty of the "most glaring breach of trust." The landed interests then in control of the assembly, he said, voted to support the soldiers in order to repay them for suppressing tenant riots in 1766 and, hence, to insure their future support in the event of further riots. Philanthropos revealed the radicals' alliance with the De Lancey mercantile forces in that his broadside contained a call to the voters to reject all lawyer-candidates to the assembly because they had a "separate interest," and suggested that a land tax was the means of relieving the tax burdens of the colony. Candidates, Philanthropos continued, should be chosen only if they promised to provide public galleries in the assembly, thereby enabling the people to have greater access to their representatives—and, it might be added, a more tangible method of pressuring their assemblymen. A further warning he issued in doggerel:

> The vile and sordid wretch who's bought and sold,
> And basely barters liberty for gold,
> Cannot, with any justice, sure complain,
> If he's compell'd to drag the galling chain.

Elections still involved a great deal of vote-buying, and neither the landlords nor the city interests were guiltless of the practice.

The division between agrarian and mercantile interests was further evidenced when one of Philip Schuyler's connections, Judge Robert R. Livingston, lost his assembly seat. Remembering the suppression

---

violent contentions in the election, on the fortunes of Judge Livingston, the leadership of New York City members of the assembly, and the animosity against lawyers and Presbyterians.

14 Becker, *Political Parties,* p. 60.

of the tenant rioters in 1766–1767, the freeholders of Dutchess County turned Livingston out of the house for his opposition to the tenants' cause.[15] Moreover, as a judge, Livingston bore the animus of lawyer which the negative campaign slogan imposed.

Lieutenant Governor Colden thought it remarkable that Judge Livingston "gave up" although "he had every thing in his Favor, which power could give him [in] the County where his Family Interest lies. Some one of the Family have been elected for above forty Years," Colden observed, but now Livingston was deprived of an assembly seat.[16] The De Lanceys trounced the Livingstons on the strength of the southern counties. North of Westchester, except for Dutchess County, the Livingstons made a clean sweep. This was Schuyler's home territory. The Hudson River counties had been defeated by the courtly, commercial city and county of New York which elected James De Lancey, Jacob Walton, and James Jauncey. These three generally directed affairs in the assembly.[17] Only one New York member, Philip Livingston, who was not of this faction, retained his seat. John De Lancey, cousin to James, sat for Westchester Borough. John Rapalje was added from Kings County. Leonard Van Kleeck and Dirck Brinckerhoff replaced Robert R. Livingston and Henry Livingston in Dutchess County. The distinct agrarians and anti-De Lanceyites came from Ulster and Albany counties, which included the constituencies of Schenectady Township and Rensselaer and Livingston manors. The Livingston majority of the old twenty-seven-member assembly was considerably reduced in the new house. Thirteen new members were elected, but most were not allies of the Livingstons. An assembly majority required a minimum of fourteen members, but the Livingstonians fell well below that number. Only nine of the members could be said to be within the agrarian pale, although of course boundaries were not tightly drawn for all cases. Some assemblymen appear to have fluctuated between the poles of the Livingston and De Lancey leadership so as to make a steady, reliable, majority-minority division very uncertain.[18]

15 Mark, *Agrarian Conflicts,* p. 158.

16 Cadwallader Colden to Lord Hillsborough, April 25, 1768. C.O. 5/1137:177.

17 *Ibid.*

18 The thirteen new assemblymen were: Schuyler, Albany County—replaced Volkert Douw; Pierre Van Cortlandt, Cortlandt Manor—replaced Philip Ver Planck; Leonard Van Kleeck and Dirck Brinckerhoff, Dutchess County—replaced Henry and Robert R. Livingston; John Rapalje, Kings County—replaced Abraham Schenck; James De Lancey, Jacob Walton, and James Jauncey, New York—replaced John Cruger, Leonard

The prospects of an election victory for the Livingston party must have been dim indeed for Philip Schuyler to have been enticed into the fray. But William Smith, Jr.'s, words likely struck a responsive chord with the colonel. Smith wrote him on January 18, 1768. "Let me persuade you not to refuse your services to your Country," he urged. What these were it was not necessary for him to explain. "After 7 Years we shall both abandon to Ease. I will promise to leave you in full & quiet Possession of your Wolves Foxes Snow Mills Fish & Lands at Saraghtoga & give no Disturbance while the remaining Lands run out." [19] How difficult for a landlord to leave his earthy pursuits while the lands had not yet "run out," and he was anxiously accumulating as much as he could. Yet there was another urgency—maintaining the dominance of the agrarian interest in the assembly. Little could Schuyler know that after seven years he would not be allowed a "full & quiet Possession" of his Saratoga estate, but that he would be caught up in the stormiest political and military controversy of his career, his later role in the Federalist movement notwithstanding.

Schuyler found it no easy matter to pull himself away from concentrations on land schemes, but neither was it altogether simple to win acceptance as a candidate for office. Candidates were "set up" by a form of private, personal arrangement—an arrangement whereby the "interests" of a few men were large enough to decide the election. For Schuyler and Albany County in 1768 the question was not, "Whom are the people for?" or "What are the candidate's principles?", but rather, "Whom is Sir William Johnson or Colonel Livingston for?" There were rumors in January that Sir William intended to produce his own candidate from the Mohawk region. These caused varied conjectures and consternation at Albany. Sir William ended the speculation by stating that neither he nor his son intended to "set up." [20]

Lispenard, and William Bayard; Selah Strong, Orange County—replaced Abraham Haring; Charles DeWitt and George Clinton, Ulster County—replaced Abraham Haasbrook and Jacobus Bruyn; John De Lancey, Westchester Borough—replaced Peter De Lancey; Jacobus Mynderse, Schenectady Township—replaced Nicholas Groot. The nine Livingston men were: Philip Livingston of New York, Jacob Ten Eyck and Schuyler (Albany), DeWitt and Clinton, Mynderse, Abraham Ten Broeck of Rensselaer Manor, Peter R. Livingston of Livingston Manor, and Van Cortlandt. Assembly Journals, Oct. 27, 1768. C.O. 5/1100:53. Cf. Werner, *Civil List* (1884), p. 311.

[19] Smith to Schuyler, Jan. 18, 1768. NYPL, Schuyler Papers Box 23.

[20] Carl Becker, "Nominations in Colonial New York," *The American Historical Review*, VI (1901), 265, 267–268.

Even so, Schuyler was not the only prospective candidate, or even the first choice. Volkert Douw, mayor of Albany, was reported to be much favored to continue in his old seat, and likewise Jacob Ten Eyck was willing to be re-elected to another term in the assembly. As late as February 22 the election remained unsettled in the Albany districts. The patroon and other friends "prevailed" upon Abraham Ten Broeck to represent Rensselaer Manor, and he expected no opposition. But it was with reluctance that Albanians accepted Volkert Douw's refusal to be their candidate. Douw declined for reasons of "interest" and health. When he refused, Schuyler became the obvious choice. Ten Broeck wrote, "Every Body is averse to a Poll it is now under Consideration to fix on a Person With Mr. Ten Eyck & I Believe I may venture to Say it Will be Mr. Philip Schuyler." [21] Schuyler evidently had been found acceptable to both Colonel Livingston and Sir William Johnson. Livingston might approve the candidate for reasons of family connections and common landed interests. Sir William tendered his support after Schuyler carefully solicited the baronet's approval.[22]

On March 3, 1768, the freemen and freeholders of Albany County assembled at the Albany city hall to make their poll for two assemblymen. Jacob Ten Eyck and Schuyler were chosen without opposition; the men of interest had decided on their candidates beforehand and with finality. So secure were they in their decision that Sir William Johnson wrote Schuyler on February 29, several days before the polling, to offer congratulations on his having been unanimously chosen to the assembly "by the Principal People of Albany"! Johnson quite approved of their choice.[23]

The election did not run as smoothly for the Livingston forces in other counties as it had in Albany and environs. The reaction against them proved stronger in districts closer to New York City. In an

21 Ten Broeck to James Duane?, Feb. 22, 1768. NYHS, Duane Papers. See also *The New-York Journal* (Holt), Mar. 10, 1768.

22 Sir William Johnson to Hugh Wallace, Jan. 25, 1769. *Sir William Johnson Papers*, VI, 608–609. Johnson's mention of Schuyler's request for his "interest *again*" is a reference to the first time Schuyler "set up," and clearly shows that Johnson gave his support in 1768. See also Johnson to Schuyler, Feb. 29, 1768. NYPL, Schuyler Papers Box 23.

23 Indenture, Mar. 3, 1768, certifying the election, signed by the county sheriff and other witnesses. NYSL, Schuyler Papers. Johnson to Schuyler, Feb. 29, 1768. NYPL, Schuyler Papers Box 23. Schuyler to Philip Ver Planck, Mar. 7, 1768. Baxter, *A Godchild of Washington*, p. 63.

agrarian society such as New York it is difficult to see why the Livingstons should lose. They remained essentially moderate in resisting
Parliament. They were rather loosely linked by a mutual "distaste
for taxes on property, fear of Parliament, an appetite for office and
patronage, and a suspicion of the lower orders." The party was no
less aristocratic than the De Lanceys, but "it was far less disposed to
obey the authorities in England"; yet its aristocratic leanings formed
its very weakness, and certain negative aspects combined to make it
unpopular. The faction included men whose varying degrees of conservatism ranged from Peter R. Livingston's blankly rightist position
to the radicalism of attorney John Morin Scott (which did not, however, satisfy the most violent of the Sons of Liberty).[24] The De Lanceys
managed to capitalize on the general disgruntlement of the electorate
who felt the lawyers' alliance with the landlords must be checked.
That the electorate of Dutchess County was even able to unseat Judge
Robert R. Livingston indicated that the landlords held no invincible
sway over tenants and lesser agrarians, notwithstanding the coercive features of the leaseholding system and the *viva voce* method
of voting.

In summary, the Livingstons' defeat in 1768 could be laid to several
causes. First were the fears of certain propertied elements who were
wary of the Livingstons' flirtations with the rabble—a mob which
might get out of hand. Secondly, the more turbulent elements who
coveted greater political power were not satisfied with the Livingstons'
cautious direction of the mob or with their more enduring connections with the establishment. Finally, the faction lost votes because
of religious labels. The Livingstons dubbed the De Lanceys the Episcopal party, and Anglicans were not likely to vote for men who
fastened such tags on politicians. Further, the Dutch Reformed voters
would not cooperate with the Presbyterians who were linked with the
Livingstons.[25]

As his friend, Sir Henry Moore must have been pleased with Philip
Schuyler's election—pleased and hopeful. As far as the general behavior of the assembly was concerned, Moore rather expected the new
house would prove more cooperative than the old one. The governor
was concerned that he had "not had interest enough in that House
to prevent" its refusal to compensate Cadwallader Colden for his back
salary and for damages incurred in the Stamp Act riots. And as for the

24 Dangerfield, *Livingston*, p. 39.
25 Alexander, *James Duane*, p. 46.

quality of assemblymen, the governor bemoaned the "misfortune . . .
that the greatest part of the . . . Assembly consists of men whose
Education has been extremely confin'd and the illiberal Notions in
which they have been brought up are not to be eradicated without
the greatest difficulty." [26] Schuyler does not appear to have fit this
category, and Moore was to find that even a switch in factions in the
house meant little abatement of partisan difficulties. Still, he hoped
for better success in the coming session because of the new members,
among whom Schuyler was numbered.

"The victory of the De Lanceys in 1768, and their emergence as a
'popular' party, only serves to deepen the mystery of colonial politics
in New York, unless we remember . . . that both Livingstons and
De Lanceys considered themselves Whigs." The Livingstons believed
more in reform. Both aimed at control of the assembly because it was
the disbursing and taxing power. And "to parties whose intellectual
existence was largely predicated upon their views on direct taxation,
and whose physical existence depended upon office and patronage,
control of this body was a matter of the first importance." [27] The
nature of the victory gave no indication that the province was first
and foremost concerned with imperial-colonial matters, but rather
that it was interested in which of the factions should be privileged to
govern and to enunciate the province's views to the royal-imperial
establishment. The De Lancey victory in 1768 and in the following
year did not mean the faction maintained its "popular" complexion.
The fact of its "reversal" and the development of the patriot attitude
of the Livingston forces suggest that the Revolution in New York was
very largely the outgrowth of local partisan struggles which were aggravated by fresh imperial administrative measures.

Once securely established in office, the De Lancey party reverted to
its true nature and became increasingly reluctant to truckle to the
popular elements. In time this so frustrated the less conservative and
the radical elements who could not hope to influence the assembly
that they turned to a greater use of extralegal methods to voice complaints and then to institute their own government. Seizing the initiative from moderate dissenters in the assembly like Schuyler, the radicals pursued a course that pulled assembly moderates with them and
resulted in a provincial congress—and independence. Philip Schuyler

[26] Moore to Hillsborough, May 9, 1768. C.O. 5/1099:249–250.
[27] Dangerfield, *Livingston*, p. 41.

was a leader of the resistance to the De Lancey variety of conservatism, but his group proved very largely ineffectual in the face of the opposition's strength. Like many other moderates, he was driven into the arms of the radicals. Once established in their camp, he endeavored to foster the conservative element there to check the Revolution, and by championing the erection of a state government based on privilege and traditional political forms, Schuyler helped wrest control from radical hands and helped restore it to an older segment of the governing class. We must remember this general line of movement in order to appreciate Schuyler's role in the history of the last years during which the New York Assembly sat under royal auspices.

Philip Schuyler was sobered by the prospects that lay before him, especially because at thirty-five he was one of the youngest men in the assembly.[28] He was without experience in a deliberative body except for the Albany City Council. But associating with close neighbors in familiar surroundings was somewhat easier than the work of settling issues affecting the entire province in the company of men whose interests could be as diverse on occasion as the parts of New York from which they were elected. Schuyler's position was important both as evidence of personal character and as a recognition of influence and interest. Barring an unforeseen dissolution of the house, he would occupy his seat for seven years. To a kinsman, Philip Ver Planck of Cortlandt Manor, he wrote to ask if he would continue to represent the manor. Schuyler hoped "to borrow part of that knowledge in public affairs, which, in the course of many years' experience joined to a luxuriant genius[,] you have acquired." The colonel realized the difficulties of assembly politics, and the complexity of the factional arrangements. "In following such a guide," he continued, "I should be in no danger of losing myself in the political labyrinth." [29]

The country squire might well hesitate before the devious ways of factionalism. William Smith, Jr., reminded Schuyler of the divisions among merchants, landlords, and lawyers that he would face in the assembly. In May, Smith warned that the disability of judges in going on circuit to hear land trials (actions of landlords against squatters, and landlords' mutual disputes over boundaries) meant the coming assembly would have to open its purse or the country must go without justice. "The Project proposed of calling Merchants to the Bench,"

[28] Lossing, I, 223.
[29] Schuyler to Ver Planck, Mar. 7, 1768. Baxter, *A Godchild of Washington*, p. 63.

Smith sneered, "appears to me as absurd, as the issuing Commissions to Statues of Wood or Stone." [30] The bench belonged in the hands of men trained in the law, men who were allies of the landlords, for the merchants clearly had no talents nor inclination to protect the agrarian interests of landholder and barrister. Here again was evidence of the abiding antagonism between city and merchants and country and landlords backed by the local bar.

Schuyler's foray into the political labyrinth was delayed when Governor Moore periodically prorogued the assembly until October. Between March and October, 1768, the landlord was occupied with matters quite separate from political interests, except for a visit from Governor Moore, who went up to Albany and thence to Fort Stanwix, where Sir William Johnson settled an Indian boundary. Ordinary business, though routine, demanded the colonel's constant attention, although larger events were stirring in New York City. There the merchants were finally rousing themselves to demonstrate their opposition to the Townshend Acts by a non-importation policy.

In April, 1768, the merchants of New York bestirred themselves to deal with the Townshend Acts. They decided to join Boston and Philadelphia in a non-importation program until Parliament should repeal the obnoxious duties. But they also proceeded to strengthen the program. Boston's non-importation scheme of October, 1767, was not as comprehensive as that proposed by the New York merchants in April, 1768, nor did the New Englanders join it until August. Philadelphia merchants objected to the program because it tended to create a monopoly; "merchants with capital to lay in a large stock of the proscribed commodities before the agreement became effective" (October 1) would have an unfair advantage. Importers thus aimed at enriching themselves at the expense of the populace, but they were also interested in resisting Parliament, and not merely in self-aggrandizement.[31] When Philadelphians declined to join the non-importation scheme, New York merchants met again late in August and devised a new association. These doings seemed not to touch Schuyler for the moment. As a landholder he had no far-flung merchant interests even though he sold staples and other goods to his tenants. A landlord had only his trade in timber, grain, and flour to consider, and non-importation plans did not much endanger his export market for the time

[30] Smith to Schuyler, May 30, 1768. NYSL, Schuyler Papers.

[31] Becker, *Political Parties*, pp. 61–62. See also *The New-York Gazette, and the Weekly Mercury*, April 18, 1768.

being.[32] He would have new worries, however, once he took his place in the assembly. It was there that non-importation and imperial legislation took on new importance for him. From his assembly seat the problems of both empire and local factional struggles assumed greater reality, stronger urgency, than they ever appeared to have when viewed from Saratoga.

– 2 –

"A GENTLEMAN OF GREAT INDEPENDENCY OF SPIRIT AND A TRUE SON OF LIBERTY"

WHETHER in anticipation of taking his family with him to a spring session of the assembly in 1768, or in planning for his children's schooling in New York City, Schuyler made inquiries of a kinswoman about their accommodations. Elizabeth Livingston informed him that two reputable boardinghouses were full, but that a Widow Grant would take two of the children for two pounds of tea, a loaf of sugar, and £50 each per year. She would mend their clothes as well. It was as good a place as Schuyler could put them, she thought.[33] The squire's family was also continuing to grow. Mrs. Schuyler was delivered of another son, Philip Jeremiah, in January.

However, the assembly was not summoned by the governor until October, and during the spring and summer Schuyler busied himself with his property and with the settlement of the sales of flour to the deputy commissary at Crown Point. He advised the Livingstons about their inquiries regarding the value of lands that they wished to sell. He visited Governor Moore, who came up to Albany for the purpose of settling an Indian boundary. He corresponded with William Smith, Jr., his attorney, respecting a mortgage and the matter of advancing funds to Walter Livingston and to Dr. John Cochran, his brother-in-law. Smith also had advice to offer about the approaching assembly session and the necessity of better support for the judiciary. It was Smith, too, who evidently kept Schuyler informed of affairs in the mother country—elections, ministerial alignments, and the John Wilkes controversy.[34]

---

[32] Becker, *Political Parties*, p. 63.

[33] Elizabeth Livingston to Schuyler, April 5, 1768. NYPL, Schuyler Papers Box 23.

[34] William Smith, Jr., Elizabeth, Robert J., and Peter R. Livingston to Schuyler, April 12, 1768; Henry Moore to Schuyler, May 16, 1768; Robert Leake to Schuyler, June 20, 1768. NYPL, Schuyler Papers Box 23. William Smith, Jr., *et al.*, to Schuyler, April 21, 1768, and Smith to Schuyler, May 30, 1768. NYSL, Schuyler Papers.

The thirtieth New York Assembly opened its session in October, 1768, with an ordinary calm. But the quiet was punctuated more and more by periodic eruptions until the final swell exploded with dissolution and an order for new elections. Its proceedings were marked both by factional struggles for local dominance and by larger questions of protest against effects of imperial economic and financial legislation. Philip Schuyler was a veritable personification of the shift in temper and interest of the body. He began the session with routine work and ended it threatened by a duel. He proved himself essentially loyal to the regime, and yet not unwilling to criticize. There were issues which gave no appearance of serious controversial division, while others drew factional lines and deepened the cleavage in each successive session until a revolutionary third party finally seized the initiative from the assembly factions and forced them to make clearer choices on the fundamental disputes over rights and power.

The novice assemblyman was in his seat on October 27, 1768, when the newly elected house met, seven months after the polling. Both assembly and council had chambers in the New York city hall, a short walk east of Trinity Church, at the juncture of Broad and Wall streets. Closer to Fort George, and at the opposite end of Broad Street from city hall, stood the Exchange, the meeting place of extralegal assemblages that were yet to come—and to replace the assembly's own functions. The governor's headquarters were in Fort George, south of the assembly chambers, and the burden of communications between the two centers was shared by turns among assemblymen in much the same fashion as they were obliged to carry legislation to and from the council.

On October 27, Justice William Smith, Sr., "qualified" the members of the assembly and administered their oaths. Governor Moore summoned them to the council chamber and ordered them to name a speaker by the following day at one o'clock. On October 28 the house displayed a notable lack of factionalism by unanimously selecting Philip Livingston and presenting him to the governor, who accepted him and then made a speech outlining the work to be done.[35] Moore informed the legislature that the Board of Trade had now given the control of the Indian trade to the colonies, and this called for special enactments. The slow pace with which the assembly responded to this new responsibility suggested that, for all their desire to regulate such

---

[35] Assembly Journals, Oct. 27, 28, 1768. C.O. 5/1100:53–54.

matters locally, the colonists were really quite unprepared to move expeditiously in assuming full self-government. The governor asked for legislation to prevent settlements beyond a line to be agreed upon by the Indians and to punish fraudulent trading. Pointing out the economies affected with royal troop supply, the governor expected further appropriate sums to be voted.[36] There was very little of anything controversial in this or in the assembly's respectful reply to the governor's address. The house promised salutary measures for the Indian trade, but declined a request for relief to sufferers in Montreal, which had lately been ravaged by a great fire. "The impoverished State of this Colony," said the assembly, "will not permit us to lay any additional Burthens on our Constituents. . . ." [37] It was a hint of things to come.

Much of Philip Schuyler's introduction to the work of the assembly consisted of routine or non-controversial business. He was a member of the committee on privileges and elections—an apparently ordinary assignment, until the committee became involved in two contested elections which rocked the house. He ran errands, seeing a tardy member "qualified" and given the oath before Justice Robert R. Livingston, waiting on the governor to inquire when he would receive the house and hear its address, or carrying bills to the council for its consideration and action. On occasion he acted as spokesman of the committee of the whole, reporting and summarizing its activities to the house—a clear indication of his forensic abilities. He sponsored several bills for the benefit of his own constituents and successfully saw them through the legislative mill: one for regulating, clearing, and further laying out highways in the county, and several allowing the county to raise money to finance various activities such as the translation and indexing of Dutch records.

Schuyler also offered gestures of loyalty to the royal establishment. He presented a bill for continuing an older statute designed "effectually" to collect the king's quitrents and to partition lands. This later proved personally advantageous, however, when he set about buying lands in 1772 for arrearages in quitrent payments. Nor did Schuyler oppose the voting of £1,800 for troop supply, or the salary bill, liquor excise, and import duties—all supports of the royal government. Indeed, these measures comprised the main business of the assembly,

[36] Moore's speech (printed) to the council and assembly, Oct. 28, 1768. C.O. 5/1099:473–474.

[37] Reply of the assembly to the governor, Nov. 3, 1768. C.O. 5/1099:477.

and there was little to threaten their passage except as peripheral matters arose to interrupt the orderly processes of legislation. But these interruptions provided the fuel for partisan fires.

Schuyler supported Governor Moore as much as he could, consistent with his other interests, for he still had favors to ask. His friend, John Bradstreet, had requests for Indian lands. In November, Bradstreet asked the colonel "please to let the Governor into" the land affair and "take his directions how I must proceed if the Lands will do." Bradstreet advised Schuyler that the assembly should "grant their Aids liberal[l]y & with dispatch" as a means of preparing the security of the frontier—advice with which the colonel appears to have agreed. Bradstreet reminded him that the colony's trade and safety were in danger and that it would be well to lay this matter before the "Gover[n]ment forcibly & soon." He gave Schuyler permission to show his letter to the governor and William Smith, Jr., and in urging him to advocate projects for advancement, Bradstreet suggested "If any Representation goes Home from your Quarter, it would be a good Oppertunity [sic] to do me Service by a Mention of my former Services . . . this Youl [sic] manage if you can as from yourself." [38] Bradstreet was also angling for a military promotion.

As long as the governor was the real center of influence with lands or sinecures to offer, ambitious men turned to him for favors and offered him support. But once they had secured their land titles and won position, their dependence upon him declined noticeably, and they could take a more independent view.[39] Schuyler, like others, tended more and more to identify himself with the assembly, with a faction, and ultimately with the patriot cause. At the same time, he was enhancing his fortunes, and reaping as great a harvest as he could from the fields of patronage and influence. The more he accumulated and the more difficult it became for him to exercise influence the less he cooperated with those in whose hands the power of the establishment rested. His gradual shift away from "the establishment" coincided with the greater measure of independence he had garnered and with the uncertainty of influence with the governors following the death of Sir Henry Moore.

When the assembly began to complain of the Townshend Acts and other imperial legislation, Philip Schuyler joined his voice in protest

[38] Bradstreet to Schuyler, Nov. 15, 17, 1768. See also Bradstreet to Schuyler, [Nov. 29, 1768]. NYPL, Schuyler Papers Box 9.

[39] Becker, *Political Parties*, p. 12.

as much as he dared. It seemed the gesture of a man appealing for support against an opposing faction that first catered to the radical elements to win leverage against the governor and then grew more and more reluctant to resist imperial authority. It seemed the partisan tactic of fighting an opponent's appeals for popularity with the radicals, when indeed that rival's bid for popularity in the debate over "home rule" was a mere subterfuge for entrenching himself in a position of power. Schuyler walked a delicate line, a middle way, that was an essentially cautious approach to factions, the assembly, and to the governor.

One of the sharpest and yet manifestly complex indications of the assembly's growing factionalism came with two election contests in which charges of bribery, corruption, and irregular procedure were raised against De Lancey men. These controversies ran concurrently during the session. One centered on John Morin Scott's charge against James Jauncey, member from the city and county of New York. Another concerned the Westchester Borough seat narrowly won by John De Lancey over Lewis Morris. A third and less important issue arose concerning election riots in Orange County. The incidence of these disputes was clear testimony of the bitterness with which the elections of 1768 had been fought.

On October 29 the assembly called for information on the charges of John De Lancey's improper election, ordered the investigation of James Jauncey's election, and summoned men to answer for the election tumults in Orange County.[40] These matters were properly the business of the committee on privileges and elections—a committee divided four to three along factional lines and reflecting the divergence of southern "De Lancey counties" with the northern "Livingston counties." [41] But the committee's business proved too explosive for the house to allow it complete jurisdiction, and a committee of the whole undertook to settle the disputes.

Within a few days the assembly disposed of the Orange County issue, resolved after an investigation that the sheriff's actions had not jeopardized the validity of the election proceedings and further directed that all petitions on elections be presented to the committee

[40] Assembly Journals, Oct. 29, 1768. C.O. 5/1100:57.

[41] The committee included Zebulon Seaman (Queens), Benjamin Seaman (Richmond), Simon Boerum (Kings), James De Lancey (New York), Abraham Ten Broeck (Rensselaer Manor), George Clinton (Ulster), and Philip Schuyler (Albany). Assembly Journals, Oct. 28, 1768. C.O. 5/1100:56.

on privileges and elections within a fortnight.[42] The Jauncey and De Lancey cases were not disposed of so easily. They dragged on for weeks, the latter until November 18 and the former for a month later.

Day after day Schuyler and the other assemblymen heard testimony. On November 8, John Morin Scott was called in to prove his allegations of the "undue" election of his opponent, James Jauncey. Scott had certain affidavits he wished to offer in evidence. A rousing debate ensued over the question of admitting this evidence, but finally the assembly voted (20 to 5) to refuse them. Schuyler voted in the minority, with Livingston, Henry Wisner, Charles De Witt, and Abraham Ten Broeck. Yet there was no evidence here of much breadth to rigid factionalism; agrarians and upper-county men like Ten Eyck from Albany, George Clinton from Ulster, and Pierre Van Cortlandt of Cortlandt Manor (lower on the Hudson) voted in the De Lancey majority. On November 8 one of the De Lanceys also moved to take Scott's charge of corruption against Jauncey out of the hands of the committee on privileges and elections and into a committee of the whole. The motion carried by an overwhelming majority, only Schuyler and Clinton contending for their committee's jurisdiction, and Ten Eyck and Livingston supporting them.[43]

The committee of the whole continued to consider the Jauncey case from November 8 to 12. In the midst of these proceedings it turned to a determination of John De Lancey's contested Westchester Borough seat, and did not resume hearing the Jauncey dispute until November 21. The Westchester election was complicated by the question of electors' qualifications and the narrow margin by which De Lancey had won his seat. According to the election writ, the returning officer was to take the votes of both freeholders and freemen, but he rejected the votes of all the freemen of the borough who favored Lewis Morris. As De Lancey had but a majority of three votes, the admission of the freemen's votes could well spell his defeat. *The New-York*

[42] Assembly Journals, Nov. 1, 1768. C.O. 5/1100:58–59.

[43] Assembly Journals, Nov. 8, 1768. C.O. 5/1100:65. Jauncey claimed he had refused the offers of forty men in New York City to sell their votes to him. He was accused of loaning money in such a way as to create favorable votes and of persuading his election agent (Nicholas Stokes) to abandon a suit against one Isaac Van Hook if Van Hook would vote for him. Jauncey denied this, but his opponents refused to take the denial seriously. Scott was accused of threatening to sue one man if he would not vote for him, and of contributing to welfare funds of journeymen and carpenters just before the election. Chilton Williamson, *American Suffrage From Property to Democracy, 1760–1860* (Princeton, 1960), pp. 54–55.

Gazette, and the Weekly Mercury reported that the law provided that the assembly franchise depended on a freehold worth £40, except for New York and Albany, where freemen were entitled to vote according to city charter. Three freemen of Westchester Borough with neither real nor personal estates nor any trade, business, or occupation within the borough had attempted to exercise the franchise. Several other ballots were also questioned on the basis of property qualification. And although the election writ had ordered that both freemen and freeholders could vote, this was pronounced contrary to the law.[44] Thus the question was one of interpretation of residency provisions of the electoral law. But it also had partisan implications.

Schuyler saw that the assembly's task now was to determine the validity of a handful of contested votes. Lewis Morris offered testimony against John De Lancey's campaign activities. On the afternoon of November 15 a certain Joshua Billop petitioned to have his name added to the poll list on De Lancey's behalf; Billop maintained he had not voted because Morris informed him he was not qualified. Billop later decided that he was entitled to the franchise after all.[45] On November 17 two crucial questions arose: Should nonresident freemen of Westchester Borough have the right to vote for its burgess? Should resident freemen have the right to vote there also? To both questions the house responded with a resounding negative vote. But to the question of the right of resident freemen to vote, Schuyler and five fellow agrarians (De Witt, Livingston, Clinton, Van Cortlandt, and Ten Broeck) voted aye.[46] Next day five new questions were raised. The first concerned the allowance of the vote of a certain Josiah Briggs who produced evidence of his property qualification as a freeholder—a deed dated eight days before that of the test of the writ for electing the borough representative. The house voted no. It also decided the poll of a second contested elector should not be counted, but that a third elector's vote be confirmed. On each of these questions Philip Schuyler voted with a large majority.[47] But on the questionable polls of two other electors the house vote was narrower and Schuyler voted in the minority against accepting these polls. At this point the house examined the Westchester poll lists, and supposing

[44] *The New-York Gazette, and the Weekly Mercury*, Feb. 29, Mar. 7, 1768. Assembly Journals, Nov. 8–21, 1768. C.O. 5/1100:65–77.
[45] Assembly Journals, Nov. 15, 1768. C.O. 5/1100:70.
[46] Assembly Journals, Nov. 17, 18, 1768. C.O. 5/1100:73–74.
[47] Assembly Journals, Nov. 18, 1768. C.O. 5/1100:74–75.

four more contested votes for Lewis Morris to be valid, without actually determining them, it declared John De Lancey by a majority of one vote had been duly elected representative of the borough. Evidently the assembly thought it needless to determine the validity of more of the polls, as De Lancey had the required majority.[48]

One disputed election resolved, Schuyler and his colleagues turned back their attention to the more controversial Scott-Jauncey case. The longer it dragged, the more bitter it apparently became. From November 21 to December 9 the house heard the arguments. On December 13 it decided to call for a summing up, and the next day by a narrow vote of 12 to 11 the house refused to allow Scott's counsel the last word to Jauncey's case. Again Schuyler found himself in the minority —a group comprised largely of the Livingston agrarians who favored Scott's cause against the 1768 De Lancey victory in New York and elsewhere.[49] For the next few days the two sides summed up their cases. On the sixteenth Peter R. Livingston attempted to instruct the committee of the whole to report the substantial part of the testimony to the house; so much time had been spent in the investigation that some members could not remember all of the evidence, while others had been absent and heard nothing. But Livingston's motion failed (15 to 7), and again Schuyler led his minority with the speaker, Philip Livingston, Peter R. Livingston, and Ten Broeck and Van Cortlandt. When the crucial vote was taken as to the truth of Scott's charge of Jauncey's bribery of electors, however, the factionalism of the house took on a peculiar color. The house voted a resounding (18) no to three ayes—Schuyler, Peter R. Livingston, and Abraham Ten Broeck. Even Jacob Ten Eyck, Schuyler's fellow Albanian, and Pierre Van Cortlandt voted with the majority. Nor was this all. Captain James De Lancey moved "That as Mr. Scott has not made out the Charge of Corruption against Mr. Jauncey, that it be declared . . . frivolous, vexatious, and litigious." But the house refused this kind of backbiting and voted no, again 18 to 3. This time Schuyler stood with the majority, and only James and John De Lancey and Jacob Walton voted aye.[50] These two votes reveal the extreme polarity of the faction

48 Assembly Journals, Nov. 18, 1768. C.O. 5/1100:76.
49 The minority consisted of Schuyler, Ten Eyck, De Witt, Holland, Wisner, Kissam, Philip and Peter R. Livingston, Ten Broeck, Van Cortlandt, and Benjamin Seaman. Assembly Journals, Nov. 21–Dec. 9, Dec. 13, 14, 1768. C.O. 5/1100:77–97, 100.
50 Assembly Journals, Dec. 15–16, 1768. C.O. 5/1100:101–104.

leadership: Schuyler, the Livingstons, and Ten Broeck at one extremity, and the De Lanceys and Jacob Walton at the other, country against city, agrarian against merchant. The rest of the members might tumble between them, falling one way or another, depending on the particular issue presented to the assembly at a particular time.

The contested elections had further consequences. On December 17 the house ordered a committee to draft resolutions to prevent "undue election practices" concerning assemblymen. Eleven days later a resolution was offered that any person or his agent who before any assembly election presented or allowed to be presented to others any money under the guise of wages, or expenses, or meat, drink, entertainment, or gifts, or who promised to give such items in return for his election should be disabled and incapacitated from sitting in the assembly. Votes given to such a candidate would be considered null and void.[51] That very day Peter R. Livingston presented a bill to prevent bribery and corruption in assembly elections. But the session closed so abruptly that any action on the measure was precluded, and the resolves and proposed act died without further ado. It is evident that they were mere protests against partisanship that each faction could make against the other. Neither group would relent in playing the game of which it accused the other of being guilty. A few days before the assembly's dissolution the house resolved that any person who prosecuted another for his testimony to the assembly would be considered guilty of a breach of the body's privileges. Several people claimed they had been arrested by reason of the evidence given in the Scott-Jauncey case. Finally, on December 30 in response to a petition by John Morin Scott, the assembly voted to allow a "scrutiny" of his charges against Jauncey. The members from Kings, Queens, Richmond, and Westchester counties were to sit as a committee of investigation the following February. The bitterness of the factions was to be prolonged and aggravated by new investigations.[52]

When the assembly first convened, Governor Moore had foreseen no difficulties about procuring the annual grant for supplying the troops, nor did the house seriously threaten not to make the grant even though it suddenly turned to considerations of its rights and grievances in December. On November 10, Moore wrote the Earl of Hillsborough

[51] Assembly Journals, Dec. 17, 28, 1768. C.O. 5/1100:105, 117–118.
[52] Assembly Journals, Dec. 30, 1768. C.O. 5/1100:122. No such hearing was held, for the house did not meet in February, and fresh elections removed the reason for further contests.

that he could not say much about the assembly so early in the session, but that he had "hitherto no reason to suppose that my endeavours to serve the Province will prove unsuccessful. . . ." [53] Moore found that the assembly was not as pliant as he might wish.

The assembly's factionalism still was not precise or fixed, but fluctuated—except for the extreme polarity of leadership revealed by the disputed election cases. Even a decision not to open the house to spectators was not made along strict De Lancey-Livingston lines, but quite the contrary. Early in November, Schuyler offered a motion "That the Doors of this House may be from henceforth open under the following Regulations": no one would be admitted without a member's introduction, nor could a member introduce more than one guest at a time; if any member desired the chamber cleared, it should be done at once; visitors must behave quietly without speaking or whispering, and to "stir out of his Place, to the Disturbance of the House" would mean immediate expulsion. These were sound restrictions, to say the least, but Schuyler's proposal proved much too "radical" for the temper of the house whose members were jealous of their independence. Indeed, the plan was a response to the sentiment expressed in the 1768 election broadside of "Philanthropos" which called for the provision of public galleries as a means whereby the people might have easier access to their representatives. If Schuyler favored this in general terms, he also was careful to limit the privilege and to prevent its exercise by those elements who might wish to intimidate the assembly by their attendance. It is more likely, however, that he proposed the measure to test the sincerity of the merchant-members' appeal to the radicals outside the house who, during the election, had suggested that public galleries be provided. Schuyler's motion failed by a vote of 13 to 12. Interestingly, the city members (De Lancey, Jauncey, and Walton) favored the motion, while the colonel's fellow Albanian, Jacob Ten Eyck, and members from agrarian areas like Schenectady Township and Dutchess and Westchester counties were opposed. Still, except for the New York City members, John De Lancey of Westchester Borough and Daniel Kissam of Queens County, Schuyler's group formed along lines reminiscent of the elections of 1768 which had divided the northern and southern counties and had led to the De Lanceys' triumph.[54]

The assembly both surprised the governor and astounded the secre-

[53] Moore to Hillsborough, Nov. 10, 1768. C.O. 5/1099:469.
[54] Assembly Journals, Nov. 3, 1768. C.O. 5/1100:62–63.

tary of state for the American Department, not so much when it addressed petitions to the king and Parliament, but because it dared to insist on reading the Massachusetts Circular Letter and to vote resolutions about the rights and grievances of the colony. Even in these questions of "home rule" it was noticeable that the struggle was more vitally one of "who was to rule at home." This latter struggle was not yet an interclass conflict but rather a contest between elements of a single class.

As an assemblyman, Schuyler faced not only provincial problems but also issues more broadly related to the empire. The first indication of the assembly's renewed concern for the imperial system came on November 8, when the house ordered a committee appointed to draw a petition to the king, a memorial to the Lords and a remonstrance to the Commons. The addresses were to present local opinion regarding the Townshend duties and to request relief from the act to raise a revenue by customs duties.[55] However, even this had partisan possibilities. Calculating politicians might hope to cultivate popular support for criticizing the Townshend Acts through a series of addresses. Yet they need not risk the dangers of objections from London or the governor for acting directly on the Massachusetts Circular Letter which invited the New Yorkers to oppose the measures. Thus, they might not only curry popular favor for asserting rights, but also prevent the dissolution of the assembly—a distinct danger if they endorsed the circular—and increase their chances for enhancing their power later.

But before the committee could compose its assigned papers yet another issue arose to complicate factional alignments. On November 21 the governor reported that, because of a "riot" staged on the evening of November 14, he had offered £50 reward for the conviction of the contrivers of the disturbances.[56] The Sons of Liberty had renewed strong agitation against the Mutiny Act, and the popular dislike and suspicion of the soldiers only increased it. The Sons of Liberty paraded with effigies, intending to burn them, but the magistrates had prevented this several times until, on November 14, the mob proved uncontrollable.[57] Now Governor Moore asked for support in taking steps to prevent future insults to the legislature—affronts

[55] Assembly Journals, Nov. 8, 1768. C.O. 5/1100:66.
[56] Assembly Journals, Nov. 21, 1768. C.O. 5/1100:77.
[57] Becker, *Political Parties*, p. 73. See also Sabine, *Smith Memoirs*, I, 46; *The New-York Gazette, or Weekly Post-Boy*, Dec. 5, 1768.

given a body which had complied earlier with the Mutiny Act and which was even then considering the grant of fresh supplies for the troops.

The following day the assembly agreed to pay the £50 the governor had offered as a reward for convicting the riot leaders.[58] While desiring relief from the Townshend duties, the assembly, like William Smith, Jr., evidently feared that rioting would only "induce the Government to turn a Deaf Ear" to its petitions.[59] Moreover, the house might well fear the popular tumults as intimidation and as a threat to its own independence.

In the council the mercantile interest, led by Oliver De Lancey, John Watts, and Henry Cruger, objected to Moore's action against the popular clamors, despite the concern it shared with the assembly for procuring relief from the Townshend duties. The De Lanceys were using the radicals for support against the governor and against the opposition faction. William Smith, Jr., urged Moore to act. The governor suspected the rioters "were set up by People of Property" with an eye to destroying harmony between himself and the assembly by intimidating the latter.[60] The house received Moore's address on November 21 and immediately named a committee to answer it. Smith coordinated the governor's address with the committee, which was headed by none other than Colonel Schuyler. The colonel immediately left the house and settled his committee in a tavern to draft a reply—an answer which Smith himself had devised and given to him to offer the assembly.

Factionalism rose to a fever pitch. Smith recorded the details of the mere outlines given by the assembly journals. Schuyler "had got my Draft nearly by Heart," he wrote, "& so scrawled out a Draft before the Committee & brought it in [to the house] that Morning [November 21]." The house received the address and ordered it engrossed the next day. One of Schuyler's committee, John Thomas, had opposed the address in the committee, and "having been visited by the Sons of Liberty . . . he . . . moved to have it rejected." [61] Thomas' motion was offered on November 23, but the assembly refused to reject the address by a vote of 17 to 5, the two De Lanceys, Jacob Walton, Daniel Kissam, and Thomas forming the minority.[62]

58 Assembly Journals, Nov. 22, 1768. C.O. 5/1100:78.
59 Sabine, *Smith Memoirs*, I, 46.
60 *Ibid.*, p. 47.
61 *Ibid.*
62 Assembly Journals, Nov. 23, 1768. C.O. 5/1100:79.

By this maneuver the De Lanceys gave proof of what William Smith, Jr., had been telling the governor all the while—proof that they wanted to lead the mob in disturbing his administration. Now they had "lost Credit also with the weighty Citizens who all disapproved the Riot. . . . If they had acted cunningly," Smith exulted, "they should knowing the sense of the House the Night before have absented themselves & not exposed their Weakness," but now their position was recorded in the journals for all to see. Nor was this the full extent of the current party furor. James De Lancey had offered resolutions "in high Terms" for a committee to correspond with other assemblies. "Schuyler shewed them to the Govr.," and Smith, together with John Morin Scott, who had been contesting James Jauncey's assembly seat, drew up a set of more temperate resolutions, which the house then preferred to De Lancey's. The four city members (De Lancey, Jauncey, Walton, Philip Livingston) heretofore comprised the committee for corresponding with the New York agent in London, but the new resolves enlarged the committee to nine, and by "this Stroke" De Lancey, Walton, and Jauncey could not "engross the Correspondence—a great Trust, as they represent & characterize the whole Province . . . & by a short Cutt thro the Agent to the Ministers have Power to make Bargains with the Crown for their own Advancement." [63] Schuyler could have rejoiced no less than Smith over the tactics employed against the De Lancey forces.

The assembly's address to Governor Moore was the voice of a conservative faction denouncing the De Lanceys' courtship of the radicals out of doors who opposed the imperial measures and who objected to the last assembly's compliance with the Mutiny Act and to the present body's inclination to vote new supplies for the troops. In its address the assembly mentioned its distress under the new duties, yet it said, "we are far from conceiving, that violent and tumultuous Proceedings, will have any Tendency to promote suitable Redress." The governor was informed of the preparation of addresses to the king and Parliament and of the assembly's abhorrence of the tumult produced by a very few persons of the "lowest class." The assembly, he could be assured, would concur in every measure conducive to good order. [64]

This profession of loyalty might have been reassuring had it ended there. But the assembly proceeded to consider resolutions asserting the colony's rights against the Townshend Acts. These, too, offered

[63] Sabine, *Smith Memoirs*, I, 47–48.
[64] Assembly Journals, Nov. 23, 1768. C.O. 5/1100:80.

fresh occasion for factionalism to run rampant and for strains between colony and empire to emerge. Indeed, political maneuvering seemed to take precedence over political philosophy as partisans used a constitutional argument between the colonies and Britain to further their local political ends. In the midst of the maneuvering Schuyler worked energetically to thwart the De Lanceys. The De Lancey forces had been put off earlier in the session when they had proposed the reading of the Massachusetts Circular Letter, a missive urging concerted action against the Townshend Acts. By arrangement the New York City members received instructions from their constituents to have the circular letter read and, in the event the assembly voted money for the troops, they were to procure a resolution that only the assembly had the right to tax its constituents. In this they eventually succeeded, but the threat to force these measures early in the session also threatened the house with dissolution.

The De Lanceys threatened to move a reading of the circular letter as a way of feeling the pulse of the house. If a majority were opposed to the reading, the cabal by its motion might monopolize credit and popularity with the radicals for themselves. It was excellent strategy to make a proposal, have the opposition vote it down, and then expose them to the popular odium. These connivings were remembered almost two years later when they were recorded and re-presented to the political community in a broadside issued by the Livingstons' "Watchman." The De Lanceys having repeatedly threatened to have the Massachusetts letter read, "many of the members saw through the artifice, which greatly incensed them, upon which Col. Sch—yl—r, a gentleman of great independency of spirit and a true Son of Liberty, being unable any longer to bear the duplicity of those political hypocrites got up and observed to the house that he was as determined to read the Circular Letter, and make resolutions, asserting the rights of the people of the colony, as any Gentleman in the house," but he warned that the welfare of the colony should be put first. The colonel "conceived it most eligible, to go through the business of the session, that the colony might not suffer for the want of the necessary and annual laws. . . ." Following the completion of this business, the resolves could then be considered, and this "would as well serve the cause of Liberty, as if they were made at the expense of the loss of those laws." If the assembly dared consider the circular letter first, Schuyler warned, it would surely be dissolved. This he had learned from the governor himself. In a circular letter of his own, Lord Hillsborough had ordered the colonial executives to prevent their assemblies from endorsing the Massachusetts circular, by dissolution if necessary. The New York City members proposed to treat the former with contempt, and the latter with respect. With the irony of feigned diffidence and with determination that the De Lanceys should not capture popular support by posing as sympathizers with the radicals out of doors, Schuyler proposed that if the house were determined to read the letter first, the members ought to save their own time and their constituents' money by getting on with it at once. Therefore, he moved that the circular be read immediately and that an answer be given to it.[65]

Schuyler's motion to read the Massachusetts Circular Letter frightened the De Lanceys and rallied support to the colonel's position. Perhaps the De Lanceys desired a dissolution in hopes that fresh elections would enable them to increase their power in the house; getting the assembly to approve of the Massachusetts letter and a series of constitutional resolves would be defiance of Lord Hillsborough's orders and bring such a dissolution. Of course any defense of American rights would be popular with the radicals. On the other hand, the De Lanceys may well have feared the risks of another election if the Livingstons could improve their reputation by support of a popular cause. Perhaps the De Lanceys wished only to cultivate credit from the Sons of Liberty by championing the cause of Massachusetts. Almost certainly the Livingstons were not willing to face the risks of an election, for unless they could embellish their public image, they faced the dangers of still further losses at the polls. But it appeared to Colonel Schuyler that the house for the most part wanted to take no notice of the instructions to the New York City members, but that most of them would support a motion to consider the circular "for Fear of the Populace. . . ." When Schuyler "put their Mettle to the Trial and exposed them to the utmost Contempt & Disgust of the House, . . . the House was thrown into the utmost Confusion." De Lancey was thunderstruck by losing the honor of making the motion and by the disgrace of opposing it out of fear of a dissolution. He begged to postpone the matter for several days on the grounds that

[65] "The Watchman, No. 5," a supplementary broadside to Holt's New-York Journal, printed April 21, 1770, and also printed as a supplement to the Pennsylvania Journal, May 3, 1770. See also Robert R. Livingston to Robert Livingston, Dec. 12, 1768. NYPL, Bancroft Collections: Transcripts, Livingston Papers, p. 19; Sabine, Smith Memoirs, I, 48.

attendance was then thin. The panic and surprise inclined the members to take the time, and Schuyler consented.[66] Thus he was "persuaded" to postpone the motion. The movement was so deftly made and so potentially explosive that even the journals record nothing of the maneuvering. When the house later ordered the Massachusetts letter read and considered, it was done in such a way that no member could win credit for it. Colonel Schuyler helped arrange that, too.

The day following the report of the committees on the addresses to the king and Parliament, Schuyler and William Smith, Jr., discussed the tactics by which they had forced a delay on the Massachusetts Circular Letter. Smith thought that Schuyler should have pushed his motion through to a division instead of allowing a postponement, for by doing so he would have denied the De Lanceys time for a counterplot against the motion. Schuyler agreed but feared his motion "would be attributed to a Desire to prevent the Judgement of the House on Mr Scott's Charge of Corruption agt. Jauncey & his own Character [would thus] suffer for Partiality." The Scott-Jauncey case was running concurrently with the assembly's weightier consideration, and Schuyler might well have feared losing himself in a political labyrinth, as he had once confided to a friend.[67]

On December 13, after the delay agreed upon, Schuyler called for his motion to read the Massachusetts Circular Letter, and "after much Altercation an Agreemt. was ent[e]red into unanimously that his Motion should be withdrawn. . . ." It was decided, however, that following completion of the assembly's regular business and the passage of acts by the governor, the clerk should "enter the Motion for a Letter to Boston as unanimously carried together with the Constitutional Resolves and so the Dissolution was to be expected and all the Members to fare alike in Point of Reputation." [68] Here then, was an assembly unanimous in its determination to pass resolves and petitions of protest, unanimous in its sympathy for the position of Massachusetts, but factionally split in opinion as to the proper moment to take action; the difference in selecting the time was calculated to solicit the favor of certain local elements or rebuff them. Clearly, the divisions within New York at this point were not determined by philosophies of home rule, but by the more practical issue of which

[66] Sabine, *Smith Memoirs*, I, 48–49. See also "The Watchman, No. 5."

[67] *Ibid.* See also Schuyler to Philip Ver Planck, Mar. 7, 1768. Baxter, *A Godchild of Washington*, p. 63.

[68] Sabine, *Smith Memoirs*, I, 49.

of two segments of a privileged governing class was to rule at home—
to savor the greater share of power and popularity.

After a committee of the whole had considered resolutions on the
recent acts of Parliament and on the rights of the king's subjects
(November 24–December 9) the house established committees to formulate addresses to the king, Lords, and Commons. At first but one
committee was named to draft the three papers, but its work was rejected by the house, and the De Lanceys agreed to add to its membership and to divide it into three committees, especially since one member was ill and another had died.[69] On December 9, Eleazer Miller
of Suffolk, Pierre Van Cortlandt of Cortlandt Manor, Peter R. Livingston of Livingston Manor, and Philip Schuyler were appointed a
committee to draft a memorial to the House of Lords. Speaker Philip
Livingston himself took charge of amending the petition to the king,
and Schuyler asked William Smith, Jr., to help make a new draft of
the memorial to the Lords (which was then styled a petition). Even
though Schuyler advocated the idea, Smith's request for an American
parliament or "Convention of Deputies" which would grant supplies
to fill royal requisitions was stricken from the memorial. On December 12 the various committees reported their papers to the house,
which approved them and ordered them engrossed. These completed,
the committee of the whole continued consideration of the resolutions on rights and grievances.[70]

From these proceedings in the assembly Schuyler could observe a
gradual shift of attention from purely local problems to the expression of complaints aimed at the imperial government. The assembly
dropped the provision bill momentarily to address statements to the
king and Parliament, papers which in fact proved offensive to the
ministry in London, although they were carefully couched in respectful language. Inasmuch as these papers reveal political thought then
current, and especially Schuyler's views as found in the petition to
the Lords, we may consider briefly both their content and their cause.

In the petition to the Lords the assembly complained that the laws
of trade were causing commerce to languish, that the jury system was

[69] *Ibid.* Assembly Journals, Nov. 24, 1768. C.O. 5/1100:84.

[70] Sabine, *Smith Memoirs*, I, 49. Smith reported that he and William Livingston
refused any legal counsel for drawing up the papers until their "Friends were . . .
added to the Committees. . . ." Smith then helped with the memorial to the Lords
and William Livingston drew up the petition to the king. See also Assembly Journals,
Dec. 9, 12, 15, 16, 17, 1768. C.O. 5/1100:96, 100–103, 105.

threatened by the extension of admiralty court jurisdiction to penalties, forfeitures and trespasses on the land, and that it was feared the colony was about to lose its legislative independence. Since the Stamp Act crisis, the petitioners complained, "our Confidence in the Tenderness of Great Britain seems to have suffered a very sensible abatement." The pre-1765 tranquillity had never been restored. Supposing their grievances had arisen accidentally and without design, the assembly avowed the colony had endured them well. But the Townshend duties for raising a revenue were too much to bear, and the Lords were requested to grant "such Relief, as may most effectually conduce to the joint prosperity of Great Britain and all her dependent dominions." [71]

To both king and the Commons the assembly professed no desire for "Independency," but insisted that it was *"not Essential"* that Parliament have the taxing power in order "to preserve the just Dependance [sic] of the Colonies." The levy of taxes such as the Townshend duties, they felt, was an infringement of an ancient right, a subversion of their "natural & constitutional Rights." And the act suspending New York's legislative power until the assembly complied with the Mutiny Act was even more alarming—yet the Restraining Act had never operated even for a day. However, the assembly grumbled that the act implied an undeserved censure upon New York representatives. Yet it assured the king that it did not claim exemption from *all* taxes except those laid by their own representatives. Taxation for the regulation of trade was permissible. But duties levied for the sole purpose of raising a revenue were "utterly Subversive of their Constitutional Rights" because New York neither was nor could be represented "equally or effectually" in Parliament.[72]

The grievances expressed in these addresses surprised both Governor Moore and the secretary of state, the Earl of Hillsborough. The Restraining Act had never gone into effect because New York had voted supplies. The provisioning of the troops had been largely settled, and "the jury system was as safe as at any time since the sugar act." Even the Townshend duties had been collected for over a year without difficulty and "almost without complaint." [73] Why then did the assembly suddenly display such an apparent change of front?

[71] "Petition to the Lords, Dec. 17, 1768." C.O. 5/1100:13–18.
[72] "Petition to the King" and "Remonstrance to the Commons," both dated Dec. 17, 1768. C.O. 5/1100:5–10, 21–24. Italics added.
[73] Becker, *Political Parties*, pp. 64–65.

The question is difficult to answer. Yet there are two evident clues. One is the striking change in general attitude in the second half of 1768, and the other is the ever-present force of assembly partisanship. New York merchants and traders signed a stringent non-importation agreement in August, binding themselves to countermand orders sent to England after August 15 and to halt the import of British goods after November 1 unless the Townshend duties should be removed. This opposition seems to have reflected discontent with the Parliamentary limitation of paper currency emission more than with the Townshend duties themselves. In view of the assembly's subsequent drive to procure new emissions of bills of credit, the discontent with the restrictions appears all the more logical a reason for action in the fall of 1768. As of that time the paper money issues of 1758, 1759, and 1760 were to be retired. Even though the Board of Trade agreed to allow New York a new issue of £260,000 without making the bills legal tender, the assembly felt that this was no concession at all. In the summer of 1768 the new Board of Customs at Boston "instructed the collector at New York to accept nothing but coin in payment of duties. Unfortunately there was no coin in the colony; because of this shortage, property began to decline in value and widespread hardship seemed certain." [74] Even Governor Moore had told the Board of Trade that the retirement of paper currency issues, together with the small silver supply, would leave the country without a sufficient medium for commerce.[75] The provincial assembly delayed action on printing paper currency, hoping the ministry would make further concessions. When, therefore, the assembly began to formulate complaints in December, 1768, it mirrored the conditions that had been cumulative: the retirement of the old currency without provision for the new issue permitted them, and the operation of the commercial duties that required payment in silver. Yet the incidence of partisanship in the formulation of complaints indicates there was no clear-cut distinction between local factional struggles for power and the broader issues of "home rule" which the Townshend, Currency, Mutiny, and Restraining acts entailed.

When one takes into account the recurring factional divisions in the assembly, it appears that the De Lanceys may also have led the house to a consideration of grievances and presentations of addresses to the king and Parliament for partisan reasons. By the earlier diffi-

[74] Flick, III, 203. See also Becker, *Political Parties*, pp. 65–69.
[75] *Ibid.*, p. 70.

culties of dealing with New York City rioters, the De Lanceys sought both popularity with the radicals out of doors (who were demonstrating against the Townshend duties) and influence with the governor by demonstrating to him their power to create difficulties. Both Sir Henry Moore and William Smith, Jr., suspected them of planning to destroy the harmony within the branches of government by intimidation of the assembly. And it was Philip Schuyler who sought to check the De Lanceys when they proposed to denounce the Restraining Act in more vigorous terms than were passed. Again, it was Schuyler who reported to Governor Moore the resolves by which the De Lanceys offered "in high terms" to establish a committee to correspond with all the assemblies on the continent. The colonel then suggested resolves of his own by which the committee to correspond with the New York agent was taken from the exclusive control of the New York City members—who were De Lanceys.[76]

The petitions forwarded to London were not the last of the assembly's complaints. The house went a step further in voicing its dissatisfaction and voted a series of resolves asserting colonial rights. It thereby invited its own dissolution.

Once the addresses to the king and Parliament were passed, the assembly turned to consider appropriations. On December 23 it voted £1,800 for the troops, and then took up the salary bill. After the Christmas recess the De Lancey-Livingston factionalism again appeared, this time on the salary provisions. On December 28, Captain De Lancey proposed postponing any salary measures until the governor should give assent to other bills. But in this he was thwarted by the leadership of Schuyler's clique, which carried the report on the salary bill without further delay. Governor Moore was embittered with the De Lanceys. "Towards the conclusion of the Session," he wrote, "they shewed plainly what their real intentions were, by opposing the support bill, without any Cause being assigned for such a proceeding. . . ." They intended to enjoy greater control by forcing the rest of the assembly to "Measures which they never wished to see adopted, but had not Resolution enough to oppose. . . . The same Faction was particularly instrumental in keeping up a Heat in the House which would not otherwise have prevailed. . . ." The essential business of the assembly had been completed. In accordance with the agreement made earlier, the clerk now proceeded to "enter the Mo-

[76] Sabine, *Smith Memoirs*, I, 46–49. See also Assembly Journals, Dec. 31, 1768: C.O. 5/1100:124; and Becker, *Political Parties*, pp. 69–71.

tion" for an answer to the Massachusetts Circular Letter, and in committee of the whole the house replied to the circular and turned to resolutions regarding the infringed rights of the king's subjects.[77]

These resolves were based on the same conditions which produced the earlier addresses to the king and Parliament—the "economic distress resulting from the financial stringency . . . the popular suspicion and dislike of the soldiers resulting from a quarrel" between Governor Moore and General Thomas Gage about precedence, and "the renewal of radical agitation against the mutiny act. . . ."[78] Again a certain amount of partisanship appeared in the adoption of the resolves. These resolutions were considered seditious. They were certainly a challenge to the authority of the imperial government and to Parliamentary sovereignty. Their provisions were contentious. First was the blow struck against the Townshend duties: "no Tax . . . can, or ought to be imposed or levied upon the Persons, Estates, or Property of his Majesty's good Subjects within this Colony, but of their free Gift, by their Representatives lawfully convened in General Assembly." Second came an objection to the Restraining Act, which had never operated to suspend the legislative powers of the assembly because the house met the requirements of voting troop supply: "the Power and Authority of the said Legislature, cannot lawfully or constitutionally be suspended, abridged, abrogated, or annulled by any power" except by prorogation and dissolution. Then followed an assertion of right to respond to the Massachusetts Circular Letter—the action which produced the assembly's dissolution: "this House has an undoubted Right to correspond and consult with any of the neighboring Colonies, or with any other of his Majesty's Subjects out of this Colony . . . either individually or collectively, on any Matter. . . ." The assembly ordered the appointment of a larger committee to correspond with the agent in London.[79]

When Captain De Lancey moved to strengthen the resolve against the Restraining Act, Colonel Schuyler's faction carried the assembly against it. De Lancey proposed that they declare the act "a high

[77] Assembly Journals, Dec. 23, 28, 31, 1768. C.O. 5/1100:110, 119, 123–125. Moore to Hillsborough, Jan. 4, 1769. C.O. 5/1138:42–46.

[78] Becker, *Political Parties*, p. 73. For the description of the distresses see pp. 70–73. Their incidence was reported in the New York newspapers and in Governor Moore's correspondence with the Board of Trade and the secretaries of state for the American Department, Lord Shelburne and Lord Hillsborough.

[79] Assembly Journals, Dec. 31, 1768. C.O. 5/1100:123.

Infringement of the Freedom of the Inhabitants" of New York which tended "to deprive them of their natural and constitutional Rights and Privileges." By a vote of 17 to 6 the house decided this was unnecessary; De Lancey's proposal was already substantially implied in the resolution stating the assembly's right of correspondence.[80]

By these actions the members were inviting Governor Moore to dissolve the house—but not until he had called them to the council chamber, where he gave his assent to thirty bills. Included were the salary bill and the grant of £1,800 for the troops.

– 3 –

COLONEL SCHUYLER AND MR. WALTON GO OUT WITH PISTOLS

BEFORE the assembly's dissolution on January 2, 1769, Philip Schuyler found himself the very particular and personal object of factionalism—the "intemperate Heat" with which the governor said the assembly had been smitten. The colonel and another member of the house, Jacob Walton, threatened each other with a duel.

It is difficult to determine precisely what were the grounds for issuing a challenge. No accounts of the affair reached the provincial newspapers, though mention of it was made in private correspondence, and doubtless there was much talk of it in private circles. Walton was a member from New York City. He was a merchant. On those two counts he was Schuyler's opponent, for the colonel was a northern county man and an agrarian. Moreover, Walton was a De Lancey follower. On only one vote recorded in the assembly journals was Walton in agreement with Schuyler—the question of opening the house to visitors. On all others they were partisan foes, but especially in the bitter Scott-Jauncey election contest and on the question of supporting the governor against city rioters, when the De Lanceys were courting the support of tumultuous radicals as a means of political leverage. In addition, one of the Walton family, William, was a member of the council (1758–1768), and from that point he and Jacob had obstructed petitions for land on which Schuyler himself had designs. In February, 1768, Governor Moore had written Schuyler of the Waltons' claims that they had permission to buy these lands as early as 1762. There was no way for the Saratoga landlord and speculator

80 Assembly Journals, Dec. 31, 1768. C.O. 5/1100:124–125.

to procure what he wanted except to allow the Waltons a share in the territory.[81]

Aside from these general reasons for animosity, the personalities of the principals themselves probably clashed. Schuyler had a lofty, perhaps an overweeningly prideful, concept of honor which could lead him to precipitous action. Yet so serious a gesture as a summons to duel probably resulted more from an extended series of irritating circumstances. Schuyler once wrote to a correspondent that "A Man's Character ought not to be sported with, and he that suffers Stains to lay on it with Impunity really deserves none—nor will he long enjoy one." [82] Perhaps Walton probed the colonel's sensitivity at too delicate a point. Moreover, Schuyler was a partisan. One of the governor's council members, Hugh Wallace, said that he had an "arbitrary, & overbearing, bul[lying] manner," and whatever the measure of Wallace's own partisanship or partiality, his estimation was to some degree true.[83] Another, more independent, observer—a Schuyler admirer—remarked that Schuyler's temperament was arduous and his feeling vehement.[84] The trenchant eruptions during the recent session did nothing to allay tempers, and Walton could not have been much different in his "heat" and temperament than Schuyler, since he got into such serious trouble with the colonel. It does not appear which one made the challenge. "Colo Schuyler & Mr. Walton went out with Pistolls but did no more, as Friends interposed," wrote Hugh Wallace to Sir William Johnson. Little more of the record has survived for us to know exactly what happened. Just before the governor dissolved the assembly on the afternoon of January 2, the house ordered Mayor Whitehead Hicks and Alderman Elias Desbrosses of New York City to appear next day "to shew what Cause they had to bind over" Schuyler and Walton to the peace.[85] The steps taken for dueling were

81 Moore to Schuyler, Feb. 28, 1768. NYPL, Schuyler Papers Box 23.

82 Schuyler to John Morgan, Sept. 16, 1776. NYPL, Schuyler Papers: Letter Book, 1776, p. 433.

83 Wallace to Sir William Johnson, Jan. 7, 1769. Sir William Johnson Papers, VI, 570–571.

84 James Kent, "An Anniversary Discourse Delivered Before the New-York Historical Society, December 6, 1828" (New York, 1829), p. 39. Kent referred to Schuyler (then in his old age) as being noted for his "constitutional ardour of temperament and vehemence of feeling" in his younger days.

85 Wallace to Sir William Johnson, May 15, 1769. Sir William Johnson Papers, VI, 758. Assembly Journals, Jan. 2, 1769. C.O. 5/1100:128.

a disturbance of the peace but the house was jealous for its members' freedom. Here the matter was dropped.

For Schuyler and others the session had been hectic, but on January 2, the governor called a temporary halt to this excitement by summoning the assembly to the council chamber. He was forced to dissolve them because of the "extraordinary nature" of the resolves passed on December 31, and he could no longer delay his action. Moore told the members he hoped their presentations to the king and Parliament were "termed" decently and respectfully; he promised to represent their proceedings to the ministry in a favorable light in order to prevent adverse misconceptions. Notwithstanding the house's "intemperate Heat," he had in general a "good opinion" of its character and work.[86] For the second time within a year the assembly factions were forced to submit to an election. This time the De Lanceys were to win an even greater ascendancy.

Philip Schuyler proved himself both a partisan and a loyal supporter of the governor in his first encounters with the provincial legislature. He had fought the De Lancey interests with vigor in the Jauncey and De Lancey election disputes, in the vote to support the governor's action against the radical rioters who favored the De Lanceys, and in the question of delaying the salary bill until the governor had passed other assembly measures. The colonel had resisted De Lancey's attempt to strengthen the resolve aimed at the Restraining Act. He insisted on a delicate approach to obtain redress from Parliament and abhorred the use of violence as a means of protest. Schuyler's good sense and responsible nature prompted him to procure a delay in the assembly's consideration of the Massachusetts Circular Letter lest it bring dissolution and leave the colony without legislation and appropriations until another session. Nor did he propose to make the province's position odious to the ministry at a time when it might consider granting relief from the Townshend duties, provided New York continued to do its duty by the Mutiny Act. The colonel supported the government's interest in maintaining collection of royal quitrents, but by this token he later was able to take advantage of the law to purchase lands put on the auction block for nonpayment of quitrents. And yet Schuyler was not wholly willing to accept imperial regulations without murmur. His role in framing the addresses to the king and Parliament and the resolves on December 31

[86] Assembly Journals, Jan. 2, 1769. C.O. 5/1100:129–130.

contributed to the governor's obligation to dissolve the assembly.[87] He did not, as he once feared he might, lose himself in the political labyrinth. Instead, Schuyler had passed his assembly novitiate, and drawn his first real breath of political life. To the Livingston forces the colonel proved himself a "gentleman of great independency of spirit and a true Son of Liberty"—a *true* son, they believed, was no radical. Subsequent sessions of the assembly proved his "independency of spirit," altered and mixed his support of the royal establishment, and led Schuyler step by step toward a position in which he ultimately found himself fighting in a great war for independence. This he protested at the outset was not what he wanted. Problems of imperial administration, added to the partisan conflicts in which he participated led him to choose a local loyalty and to oppose the empire whose cause the De Lancey faction embraced and against which they refused to allow as effective a criticism as Philip Schuyler preferred.

[87] Lossing, I, 233, says Schuyler was probably the author of the Dec. 31 resolves. If he was not, he nevertheless appears to have been active in procuring their adoption.

CHAPTER V

The Emergence of a Partisan Leader

THERE IS perhaps a clue to Philip Schuyler's attitude to public life before 1775, a hint of his development from provincial partisan to the patriot in revolution, given in a letter he addressed to Congress in 1776. "Had I considered meerly my own Inclinations," he wrote, "I should not have ventured on the Storms of Public Life, well knowing that my Want of Abilities would expose me to a Thousand Difficulties & deprive me of the Inestimable Comforts of Domestic Life. . . ." These were the words of a rebel general; yet how revealing they are of his civilian and political occupations! Before 1768, Schuyler had been content to conduct his private affairs and was reluctant to leave Saratoga for the assembly. But once into the political current, only briefly did he seriously entertain an inclination to leave it, and that was at the election held in 1769. He said to Congress in 1776 that he had taken his military position "well knowing . . . that I should be envied by those weak Minds who are dazzled with Power but have not Elevation of Sentiment enough to conceive that to some Men It has no Charms." [1] This was strange talk for a man who had seemed anything but disinterested in provincial politics. His knowledge of the envy of "weak Minds" without "Elevation of Sentiment" and men "dazzled with Power" came very largely from his experiences in the colonial assembly. Yet whatever partisanship he displayed, Schuyler showed himself a man of some philosophy, idealism, and what he termed, "Elevation of Sentiment." We must note these characteristics in the last sessions of New York's provincial assembly as well as the partisanship that he displayed there.

– 1 –

THE ELECTIONS OF 1769

IN RETALIATION for the passage of resolutions against the imperial government and for reading the Massachusetts Circular Letter in di-

[1] Schuyler to the President of Congress, Feb. 20, 1776. NYPL, Schuyler Papers, Letterbook 1775–1776, p. 368.

rect contravention to the secretary of state's instructions, Governor Moore dissolved the New York Assembly on January 2, 1769, and ordered new elections. The campaign that followed was fought on the old religious battlefield of Anglican versus Presbyterian, and the Livingstons "prepared for a stern ordeal but a victorious issue." [2] The ordeal proved more certain than the victory. One newspaper did not doubt "but the same Members who have in a Capital Instance, acted so highly to the Satisfaction of their Constituents, and made such an honourable Exit, will be re-elected." [3] As it happened, the province generally approved the old assembly's conduct by returning most of its members. However, the Livingston faction almost entirely collapsed in the face of the De Lancey onslaught that followed the election. The contest of 1769 also marked the appearance of the mass meeting as a distinctive political device. Added to the basic feud between Livingston and De Lancey, or Presbyterian and Episcopalian, was the issue of British control. On the surface this perplexing combination of personal and partisan contests with questions of principle [4] suggests that New Yorkers were more concerned with imperial affairs at the time than they actually were. The election and the subsequent partisan expulsion of the De Lanceys' opponents from the assembly were but additional evidence that politics in New York were not centered so much on imperial questions of state as they were based fundamentally on partisan struggles for power. There was little disagreement about the former assembly's expressions regarding rights and grievances and the imperial program, but the disagreement about who was to control the assembly was sharp.

The election contest of 1769 was more bitter than that of 1768, and the De Lancey-Episcopalian victory considerably reduced the whiggish opposition. Yet what remained of the minority was vocal, although still fundamentally conservative. But the De Lanceys became so conservative in the long run that the assembly provided less and less effective "leadership in the campaign against parliamentary aggression. . . ." Had it been otherwise, there might have been no need for extralegal committees until much later, and New York might "have been even slower . . . to arrive at the decision to declare independence." [5] A protesting minority headed by Philip Schuyler was slowly

2 Dangerfield, *Livingston*, p. 39.
3 *The New-York Gazette, or Weekly Post-Boy*, Jan. 9, 1769.
4 Becker, "Nominations in Colonial New York," p. 274.
5 Spaulding, *George Clinton*, p. 25.

but steadily driven into the arms of the radicals, and it was this leaven which worked to modify the radicals' movement until the state constitution of 1777 finally solidified the old conservative agrarians' influence—the middle ground between the De Lancey right and the radical left.

The religious heats of the 1769 elections were apparent in a number of ways. New Yorkers were presented a vitriolic broadside offering "Reasons For the present glorious combination of the dissenters . . . against the further encroachments and strategems of the episcopalians." [6] The reasons were numerous and minute. They comprised a lengthy list of incidents as ancient as 1693, when a law established "episcopacy" in the four lower counties under the pretense of supporting a ministry. In 1704 the wardens and vestry of Trinity Church had won the privilege of calling their rector instead of allowing the general Anglican populace of the city to help select him. The Episcopalians had seized possession of a Presbyterian church at Jamaica. Presbyterian ministers had been prosecuted for preaching without the governor's license. The Episcopalians had persuaded the assembly to appropriate money for a church college. They opposed Lutheran and Presbyterian applications for chartering their own churches, and they engrossed positions on the governor's council. They had tried to ruin the Dutch church by preventing the introduction of English preaching, thereby hoping to drive its non-Dutch-speaking communicants elsewhere. The broadside charged the Episcopalians with designs of introducing "that curse of curses an American Bishop" with all his spiritual courts and great power, and with refusing dissenters' overtures to nominate two of the city's four candidates to serve in the assembly. If the dissenters raised such heated protests, it was because they opposed the politics of the Established Church, its domineering spirit, its pride and thirst for universal domination. So the dissenters charged. But it would be a mistake to interpret the religious element in the elections as any real issue or as anything other than practical politics. Both family factions seemed to understand and accept the value of appeals to such prejudices.

For their part, the De Lanceys referred to their "presbyterian" opponents with no less charity. "Damn them all," wrote John Wether-

[6] Broadside, Jan. 1769. "Reasons For the present glorious combination of the dissenters in this city, against the further encroachments and strategems of the episcopalians, from a brief recollection of what the latter have already done, to exalt their own party on the ruins of every other religious persuasion amongst us." NYPL.

head to Sir William Johnson, "a pack of hipocritical, Cheating, Lying, canting, illdesigning Scoundrells . . . I am not the least afraid but we Shall Carry our Election All Hollow against the Miscreants." He informed Sir William that "Schuylers Conduct in the House has Certainly [made] him the laughing Stock of every body, except the Faction of [   ] Presbiterians So far we will laugh at him." Wetherhead urged Sir William not to "fix upon Such a person" as Philip Schuyler who, he feared, would be a "paltry Tool & meer Machine of a Faction" in New York City. William Smith, Jr., he termed a "Snake in the Grass." [7]

The choice of New York City candidates was but one of several points at which the dissenters leveled their "religious" broadside. But it was perhaps the most immediate issue in the 1769 elections, and it was responsible for the Livingstons' loss of their single remaining assembly seat from New York City-County. The division of candidates there illustrated the factionalism. Lieutenant Governor Colden divided the city into two parties along lines slightly different than religious. One, he said, consisted of the new members chosen for the last assembly, and the other of those supposed to be favored by the governor.

The choice of candidates for New York's assembly seats provided a clear-cut division of parties. When it was proposed that the four old members "set up," delegates from all the dissenting churches held a meeting and offered a counter-proposal that the De Lancey-Episcopalians name two candidates and that the dissenters be allowed to propose the other two. But the Episcopalians refused, and with that answer several hundred dissenters met in the Fields to nominate four men to run against James De Lancey, Jacob Walton, James Jauncey, and John Cruger; they were Philip Livingston, Peter Van Brugh Livingston, John Morin Scott, and Theodore Van Wyck. Philip Livingston declined being a candidate, and although he was replaced with John Cruger, the Livingston faction continued to center their hopes on him as one of the two men they might elect. Apparently they doubted that they could unseat all four De Lancey men, but they hoped to win at least two of the four posts at stake.[8]

---

[7] Wetherhead to Johnson, Jan. 9, 1769. *Sir William Johnson Papers*, VI, 574–575. Cf. Sabine, *Smith Memoirs*, I, 50.

[8] William Smith to Robert R. Livingston, Jan. 5, 1769. NYHS, Robert R. Livingston Collection. Peter R. Livingston to Schuyler, Jan. 16, 1769. NYPL, Schuyler Papers Box 23.

Livingston, however, bore the animus that Scott still carried as a lawyer. And the Episcopalians, merchants, and Sons of Liberty assured a complete victory for the De Lanceys, who thereby increased their assembly seats from three to four. Cruger was elected with De Lancey, Jauncey, and Walton, and although he had Livingston backing, Cruger did not prove to be much of a Livingston supporter. Philip Livingston was chosen to sit for his family manor, and this caused a subsequent furor when the De Lancey assembly refused to seat him because of nonresidency.

The Livingstons fought vigorously to elect their candidates, believing they could keep the De Lanceys from enjoying an undue share of assembly seats. Schuyler had less trouble in Albany County with his re-election; but his interest in his faction's prospects elsewhere was strong. Peter R. Livingston wrote him on January 16 that their New York party was hard at work. "I think the Prospect has a good Aspect," he said, "and at all Events Jauncey must go to the Wall this time. I make no doubt if we can keep the people to the promises they have made that Philip & Scott will be two, and if the opposite party pushes Old John Cruger I am of oppinion they will push one of the other two out." But it so happened that Livingston and Scott, not two De Lancey men, were pushed out. Peter R. Livingston's hope that cross-voting would insure his faction of control of two seats proved empty. Instead, cross-voting apparently helped elect the De Lancey men. Still, he trusted the "good management of the Votes" and the "high Spirits" of "our people." If no fair play was shown, Livingston vowed "there will be blood shead [sic] as we have by far the best part of the Bruisers on our side who are determined to use force" if the De Lanceys used any foul play. Livingston invited Schuyler to extend the fray to Albany, asking that he "scatter" some of William Smith's propaganda sheets which had "done us a great deal of good" in the city.[9]

While his faction in New York was embroiled in the bitter election struggle, Philip Schuyler did not pass his election without peculiar difficulties of his own. The support from the two greatest men of interest in the county, Livingston and Johnson, seemed uncertain. Relations with them were personal, however, and evidently involved

---

[9] *Ibid.* This propaganda may have included "an old rascally sermon, called 'Masonry the sure Guide to Hell,' reprinted" by Smith and William Livingston. John Wetherhead to Sir William Johnson, Jan. 9, 1769. *Sir William Johnson Papers*, VI, 576.

neither Schuyler's partisan position nor his political philosophy as such.

During the recent assembly session, Schuyler referred to Sir William Johnson's handling of the Treaty of Fort Stanwix in a manner that raised Johnson's suspicions and the ire of one of the baronet's friends, Hugh Wallace, who sat on the governor's council. Wallace told Johnson that he had heard Schuyler had made some disrespectful comments about Sir William's character and conduct. To determine the accuracy of the report, Wallace "got into his Company, & introduced a discourse about that Affair," but Schuyler gave no indication of criticism of Sir William. "His tone was different," said Wallace, "or By God his Bones would have paid for it." Wallace suggested that Johnson exert his influence to prevent the colonel's re-election. And John Wetherhead, another correspondent, also provided a report about Schuyler—that "bullying, courageous Gentleman"—leaving Sir William to "resent as you think proper." [10]

Following receipt of Wallace's report, Johnson received a letter from Schuyler and his assembly colleague, Jacob Ten Eyck. They requested Sir William's "interest" in the election, but Johnson refused to give them an answer until he should receive an explanation from Schuyler about the question Wallace had reported. Johnson expected Schuyler could assure him that the charge was without foundation. He would "suffer" no man "to treat me Ill with Impunity," but neither was he willing to "admit" such a charge against a person whom he had long esteemed. Johnson asked about Schuyler's accusation that the baronet misrepresented the behavior of certain missionaries in the Indian territory—possibly another nuance to the political-religious controversy. He also asked if an attempt to procure a law preventing council members from "Voting Intermeddling &ca" in Indian matters was leveled at himself, "however Unusual or Extraordinary such a Step may appear. . . ." [11] Johnson was also a member of the council. He promised he would suspend his "belief" until the matter was explained.

Apparently Johnson did not reject Schuyler's petition for support

10 Ibid., pp. 574–575. Wallace to Johnson, Jan. 7, 1769. Sir William Johnson Papers, VI, 570–571. Cf. Becker, "Nominations in Colonial New York," p. 269, for the full text of what is now missing in the Johnson Papers.

11 Johnson to Schuyler, Jan. 17, 1769. NYPL, Schuyler Papers Box 23. Cf. Sir William Johnson Papers, VI, 575 n. and 589–590. Schuyler had moved to prevent members of the council from interfering in elections, according to p. 575 n.

in the election. Candidates were very scarce in Albany County, and Sir William felt that there was little choice because few men of ability were available. He had given his blessing to the colonel's candidacy in 1768 when his "Conduct was such as admitted of no objection." And after Schuyler sent what seemed to be a satisfactory explanation of charges against his conduct toward Johnson, Sir William again did not withhold his "interest." Schuyler denied and explained away the charges and evidently was able to write in such a manner that it would not be altogether "Justifiable" for Johnson "to Condemn him at once." [12]

Another personal difficulty troubled Schuyler: support from Robert Livingston, Jr., third lord of the manor, the other key man with interest and influence in Albany County. The colonel almost considered withdrawing from his race, apparently because of a question of Livingston's backing. On January 23, Livingston's son, Peter R., wrote Schuyler of their apparent success at the polls in New York City. His count of the vote would have given the four assembly seats to Scott, James De Lancey, Philip Livingston, and John Cruger. But not one of his faction had succeeded in spite of his belief in their "most solid Interest and by getting our Sheriff to take none but those that had Votes I am of oppinion that we shall gitt Philip & Scott in at least, but I find Industry alone does the business." Peter Livingston offered Schuyler some reassurance on his personal campaign, for the colonel had thought Peter's father opposed his re-election. It is not clear what strained their relations. Perhaps Schuyler's connection with his father-in-law's boundary dispute with Livingston Manor was enough to dampen the third lord's ardor for him. But Peter assured Schuyler that he had asked his father to support the colonel "in all his power" if Sir William Johnson or anyone else opposed him, and he begged Schuyler to "come again and not think of staying back." [13]

The Livingstons were clearly in trouble—in New York City, in Dutchess County, and in Albany, where Schuyler was confronted with the possibility of Sir William Johnson's opposition and the unenthusiastic support of the lord of Livingston Manor. Robert R. Livingston

[12] Becker, "Nominations in Colonial New York," pp. 269–270. Cf. Johnson to Wallace, Jan. 25, 1769. *Sir William Johnson Papers*, VI, 608–609. Becker indicates that he consulted the Johnson papers before they were damaged, and he thus provides words omitted in the editing of the Johnson letter.

[13] Peter R. Livingston to Schuyler, Jan. 23, Feb. 6, 1769. NYPL, Schuyler Papers Box 23.

of Claremont was not altogether certain of his own position in Dutchess County, where he could only "believe I shall be again set up." Livingston called on Schuyler for information about the factional struggles of the recent session in order to use it in his campaign.[14] From Peter R. Livingston, Schuyler also heard of likely difficulties both in the elections and in the assembly session to follow. After telling the lord of Livingston Manor he would postpone his polling until the New York City elections were over, the patroon of Rensselaerwyck supported Abraham Ten Broeck for Rensselaer Manor's seat. In the event the patroon's father-in-law (Philip Livingston) was not elected from New York, Rensselaer had offered to get him elected in his own manor. Yet it is not clear what caused this alteration in strategy, but Ten Broeck was elected from Rensselaerwyck, and Philip Livingston was left without a seat. Amazed at these developments, Peter R. Livingston gave his place from Livingston Manor to his kinsman because Philip had been the assembly speaker; it was in the family's interest that their representatives enjoying the greatest position remain in office. Peter Livingston told Schuyler he would "be deprived of the pleasure of contributing my little assistance to your aid in any points you may have Occasion to push in the next session." [15]

It was evident that Schuyler had risen to a position of leadership. This was particularly significant inasmuch as the positions of several of the Livingstons were threatened. Judge Robert Livingston might have trouble regaining the Dutchess County seat which he had lost in 1768. Peter Livingston could only hope his own inability to help Schuyler in the house would be compensated by the judge's service. However, the judge's opponents had "great interest" and he, too, was to be prevented from offering Schuyler any service in the house. The judge failed in his bid for election from Dutchess County because the Beekman and R. G. Livingston tenants voted against him. Shades of the "Great Rebellion" of 1766! Even Philip Livingston was to be deprived of his seat for the manor after he reached the assembly, for John De Lancey of Westchester Borough was already laying plans to oust Assemblyman Lewis Morris on the issue of nonresidency, and what could be used against Morris was a likely weapon against Livingston too.

14 Robert R. Livingston to Schuyler, Jan. 28, 1769. NYPL, Schuyler Papers Box 23.
15 Peter R. Livingston to Schuyler, Feb. 6, 27, Mar. 13, 1769. NYPL, Schuyler Papers Box 23.

Thus Schuyler was re-elected to his assembly seat in the midst of much campaign furor—a campaign which momentarily tempted him to withdraw from the hustings. Yet his friend William Smith, Jr., congratulating him on his victory in February, assured him that even the "Dutch and other Dissenters" in New York City were gratified at the colonel's election. As for his opponents' chagrin, Smith said, "Their Disappointment will be of service & has raised a spirit that will render our City Members more tame and fearful of another Dissolution. This religious Quarrel will be of service to Sir H[enry Moore] and not unfriendly to the Colony in many Respects; however hateful in other Points of View." Smith also reported other developments resulting from the work of the previous assembly. Schuyler's "Representation" to the king and Parliament, Smith felt, would be resented as much as the Virginia Remonstrance, and as things were "drawing to a Crisis," Smith suspected "we shall be obliged next to send Home special Agents" to present New York's case to the ministry. Smith vowed if he "had a Voice," Schuyler and Judge Robert R. Livingston "should be urged to see England in this momentous Embassy." [16] Were there to be such places to fill, the rival factions might find fresh cause for dispute.

Prior to the meeting of the new assembly there was quite as much maneuvering as during the election, although now it was directed toward planning strategy within the house instead of means of winning places to it. From Claremont, Judge Livingston proposed to Schuyler that he "should be very glad of a Little Conversation with You before You meet in the House." [17] Perhaps the colonel could stop to see the judge on his trip downriver to Manhattan for the session. Peter R. Livingston prepared his friend for the meeting of the assembly by reporting the intended movements, more than glad that Schuyler had been re-elected, "as Men of your Parts and Station of Life are more necessary now than ever I mean men that will not be swaed [sic] by passion or Interest but steadyly pursue the Interest of the Public Weal." It would be nonsense to deny that Schuyler had an "interest," but it is apparent that members of the Livingston faction, thinking themselves free from selfish partisanship, typically cast themselves in the role of guardians of the public weal. Peter Livingston also told Schuyler the opposition was "greatly vexed at my given [sic] up my place to Uncle Philip [Livingston] and are determined that he shall

16 Smith to Schuyler, Feb. 11, 1769. NYPL, Schuyler Papers Box 23.
17 Robert R. Livingston to Schuyler, Feb. 21, 1769. NYPL, Schuyler Papers Box 23.

not be Speaker as they have fixed the plan to turn out all New [non?] Residents particularly pointed at him and Lewis Morris. . . ." He warned Schuyler that all their friends who wanted to keep both Morris and Livingston in the house and Livingston as speaker "must make a point of being here on the day the House meets. . . ." As for the wider problems of imperial legislation, Peter Livingston noted some rumors that the Townshend duties would be repealed. Others said not —that the ministry was to take action against America and that no goods whatsoever would be shipped that spring. The last "would occasion a rumpus amoung the poorer people at home by next fall." [18]

The Livingston missives bore a remarkable likeness to the British circular letter—a device for arranging specifically appropriate votes and the general support of members of Parliament for or against government measures. The use of such a whip in Britain and His Majesty's province testified not only to the absence of strict party organization and party discipline but to the essential condition of politics as well: a sizable measure of independence among representatives, dependence on factional leaders, and shifting alliances when not each and every issue before Parliament or the provincial assembly was a "party" one.

In March, while Schuyler succumbed momentarily to his old sickness, he heeded Peter R. Livingston's urgings that he and other house members from upriver be punctual in meeting on April 4 "to prevent any surprizes." [19] The colonel managed to be on hand for the opening of the assembly. More serious factional disputes were afoot.

– 2 –

THE POST-ELECTION SESSION

GOVERNOR MOORE called the assembly to meet on April 4, 1769. The house contained but six new faces—John Cruger, Nathaniel Woodhull, Christopher Billop, John De Noyellis, Samuel Gale, and Lewis Morris. Morris, who had lost the disputed election with John De Lancey in the previous session, had finally won a seat, though he was soon to be expelled. Philip Livingston, who once represented New York City-County, now sat for the manor, but he, too, was to be expelled. Most of the new men were members of the De Lancey faction, and although the old Livingston interest had withstood de-

[18] Peter R. Livingston to Schuyler, Feb. 27, 1769. NYPL, Schuyler Papers Box 23.
[19] Peter R. Livingston to Schuyler, Mar. 13, 1769. NYPL, Schuyler Papers Box 23.

cline rather well, the expulsion of Lewis Morris and Philip Livingston, when combined with the loss of another member or two, left the De Lanceys largely victorious. The "whigs," a group of upcountry men with mixed racial stock, farming and religious minority interests, had captured only one seat south of Cortlandt Manor. And by that degree their opposition to the seaboard, mercantile, and Established Church interests, and to Parliamentary government, was weakened.[20] The governor had written that the old assembly was largely "compos'd of plain well meaning Men, whose notions from their education, are extremely confin'd," [21] but it is doubtful that the new house was any different. The only men of any real stature, as events later proved, were Philip Schuyler and George Clinton. A few others were only slightly more able than most of their fellows.

Governor Moore had called "the new Assembly together, sooner than the usual time . . . on account of some additional Provision to be made for the troops. . . ." [22] The old assembly had been generous with the purse, but as for its addresses to the king and Parliament, the secretary of state told the governor that the monarch was displeased at the failure of the assembly to transmit its petition through Moore. Also, the petition contained claims inconsistent with the constitution—claims denying the supreme authority of Parliament.[23] Only time would tell what the assembly might say to this.

The political complexion of New York was mottled. The De Lanceys' victory in 1768 and their emergence as a "popular party" rather deepened the mystery of colonial politics. But the two factions were plainly after power, and the "De Lanceys were perfectly capable of taking over the role of the Livingstons, of becoming Whigs with radical connections, of leading the battle against the encroachment of Parliament, if this was the best way to exploit the unpopularity of the Livingstons and regain command of the Assembly." This was precisely what they had done in the assembly in 1768–1769. "They led the assault against the Townshend Revenue Acts," which were threats to the assembly's control of salaries—and against the Restraining Act.

[20] Spaulding, George Clinton, p. 25. The lone member the Livingstons added from south of Cortlandt Manor was Woodhull of Suffolk County. They had lost Philip Livingston's New York seat. His transfer to the manor was soon brought to nought and the manor was left without representation.

[21] Moore to Hillsborough, Jan. 4, 1769. C.O. 5/1100:40.

[22] Moore to Hillsborough, Jan. 24, 1769. C.O. 5/1100:141–143.

[23] Hillsborough to Moore, Mar. 24, 1769. C.O. 5/1100:240–241.

They bargained with the governor, conceding a bill for provisioning troops in return for his promise to intercede with the ministry to allow New York to issue £120,000 in bills of credit.[24] And then, although they kept control of the house, their popularity began to vanish. This process began with fresh partisan disputes in the session of the assembly from April to May, 1769—disputes that helped drive Philip Schuyler farther away from the empire by reason of his exclusion from a substantial share of power and because at the same time there developed a divergence on political principles. He remained a member of the governing class, but the faction of the class to which he belonged was denied the degree of power held by their peers. Local partisan struggles apparently determined or at least framed his attitude toward the empire and formed the basis for choosing between a sovereign Parliament and an extralegal Continental Congress.

The first indication of the abiding partisan temper of the assembly came on the very day the new house was called to order. The De Lanceys replaced Philip Livingston with John Cruger as speaker. The following day they began maneuvering to unseat two of their opponents, Lewis Morris and Philip Livingston. They accomplished this by interpreting the law on residency. Before the De Lanceys managed to unseat the two members, Philip Livingston proposed to strike a blow for his own faction. He suggested a bill to vacate the seat of every member who accepted any post or place of "honor, profit or trust" under the Crown after being elected to the assembly.[25] This might prevent the De Lancey members from using their assembly stations as steppingstones to other offices while still retaining their seats. Two days later, on April 12, John Thomas moved Livingston's dismissal on the grounds that as a resident of New York City he could not represent Livingston Manor in Albany County. The act of 1699, he said, provided that a nonresident could not represent a district. The house then voted on the question to reject Thomas' motion, but it was saved by a vote of 16 to 8; Schuyler led the minority's attempt to quash it. The agrarian aristocrats clearly believed a man could represent a constituency without actually residing there, and that no urban, mercantile group should prevent the possibility. Thomas' motion was postponed; George Clinton offered one of his own, however. Clinton moved that Thomas be charged with the payment of costs in case his motion to dismiss Livingston proved "vexatious" and "friv-

24 Dangerfield, *Livingston*, pp. 41–42.
25 Assembly Journals, April 4, 5, 10, 1769. C.O. 5/1100:351–352, 369.

olous." [26] Again the factional lines held, the De Lanceys voting nay 14 to 9.

On April 13 the house discussed another election contest. This time John De Lancey disputed Lewis Morris' election from Westchester Borough.[27] The next day the election issue assumed wider importance when it extended to the larger questions of taxation without representation and virtual as opposed to actual representation! The local struggle over residency qualifications of assembly representatives was in a sense but a microcosm of the wider colonial-imperial dispute over virtual and actual representation—and taxation.

Charles De Witt of Ulster County, a new member of Schuyler's clique, offered a lengthy motion with startling implications: no tax must be levied except as a free gift; virtual representation was a "pernicious" doctrine; exclusion of a member having a freehold in a constituency from which he was elected because of nonresidence might draw into question the rights of the electors themselves to choose representatives in places where they did not reside; taxation of estates of nonresident freeholders *who were excluded from the position of representatives* would imply approval by the assembly of a principle held by its "enemies" who proposed to tax the province on the basis of virtual instead of actual representation. Thus De Witt cleverly linked the British practices of taxation without representation and virtual representation with the De Lanceys' move to use the nonresidency law to expel their opponents. De Witt moved that the house "abhor" these practices, that it declare the possession of taxable freeholds entitled even a nonresident freeholder the right to representation, and that no person having a sufficient freehold might be taxed without his consent given *as a representative* in the assembly! De Witt wanted these points determined *before* the house decided Lewis Morris' right to represent Westchester Borough. Evidently he proposed them as a diversionary tactic, a means of encouraging debate and thus of postponing a vote on unseating Morris. If De Witt's motion passed, Morris could not be expelled. He would then be able to qualify as a representative under the proposition that taxable freeholds (which Morris had) entitled the holder to freedom from taxation unless he

[26] Assembly Journals, April 12, 1769. C.O. 5/1100:372–373. The eight were Schuyler, Ten Broeck, Morris, Ten Eyck, Mynderse, Clinton, De Witt, and Van Cortlandt. On the second vote the minority held fast except for the addition of one of the Seamans' vote. Philip Livingston did not vote on either motion.

[27] Assembly Journals, April 13, 1769. C.O. 5/1100:374.

was able to give his consent (as a representative as well as an elector) in the assembly.

At this point the De Lanceys faced a dilemma: allow the resolution to pass and thus be defeated on a partisan tactic, or fight De Witt's proposal and thus appear as opponents of colonial rights. The De Lanceys extricated themselves by use of a motion for the previous question. They voted down the proposal to act on De Witt's motion before the Morris case was settled, and they demanded an early decision of Morris' eligibility by ordering a prompt summation of the argument between Morris and John De Lancey.[28]

When Morris proceeded to sum up his own case on April 15, he was obliged to interpret the law of 1699 regarding residency. Morris maintained that the law which allegedly required a man to reside in the district he represented did not apply to Westchester Borough, but that it simply required all assemblymen sitting for cities, counties, and manors to be residents of the *province*. Moreover, he insisted that his possession of an estate in Westchester entitled him to be a representative because ownership implied residency.[29]

The controversy dragged on until April 20. One of the Seamans (representatives of Queens and Richmond counties) offered a motion to decide Morris' residency. Colonel Schuyler found himself in the minority when the house voted 15 to 8 to put the Seaman motion. The colonel then offered a parliamentary diversion. He suggested that before the vote on Morris' residency was taken, a committee be named to investigate old assembly journals and determine whether or not other persons had ever represented constituencies in which they did not actually reside. Perhaps the argument of ancient practice would prevail over strict legal construction used as a political weapon. James De Lancey moved the previous question, thus by-passing Schuyler's motion, and by a vote of 15 to 8 the house decided to vote on whether or not Morris was entitled to a seat. On the crucial issue the assembly voted 12 to 11 to dismiss Morris on the grounds of his nonresidency. Schuyler's minority was narrowly defeated. Almost a month later, the assembly decided that Morris' opponent, John De Lancey, had been duly elected as the member from Westchester Borough. Thus

---

[28] Assembly Journals, April 14, 1769. C.O. 5/1100:375–376. The vote on the previous question (to decide the Morris case without first voting on De Witt's motion) was 15 ayes to 9 nays. Schuyler, De Witt, Livingston, Clinton, Morris, Ten Broeck, Van Cortlandt, Ten Eyck, and Mynderse formed the minority.

[29] Assembly Journals, April 15, 1769. C.O. 5/1100:377.

having decreased the Livingston minority, the De Lanceys added another vote to their own majority.[30]

As far as the general membership of factions was concerned, the agrarian-mercantile lines were drawn rather broadly. The leadership of the two sides was distinctly divided, while others fell between them for varying and immediate reasons we probably shall never know. The disputed election was complicated by an auxiliary issue: Did nonresident freeholders have a right to vote for assemblymen of the districts in which their freeholds lay? A nonresident, it had been decided, could not represent a district, but by a vote of 13 to 11 (on April 26) the assembly affirmed his right to help select the representative of the district in which his freehold lay. Philip Schuyler's support of this decision was nothing less than an affirmation of his beliefs about property as the foundation of the franchise and of other political privilege. Another upshot of the dispute was that James De Lancey proposed to amend the act regulating the election of assemblymen— an amendment which would specify the qualifications of members of the house. De Lancey pushed through his legislation explaining the 1699 law. It provided a definition of residency, and allowed nonresidents to vote for assemblymen, but stipulated that no candidate could be elected to the assembly unless he had actually resided in his district six months before the test of the election writ, and unless he possessed a sufficient freehold for that period.[31] Although Governor Moore suggested that the Privy Council disallow the new law as contrary to the New York charter, the province's practices and to Parliamentary usage, the government did not interfere. Meantime, the Livingstons and De Lanceys turned to new battles.

Notwithstanding the efforts of Schuyler and his cohorts to prevent it, Philip Livingston was dismissed from the assembly on May 12, scarcely more than a week before the house was prorogued. But why so tardy an action? For the De Lanceys to allow Livingston to compensate for the seat lost in New York City by offering himself as a representative of Livingston Manor would be to accept less of a vic-

[30] The minority included Schuyler, Ten Eyck, Ten Broeck, Boerum, Livingston, Van Cortlandt, Mynderse, De Witt, Clinton, Woodhull, and Colonel Seaman. Assembly Journals, April 20, May 18, 1769. C.O. 5/1100:383–384, 424–425.

[31] Assembly Journals, April 26, May 20, 1769. C.O. 5/1100:389, 429. See also a copy of the act explaining and amending the 1699 law in C.O. 5/1100:468–469; and State of New York, *The Colonial Laws of New York From the Year 1664 to the Revolution* (5 vols.; Albany, 1894), IV, 1094–1096, gives the statute of 1769; Appendix C, *infra*.

tory than they had won at the polls. And they were in no mood to permit the Livingstons to turn adversity into triumph. The controversy which centered on the former speaker was also that of residency, and it threatened the seat of still a third member of the house—another agrarian. The Livingston Manor freeholders headed by Lord Robert, Jr., Robert R., and Peter R. Livingston petitioned the assembly against John Thomas' motion to unseat Philip Livingston. They, too, insisted that the act of 1699 applied not to the residence of assemblymen, but of electors, and that according to law, a person's residence depended on the place of his freehold, not on his actual residence in a dwelling. They argued from precedent and custom that nonresidents could represent a constituency. Had this not been the practice of the past? The British doctrine of virtual representation, they said, was pernicious, and it would surely be strengthened if people were taxed for their estates without representation. According to the argument thus implied, a nonresident freeholder who merely possessed the right to vote and not the right to be elected to the assembly had not the substantial political liberty to which he was entitled. The vote to dismiss Livingston was less evenly divided than was that cast on Lewis Morris; Philip Schuyler and only five others opposed the seventeen votes the De Lanceys mustered to oust him. But this was not all. John De Noyellis then charged Abraham Ten Broeck with nonresidency in Rensselaer Manor, and thus suggested that he be ejected from his seat as well! [32]

The issue of residency continued to encourage factionalism, and it was soon linked with another question—that of allowing provincial officials to sit in the assembly. On the residency issue the Schuyler faction resisted even a consideration of the De Lancey bill to alter the 1699 act regulating the election of assemblymen. It was as if they fought to maintain an ancient liberty against encroachment and innovation. When the house voted on whether or not to proceed with a bill vacating assembly seats of men who occupied other Crown offices *after* their election to the house, Schuyler somehow managed to get the issue laid aside. The De Lanceys persisted, however, and when they found the bill regarding assemblymen holding royal offices in general was postponed, they promptly offered a more specific motion to prevent supreme court judges from sitting in the assembly. They passed this on May 17. It was a shaft aimed specifically at Judge

[32] Assembly Journals, May 12, 1769. C.O. 5/1100:407–410. Schuyler's minority dwindled to De Witt, Van Cortlandt, Ten Broeck, Ten Eyck, and Mynderse.

Robert Livingston, who was elected a representative from Livingston Manor after Philip had been ejected from his seat. The judge could not be ousted on the grounds of nonresidency, but the De Lanceys managed to exclude him with a resolution that one could not be both a judge and an assemblyman; their argument was that this was contrary to political custom and to the spirit of the British Constitution. But before the De Lanceys could accomplish their move, Schuyler offered a more comprehensive motion to test their true interest in the principle of excluding royal officers from enjoying assembly seats as contrasted with their partisan concern for eliminating the Livingstons.[33]

Schuyler "was so averse" to the motion excluding supreme court judges from the assembly "that he ventured to tell the House, that they may as well put Judge Livingston's Name in the Votes; for that he apprehended that the House had nothing else in view, but to *exclude him:* And in order to try them, he proposed by a Vote, to exclude all Persons, who held any Place of Honour or Profit under the Crown." [34] Several assemblymen, mostly De Lanceyites, thereby stood to lose their seats. Schuyler's maneuver proved to be an almost fruitless gesture except that he forced the De Lanceys once again to make their true intentions a matter of record. They carried their motion to refuse supreme court judges an assembly seat and voted down Schuyler's resolution to exclude *all* persons "holding any Place of Honour, Profit or Trust, whatever, under the Crown" from the assembly. The resolution would have required members to resign such an office within six weeks after its passage or forfeit their positions in the house. These "angry partial Feuds," as William Smith, Jr., called them, showed a shift of the New York City members from their former attachment to nonresident members, whereas the country representatives' jealousy of the city members' influence in legislation and in the council made the feuding even hotter.[35] Moreover, the partisan agitation over the law on residence qualifications and the resolution

---

[33] Assembly Journals, May 17, 1769. C.O. 5/1100:414–415.

[34] Broadside, "The Case of the Manor of Livingston and the Conduct of the Honourable House of Assembly, towards it, considered." [1769] NYPL. Cf. Assembly Journals, May 17, 1769. C.O. 5/1100:415.

[35] Sabine, *Smith Memoirs*, I, 51, 66. The men who stood to lose their assembly seats, had Schuyler's motion passed, were Thomas (judge of Westchester County), Kissam (a justice of the peace), Boerum (clerk of Kings County), and Nicoll (clerk of Suffolk County). None of them voted for Schuyler's motion.

on plural officeholding for legislators offered significant additions to the American Revolution in New York. Because of the circumstances the De Lanceys' alteration of the law by amendment and resolution might better be termed evolutionary than revolutionary, and certainly these changes were motivated more by practical and expedient considerations of the moment than by any idealistic or principled philosophy of foresight. But perhaps the political implications of the alteration were extensive enough to justify the label "revolutionary."

Philip Schuyler's religious persuasion can only be intimated by the facts that he was a member of the Dutch Reformed Church and that he took a clear stand on the issue of religious privilege regarding the support of the Church of England and other dissenting bodies. The latter position was also colored by partisan politics.

Partisanship in the 1769 spring session of the assembly over religious questions was less apparent than real, nor was the evidence of it clearer for the greater attention given to issues of residency and officeholding. Still, religious partisanship was as continuing a phenomenon as the heats of the successive election campaigns. Early in the session Lewis Morris presented a bill to exempt all dissenters in Westchester, Queens, Richmond, and New York counties from paying taxes to support the ministry of the Established Church. In these four counties the Anglican establishment had been rooted since the Ministry Act of 1693. Morris' proposal was dear to Schuyler's heart insofar as the colonel himself was a dissenter and an opponent of the De Lancey-Episcopalians. The assembly passed Morris' bill on May 15 and sent it to the council, but the ostensible absence of controversy was misleading.[36] The De Lancey forces evidently did not protest or thwart the measure in the house as they might have, but trusted that the governor's council would reject the measure for them. Their confidence that it would do so made a violent display unnecessary.

On April 27, Schuyler offered another bill aimed at giving dissenters some relief from their relatively disadvantageous position with Episcopalians. Based on the necessity of promoting settlement, which he maintained could be assisted by encouraging "the Worship of God upon generous Principles of equal Indulgence to loyal Protestants of every Persuasion," Schuyler's bill offered "every Church or Congregation of reformed Protestants" in Albany County "without Discrimination, to take and hold real Estates . . . given to them for the Sup-

[36] Assembly Journals, April 6, May 15, 1769. C.O. 5/1100:356, 412. Cf. Assembly Journals, Jan. 25, 1770. C.O. 5/1219:107.

port of the Gospel. . . ." [37] Here was a means of providing support for all denominations without imposing taxes. And insofar as it might encourage settlement, the proposal was rather advantageous to the interests of a landed magnate. This measure ran into difficulty when it was suggested that the bill might be repugnant to several acts of Parliament, the Statutes of Mortmain. When some members suggested that the judges of the supreme court be invited to comment on this possibility, Schuyler successfully opposed the diversion, but more study of the measure was judged necessary. The bill was finally satisfactorily amended and on May 11, Schuyler and Jacob Ten Eyck presented it to the council.[38]

Neither of the religious bills became law, however. Within a fortnight after receiving the bill, the council refused to exempt dissenters in the four lower counties from taxes to support the Established Church, and it refused to consider further the Albany County bill allowing Protestant churches to hold property for their support.[39] The council proved its ability quietly to quash matters that the De Lancey forces in the assembly did not choose to quarrel about. Even in the council the majority faction benefited from Oliver De Lancey's position. The religious issues, however, were not yet settled; they arose again in subsequent sessions of the assembly.

The assembly of 1768–1769 had complained against the imperial regime. It remained to be seen if its successor would persevere in the same spirit or if its opposition to the Townshend duties would collapse. There was definite continuity between the two houses, separated as they were by the elections, several months of waiting and the appearance of six new members. Yet New York's position clearly became more moderate than initial developments suggested. The De Lanceys began to veer away from courting the radical segments of the populace, and both factions, uniting as a corporate entity—the assembly—began to bargain with the governor for the emission of paper bills of credit. They proposed to grant supplies for the royal troops in return for the governor's promise to intercede with the ministry in London on the paper money issue. There was great need for a circulating medium.

Moore had summoned the assembly in April, 1769, because of the

37 Assembly Journals, April 26, 27, 1769. C.O. 5/1100:390, 392.
38 Assembly Journals, May 9, 10, 11, 1769. C.O. 5/1100:402–403, 406.
39 *Journal of the Legislative Council of the Colony of New York, 1691–1775* (2 vols.; Albany, 1861), II, 1698, 1706.

shortage of money. The greatest part of the appropriation previously made for the troops had been used to pay debts, and the forces required fresh supplies. No sooner had the governor pointed this out than Philip Livingston raised the proposal of a new issue of paper currency—an appealing suggestion for New Yorkers. Accordingly, a bill to print £120,000 was presented to the house. Philip Schuyler, as head of a committee to prepare a reply to the governor's message, reported on an address on April 6. The colonel had drafted an absolute refusal of troop supply—another gesture aimed at currying popularity—and George Clinton supported him. But when the house slightly amended the address on the issue of military provisions, it coyly avowed that the sums already granted to the regulars were considerable, and that repeated applications for money would ruin a colony whose trade was restricted. As the province was short of paper currency, the assembly would say only that the request for supplies "demands our most serious Consideration." [40] It thereby suggested that the governor offer a *quid pro quo*.

On April 11, Governor Moore promised to send word to the house as soon as any news arrived about the ministry's orders regarding the paper currency shortage. A few days later, the house called for a bill to raise £1,800 in troop supplies. By May 6 it had passed the paper money bill, and sent Schuyler and a colleague to the council to request ratification. The bill provided for paper money based on the issuance of loan office bills borrowed at 5 per cent interest. Security was to be given in the form of a mortgage of double the value in lands, tenements, and hereditaments, and three times the value in houses. The bills were to be retired over a fourteen-year period. The interest would help finance the government. It was calculated that the interest raised for the first four years would bring in £6,000 per year, and for the next ten years, £3,000 per year—£54,000 in all. The bills would both raise a revenue for paying debts and creating an exigency fund and provide a circulating medium. At the same time the assembly ordered an address prepared and urged the governor to pass the paper money bill. The address maintained that the circulating medium was scarce, that estates were selling at half value, and that merchants were unable to pay their overseas creditors. The supply acts for government officials had fallen short because of the decay of trade; hence, debts increased. Public funds were deficient and more taxes would only

[40] Assembly Journals, April 4, 5, 6, 7, 8, 1769. C.O. 5/1100:351, 354, 356, 364, 368. Sabine, *Smith Memoirs*, I, 62.

overburden the populace. The interest from a loan would be the easiest method of paying debts under the circumstances.[41]

The governor passed the bill supplying the troops, but he gave his assent to the currency bill only until the ministry made a final ruling. Moore evidently agreed with the assembly's request for paper currency, for he forwarded its arguments to the secretary of state as his own. He commended the house's "great Cheerfulness" in voting the supplies and warned the ministry that there were no more funds and that it would be impracticable to tax estates in such distressing times. Both he and Lieutenant Governor Colden urged the ministry to approve the paper currency act as a means of assuring troop supply, of keeping the colony as peaceful as possible, and as a way to encourage consumption of British manufactures. In view of the recent resolves of the Virginia Assembly and the urgings from Massachusetts that New York merchants refuse British imports, approval of the currency emission would be highly expedient.[42] The assembly had but to wait to see what would become of its choice piece of legislation. This then was a key to the pacification of New York; when the ministry finally granted permission to emit paper currency, New York returned to a posture of easy subordination within the empire. Yet for all the quiescence, local factionalism persisted.

The spring session of the New York Assembly in 1769 did not altogether satisfy the ministry in London, however. The house, for example, had ignored the governor's recommendation that the colony's agent be chosen by the joint action of the assembly, council, and governor.[43] On April 8 the assembly informed the governor in no uncertain terms "with that Freedom which is the Birth-right of Englishmen, that it would be sacrificing the Rights, and diminishing the Liberties of our Constituents, to adopt any other Mode of Appointment, than that which has been practised in this Colony for many Years past." [44] An innovation and encroachment on executive power made effective but twenty years earlier was now regarded an established liberty. There was then, for all the assembly's compliance with

[41] Assembly Journals, April 11, 14, May 6, 1769. C.O. 5/1100:371, 375, 401. Extract from the act emitting bills of credit in C.O. 5/1100:329. See also Assembly Journals, May 20, 1769. C.O. 5/1100:427–430.

[42] Moore to Hillsborough, May 26, 29, July 11, 1769. C.O. 5/1100:313–314, 322, 489–490. Colden to Hillsborough, Oct. 4, 1769. C.O. 5/1100:555–556.

[43] Assembly Journals, April 4, 1769. C.O. 5/1100:350. Hillsborough to Moore, June 7, 1769. C.O. 5/1100:291. Moore to Hillsborough, May 12, 1769. C.O. 5/1100:299–300.

[44] Assembly Journals, April 8, 1769. C.O. 5/1100:368.

imperial authority, a certain resistance, a minimal position behind which they would not recede even in the face of Parliamentary sovereignty. And local partisanship might always threaten even the best possible relations between province and empire. Indeed, New Yorkers did not demonstrate much concern about the dangers of exploiting imperial difficulties for local advantage. The Earl of Hillsborough also told Governor Moore that the king did not like Philip Livingston's motions to thank the merchants for continuing the non-importation program until Parliament repealed the acts declared unconstitutional by New York. Nor did he approve of excluding judges from the assembly, or of the resolutions for concurring in the "violent" resolves of the former assembly.[45] However, it was James De Lancey who had moved that the addresses to the Crown and Parliament be entered on the journals and printed in the newspapers,[46] and these motions scarcely indicated that the factions had violently disagreed about the assembly's posture toward the imperial administration at the time the addresses were passed. De Lancey's motions appear to be little more than a weak gesture of compensation for the opposition's recent and popular proposals to print more paper money and to open the chamber to the public. Moore blamed the assembly's resolutions on the Sons of Liberty, but he was obliged to admit defeat in trying to prevent their entry in the house journals.[47] In this way the assembly persisted in its semi-belligerence, but its unwillingness to act further until the London government responded indicated an underlying current of quiescence and cautiousness, and, on the whole, a moderate temper.

On one other notable issue both Philip Schuyler and the New York Assembly proved their essentially conservative approach to the imperial system. Likewise, the Livingstons again demonstrated their persistent efforts to cultivate popular support and to paint their opponents in less than flattering colors for the scrutiny of the electorate—this by driving the De Lanceys into a contrary position. On April 8, 1769, Schuyler offered a significant motion:

As the repeated Resolves and Applications of the Colonies, relative to parliamentary Taxations, and the embarrassed State of our Commerce, and several other Grievances, have not been attended with the Success so ardently wished

45 Hillsborough to Moore, July 15, 1769. C.O. 5/1100:449–450.
46 Assembly Journals, April 7, 10, 1769. C.O. 5/1100:357, 369.
47 Moore to Hillsborough, June 3, 1769. C.O. 5/1100:431–432.

for, and so mutually conducive to the Tranquility of the British Empire; and as the growing Distresses of our Constituents loudly call for our most earnest Attention to Measures best calculated to preserve the Union between Great-Britain and her Plantations, and restore a lasting Harmony founded in mutual Affection and Interest; I therefore move that a Day may be appointed for taking the State of this Colony into our most serious Consideration, and for the Appointment of special Agents of approved Abilities and Integrity to be sent home, instructed to exert their most strenuous Efforts, in Conjunction with such Agents as the other Colonies have sent or may think proper to send, in soliciting the important Affairs of this Country at the Court of Great-Britain, and before the two Houses of Parliament, during the Course of the next Session.[48]

The motion was referred to a committee of the whole house. It is interesting to note the phraseology of Schuyler's discontent, for the terms he employed indicated no interest in radical change: "preserve the Union," "restore a lasting Harmony," "Agents . . . sent home." Such language shows no threat of independence. Only the motivation behind the proposal suggests a discontent which, if borne long enough and multiplied or aggravated, might help incline disappointed and disgruntled colonists to such a course, however reluctantly, or indeed unconsciously, they might move. But Schuyler's motion, though promised consideration, was repeatedly postponed. His suggestion was little but the discreet expression of judicious concern. Yet the disposal of it was even more prudently executed. Six times it was deferred until on May 4 the committee of the whole finally took the proposal under consideration.[49] The house had been preoccupied with other matters, and its "Dread of a Dissolution had . . . extinguished the Zeal for Liberty." [50] Schuyler's proposals added something to the body's bargaining power with the governor concerning troop supply and the issuance of paper money. After the many delays and but brief consideration given his motion, the assembly did no more than name its members from New York and Kings counties as a committee to correspond with the New York agent in London, Robert Charles. It is not difficult to understand why the colonel gradually found less and less with which to be satisfied in the provincial power arrangement

[48] Assembly Journals, April 8, 1769. C.O. 5/1100:366.

[49] Assembly Journals, April 12, 14, 21, 25, 26, May 2, 4, 1769. C.O. 5/1100:373, 375, 385, 388, 391, 398, 400.

[50] Sabine, Smith Memoirs, I, 63.

when his suggestions were so slightly received, but he would need many such disappointments before he would abandon close adherence to accepted procedural method. On May 20, its essential business of appropriations over, the governor prorogued the house.[51]

In 1769, Philip Schuyler clearly did not oppose "every measure that was proposed in the Assembly for a reconciliation" between Britain and her colonies, nor did he wish, as one Tory historian wrote, "all the petitions, remonstrances, and complaints, sent from the Colonies to England at the bottom of the sea." [52] His partisanship in the disputed elections was evident. That was a local matter. But his proposals that the assembly consider the state of the colony and the appointment of agents to visit London were consonant with the generally moderate temper of the assembly toward the governor and the imperial government. Perhaps Schuyler the partisan also warmed to William Smith, Jr.'s, suggestion of February 11 that he and Judge Robert R. Livingston would make suitable agents to send to London if the assembly would but appoint them. His proposal that the assembly send agents "home" may well have reflected his ambition for an appointment. In mid-May Hugh Wallace reported to Sir William Johnson that Schuyler had "been much more moderate this Session than last. The De Lancey Interest prevails in the house greatly, & they have give ye Livingston Interest prooff of it, by dismissing P: Livingston . . . as a non resident. . . ." [53] Johnson fancied Schuyler's moderation "may be accounted for, That party Visibly droops and will lose their Spirit with their Influence," he wrote.[54]

Other developments in the spring and summer affected Schuyler. His own limited power of patronage was challenged,[55] and there were signs of increasing tempers for the winter assembly session. The death of Governor Moore in September meant the loss of a patron and threatened the colonel's prospects for procuring land he and Philip Livingston, Jr., coveted.[56] William Smith, Jr., reported in August that "Great Preparations are making in the Southern Counties for the

[51] Assembly Journals, May 20, 1769. C.O. 5/1100:429–430.

[52] Jones, History of New York, II, 317.

[53] Wallace to Johnson, May 15, 1769. Sir William Johnson Papers, VI, 758.

[54] Johnson to Wallace, May 26, 1769. Sir William Johnson Papers, VI, 780.

[55] Solomon Hutchinson, et al., to Moore, Mar. 12, 1769. Sir William Johnson Papers, VI, 642.

[56] Philip Livingston, Jr., to Schuyler, Oct. 8, 1769. NYPL, Schuyler Papers Box 23.

Reversal of [Lewis] Morris's attempt about the Church tax. The Wind is come about in Suffolk & Orange & People in all Quarters" seemed determined that the assembly be pressured to pass Schuyler's bill for incorporating the dissenters' churches. Persisting religious issues mirrored the partisan political divisions. And antagonism toward the Established Church increased with discussion of the possibility of establishing an American episcopate. Vandals broke into St. Paul's Church, slashed cushions, scattered feathers, and carried off damask coverings after failing to break into the vestryroom.[57] The incident was but the symptom of a condition. Smith told Schuyler that "The Ministerial Rebuff to the Bishop Scheme" had animated "the non Episcopal Patriots & has brought the Tories to Reason." [58] Again in September he told the colonel, "The Spirit of the People is changing fast." [59] Perhaps the coming session would be even more lively than the previous one.

– 3 –

MAC DOUGAL, MONEY, AND MANORS

THE ASSEMBLY'S winter session, November, 1769–January, 1770, came only after several prorogations and the death of Governor Moore, who finally succumbed to the burdens of his eighty-third year. Although new annual supplies were required, Lieutenant Governor Colden delayed calling the house because he hoped to receive some news from the ministry about the paper currency bill.[60] Though it had word that the ministry did not intend to lay any further taxes for revenue purposes, the assembly decided to resist Colden's attempt to secure a provision bill until the king approved the currency act. The house again coyly suggested that it would give "serious Consideration" to Colden's request, thereby hinting that he must bargain with them for the supplies by supporting the issuance of bills of credit.[61]

Colden was determined to win these appropriations, and he agreed to sign a new paper currency act in order to get the assembly to vote supplies. He knew Hillsborough questioned the first currency act, and the second contained the same objectionable provisions. Hillsborough

57 *The New-York Gazette, or Weekly Post-Boy,* July 17, 1769.
58 Smith to Schuyler, Aug. 21, 1769. NYPL, Schuyler Papers Box 23.
59 Smith to Schuyler, Sept. 12, 1769. NYPL, Schuyler Papers Box 23.
60 Colden to Hillsborough, Dec. 4, 1769. C.O. 5/1138:117.
61 Sabine, *Smith Memoirs,* I, 70.

wanted to know if the bills of credit were meant to be legal tender at the loan office and the treasury.[62] Moreover, he objected to Colden's informing the assembly of the "greatest possibility" of the repeal of the Townshend duties, and to the framing of a second bill to emit paper currency. Even the assembly's adoption of the Virginia Resolves did not appear proper.[63] Yet William Smith, Jr., believed that the assembly should have been more vigorous in supporting the Virginia Resolves. But for the De Lanceys, who led a "silent Desertion from the Common Standard of the Colonies," Smith thought the "Recent & Subsequent Advices from Home of the Embarrassments of the Ministry might have emboldened [the house] to use superior Freedom of Expression" in criticizing the government for sending troops to Boston.[64]

In the discussion of the supply and paper currency bills Philip Schuyler at first was conspicuously absent. At least he did not vote on two motions of December 15, regarding the grant of supplies. The fact was that he had fallen ill with his old ailment—the rheumatic gout—and was unable to leave his chambers. Schuyler's report to John Bradstreet, who was living with the colonel's family in Albany, raised Mrs. Schuyler's alarms. Bradstreet could not persuade her to stay at home. Her husband's assurances that his danger had passed and that he was growing better failed to satisfy her, and Mrs. Schuyler insisted on crossing the river in a rainstorm in her haste to reach New York.[65] Perhaps she provided the homely comforts so much needed and welcomed by a man who was harried by illness and faced by the partisanship of the new session.

On December 15 the assembly heard a motion by John De Noyellis to grant not more than £2,000 for the troops from the loan office money *after* the king approved the act to emit bills of credit. The motion was narrowly rejected by a vote of 12 to 11, and although the De Lancey forces generally opposed the motion, some of their number (including John De Lancey) voted for the measure. When this failed,

[62] Becker, *Political Parties*, pp. 78–79; Hillsborough to Colden, Dec. 9, 1769. C.O. 5/1100:659; Colden to Hillsborough, Dec. 4, 1769. C.O. 5/1101:1–2.

[63] Hillsborough to Colden, Jan. 18, 1770. C.O. 5/1101:16–17. The Virginia Resolves asserted that the sole taxing power lay with the governor and legislature, implied a censure on the British ministry for denouncing the Massachusetts and Virginia circular letters, and condemned a proposal that American malcontents be taken to England for trial.

[64] Sabine, *Smith Memoirs*, I, 70.

[65] Bradstreet to Schuyler, Dec. 8, 1769. NYPL, Schuyler Papers Box 9.

William Nicoll moved to grant £2,000 for troop supply, half of which would be paid immediately from the treasury and would be replaced by the first money raised from the loan office bill, and the other half to be raised from the same source as soon as the paper currency bill passed into law. This motion carried by the vote of 12 to 11 with the same alignment as before.[66] At this point a fresh radical outburst against any compliance by the assembly with the Mutiny Act renewed the partisan furor, and Philip Schuyler suddenly appeared at the head of the opposition to the De Lanceys—evidently none the worse for his recent bout with the gout.

Radical sentiment outside the assembly was directed against any compliance with the Mutiny Act whatsoever.[67] This sentiment was voiced in a public meeting and was embodied in a broadside issued on December 17 "To the betrayed Inhabitants of the City and Colony of New-York" by Alexander MacDougal, who had signed himself as a "Son of Liberty."[68] MacDougal maintained that New York's easy compliance in granting supplies was an admission of Parliament's authority and of the obligatory nature of the revenue acts. He charged the De Lanceys with conniving with Colden to secure power and prevent the dissolution of the assembly. Colden stood to benefit from his "promise" that the king would pass the currency act by receiving a salary appropriation. It was a farce, MacDougal charged, for the assembly to thank the merchants for their non-importation policy— aimed at procuring the repeal of the revenue acts—while at the same time it voted money to support a military establishment that "enslaved" the people. Finally, the "Son of Liberty" called for a public meeting in the Fields, an open area at the northern edge of the city (now the site of city hall). There public opinion might be polled for the benefit of the house. He assumed the public would oppose the assembly's position, for he suggested that after the poll the meeting go in a body to the assembly to insist that it refuse the bill for troop supply. This was a direct threat to the independence of the assembly.

The MacDougal broadside appeared on Sunday. On the following Tuesday the assembly wrathfully turned against this outburst. John

[66] Assembly Journals, Nov. 21–Dec. 15, 1769. C.O. 5/1219.

[67] Colden to Hillsborough, Jan. 6, 1770. C.O. 5/1138:128–129. See also Becker, *Political Parties*, pp. 77–81.

[68] Assembly Journals, Dec. 18, 1769, carries a copy of the broadside. C.O. 5/1219. See also Sabine, *Smith Memoirs*, I, 71–72, and *The New-York Journal, or the General Advertiser*, Feb. 15, 1770.

De Lancey carried a motion "that the Sense of the House be taken, whether the Paper . . . is not an infamous and scandalous Libel?" The house agreed by a vote of 20 to 1, Philip Schuyler alone dissenting. The house next decided the paper was "a false, seditious and infamous libel." But Schuyler's opposition to taking the sense of the house suggests that the resolution was slightly less than a unanimous expression of the assembly's feeling.[69] After seeing the overwhelming sentiment against him, the colonel may either have failed to object further to a declaration that the paper was a libel, or if he joined in assenting, it seems he did so for the sake of defending the prerogatives of the house. His initial vote, however, revealed both his partisanship and "independency of spirit." Without objection the house passed other resolves: that the paper, calculating to inflame the minds of the populace against their representatives, reflected on the honor and dignity of the house; that the proposal for a popular march on the assembly was "an audacious Attempt to destroy the Freedom and Independence of this House," and that the threat induced anarchy and confusion; that the author(s), aiders, and abettors of the paper were guilty of a high misdemeanor; and that the assembly would ask Lieutenant Governor Colden to proclaim a £100 reward to discover the author(s) and his cohorts. The assembly dealt in the same fashion with a paper signed "Legion," which called a public meeting of protest.[70]

Schuyler's lone stand on the initial question may have been designed to remind his colleagues that the definition of libel was no easy undertaking, or he may have objected to making it an issue, but his seeming

[69] Sabine, *Smith Memoirs*, I, 72. Cf. Assembly Journals, Dec. 18, 19, 1769. C.O. 5/1219. Smith states that the house declared the paper "a false, seditious, and infamous Libel. Resolved, Nemine Contradicente." However, according to the journals, the house first decided the question of *whether or not to take the sense of the house* as to the infamous and scandalous nature of the libel. After it did so by the vote of 20 to 1, the assembly *then* "Resolved therefore, That the said paper is a false, seditious and infamous libel." And finally, the *nemine contradicente* decision was made with respect to a number of subsequent resolves and not to the declaration of the libel. It does not appear that the 20 to 1 vote refers to declaring the libel but rather to the question "that the Sense of the House be taken. . . ." If the vote was for declaring the libel, one wonders why the nature of the libel was described in different terms. On the motion for taking the sense of the house the libel is called infamous and scandalous. But when it was decided that there was a libel, the words used are "false, seditious and infamous."

[70] Assembly Journals, Dec. 19, 1769. C.O. 5/1219.

concurrence with the other resolves indicated his aversion to the activities of the rabble and their leaders. He had shown both his persistent opposition to the De Lanceys and his distaste for anything less than keeping control of even moderate protest in the hands of established government. However, the uproar caused by the broadside did not prevent the passage of a supply bill. And when the author of the paper was finally detected, arrested, and jailed for seditious libel because he refused to pay bail, New Yorkers thought they had the equivalent of England's John Wilkes—a man who personified resistance to tyrannical authority. But whereas Wilkes had gained notoriety by opposing what some called royal tyranny, MacDougal's fame was really based on an opposition to the "tyranny" of a representative body controlled by a privileged faction.

On the question of granting £2,000 for troop supply (December 20) Schuyler and ten others voted nay, but the De Lanceys, cooperating with Colden, passed the appropriation on its second reading by a bare majority of one. When the bill went before the committee of the whole, Schuyler and George Clinton attempted to amend it by providing that the treasurer pay the money from the loan office, but not until the paper currency act became law! Again the vote was close: 12 to 10 against the amendment. Holding the same alignment, the Schuyler-led Livingston forces also failed in their attempt to prevent the supply bill from reaching the floor of the house, and again in the vote to engross the bill. The supply bill was passed (12 to 10) on December 30; Schuyler remained in the forefront of the opposition, thereby suggesting a degree of resistance to the assembly's tacit recognition of Parliamentary sovereignty which it gave by complying with the Mutiny Act.[71] Perhaps he would not have done this had the paper currency bill been allowed.

Within a week both the £2,000 supply bill and the second act emitting £120,000 in bills of credit received the governor's approval. The supply bill, however, provided that £1,000 be granted immediately, and that the other £1,000 be paid from the interest arising from the loan office bill after it had become law.[72] Thus the De Lanceys managed a compromise, but the Livingston-Schuyler group which opposed it objected not to voting supplies, but wished rather to make the appropriation depend fully—not partly—on the governor and the Crown's approval of the loan office bill.

[71] Assembly Journals, Dec. 15, 20, 28, 29, 30, 1769. C.O. 5/1219.
[72] Assembly Journals, Jan. 5, 1770. C.O. 5/1219.

The narrow division of the assembly over the supply bill was not due to one faction's advocating unqualified compliance with the Mutiny Act and to the other's flat refusal to grant any supplies whatsoever (as called for by MacDougal's broadside). Neither one was interested in following MacDougal's proposals. The aim of both was to bargain for paper currency, but the one wanted stricter terms than the De Lanceys would allow. The Schuyler forces were more responsive to the suggestions of the MacDougal broadside that compliance was an admission of Parliament's authority; they were more responsive only because their position happened to be closer to that of the broadside than was the De Lanceys'. By insisting that at least half the appropriation be made at once and allowing the other half to depend on the king's assent to the currency or loan office act, the De Lanceys showed they were more inclined to an easy compliance. Schuyler's following had insisted throughout that the entire £2,000 supply be contingent on the approval of the currency act, and steadfastly opposed the De Lancey arrangement. Resistance was a matter of degree. It was a partisan matter. The position adopted by the colonel and his cohorts was more of a partisan tactic than an ideological agreement with MacDougal's opposition to Parliamentary sovereignty. And yet the division carried the faint suggestion of how men like Colonel Schuyler might one day be driven from one camp into another, because of the slightest identification of a conservative faction's tactics with the ideological position of a radical third party.

Philip Schuyler apparently won his position of leadership and played a key role in the opposition largely because of the forced absence of Judge Robert Livingston. Five times Livingston was elected for the manor, and five times the De Lanceys rejected him. They refused to alter a resolution passed the previous session against seating supreme court judges, nor would they retreat when in 1770 the law barring judges from the house was disallowed by the king in council! In vain the judge appeared before the house to present his case for being "qualified" as a duly elected member, and in vain the manor electors re-elected him.[73]

The De Lanceys also tried to eject Schuyler's friend, Abraham Ten

[73] Robert R. Livingston to General Monckton, Dec. 4, 1769. NYPL, Chalmers Papers, IV, 53. See also "The Address of Mr. Justice Livingston, to the House of Assembly, In Support of his Right to a Seat," NYPL, Chalmers Papers, IV, 50–51; the broadside, "The Case of the Manor of Livingston and the Conduct of the Honourable House of Assembly, towards it, considered," NYPL; Sabine, *Smith Memoirs*,

Broeck, who sat for Rensselaer Manor. A question of Ten Broeck's residency in the manor was the ostensible excuse, but the Schuyler forces managed to attract enough votes from less consistently partisan De Lancey men to declare him qualified to represent Rensselaerwyck. Personal partisanship seemed to count more than principle, else Ten Broeck would have followed Judge Livingston to the doors.

The De Lanceys attempted still another measure aimed against representation of the manors, and thus against Livingston and other agrarian or "country" interests. Their bill was designed to subject members then eligible to represent boroughs, manors, or towns to a vote of all the freeholders of the counties in which such constituencies lay. The members so affected immediately protested, and by a bare majority of one, Schuyler's opposition prevented the passage of the act.[74] The maneuvering had the earmarks of a struggle against innovations and for the maintenance of well-established forms which made up mixed government.

For the remainder of the 1769–1770 session Schuyler's activities centered on issues which illustrated a certain liberal tendency within the broader context of his conservatism and partisanship. Either dissatisfied with the work of Agent Robert Charles, or preferring Edmund Burke, Schuyler in December, 1769, moved that the assembly name Burke its agent. The house had passed both the controversial paper currency bill and the £2,000 troop supply measure. Perhaps he believed Burke would more effectively represent New York's needs and wishes within the complex of empire and the passage of these measures. Schuyler's motion came on the heels of an attempt by John Thomas to name Stephen Sayre as assistant to Charles, but Thomas' motion was rejected, and the colonel's suggestion was postponed from day to day. Only after Charles died was Burke finally named, during a session in which Schuyler was absent. The De Lanceys' postponement of the choice of Burke suggests, therefore, their opposition to

I, 69; *The New-York Journal* (Holt), Aug. 23, 1770; Assembly Journals, Jan. 26, 1770. C.O. 5/1219. The law barring judges is in *Colonial Laws of New York,* V, 73–74. See also Livingston, *The Livingstons of Livingston Manor,* p. 182.

74 Assembly Journals, Jan. 13, 26, 1770. C.O. 5/1219. It is interesting to note that on the various votes regarding the bill, John De Lancey of Westchester Borough joined the Schuyler group, thus voting according to local interest just as did the representatives of Rensselaer and Cortlandt manors, and Schenectady Township (Ten Broeck, Van Cortlandt, and Mynderse, respectively). Livingston Manor was not represented at the time, else its assemblyman would doubtless have been part of the Schuyler forces too.

Schuyler, from whom it appears they wished to keep the credit for the appointment.

Schuyler's proposition to name Burke appears a curious gesture, suggestive of his opposition both to the Townshend duties (which Burke opposed as inexpedient) and to the De Lanceys, who comprised the committee charged with corresponding with the New York agent. Burke was perhaps a strange choice for the agency. For all his support of colonial interests, he was a staunch believer in Parliamentary supremacy—and the Declaratory Act—which many colonists seemed to have forgotten. Yet even his position was not one without partisan foundation, for Burke's stand developed from political experience— the workings of party. Perhaps Schuyler believed Burke to be quite suitable for New York's needs, notwithstanding his support of the basic authority which seemed to thwart colonial aspirations for freedom from imperial regulations. Perhaps Schuyler did not fully realize Burke's position, or believed that Burke would be less amenable to the De Lancey interests who controlled the committee of correspondence that bridged the gap between the assembly and the home government. Perhaps he simply suggested Burke because he identified him with the local minority opposition just as Judge Robert R. Livingston said that Burke was "the Kings personal Enemy & . . . the most detested of any Man in the Opposition." [75]

In response to a popular desire for opening the assembly to visitors, Philip Schuyler had moved in his first session to allow public spectators. The motion had narrowly failed by one vote in November, 1768, but on December 6, 1769, the assembly agreed to open its doors to spectators under certain regulations—conditions that the visitors remain quiet and that they leave upon any division of the house. [76]

[75] Dangerfield, *Livingston*, pp. 42–43. Assembly Journals, Dec. 20, 1769. C.O. 5/1219. The move to name Stephen Sayre as joint agent with Robert Charles was backed by the Sons of Liberty led by Isaac Sears who wanted to get rid of Charles. Charles owed his appointment to the De Lanceys. When he refused to defend Americans' claim to the exclusive right of taxing themselves, he roused the animosity of the Sons of Liberty, who tried to get the Livingston forces to oust him. Sayre had been critical of Charles as a ministerial placeman, but the vote failed, 16 to 6, with only John Thomas, Abraham Ten Broeck, Charles De Witt, George Clinton, Nathaniel Woodhull, and John Rapalje favoring Sayre. It was then that Schuyler proposed Burke, but the assembly refused further action until Charles died in 1770. Nicholas Varga, "Robert Charles: New York Agent, 1748–1770," *The William and Mary Quarterly*, Third Series, XVIII (April, 1961), 213, 217, 233–234.

[76] Assembly Journals, Nov. 3, 1768. C.O. 5/1100. Cf. Assembly Journals, Dec. 6, 1769. C.O. 5/1219.

This was in a way a liberal gesture. But it also coincided with the general courtship of radical support by the De Lancey forces.

Schuyler also favored a bill that would order the use of the secret ballot in the election of assembly members. This issue proved the partisan division of the assembly once again. The New York City members had received instructions from their constituents to oppose any alteration of the old *viva voce* method. The secret ballot, they said, was a dangerous innovation against the laws and customs of the realm. It would mean a surrender of the privilege of declaring one's sentiments openly on all occasions! The argument that a secret ballot would deliver the poor from the influence of the rich was weak, they said, for it assumed that honest men would sell their birthright for a mess of pottage. Secrecy would not prevent frauds and imposition, but breed more secrecy and craftiness instead.[77]

The Schuyler clique, which was distinctly agrarian, a faction of landlords who, it has been charged, favored the advantages of controlling their tenants' votes by the *viva voce* method,[78] now favored the secret ballot proposal! The assembly was tied (12 to 12) until Speaker Cruger broke the division and voted with the urban-mercantile De Lanceys to defeat the measure. It was clearly the urban, merchant interest that favored the *viva voce* method by which elections could be more easily manipulated and representatives more easily intimidated in cities no less than in the country. The division indicated how parties proved either willing or reluctant to alter existing institutions in order to advance their own political power.

Finally, the 1769–1770 session not only indicated the continuation of the religious element in politics but also the position of Philip Schuyler as a dissenter, a "religious liberal," and an opponent to the De Lancey-Episcopalians. True to the warning that William Smith, Jr., had given Schuyler in August that the dissenters were planning to pressure the assembly for an end to the Ministry Act of 1693, a petition was laid before the house on January 8, praying relief from

77 *The New-York Gazette, or Weekly Post-Boy,* Jan. 15, 1770.

78 Becker, *Political Parties,* pp. 14–15. Assembly Journals, Jan. 9, 1770. C.O. 5/1219, shows the following agrarians and landlords favoring the secret ballot by which they stood to lose influence with subservient tenants, freeholders, and freemen, provided of course that this was their practice and concerted aim: Van Cortlandt (Cortlandt Manor), Schuyler and Ten Eyck (Albany), Ten Broeck (Rensselaer Manor), Mynderse (Schenectady Township), Thomas (Westchester County), Van Kleeck (Dutchess County), and Charles De Witt and George Clinton (Ulster County).

taxation for the support of the Anglican Church.[79] Significantly, the petition was offered on behalf of the four southern counties by certain freeholders of Albany County, Schuyler's own constituency.

The bill favoring property-holding for dissenting churches in Albany County and the bill to exempt dissenters in the four lower counties from taxes to support the Established Church were both reintroduced in the assembly after the council had rejected them during the preceding session. A third bill to exempt Protestants from paying any clergy by a compulsory tax was added. As the session drew to a close, Schuyler and Charles De Witt visited the council to inquire about the progress of two of the measures. The council rejected both the bill allowing Reformed churches of Albany County to hold property and the bill exempting Protestants from paying any clergymen by compulsory taxation. It refused to pass such acts without a suspending clause (a device deferring execution until approved by the Privy Council), and when the De Lanceys refused to add such a clause, they thereby assured the rejection of the acts by the council, just as they had done in the previous session.[80] Thus these attempts again fell by the board. But on the other proposal to exempt dissenters in the four lower counties (New York, Richmond, Westchester, Queens) from supporting the Established Church, the assembly factions quarreled noticeably and so delayed its passage that by the time the house was prorogued, the council had given no final ruling on it. The attempt, in effect, failed again. But the maneuvers in the assembly's committee of the whole were typically partisan.

James De Lancey moved to strike out certain words from the bill exempting people from supporting churches to which they did not belong. He proposed to drop the provision, "Except such as are or profess themselves to be of the episcopal Denomination, and more frequently or ordinarily attend Divine Service, according to the Rites of the Church of England." The words were stricken by a vote of 14 to 9. Schuyler, who led the minority favoring the retention of the exception, evidently did not oppose the taxation of Anglicans for Anglican purposes. Indeed, it appears that he believed they alone might be subjected to a coercive feature which had been extended to

[79] Smith to Schuyler, Aug. 21, 1769. NYPL, Schuyler Papers Box 23. Assembly Journals, Jan. 8, 1770. C.O. 5/1219.

[80] Assembly Journals, Nov. 29, Dec. 11, 1769, Jan. 25, 1770. C.O. 5/1219. See also the *Journal of the Legislative Council of New York*, II, 1742, and Sabine, *Smith Memoirs*, I, 70.

dissenters. But the colonel did not approve forcing the support of the church by those not within its fold. John Cruger then moved to reject the entire bill, but on this the De Lanceys lost by an overwhelming vote of 19 to 3. Schuyler managed to amend the measure to declare that all persons not in communion with the Church of England "be exempt . . . from paying any Part of the said Tax." The bill thus amended was sent to the council, where it died when the assembly was prorogued three days later.[81]

By the close of the session in January, 1770, Philip Schuyler had emerged as the "acknowledged leader of the opposition in the assembly, and the special favorite of the more conservative patriots. . . ." His political inclinations were perhaps suggested by his presence at a meeting of the Sons of Liberty in the preceding November. He joined them in celebrations commemorating the repeal of the Stamp Act, but he was not one of their members. He joined in their toasts of loyalty to the king and his *honest* councilors, but also drank to the Massachusetts General Court and all colonial assemblies for resisting what some called arbitrary power. But if he was a leader in the assembly, it was not so much a position of clear opposition to the imperial government which he occupied as it was one of ambitious resistance to what Judge Robert Livingston so aptly designated as "a party now triumphant in the House. . . ." [82] This then was the measure of his conservative patriotism.

81 Assembly Journals, Jan. 25, 1770. C.O. 5/1219. The minority of three consisted, significantly enough, of Cruger, Walton, and James De Lancey—the New York City members.

82 Lossing, I, 246, 250. Robert R. Livingston to General Monckton, Dec. 4, 1769. NYPL, Chalmers Papers, IV, 53.

CHAPTER VI

Accommodation

– 1 –

THE 1770–1771 SESSION

THE SPRING and summer of 1770 passed quietly and were largely uneventful for Colonel Schuyler and also for New York, despite earlier excitements—the January 18 "Battle of Golden Hill" between the Sons of Liberty and soldiers who cut down a liberty pole in New York City, and the "massacre" of March 5, when a squad of British regulars was provoked into firing on a Boston mob. As for political quiescence, even Lieutenant Governor Colden commented that Schuyler surprised him by proposing that the assembly grant Colden the same salary Sir Henry Moore had enjoyed. Remarkably enough, Colden did not "so much as know" the colonel by sight.[1]

The colonel and his lady suffered some personal sorrow and distress in July, 1770, when Mrs. Schuyler presented him with triplets who died at birth. For a time her life was also endangered during her confinement, but she managed to survive.[2]

Between December, 1770, and March, 1771, the assembly under the governorship of the Earl of Dunmore met without Philip Schuyler. Recurring attacks of rheumatism and gout, and possibly the administration of his estate, prevented him from making the long trip south. Two years passed before he took his assembly seat once again, and by that time the critical situation in New York had for the most part passed. In the colonies as a whole these years were quiescent, threatened only by the Boston Massacre (March, 1770) and hardly again until the tea controversy (December, 1773).

Although he was kept from the assembly session of 1770–1771, Schuyler was not altogether politically inactive. Business demanded his presence in New York. In February, 1770, he was implicated in a

[1] Colden to Sir William Johnson, Jan. 28, 1770. *Colls. N.Y. Hist. Soc. for 1923* (New York, 1923), LVI: Colden Papers, VII, 165.

[2] Schuyler family Bible, Albany mansion. See also John Cochran to Schuyler, July 15, 1770. NYPL, Schuyler Papers Box 23.

dispute between General Thomas Gage and John Bradstreet about quarter-master accounts. He was also obliged to deal with the governor about John Van Rensselaer's land claims and Henry Van Schaack's contest over the Van Rensselaer militia district. Schuyler was further involved in the autumn of 1771 with the revival of the Hampshire Grants controversy. Governor William Tryon sent him to Boston in a semi-official capacity to confer about the boundary dispute with Massachusetts authorities. But the dispute over the New York–Massachusetts line remained unsettled.[3]

The relative calm that settled upon the colonies in general and New York in particular was the product of several influences: the basic conservatism or indifference of the leaders and the people, the mutual concessions of both the ministry and the colony, and the willingness of the London government to compromise by easing restrictions without really sacrificing the principle of Parliamentary supremacy. The repeal of the Stamp Act was accompanied by an act declaring Parliament's authority to legislate for the colonies in all cases whatsoever. The molasses duty had been reduced from three pence to a penny, but the revenue was still devoted to the expenses of colonial defense, and the colonies acquiesced in the matter. In 1768 there had been a partial withdrawal of troops, and the colonists were given control of Indian affairs, although it was only haltingly that New York attempted to form regulations for the Indian trade.[4] Assumption of responsibility came slowly, when it came at all.

There were other indications that a satisfactory arrangement within the empire had been achieved. The 1769–1770 session of the New York Assembly had approved the Virginia Resolves asserting the sole taxing power lay with the governor and the assembly, but by merely entering the resolves in the journal, the house made no great display or issue of the contention. On March 5, the day of the so-called Boston Massacre, Lord North moved to repeal the Townshend duties except for the tax on tea and pledged that no new taxes would be levied on the Americans.[5]

3 Smith to Schuyler, April 22, June 8, Nov. 9, 1771; Stephen Williams to Schuyler, Oct. 18, 1771. NYPL, Schuyler Papers Box 23. See also Schuyler to William Smith, Jr.?, Feb. 5, 1770, NYSL; Lossing, I, 258; Sabine, *Smith Memoirs*, I, 110.

4 Sosin, *Whitehall and the Wilderness*, pp. 155–156, 167–168, 180, 211–218, 238, 251. See also Assembly Journals, Jan. 26, 1770, Jan. 22, Feb. 15, 1771. C.O. 5/1219. Cf. Assembly Journals, April 6, 1769. C.O. 5/1100.

5 Assembly Journals, Nov. 29, 1769. C.O. 5/1219. See also Becker, *Political Parties*, pp. 69, 83–85.

New York had still other cause to adopt a conciliatory attitude toward Britain. The Privy Council had disallowed two paper currency acts because the clauses making the bills payable at the treasury and loan office were contrary to the act of Parliament which forbade the use of paper currency as legal tender for payment of any "debts, dues or demands, whatsoever." But Parliament also passed a special act allowing New York to circulate paper money as legal tender when presented at the colonial loan office and treasury—though it was not legal tender for private debts owed, for example, to London merchants. Nevertheless, the shortage of currency in New York was relieved, and the colony bowed to the principle of Parliamentary authority by accepting the act. In its 1770–1771 session the assembly took advantage of the law to emit £120,000 in bills of credit. In June, 1773, Parliament amended the currency act of 1764 so as to allow other colonies to issue paper money too—provided that the currency was backed by taxes, that it was systematically retired, and was legal tender *only* at the local treasury for payment of taxes, excise duties, or debts due the colony.[6]

In return for the concession on paper money the New York merchants were inclined to call a halt to non-importation, and after some hesitation to see what other colonies would do, they finally lifted the ban early in July, 1770. The assembly also indicated its loyalty by unexcitedly voting supplies for the troops every year until 1775. Indeed, in the 1770–1771 session when Schuyler was absent, only two of his colleagues (George Clinton and Nathaniel Woodhull) voted against granting supplies.[7]

This same session was notably free from disturbance except for two minor incidents. The De Lanceys again refused to seat Judge Robert Livingston, who had counted on Schuyler's presence and support for his case,[8] and the house voted Alexander MacDougal guilty of contempt, and jailed him until April, 1771. MacDougal maintained that he need not answer the question of his authorship of a broadside

[6] Hillsborough to Colden, Feb. 17, June 12, 1770. C.O. 5/1101:83–86, 119.

[7] Becker, *Political Parties,* pp. 88–89, 92. See also *The New-York Gazette, or Weekly Post-Boy,* Aug. 20, 27, 1770, about Albany's initial protests at relaxing non-importation and her subsequent acquiescence with New York City; Assembly Journals, Feb. 7, 1771. C.O. 5/1219.

[8] Assembly Journals, Dec. 20, 21, 1770; Jan. 25, 1771. C.O. 5/1219. See also "The Watchman, No. 5," a supplementary broadside to Holt's *New-York Journal,* April 21, 1770, NYPL; and Robert R. Livingston to Robert Livingston, Jan. 7, 1771. Robert R. Livingston Collection, NYHS.

critical of the assembly; he clung to his rights against self-incrimination. Moreover, he asserted that as he had been indicted for libel by a grand jury, the assembly could not try him on a criminal charge still being considered by a court of law. But to no avail. The house directed his imprisonment. The courts could not proceed against him for want of evidence; the witness had died, and MacDougal finally went free. In both the Livingston and MacDougal cases a small opposition group found itself quite overwhelmed by a determined majority and was unable to prevent either Livingston's expulsion or a declaration of MacDougal's contempt.[9]

Following Schuyler's promptings in the previous session, the house quietly elected Edmund Burke agent on December 21, 1770—though it did this without the governor's knowledge and contrary to the government's wishes for joint election by governor, council, and assembly. It also voted troop supplies, salaries, excise taxes and even began to make some progress with regulation of the Indian trade, although it complained to the governor that the execution of this function, relinquished by the imperial government in 1768, was being delayed by the lack of intercolonial cooperation and the time required for collecting information.[10]

– 2 –

TEDIUM AND PARTY SPIRIT

THE CALM marking the years 1770–1772 when Philip Schuyler largely withdrew from the political stage gave no indication of much colonial dissatisfaction with the imperial government and no suggestion of great concern about questions of "home rule." In August, 1770, following the Boston Massacre, New York erected a statue of the king and dropped the non-importation program. Two new governors arrived, the Earl of Dunmore in October, 1770, and William Tryon in July, 1771; Dunmore was toasted with a wish for the "total Abolition of all Party-Spirit, by [his] just and equal Administration." While Tryon was received with less enthusiasm, he was greeted with customary politeness.[11] The wish to abolish party spirit seemed attain-

9 Assembly Journals, Dec. 13, 1770. C.O. 5/1219.

10 Assembly Journals, Jan. 22, Feb. 15, 1771. C.O. 5/1219. See also *The New-York Gazette, or Weekly Post-Boy*, Feb. 5, 1770.

11 *The New-York Gazette, or Weekly Post-Boy*, Oct. 22, 1770. See also Tryon to Hillsborough, July 9, 1771. C.O. 5/1138:233, and Sabine, *Smith Memoirs*, I, 108.

able in the context of imperial-colonial relations more than in local intraparty struggles. For the following three sessions (January–March, 1772; January–March, 1773; January–March, 1774) the assembly showed scarcely a sign of local discontent with the empire. Commotions in the house were fixed largely on local, partisan issues and the conflicts between factions. The De Lancey party outnumbered the minority about two to one.

Indeed, the lack of contest over imperial measures in these "quiet years" suggests that the earlier protests which had reached a peak in 1769–1770 were determined less by reasoned, well-founded objections to imperial policy than by local factional and partisan struggles for power—not issues of "home rule," which was scarcely threatened, but rather controversies centering on the question of who was to rule at home. The persistence of local partisanship and its subsequent connection with later outbursts likewise suggests that it was the determining factor in the colonial-imperial quarrels. The fundamental undercurrent of partisan politics provided the framework of revolution. Local partisan divisions tended to carry over and merge with the broader issues of provincial relations with royal authority, Parliamentary supremacy, and the imperial system. Factional differences in the quest for local power largely determined the manner and spirit of later colonial contentions against Parliament and the empire.

The New-York Gazette pronounced the assembly session of January–March, 1772, a "tedious and Singular Session," and George Clinton thought the "Opposition by the Minority [was] more Spirited." [12] It proved to be both tedious and sporadically spirited. It was tedious insofar as the house was occupied with solid, ordinary legislation, and spirited inasmuch as there were occasional outbursts of partisanship. Even the governor told the secretary of state for the American Department that the session passed favorably except for the issue of excluding judges from the house. There was nothing extraordinary for Governor Tryon to request of the assembly when he opened the session in January. He reviewed the need for a militia bill and the usual troop supplies, salary grants, and excise duties. The assembly had nothing to say in return but that "The several Matters recommended by your Excellency, shall be considered with the utmost serious Attention." There was no controversy about voting appropria-

[12] *The New-York Gazette, or Weekly Post-Boy*, Mar. 23, 1772. George Clinton to Peter Tappen, Jan. 8, 1772. NYHS, Misc. MSS (Clinton).

tions. The house did, however, resolve that the governor's demand for payment of arrears for quartering the king's troops be disallowed. But it reversed itself when Tryon asked that the delinquent sums be paid as a matter of public faith and honor. The arrears had resulted when the 1769–1770 session granted £1,000 from the treasury but withheld the other £1,000 because the king had refused the paper currency bill. The record shows that Philip Schuyler neither opposed this as did six of his colleagues, nor did he vote to pay the sum.[13]

Routine legislation mainly occupied the assembly during the 1772 session, and Schuyler himself was charged with instructions from his constituents to bring several private as well as other bills before the house.[14] But the old partisan temper remained. Schuyler and his fellow agrarians (Abraham Ten Broeck, George Clinton, Nathaniel Woodhull, Pierre Van Cortlandt, Charles De Witt) again failed to have Judge Robert Livingston seated.[15] They managed, however, to defend Treasurer Abraham Lott from censure and removal from office, but this was possible only because some of the less staunch De Lanceyites joined them, and the pattern of voting revealed the extreme polarity of the factional leadership more than any sharp division of each group's following as a whole. James De Lancey had questioned Lott's handling of provincial funds, and if the treasurer had been removed, the vacant post would have been another piece of patronage over which to wrangle.[16]

The newspapers had their own comments for the "tedious and singular Session" of the assembly when Governor Tryon prorogued it on March 24. Indeed, one made a scathing commentary on the very instructions with which Albany had furnished its members, Schuyler

---

[13] Tryon to Hillsborough, Mar. 31, 1772. C.O. 5/1138:278–280. Assembly Journals, Jan. 13, Mar. 13, 14, 17, 1772. C.O. 5/1219.

[14] Instructions of the Mayor, Recorder, Aldermen and Commonalty of the City of Albany to Jacob Ten Eyck and Philip Schuyler, Jan. 6, 1772. NYPL, Schuyler Papers Box 42. The instructions concerned explanatory legislation for assembly elections, preventing freeholders who elected representatives from townships and manors from also voting for county members; they also included plans for dividing Albany County into poor relief districts, inspecting pot and pearl ashes, preserving forests, preventing any division of the county from prejudicing the city's rights and interests in Mohawk valley lands, and allowing Albany to raise money to finance street lighting and a night watch.

[15] Assembly Journals, Jan. 8, 16, Feb. 5, 1772. C.O. 5/1219. See also Robert Livingston, Jr., to James Duane, Feb. 17, April 6, 1772. NYHS, Duane Papers.

[16] Assembly Journals, Feb. 19, 21, 1772. C.O. 5/1219.

and Ten Eyck, regarding the franchise of electors of manors and townships that lay within county constituencies. Schuyler had helped pass a measure in accordance with his city's instructions to prevent manor and township electors from casting a ballot in county elections as well. "The Party-Bill for depriving the Freeholders of Manors and Towns, of their Votes, for the Members of Counties, which was rejected last Year by Lord Dunmore," ran one account, "met with the some Fate . . . upon its being presented to Governor Tryon . . . This Piece of political Cookery was first served up with such gross Marks of Partiality as rendered it too disgusting to his Lordship's Palate." This commentary, like an earlier one, suggested how "tedious," yet how partisan, the assembly had been in its latest work. "It was natural to suppose, that the Check upon Ambition and Party Rage, under the Administration of a new Governor, in high Reputation for Courage and Abilities, and made independent by the Crown [by a royal salary provision] would drive our Politicians to Art and Strategem." *The New-York Gazette* promised to publish an account of the recent partisan maneuvers for the province's information.[17]

– 3 –

PATRONAGE AND SHERIFF'S SALES

THE DIVISION of Albany County into three new units (Charlotte, Albany, and Tryon counties) opened questions of patronage after the assembly session of 1772. Coupled to this was a new militia bill which failed to provide that every militia officer be a resident of the county for which he was commissioned. This enabled those who wielded patronage greater freedom in their selections. In April, Schuyler and Ten Eyck with their brother assemblyman from Rensselaer Manor, Abraham Ten Broeck, took the lead in presenting to the governor requests for local patronage. At stake were a number of magisterial posts for both the city and county of Albany. Schuyler had corresponded with Sir William Johnson earlier in the year when the bill for partitioning Albany County was still under consideration. He invited Johnson to furnish directions about proper subdivisions of the county to be erected in the baronet's bailiwick and also reminded him to send down a list of "persons proper to be commissioned" for various official positions. Johnson obliged the colonel and told him

[17] *The New-York Gazette, or Weekly Post-Boy*, Mar. 23, 30, 1772. It does not appear whether the *Gazette* published the account or not.

that he and the others advocating the division bill should take care of the necessary offices "&c so that I need not to Enlarge." [18] The correspondence indicates that the two principals understood each other well if the present-day reader is not able to discern the details.

In April, 1772, there were complaints from a third quarter about how very active a "certain set" of men were in altering militia appointments. Henry Van Schaack also objected to Colonel Schuyler's "recommending two Dram Shop Keepers for the Office of Justices for . . . [Kinderhook] Township"—men who had "not one single quality to recommend them; except that of espousing the interest of Col. Rensselaer [Schuyler's father-in-law] in opposition to that of the Place they live in." Following the practice of allowing men of prominence to nominate local officials, Governor Tryon had invited Schuyler to draw up lists of officers for the Kinderhook militia. Van Schaack's brother tried to counteract this by telling Tryon that Schuyler's interest was directly contrary to local interests, for Kinderhook wanted more direct control of its own militia officers. Van Schaack's letter to Johnson revealed that Schuyler's interest was contrary to the Van Schaacks' political influence inasmuch as Henry's father feared that his regiment would be "New Modelled" without his being consulted. Van Schaack complained to Johnson because Sir William was the brigadier general of the district into which Schuyler's and Van Rensselaer's regiments fell. Again after Governor Tryon visited Schuyler at Albany in July, the Van Schaacks importuned Sir William to intercede on their behalf and to recommend that the governor retain the present militia establishment. Schuyler and Van Rensselaer had presented militia nominations to Tryon, and Henry Van Schaack believed "if they can't succeed in getting things established as they had them in Sir Harry's time," they would try to have the Kinderhook regiment divided in such a way as to get command of the eastern

18 E. B. O'Callaghan (ed.), *Calendar of Historical Manuscripts in the Office of the Secretary of State, Albany, N.Y.* (2 vols.; Albany, 1865–1866), II, 805–806. See also *The New-York Gazette, and the Weekly Mercury*, Mar. 16, 1772; Schuyler to Johnson, Jan. 18, 1772, and Johnson to Schuyler, Jan. 29, 1772. *Sir William Johnson Papers*, VIII, 369, 383–385. The county officers included both elective and appointive positions. The elective ones were: surveyors of highways, collectors, assessors, constables, and assemblymen. The appointive posts were: justices of the peace, judges, sheriffs, clerks, coroners, and militia officers from colonels down to cornets and quartermasters. Favored individuals and men of prominence were allowed to nominate local officials for appointment by the governor. Naylor, "The Royal Prerogative in New York, 1691–1775," pp. 232–233, 245–249.

district. Van Schaack's complaints appear to have been fruitless, however, for Governor Tryon told the secretary of state in January, 1773, that the militia law was well received, new units had been raised, and commissions were given to gentlemen of first families and distinction.[19]

Patronage was a relatively minor matter in 1772, compared with the new method Schuyler discovered to acquire lands. Between sessions of the assembly in 1772 and 1773 he recovered from an attack of the quinsy (which had forced him to bed) in time to attend a public auction of lands put on the block for arrears in quitrents.[20] The auctions proved both a profitable and controversial way to augment his growing landed estate.

Sir Henry Moore did not live long enough for Schuyler to exploit fully the obligations under which he had laid the governor. With his death, Schuyler could but turn to a new head and recommence the creation and exploitation of another connection. He was not able to make advances equivalent to those of the 12,000-acre purchase and a militia colonelcy won under Moore, but he launched another venture which created something of an uproar and momentarily threatened to check his agrarian ambitions. This was the Cosby Manor sale in July, 1772, for which John Bradstreet was his coadjutor and source of funds.

Whether inadvertently or by cautious foresight, Schuyler laid the foundation for his use of sheriff's sales to procure more lands; the sales resulted when landowners failed to pay the quitrents long overdue on their holdings. In the 1768–1769 session of the assembly the colonel had sponsored a bill to continue and amend the law by which the king's quitrents were collected. The amendment permitted the partial sale of large tracts—the sale of enough territory to raise the money to pay any arrears that might be due the government. Schuyler's efforts

[19] Henry Van Schaack to Johnson, April 17, July 27, 1772, and Cornelis Van Schaack to Johnson, Sept. 2, 1772. *Sir William Johnson Papers*, VIII, 448–450, 549–550, 589–590. See also Tryon to Schuyler, May 25, 1772. NYHS, John W. Francis, "Old New York" (New York, 1865), XIII, 17; Tryon to Dartmouth, Jan. ——, 1773, C.O. 5/1138:350–351. For other Van Schaack–Schuyler friction see the letter of Peter Van Schaack to Peter Vosburgh, *et al.*, Mar. 30, 1772, in the Peter Van Schaack Papers, Columbiana, Columbia University. In 1769 the farmers of Kinderhook had asked Governor Moore to draw militia commissions so they would not "create a presumption in favor of the Van Rensselaer claim to the area." They were so aroused that Henry Van Schaack told Johnson that seven-eighths of the county would follow him should he choose to run for office. Mark, *Agrarian Conflicts*, p. 160.

[20] Schuyler to Nicholas Bayard, July 1, 1772. NYHS, Misc. MSS (Bayard).

succeeded, and the bill became law on December 31, 1768.[21] So favorable a piece of legislation could hardly be disallowed by the king.

Taking advantage of several sheriff's sales for arrears in quitrents in 1772, Schuyler added to his holdings on the east side of the Hudson and on the banks of the Mohawk. If he could not procure new patents, he might benefit from the misfortune or carelessness of other patentees. With his own resources, those of a well-to-do friend, and with collaborators, Schuyler was able to speculate handsomely. Three of the additions to his interest were made without any apparent hitch. For 11,000 acres, a patent east of the Hudson once granted to Abraham D. Schuyler and others, Schuyler paid the sheriff of Albany County £612 5s. at public auction. In a solitary venture he procured 19,500 acres, and in a cooperative undertaking with John Morin Scott, John Bradstreet, Rutger Bleecker, Jacob Ten Eyck, and Volkert Douw, he purchased almost 17,000 acres more—all this merely by paying the arrears in quitrents.[22]

But the fourth sale, containing the largest acreage of all, caused a minor furor and an almost interminable contest. The heirs of Sir Peter Warren, represented by Oliver De Lancey, owned a large tract of land on the banks of the upper Mohawk known as Warrensburg or Cosby's Manor.[23] They had, supposedly, withheld quitrent pay-

21 Assembly Journals, Dec. 9, 22, 24, 29, 31, 1768. C.O. 5/1100:97, 109, 115, 120, 126.

22 Copy of a note signed by Schuyler to Sheriff Henry Ten Eyck, 1772. NYPL, Schuyler Papers Box 22. See also Sheriff Ten Eyck's endorsement of July 4, 1772, on Chief Justice Horsmanden's directions to sell lands, dated May 7, 1772. NYSL, Schuyler Papers. Exactly where the 19,500- and 17,000-acre parcels were located is not clear from Schuyler's inventory of Bradstreet's lands, Nov. 29, 1774, in NYPL, Schuyler Papers Box 9. The list indicates that the 1772 purchases were as follows: 11,500 acres by Schuyler alone (east of the Hudson) and this purchase is cited as 11,000 in a copy of a note signed by Schuyler to Sheriff Ten Eyck, *supra;* 16,950 acres by Schuyler, Bradstreet, Scott, Bleecker, Ten Eyck, and Douw; 19,500 acres by Schuyler alone; 21,850 acres (the Cosby Manor purchase) by Schuyler, Bradstreet, Scott, and Bleecker.

23 The lands were known as Cosby Manor because they had fallen into Governor William Cosby's hands after a number of petitioners combined to apply for large grants in accordance with the policy of limiting grants to one or two thousand acres per patentee. The grants were made in two parcels in 1734 of 22,000 and 20,000 acres, one to Joseph Worrel and others, the other to John Lyne and others. New York Colonial Manuscripts indorsed Land Papers, in the Office of the Secretary of State of New York, Patents, 1731–1739, XI, 102–103, 118–119, 121–122, 165–169, 170–174. To illustrate the tangled relationships and circumstances in which Schuyler was involved it is interesting to note that Sir Peter Warren was Sir William Johnson's uncle. Schuyler's threat to the Warren heirs was therefore an indirect blow to Johnson,

ments until these should be absolutely required by the provincial government, perhaps because it was preferable to retain the money for other uses and to pay the rents only when they could no longer be evaded—when non-payment would actually threaten forfeiture. By July, 1772, their quitrents were long overdue, and Schuyler, together with Bradstreet, Scott, and Bleecker, concerted to take advantage of the government's proceedings against the owners for arrearages and thus acquire at public vendue thousands of acres for speculative purposes.

Writing to John Bradstreet's daughters in 1775, Schuyler explained the transaction:

I purchased in the year 1772 Sundry tracts of land at vendue amounting to about forty thousand Acres. Mr. Scott . . . Mr. Bleecker . . . were to have One half and the General [Bradstreet] and myself the other half. Bills in Equity were intended to be placed against me soon after the purchase, by the former proprietors that the General did not chuse that it should be known to any person that he was concern'd, (because people of great Interest & Influence at home were of the former proprietors) and that therefore he would not take a deed from me for the land altho he had paid me the amount of his share[.] [P]erhaps you may think it prudent that it should still remain a Secret untill a decision if any is brought on.

For this venture Bradstreet loaned Schuyler £1,300 and also advanced over £950 for his share of the purchase.[24]

But what Schuyler did not tell Bradstreet's daughters was the curi-

---

who had created an immense estate for himself on the upper Mohawk. Sir Peter Warren's wife was the sister of Lieutenant Governor James De Lancey, Councilor Oliver De Lancey, and Assemblyman Peter De Lancey. Hence, Schuyler's threat to the Warren property was an affront to the De Lancey forces with whom he fought in the assembly. Flick, III, 149. Yet the De Lanceys and Schuyler were cousins! The mother of Lieutenant Governor James De Lancey and Oliver De Lancey was Philip Schuyler's aunt, Anne Van Cortlandt, the sister of Schuyler's mother, Cornelia. And Lady Warren was also therefore one of Schuyler's cousins. Schuyler, *Colonial New York*, I, 201, 203.

[24] Schuyler to Agatha Butter and Martha Bradstreet (copy), Feb. 1, 1775. NYPL, Schuyler Papers Box 9. See also "The Answer of Philip Schuyler . . . to the Bill of Complaint of John Evans . . . and Agatha his wife [1788]." Box 10. Bradstreet was angling for a promotion at the time and probably did not want to endanger his prospects of winning it by news that he was involved in a measure that threatened the interests of the Warren heirs, who numbered among them the wife of the Earl of Abingdon, Mrs. Charles Fitzroy, and Mrs. William Skinner. See copy of a petition to the governor in chancery, July 14, 1772. NYPL, Schuyler Papers Box 16. See also Charles Gould to Schuyler, April 6, 1773. Box 9.

ous manner in which the sale had taken place. To some it had all the earmarks of a conspiracy, in spite of the fact that the sheriff's vendue was fully publicized and arranged in accordance with legal form. The order for the sale at Albany was given by Chief Justice Horsmanden on May 7, 1772. A full year had passed after a notice was published that quitrents were due. The receiver general requested relief, and the chief justice then advertised for the proprietors of the Cosby Patent to appear before him in December, 1771, to show cause why their lands should not be sold for the arrears in the quitrents. Neither the proprietors nor their attorney appeared. They owed over £1,100; hence, on May 7 the chief justice ordered the public sale of "so much of the Lands contained within the . . . Patent . . . as will pay the said sum." The sheriff was to act within sixty days.[25]

Schuyler rode down to the Albany marketplace on July 4 when the auction commenced. The procedure of the sale was such that in protesting its validity, the attorney for the Warren heirs, James Duane, charged that the sheriff and prospective buyers had "previously concerted a plan for this purpose." Instead of auctioning only so much land as would pay the quitrents, the sheriff was accused of "combining and confederating" with Schuyler and others to sell the entire Cosby Patent. No one offered to bid against the colonel because, it was said, the public was of the general opinion that the proceedings were irregular and hence invalid, the sale was considered a hardship on the absentee proprietors, and because one person present to attempt the purchase on behalf of the Warren heirs was prevented from even offering a bid. Moreover, the bidding, though scheduled to last from nine o'clock until noon, was conducted in a brief fifteen minutes "in a scene of hurry and Confusion." [26]

It is impossible to determine whether or not Schuyler was fully cognizant of the difference between the chief justice's order to sell only enough land to pay the quitrents and the sheriff's sale of the entire Cosby Patent, or whether Sheriff Ten Eyck himself perceived the exactitude of his instructions or unwittingly proceeded to sell all instead of merely part of the patent. It is likewise impossible to know whether Schuyler realized the risk of incurring the ire of the De Lanceys who managed the Warren interests. Perhaps it was an honest

[25] Chief Justice Horsmanden's order to the Sheriff of Albany, May 7, 1772. NYPL, Schuyler Papers Box 16.

[26] Copy of a petition entered in chancery, July 14, 1772, by James Duane, attorney for the Warren heirs. NYPL, Schuyler Papers Box 16.

mistake. Perhaps Schuyler and his colleagues were not forced to back down on their intended purchase, but courteously admitted their mistake and conscientiously endeavored to rectify the error. John Bradstreet wrote Oliver De Lancey that the colonel had "informed" him of the purchase and that he, Bradstreet, then learned that De Lancey held an interest in the lands. Bradstreet did not doubt that Schuyler would act properly with his cousin. Indeed, Schuyler assured the general that De Lancey would be dealt with honorably and that John Morin Scott, one of the partners and a lawyer, would call on him to settle affairs. Perhaps Bradstreet was worried. His part in the proceedings was secret, and he carefully asked De Lancey to "Take no notice of your receiving this letter to any Person." [27]

Oliver De Lancey was angry, as might be expected. He quickly warned people in the disputed area to make no transaction with "the Supposed Purchasers as they will do it at their Peril and forfeit all future favor as they may be assur[e]d the Property will Remain in the family of Sr. Peter Warrin." Within a fortnight after the sale, De Lancey had received a release of part of the purchase.[28] Schuyler and company had made a hasty adjustment. Even before they had been able to get the sheriff to execute a deed for the lands, De Lancey had procured an injunction from the chancery court. Although they then agreed to hand back part of the purchase, should the entire patent pass to them by sale, they nonetheless proceeded to petition the governor for their own case.

It happened that Governor William Tryon paid a visit to Albany in July, 1772, two weeks after the controversial sheriff's sale. Tryon and his wife were greeted by the mayor, corporation, and "principal gentlemen of the city" with toasts, addresses, and "elegant entertainments." Oddly enough, Tryon's visit to Sir William Johnson later in the month coincided with the "perfection" of large purchases of Indian lands. What better opportunity could there be to gain the ear of the governor than such a visit? Schuyler had been asked by Tryon to arrange passage to Albany for himself and his party, and Mrs. Tryon was most happy to accept an invitation to be the Schuylers' guest. A governor under his own roof who had an eye to land purchases afforded Schuyler the chance to consult with him and per-

[27] Bradstreet to De Lancey, June [July] 5, 1772. NYHS, De Lancey Papers.
[28] Oliver De Lancey to Abram Hodge, July 17, 1772. See also Indenture, July 17, 1772, Philip Schuyler, Rutger Bleecker, and Oliver De Lancey. NYHS, De Lancey Papers.

sonally offer a chancery petition against the injunction that De Lancey had inaugurated to prevent execution of the sheriff's sale. If Tryon occasionally favored the Livingston interests in the assembly, he might also promote those of an individual member of that faction, as he in fact did in Schuyler's concern for John Van Rensselaer's land troubles and in the Massachusetts boundary dispute.[29]

On July 14, James Duane offered charges of irregularities in the Cosby Patent sale, but John Morin Scott filed counterclaims a week later, and Schuyler did what he could to present his case personally to the governor, in whose court of chancery the disputes had fallen. Schuyler and his associates insisted that the injunction against them was irregular because it delayed the execution of a law, and that it was in opposition to the king's right to a prompt payment of quitrents due him. They therefore petitioned that the injunction be dismissed.[30] The injunction and protests delayed a settlement of the business. As in all litigation involving land titles, the resolution of this problem dragged on. First, Schuyler could not get title from the sheriff. The injunction prevented that. Two years after the sales had been made, John Morin Scott was writing the colonel of his sorrow that "we could not compleat our affairs relating to our purchase." Oliver De Lancey canceled part of the sale insofar as the more extravagant extent of it was concerned. This he did by getting Schuyler and Bleecker to agree to return a portion of the lands to the Warren heirs and to be satisfied with only enough land as was required to be sold for raising the quitrents.[31] Schuyler signed the agreement, but De Lancey had difficulty getting Bleecker to offer his signature. Indeed, despite his promise to sign, Bleecker does not appear to have

29 The New-York Gazette, or Weekly Post-Boy, Aug. 3, 1772. The New-York Journal, or the General Advertiser (Holt), Aug. 6, 13, 1772. Tryon to Schuyler, May 25, 1772. NYHS, John W. Francis, "Old New York" (New York, 1865), XIII, 17. Schuyler, Rutger Bleecker, John Morin Scott petition to Governor Tryon in chancery, July 21, 1772. NYPL, Schuyler Papers Box 16. Jones, History of New York, I, 557.

30 Schuyler, Rutger Bleecker, John Morin Scott petition to Governor Tryon in chancery, July 21, 1772. NYPL, Schuyler Papers Box 16. Here the total Cosby Manor purchase is given at 18,996 acres. However, the Inventory of Bradstreet's Lands, Nov. 29, 1774 (NYPL, Schuyler Papers Box 9) suggests another figure: 21,850. Cf. Partition Deed between Rutger Bleecker and Philip Schuyler, Dec. 19, 1786, which offers 21,900 acres as the figure. NYPL, Bleecker Papers Box 2. The discrepancy in figures may be due to the imprecision of surveys even as late as 1772–1786.

31 John Morin Scott to Schuyler, July 8, 1774. NYPL, Schuyler Papers Box 16. Indenture: Philip Schuyler and Rutger Bleecker with Oliver De Lancey, July 17, 1772. NYHS, De Lancey Papers. This indenture carries only Schuyler's signature.

done so. Under these circumstances De Lancey managed to protect about half of the approximately 40,000-acre Warrensburg tract.[32]

As for De Lancey's success in filing a bill in chancery against the sale, Schuyler could not remember in 1803 whether any proceedings resulted from this legal maneuver. It appears that the settlement was not directed by any court, or if the court acted, it did not deprive Schuyler of his purchases. A private, semi-official arrangement was made, confirming part of the Cosby Manor sale, but preventing its extension to the whole patent. It limited it instead to only enough acres as would raise the money needed to pay the arrears of the quit-rents.[33]

At the very time the Cosby Manor sale was questioned, Schuyler's purchase of the old Abraham D. Schuyler patent of 11,100 acres east of the Hudson also was assailed. Charges were made that the sheriff had proceeded irregularly; his notification of the scheduled sales was technically late by reason of posting advertisements of the auction after sunset. He also failed to put up all the notices in the county. There were those who believed that these irregularities were grounds for preventing the execution of deeds to the purchaser. James Duane's complaints about the Warrensburg sale were applicable to the other

[32] Oliver De Lancey to Schuyler, Aug. 5, 1772. NYHS, John W. Francis, "Old New York" (New York, 1865), XIII, 114. Although Bleecker was reported ready to execute a deed, it seems unlikely that he did so. Schuyler held half interest in the sale for himself and Bradstreet. By his signature he relinquished half of the 40,000 acres. But Bleecker held one-fourth and Scott held one-fourth, and their failure to surrender their shares meant that about half the tract—a figure varyingly reported at 18,996 acres (Schuyler, Bleecker, and Scott's petition to Governor Tryon in chancery, July 21, 1772. NYPL, Schuyler Papers Box 16), 21,850 acres (Schuyler's inventory of Brad-street's estate, Nov. 29, 1774. NYPL, Schuyler Papers Box 9), and 21,900 acres (Sheriff Ten Eyck's lease and release to Philip Schuyler, July 18, 20, 1772. NYPL, Bleecker Papers Box 1; Sheriff Ten Eyck's indenture of sale to Schuyler, July 24, 1772; Parti-tion Deed between Rutger Bleecker and Philip Schuyler, Dec. 19, 1786. NYPL, Bleecker Papers Box 2)—remained in the partners' hands. See also a copy of an indenture of the Cosby heirs with Philip Schuyler, Mar. 6, 1793 (NYPL, Bleecker Papers Box 2), which mentions two parts of Cosby Manor, one 22,000-acre tract south of the Mohawk in what was then Herkimer County, and a 20,000-acre tract evidently north of the river. Cf. footnote 23, supra.

[33] Philip Schuyler's Deposition, July 19, 1803. See also Schuyler to Barent Bleecker, Feb. 28, 1798. NYPL, Bleecker Papers Box 2. Schuyler said the attorneys for the Cosby family wanted $5,000 for a release of what he had bought in 1772, and for that part which was not sold the attorneys offered a price that Schuyler did not choose to reveal by post because "the property would sell for an advance beyond what we should pay them" if anyone else learned that the price was so low.

sales in which Schuyler was involved. Duane said the sale was altogether invalid, in law and in equity. The sheriff's notices, he believed, were irregular in point of time, and so many estates had been put up for sale at the same time and the vendue conducted in such haste that he felt the act for collecting His Majesty's quitrents had been abused.[34]

None of the objections mentioned resulted in any loss of land for the colonel, however. His old friend and legal adviser, William Smith, Jr., insisted that by paying for the land (i.e., paying the quitrents due) Schuyler had title to it, even though the sheriff would not execute a deed. The deed, Smith said, was only evidence of a title; and according to the act for the collection of quitrents, the deed was not the only evidence of the title. Neither did the instrument itself constitute the title. Smith's argument prevailed. But it was some time before Schuyler won official sanction of the purchase by proper deeds, and not until 1786 did he divide the lands with Rutger Bleecker. Some twenty years after the sheriff's sale Schuyler extinguished all claims to the lands by a payment of $10,000 to the Warren heirs. He was also obliged to sue for ejectment against persons occupying the lands contrary to the purchasers' rights, and these actions he won with little difficulty. If these troubles were more than the colonel bargained for when he struck upon the use of quitrent sales to obtain land, Philip Schuyler proved his tenacity in holding what he acquired as much as his ambition and daring in adding to his landed estates.[35] The colonel's ventures also suggest the parallel relationship of assembly partisanship to wilderness speculation; his economic enterprises, no less than his

[34] Copy of Sheriff Ten Eyck's indenture with Schuyler, Oct. 9, 1773. NYPL, Schuyler Papers Box 16. A written advice by Whitehead Hicks, Sept. 21, 1772. The Albany Institute of History and Art. See also James Duane to Robert Yates, Sept. 23, 1772. NYHS, Duane Papers.

[35] That Schuyler did not lose the lands, see Partition Deed between him and Rutger Bleecker, Dec. 19, 1786, and Schuyler's Deposition, July 19, 1803. NYPL, Bleecker Papers Box 2. The deposition reveals how Schuyler worked out adjustments with various claimants. See also Ellis, *Landlords and Farmers*, p. 47; William Smith's Opinion, Sept. 17, 1772, NYPL, Schuyler Papers Box 22; for the official recognition of his 11,100-acre purchase see a copy of Sheriff Ten Eyck's Indenture, Oct. 9, 1773. NYPL, Schuyler Papers Box 16. Also for the settlement with the Warren heirs see Barent Bleecker to _____, Aug. 7, 1794. NYPL, Bleecker Papers Box 2. To avoid tedious litigation against the Warren heirs' claim to land south of the Mohawk, they were paid $10,000. See also receipts from the state auditor which show that Schuyler paid quitrents due from his lands to the state of New York for the years 1748–1787. Most of these were for the years 1772–1787. Finally, see the partition of Schuyler's Cosby Manor lands among his heirs, Nov. 12, 1806. NYPL, Schuyler Papers Box 11.

political machinations, revealed how an ambitious man was obliged to deal with the prevailing structure of New York politics and the existing means for social and economic advancement.

– 4 –

"THE GREATEST TRANQUILITY AND GOOD ORDER"

GOVERNOR TRYON, writing the secretary of state in March and April, indicated how quiet a session he enjoyed with the New York Assembly in 1773. "The Business," he said, "has been carried on without any Occurrence sufficiently remarkable to merit Your Lordship's particular Attention." It was conducted "with the greatest Tranquility and good Order." Even the partisan struggles of the factions were comparatively lessened with respect to the performance of earlier sessions. There was no other particular theme to characterize the session; it was neither preoccupied with "home rule" nor did it show excessive concern for the question of who was to rule at home. Yet the partisan undercurrents lingered, always susceptible to new outbursts. The furor over tea followed the assembly's prorogation, else the divisions within the house may well have formed the framework for new complaints against the imperial government. The only disturbance to be noted in New York City in January was caused by burglars; when Colonel Schuyler came down for the session he noted that the papers warned inhabitants "to be careful of their Doors, Windows, &c. as there are a set of House breakers now in Town." [36]

Schuyler arrived in New York well in advance of the new session. On January 3 he dined with his cousin, Councilor Oliver De Lancey. Partisan divisions did not keep relations apart, nor did the past year's trouble over the Cosby Manor sale. But Schuyler used the social occasion to good advantage, noting the De Lanceys' endeavors to embroil the governor in party matters whenever possible as a means of controlling him. From De Lancey's table Schuyler moved next day to the governor's, there to listen to Tryon's observations about the "Spirit of Party." After the session opened he obliged the governor with information about the conduct of the assemblymen toward him. It was no idle report that Tryon gave to Lord Dartmouth, the secre-

[36] Tryon to Dartmouth, Mar. 4, April 6, 1773. C.O. 5/1104:445, 477. *The New-York Gazette, and the Weekly Mercury,* Jan. 4, 1773.

tary of state for the colonies, about a governor's position: unless governors were "allowed on extraordinary Emergencies to put a liberal Interpretation" on their instructions, and unless the king's ministers put "as liberal a Construction on the Governors' Conduct, the most faithful Servant of the Crown . . . cannot long keep his Ground, or preserve his Government in peace." [37]

The formation of Tryon County meant the addition of two new assemblymen to the house, a matter which occasioned Councilor Hugh Wallace to comment about Colonel Schuyler's latest political behavior. One of the new members was Colonel Guy Johnson, Sir William's nephew and son-in-law. Wallace told the baronet he had heard "Colo. Schuyler has paid great Attention [to] Colo Johnson—Times are changed." Indeed, they seemed to be as far as zealous partisanship was concerned, or perhaps Schuyler was merely cultivating a possible ally. Wallace also noted another strange turn of affairs. Schuyler's Albany constituents had instructed him and Jacob Ten Eyck to vote against admitting Judge Livingston to the house after the many years during which they had supported the judge.[38] But it was not until a year later that Livingston was refused a seat for the last time, and Peter R. Livingston was finally admitted as a member from the manor. The judge did not present himself for admission to the house in 1773.

While Schuyler attended the assembly, Mrs. Schuyler was delivered of their twelfth child—a son born on January 29. He was named Rensselaer in honor of his maternal grandfather, whose difficulties with intruders and claimants for his lands had only recently been settled by the governor and council. This, too, explains Schuyler's subdued partisanship of the moment, for he was enjoying a measure of influence with men of power. Guy Johnson observed, "Schuyl[e]r. is very Complaisant. . . ." The colonel's presence in the assembly worked both to the advantage of his father-in-law and to Governor Tryon. William Smith, Jr., had told him that it was a good maxim to keep the power one had; now he said the confirmation of Van Rensselaer's land titles was due to "Schuyler's being in the Assembly & friendly to him [Tryon] in the Opposition to the Bill for changing the last Paper Emission. . . ." And Smith added, "50,000 guineas would not procure more" than what Schuyler's "Seat in the House got for" Van

[37] Sabine, *Smith Memoirs*, I, 136–137. Tryon to Dartmouth, Feb. 8, 1773. C.O. 5/1139:14.
[38] Wallace to Johnson, Jan. 12, 1773. *Sir William Johnson Papers*, VIII, 690–691.

Rensselaer. The aid with which he had repaid the governor in the counterfeit bill was more valuable than money.[39]

The bill for changing the paper currency emission had its distinctive origins, but it was related to Van Rensselaer's happy resolution of land troubles. The De Lanceys hoped to ensnare Governor Tryon by a new bill to issue £120,000 in bills of credit. In accordance with Parliamentary policy and royal instructions, Tryon would be obliged to reject such a measure, thus appearing in the popular mind as an opponent of paper currency. This in turn would subject him to radical criticism. The De Lanceys might then benefit from popular support or pose as rescuers of the governor and force greater influence with him. But Schuyler helped Tryon escape this danger. William Smith, Jr., and George Clinton joined the colonel to devise a substitute counterfeiting bill stipulating that no new issue of currency was intended. It was rather designed to devise a mark for distinguishing genuine bills then in circulation. This the assembly passed by a vote of 17 to 7; the De Lancey minority was a small one, but its membership was formed of the staunchest men of their interest. Clinton and Schuyler had conferred in advance with the governor; so hastily had they moved that they "knocked Mr Tryon up early" the morning of February 5 in order to divulge the scheme and get his approval. Smith urged them to act quickly to make certain the De Lanceys did not adopt the scheme "& then pretend that the Project was of their Contriv[in]g." Schuyler did not introduce the anti-counterfeit bill merely for the purposes of political maneuver. There was a real need for the measure, but oddly enough he did not cast a vote on his own proposal. However, the De Lancey forces were disgraced and then tried to "sink the Minutes of this Days Transactions." [40]

It was only on the anti-counterfeiting bill that Schuyler showed any notable difference with the members of the De Lancey faction. There were few other matters on which much partisanship was evident.

---

[39] Guy Johnson to Sir William Johnson, Feb. 2, 1773. *Sir William Johnson Papers,* VIII, 702–705. Johnson said "Col. Rensr. . . . gives up abt. 60,000a. & Patents the rest." Sabine, *Smith Memoirs,* I, 137. Smith to Schuyler, July 5, 1773. NYPL, Schuyler Papers Box 24.

[40] Sabine, *Smith Memoirs,* I, 128, 138. See also the Assembly Journals, Jan. 6, Feb. 5, Mar. 8, 1773. C.O. 5/1201; Kenneth Scott, *Counterfeiting in Colonial America* (New York, 1957), pp. 124–126, 189, 196, 203–204, 208–209, 212, 216, 219–221; John H. Hickcox, *A History of the Bills of Credit or Paper Money issued by New York, From 1709 to 1789* (Albany, 1866), pp. 40–47.

Indeed, Schuyler's dealings with the De Lanceys suggested cooperation that may have been aimed at currying favor with the governor for patronage. They also suggested that he had little cause to play the partisan game when he enjoyed and expected political influence. The smooth disposal of patronage hinged on the absence of effective opposition (which the De Lanceys might offer, especially through their connections in the council) almost as much as it depended upon influence with the governor. Schuyler apparently abandoned some of his old colleagues who maintained a more consistent opposition to their opponents than the colonel was interested in making.[41] William Smith, Jr., observed that the abatement of factionalism was due to the loss of influence of the De Lanceys, Waltons, and Crugers and that this in turn resulted from a popular discovery "in the 3 Families a Rage for Offices," and a detection of their "Design *to govern the Govr.* or drive him away for the Return of Ld. Dunmore." [42]

Assembly factionalism was also less noticeable in the old New York boundary controversy. In February, 1773, Schuyler headed a committee appointed to draw up a statement of New York's claims to the New Hampshire Grants. The statement was a full historical review of the jurisdictional dispute among New York, Massachusetts, and Connecticut. An able defense of New York claims, it was sent to the colony's agent in London for presentation to the Privy Council. Significantly, the paper was replete with references to the Van Rensselaer patent and suggested that Schuyler had carefully inserted a reminder that the holdings of his father-in-law's family were a matter of right, not of favor, because they had been Dutch grants recognized by the English government.[43] But this business occasioned no partisan tumults. It was too much a common interest of all factions who, when faced by threats from neighbors, could close ranks as Yorkers.

Schuyler's other major activities supporting the government in 1773 were signs of a wider satisfaction—and accommodation—with both the establishment and prosperity. There was very little opposition to voting funds for the government—repairs to Fort George and the mansion house, salaries, expense accounts, powder and field pieces, and troop supplies. On a vote in a committee of the whole considering the governor's request for increased troop supply, the chairman broke a tie

[41] Assembly Journals, Feb. 11, 12, 18, 19, Mar. 5, 1773. C.O. 5/1201.
[42] Sabine, *Smith Memoirs,* I, 140, 146.
[43] Assembly Journals, Mar. 6, 8, 1773. C.O. 5/1201. See also Lossing, I, 264–265.

to pass the motion. Schuyler voted for these supplies, and even joined the De Lanceys to increase the sum again. His old colleagues, George Clinton and Nathaniel Woodhull, however, voted against the increase; they opposed the government's measures and the ruling faction more consistently than did Schuyler.[44] The two men were to prove his strong supporters two years hence when new difficulties arose.

The colonel's amenability in the 1773 session did not allow him to fish for patronage without difficulty, however. William Smith, Jr., had correctly referred to the "Rage for Offices" plaguing the De Lanceys, Waltons, and Crugers, and their penchant arose again to plague the squire of Saratoga. Schuyler preferred to exercise his interest in Charlotte County without difficulty. The county had been created in 1772 when Albany County was subdivided. Charlotte County lay north of Albany and included territory in which Schuyler had a landed interest. Moreover, the county officials there would have power to deal with the Hampshire Grants intruders, who periodically caused considerable commotion. It was to Schuyler's advantage, therefore, to make certain that proper persons were named to local office.

Charlotte County was not organized until the summer of 1773, and then it seemed that the colonel's share in the patronage was to be threatened by the maneuvers of his cousin, Oliver De Lancey. De Lancey may well have designed a revenge for the Cosby Manor troubles of 1772. In July, William Smith, Jr., informed Schuyler of the developments when the colonel's residence in the country removed him from the center of patronage bargaining. De Lancey had been given the responsibility in the council for forming a list of justices of the peace for the county, "for it was long ago settled in Council that the Judges should be" Schuyler, Philip Skene, and William Duer "in the order I mention them," wrote Smith. De Lancey, Duer, and Colonel Joseph Reade (a councilor) presented the governor "with a List not only of Justices but of Judges," but Skene headed the roster instead of Schuyler. All was "set right," however, as Smith believed. Tryon was displeased with the alteration and declared Schuyler "wou'd not serve out of the plan first designated & known abroad." Smith insisted Skene should be named last, if named at all, and he warned Schuyler that for all his professions of friendship, Skene had shown his true colors. Tryon would not disappoint Schuyler, and from

44 Assembly Journals, Feb. 18, 19, Mar. 3, 5, 1773. C.O. 5/1201. See also Spaulding, *George Clinton*, p. 35.

1773 until May, 1777, the colonel held office as judge of Charlotte County. Duer succeeded him in 1777 under the newly formed state government.[45]

Notwithstanding auxiliary diversions with patronage and politick-

[45] Smith to Schuyler, July 5, 1773. NYPL, Schuyler Papers Box 24. Werner, *Civil List* (1884), pp. 387, 392. Smith was understandably agitated over the danger that Schuyler might lose an appointment as county judge. By dividing an old county into new ones, interested and influential New Yorkers were able to procure a more adequate number of law officers, sheriffs, and judges. Thus by patronage they could provide the machinery to execute ejectment actions against squatters and deal with offenders of various kinds. Alexander, *James Duane*, p. 77. The post of judge was of considerable standing. The three judges of a county (or a judge assisted by justices of the peace and a clerk) comprised an Inferior Court of Common Pleas which had jurisdiction over real, personal, and mixed actions involving sums over £5 value. These courts met twice each year. They occupied a position above that of the justices of the peace. Errors could be corrected by writs to the supreme court, and appeals could also be taken to that court when the value exceeded £20 currency. Naylor, "The Royal Prerogative in New York, 1691–1775," pp. 245–246. Lossing, I, 266, says Schuyler did not get the appointment because he "would not take a subordinate station upon the bench, and he was left in the field of politics, untrammeled by official restraints, to serve his country more profitably than if wearing the mantle of judicial dignity." This assumes that being a judge somehow compromised one's politics. Schuyler was not as unsympathetic to royal government as Lossing suggests, and Werner's *Civil List* indicates that Schuyler was made a judge. Moreover, there is no record in the *Civil List* that Skene ever served as a judge or that Duer served before Schuyler. The problem of the judicial appointment is complicated, however, by a letter Governor Tryon had written to Schuyler on May 25, 1772, in which he promised the colonel to consider a "Mr. Schuyler" for an appointment, "should a change in that Office take place." Although it may have been a judgeship, the office is undesignated, and it is not clear whether any appointment was ever made. Moreover, as this was the time Schuyler was active in soliciting other patronage, the mysterious "Mr. Schuyler" may have been a nominee for a militia or lesser magisterial post. NYHS, John W. Francis, "Old New York" (New York, 1865), XIII, 17. There is also evidence that Schuyler acted as a judge in an affidavit sworn before him by one John Duguid, Aug. 2, 1775. Although there seems to have been another Philip Schuyler living at the time (Schuyler, *Colonial New York*, II, 151) who might be confused with the subject of this study, the affidavit is signed in what appears to be the handwriting of the then General Schuyler. See National Archives Microfilm Publications: Microscopy No. 247, "Papers of the Continental Congress, 1774–1789" (The National Archives and Records Service. General Services Administration. Washington, 1959), Roll 172, vol. I, pp. 93–96. Nor does it seem probable that another Philip Schuyler held this post of judge inasmuch as William Smith's letter to the colonel of July 5, 1773, clearly indicates that it was the colonel who was involved in the appointment—not another man with the same surname and Christian name. Smith referred to the list of judges as "yourself [meaning Colonel Schuyler], Skene & Duer. . . ."

ing, land speculation continued to occupy the landlord's interest and attention. In March, 1773, the assembly had delayed consideration of a bill securing lands to the Indians on the lower Mohawk. Schuyler's vote had helped postpone the measure, thus assisting Governor Tryon's policy of making purchases from the Indians to satisfy the land hunger of Albany petitioners. Land speculating fever began to revive. Schuyler wrote his friend, William Duer, that recent purchases would bring Tryon over £22,000 in fees, "a good summer's work that." The land jobbers in New York, he said, would offer a large premium to "any ingenious artist who Shall contrive a machine to waft them to the moon," provided "any eminent astronomer" could assert discovery of "large vales of fine land in that luminary. I would apply to be a commissioner for granting the land, if I knew to whom to apply for it." [46] Thus, the humor or sarcasm of an observer who was little less smitten with land hunger than the New York jobbers of whom he wrote.

Tryon explained his Indian purchases to the ministry in terms favorable to New York landlords, although it was in his own interests to make them for the fees. In June, 1773, he wrote Lord Dartmouth that many New Yorkers had laid out funds to explore and survey lands in anticipation of government purchases from the Indians. When their patents were not confirmed, they blamed the governor. And the governor thought that "Men of Property in a Country where the soil is of little value, must have it in their Power to purchase large Tracts, if they chuse this Method to lay a foundation to raise their Families." Moreover, Tryon believed "it a good Policy rather to encourage than to check such a Spirit. The subordination which arises from a distinction in Rank and Fortune, I have found from experience, to be friendly to Gov't. and to be conducive to the strengthening the Hands of the Crown, and perhaps it will prove the only Counterpoize against a Republican & levelling Spirit which the popular Constitutions of some Colonies, and the Tempers of their Inhabitants . . . so naturally excite." [47] For the moment Philip Schuyler's behavior suggested that Tryon was right, for the colonel seemed to be warming to the establishment by virtue of his enjoyments and expectations of more influence. He always posed as a supporter of gubernatorial land transactions, and certainly the governor had not acted toward him

[46] Schuyler to Duer, Sept. 21, 1773. Lossing, I, 263. See also Assembly Journals, Mar. 3, 1773. C.O. 5/1201.

[47] Tryon to Dartmouth, June 2, 1773. C.O. 5/1139:61–66.

without promise. But would it last? Tryon was not altogether correct in his assessment. "Men of Opulence," wrote William Smith, Jr., "live more independently." [48]

Tea kindled a new flame in the colonies and upset the equilibrium that Philip Schuyler was beginning to enjoy. His trickle of patronage was relatively small. But loyal support of the governor and a providential shift in party dominance might offer better times.

[48] Sabine, *Smith Memoirs*, I, 148.

CHAPTER VII

Conservatism Thwarted

– 1 –

"THE CONTROVERSY . . . BEGINS TO WEAR A DARK & DISAGREEABLE ASPECT"

PHILIP SCHUYLER did not attend the assembly in 1774. Either recurring illness prevented a trip to New York, or he chose to avoid the possible controversy of another session and preferred to devote his energies to his private affairs. His absence, when viewed in the wider context of the events preceding and following the 1774 session, almost suggests a calculated aloofness, a studied effort to observe which direction the political winds were blowing before he would once more plunge into the fray.

In May, 1773, Parliament passed an act to rescue the East India Company from bankruptcy. It thereby prompted a new furor in the colonies. The company had millions of pounds of tea stored in English warehouses. In order to facilitate its disposal, Parliament provided a full remission of all British duties on teas exported to the American colonies. But an import tax of three pence per pound in America was retained. The company could sell tea directly to specified consignees in the colonies, and the drawbacks given by the government enabled it to cut the price of tea, even with the duty, and to undersell both colonial merchants who bought higher priced tea from middlemen and colonial smugglers who bought tea in Holland. Colonists objected to the East India Company's concession as a monopoly, and some were quick to suggest that the tea duty was merely a tax that did not have the consent of local assemblies.

When the New York Assembly met in 1774, the province was not yet disturbed by the actual arrival of the tea ships. Excitement was caused only by news of the East India Company Regulating Act and by the prospects of the tea's arrival. The furor over dumping tea in Boston harbor in the previous December did not noticeably affect the assembly which met from January until March, 1774. Perhaps this was due, in part, to Governor Tryon's promise not to use military force to land any tea in New York and to his avowal that "he would thro'w himself . . . into the Arms of the Citizens. . . ." [1] The assembly cooperated with the governor, voting the usual appropriations, import duties, salaries, the governor's travel expenses and money for the repair of Fort George. Only three members, led by George Clinton, opposed the grant of £2,000 for troop supplies. And on March 17 the house approved an address glowing with terms of esteem and respect for the governor, who was about to embark for London.[2] The serious conditions in the Hampshire Grants obliged Tryon to take New York's case to the ministry in person in an effort to resolve the controverted claims of jurisdiction.

There were hints of trouble both within and without the assembly. The house named a new committee of correspondence, on the whole a moderate group, but controlled by the De Lancey interests. This was a gesture of protest to the tea measure. The old partisan spirit, never entirely absent, but previously reduced, rose again when Judge Robert R. Livingston once more asked to be seated for Livingston Manor. Schuyler was not present to aid the judge's cause, and he was again denied entry to the house. A few weeks later, Peter R. Livingston, son of the third lord of the manor, was seated as its representative; the manor lord and freeholders had finally relented in their stubborn determination to seat the judge contrary to the De Lancey faction's ruling.[3]

Further partisanship resulted from a question of attendance in the assembly. The house was faced by the propagation of a report of "some designing Person" who was critical of its action because so few members were present to vote. The report said only fifteen assemblymen were in attendance when the house passed a number of bills, including one to raise £12,000 for the government by a lottery. This the assembly voted was "false, scandalous and malicious, and a high Contempt against the authority and dignity of this House, and calculated to inflame the Minds of the Inhabitants of this Colony." [4] They had already been inflamed against the landing of the tea.

Another partisan measure passed by the house was a militia bill to disqualify nonresident officers by which William Bayard, an enemy of a De Lancey faction member, could be turned out. The governor's

[1] Sabine, *Smith Memoirs*, I, 159.
[2] Assembly Journals, Jan. 22, 25, Feb. 7, 9, 14, 15, 17, 1774. C.O. 5/1201.
[3] Assembly Journals, Jan. 20, 26, Feb. 21, 1774. C.O. 5/1201.
[4] Assembly Journals, Mar. 14, 18, 1774. C.O. 5/1201.

council, however, refused the measure to allow the De Lanceys to reward John De Noyellis by providing him with legal revenge against Bayard (with whom De Noyellis had law suits). And the defeat for the De Lanceys suggested their power was hardly absolute.[5]

After the assembly had been prorogued, William Smith, Jr., wrote Schuyler of what he called a long and disagreeable session. Smith wished Schuyler "had taken a Part [in it] not because I wish you Trouble," he said, "but that you might have shared in the Credit which [George] Clinton has acquired in the Course of it." Exactly what credit is difficult to say. Clinton had voted against the troop provisions and for seating Judge Livingston. But Smith was probably referring to Clinton's general opposition to the De Lanceys, who were ambitious to control the governor but could not manage it to the degree they desired. Smith told Schuyler there was "a surprizing Change both within Doors and without[,] the Spirit of Party being in great disgrace, to the Confusion of those who led it . . . Their Impatience under a Govr. who scorned to be purchased excited them to another Effort to humble him but they found themselves baffled" in the council and in the house, especially in the controversy over the militia bill.[6]

Early in April, 1774, Governor Tryon embarked for England. Before his departure he was feted with great affection, but he had scarcely put out to sea when the tea ships began to arrive. The province was thrown into new excitement which steadily increased the party spirit and renewed criticism of the imperial regime. Before this, William Smith, Jr., said the De Lanceys had "distinguished themselves in their Coolness towards the Govr. & sank into Contempt." He told Schuyler that the political system had changed entirely; "Some Persons have fallen into the Dust who were at the Top of the Pinnacle." [7] But the tea controversy occasioned still further competition between various groups seeking power. And the assembly conservatives and governing classes were challenged by a third party of more radical elements of the population. Eventually, the anti-British movement passed out of the hands of the assembly to the extralegal bodies. Meantime, conservatives within and without the assembly attempted to control the activities of the radicals.

[5] Sabine, *Smith Memoirs*, I, 177.
[6] Smith to Schuyler, Mar. 22, 1774. NYPL, Schuyler Papers Box 24.
[7] Sabine, *Smith Memoirs*, I, 182. Smith to Schuyler, April 7, 1774. NYPL, Schuyler Papers Box 24.

Despite the agreement by certain partisans to boycott the tea as a means of checking violence while placating the radicals, tumults followed, and the radicals dumped the weed in New York harbor (April 22, 1774). Conservatives then realized that if the colony's policy was to be directed by moderate men of property rather than by a mob, they must win control of the Sons of Liberty. This they proceeded to do by participating in public meetings which elected a committee charged with the direction of non-importation. The radicals favored absolute non-importation, the conservatives only modified non-importation, moderation, and hesitation. In the face of the "coercive acts" passed by Parliament to deal with the situation in Massachusetts, the New Yorkers feared to refuse or to grant the request of the Bay Colony for total non-intercourse, and a local committee of fifty-one supported the suggestion for a continental congress to present colonial grievances to the mother country.[8] The congress was to formulate a general course of action on which all the colonies might unite for the most beneficial and effective results. Meantime, it was hoped the factions in New York might be freed from the task of leading resistance to the imperial government, for they had thrown their problem into the lap of an organization outside the boundaries of the province.

The election of delegates to the First Continental Congress offered still another opportunity for conservatives to resist the radicals. The

[8] Becker, *Political Parties*, pp. 111–116, 118. Roger Champagne, "New York and the Intolerable Acts, 1774," shows how these laws provided an opportunity for the factions to gain political advantage over their rivals, and how popular leaders used colonial-imperial difficulties to advance themselves in provincial affairs with the electorate. Both factions hoped to gain support of the people by posing as defenders of American freedom. And radicals such as Isaac Sears, John Lamb, and Alexander MacDougal hoped to regain an influence they had lost since the tumults of the Stamp and Townshend acts. P. 196. Champagne also indicates that the committee of fifty-one was originally created by radicals, who, only after the conservatives or "aristocrats" had captured the committee to divert it from reviving non-importation, *then* proposed their committee of twenty-five as an alternative to the larger committee. It was the De Lanceys who proposed a larger, more unwieldy, committee as a means of impeding action, and the fifty-one included 26 De Lanceys, 15 Livingstons, and 10 men whose factional alignment is unknown. Pp. 197–198, 203–205. Sears, Lamb, and MacDougal stimulated conservatives to hold public meetings and appoint committees. And whereas the conservatives or "aristocrats" were in control, their future was uncertain because having recourse to popular meetings was a "breach in the aristocratic fortress." Gouverneur Morris observed, "The mob begin to think and to reason. Poor reptiles! it is with them a vernal morning, they are struggling to cast off their winter's slough, they bask in the sunshine, and ere noon they will bite, depend upon it. The gentry begin to fear this." Pp. 206–207.

choice of representatives indirectly raised a question of future policy. A committee of mechanics offered its own radical nominees as rivals of those selected by the committee of fifty-one. In July, William Smith, Jr., reported these happenings to Schuyler, then at Saratoga. "The political sky at this Place is cloudy," he wrote. Some of the committee of fifty-one "made a secession" when the majority disapproved the resolves made by a mass meeting in the Fields—resolves empowering New York delegates to the Congress to bind the province to a policy of non-intercourse if the Congress so chose. Smith told Schuyler that it was "Strange that the colony who had the first Intelligence of the Parliamentary Measures [i.e., Coercive Acts] is behind all the Rest." South Carolina's delegates were already bound to non-intercourse should Congress so direct, and Smith said their merchants had agreed to suspend their commerce in the interim. He also suspected that the "Military mean to interrupt the Congress," but for this he had no proof, and asked the colonel not to divulge his suspicion.[9]

In electing delegates to the First Continental Congress the New York Committee of Fifty-one was obliged to recognize the radical committee of mechanics and allow the franchise to others than freemen and freeholders. Thus, not one, but two committees emerged to compete for leadership and control of the populace. The partisans in the assembly seemed unable to prevent a third force from challenging their position, and the assembly minority tended to gravitate toward the radical camp as a means of rivaling its old De Lancey foes. Several weeks of maneuvering were required before the rivals could even agree on a means of electing delegates to the Congress. Finally, they decided that the city and county should elect five delegates. Freeholders, freemen, and persons who paid taxes were allowed to vote. On July 28, the conservatives managed to elect their nominees for delegates, but they did not pledge to work for a general non-importation agreement in the Congress as the best means to procure a redress of grievances. They did no more than state that they "were *at present* in favor of" such an agreement. At the Congress they would "work for whatever seemed *then* for the best interests of the country." [10]

Philip Schuyler's role in this extralegal movement, or rather his initial inaction, was largely determined by his illness. But he also may have been more interested in his land dealings, and he was not to join

[9] Becker, *Political Parties*, p. 123. Smith to Schuyler, July 9, 1774. NYPL, Schuyler Papers Box 24.
[10] Becker, *Political Parties*, pp. 128, 133–135.

boldly in questionable activities that might compromise his own standing with the royal establishment—at least not yet.

The New York Committee of Fifty-one sought rural support for its course of action, chiefly as a means of insuring that the partisan leaders kept control of provincial affairs out of radical hands. Late in May the committee called upon county supervisors to procure the election of local committees of correspondence. There was almost no response. Again, late in July, the committee asked counties to elect delegates to the Continental Congress or to authorize New York's delegates to act for them. The response was somewhat better. Three counties sent their own delegates, and four authorized New York's delegates to act for them.[11] One of the four was Albany County, Schuyler's own bailiwick.

Albany had hesitated in forming a committee of correspondence, but by August, 1774, such an organization was functioning, and Philip Schuyler was one of its members. On August 13 the colonel proposed that delegates be named for the Continental Congress "out of the Body of the City and County of Albany." Although Schuyler's motion passed, the colonel himself voted against it! His action may have been a means to test sentiment, perhaps to determine where he himself stood as a possible candidate.[12] But the committee named Robert Yates, Henry Van Schaack, and Peter Silvester as delegates, provided the various districts of the city and county approved them within ten days. This was decided because "several gentlemen of the committee" believed they had no power to name the delegates. Perhaps this was the reason why Schuyler voted against electing representatives.

On August 23 the committee again assembled; this time Schuyler was absent. When it learned that only Livingston Manor and Schenectady Township had approved its choice of representatives, the committee decided to name but one delegate, and Philip Schuyler was chosen by a large majority. But by this late date Schuyler was not inclined to undertake a trip to Philadelphia. When the committee of

[11] *Ibid.*, pp. 136–141. Becker (p. 137) says that it was only "likely" that Albany County named a committee of correspondence. But by August, 1774, Albany did have such an organization. See Albany Committee of Correspondence Minutes, Aug. 13, 1774. Peter Van Schaack Papers, Columbiana, Columbia University.

[12] Schuyler's role in the committee of correspondence has been misstated by Jones, *History of New York*, II, 317: "Schuyler took the lead in Albany, and was chairman both of the City, and County Committee." This seems largely erroneous, according to the Minutes of the Albany Committee, Peter Van Schaack Papers, Columbiana, Columbia University.

correspondence met on August 30, Chairman Jacob Lansing produced a letter from the colonel, saying that rheumatic pains and fever prevented him from attending the First Continental Congress. With that the Albany committee authorized the New York delegates to act as its own.[13]

By declining to attend the First Continental Congress, Philip Schuyler did not fully join the extralegal movement for the moment. He refused the appointment on grounds of illness, but within a month he was able to travel as far as New York City. The coincidence of illness at the time of his election was excuse enough for not going to Philadelphia, and despite his position on the Albany committee, one wonders how anxious he was to be caught in the main channel of the extralegal current. His behavior is all the more curious, for within a few months he espoused the cause of the Continental Congress. While New York City was caught in the throes of political maneuvers in the summer, and while the First Congress met, Schuyler remained occupied with land speculation, John Bradstreet's estate and his own thoughts of the next session of the assembly—the last ever held under royal auspices.

William Smith, Jr., had invited the colonel's attention to speculation in July when he wrote that Lieutenant Governor Colden, in Governor Tryon's absence, was "granting Lands in the Face of the last Instructions in the New Hampshire District." People had no money to pay the fees for such grants, and Smith was offered lands between the Connecticut River and Lake Champlain for eighteen pence per acre. "If you have a Mind to be concerned," he told Schuyler, "I will execute any Trust you think fit to give me." But Schuyler must hurry if he meant to make any purchase, "for the next Packet may close the present Scene in which the King's Property is to be disposed of agt. his Will. Let all this be a Secret," he cautioned. The colonel seized the advantage, and Smith promptly wrote that if he bought 10,000 acres, Schuyler should send various sums totaling £750 to the lieutenant governor, Surveyor General Alexander Colden, and Attorney General Kempe. The sooner he acted, the better, but Colden's impatience to issue the patents might also mean he would reduce the fees from eighteen to fifteen pence per acre, or even to a shilling.[14] The outcome of these dealings remains unknown, although there is no evi-

---

[13] *Ibid.* See also Jacob Lansing, Jr., to Schuyler, Aug. 23, 1774. NYPL, Schuyler Papers Box 24.

[14] Smith to Schuyler, July 7, Aug. 10, 1774. NYPL, Schuyler Papers Box 24.

dence Schuyler procured any grant directly in his own name. If he acquired the 10,000 acres, he made the transaction with the aid of others who later transferred the land title to him, and although he may have made a sizable addition to his holdings, he also embroiled himself with Yankees who had their own designs for lands north and east of Saratoga.

By late September, Schuyler had sufficiently recovered from his illness to travel to New York where his aging friend, General John Bradstreet, lay dying. Before the old man expired on September 24, Schuyler persuaded him to alter his will so as to benefit the general's wife and daughters. It was a magnanimous suggestion. On the following Monday, Bradstreet was buried in Trinity Church with the honors of war. His funeral cortege provided something of a display in the city. General Frederick Haldimand rode as chief mourner, accompanied by Schuyler, William Smith, Jr., council members, judges, the mayor and corporation, and various militia officers. Bradstreet's death brought Schuyler both profit and distress. The estate he administered was handsome, but many years passed before he settled it with the contentious heirs, who suspected they were deprived of some of their father's property. Bradstreet canceled a debt of almost £3,500 Schuyler owed him out of an estate the colonel calculated at over £33,500. Schuyler's family also received bequests: Mrs. Schuyler was given Bradstreet's horses and carriages; Margaret was given money, and Bradstreet's namesake, John Bradstreet Schuyler, received a farm together with the general's books, arms, and clothing.[15]

Faced with an impending session of the assembly and the conduct of the deceased Bradstreet's affairs, not to mention his own business, Schuyler did not lack time to speculate about the larger political milieu from which his residence in the country momentarily kept him. William Smith, Jr., aided him in these contemplations by providing a hint of what to expect from some of the "old Politicians" in the next meeting of the assembly. The conduct of the house was to be determined very largely by the activities of the First Continental Congress, which met in September and October, 1774.

---

15 Schuyler to John Glen, Sept. 3, 1774. William L. Clements Library, Misc. MSS, reveals Schuyler's sentiments regarding Bradstreet who, being past hopes of recovery, made Schuyler "feel much on the Account of so good a friend. . . ." See also Rivington's *New-York Gazetteer*, Sept. 29, 1774; Schuyler to Charles Gould, Oct. 2, 1774. NYPL, Schuyler Papers Box 9. A copy of Bradstreet's will and other estate papers are in Boxes 9 and 10.

Both the New York Assembly factions and the men who made up the more radical extralegal groups outside the house had "virtually agreed to throw the burden of formulating a policy of resistance upon a power outside the colony" when the extralegal bodies were permitted to send delegates to Philadelphia in 1774. New York would likely be obliged to follow the policy and program of the Congress or risk the appearance of countenancing Parliamentary measures. While radicals hoped to revive non-intercourse, more cautious men preferred conciliation. Moderates seemed to balance both extremes, and men like John Jay and James Duane—and if we may judge by his overall behavior, Philip Schuyler—"hoped for a firm union of the colonies in measures that were free from any charge of undue submissiveness." [16] The inability of the factions to resolve the leadership problem within New York and the fact that they passed the initiative to the Continental Congress suggested that provincial politics had indeed been largely centered in partisan struggles for dominance, and not on questions of colonial-imperial relations.

Philip Schuyler has left no evidence of any philosophical or theoretical approach to the new crises, the nature of the empire, or the colonial view of the locus of power. Like a true Briton, he was much more the pragmatist than the philosopher. It was such an approach that led colonists to war when their theorizing, if taken alone, may not have done so. For all its guarded expressions of loyalty the First Continental Congress proved in the final instance that it was essentially radical by adopting the Association—a specific scheme for enforcing non-intercourse which in a way negated most of its protestations of loyalty. The resolutions of the people of Suffolk County, Massachusetts, calling for non-importation, armed defense, and the beginning of extralegal government, when considered by the Congress at Philadelphia, meant the mere presentation of a petition was not protest enough. The vote on the Suffolk Resolves may have laid the foundation of military resistance and marked the beginning of the moderates' despair of seeing any good produced by the Congress. If so, Philip Schuyler hardly seems a moderate. However, he too continued to profess loyalty. A stronger course of action seemed only to lead to more action, and ultimately to the last step—open avowal of independence.

Proclaiming allegiance to the king was practically meaningless when

[16] Becker, *Political Parties,* pp. 142–143.

the Association in effect announced that royal government no longer bound the colonists. The action of Congress thus obliged men to choose their allegiance, and Schuyler, together with his fellow partisans in the New York Assembly, was obliged to choose between "parties asserting allegiance to different authorities." [17] Again the fundamental importance of the power struggle *within* New York became quite evident as the men who enjoyed the greatest influence in the establishment tended to support those institutions on which their power was based (royal government, Parliamentary sovereignty) while the men who enjoyed less power, the old Livingston interests led now by Philip Schuyler, tended to embrace the extralegal movement; they found in the protests to imperial administration a means of challenging their opponents' position and claims to leadership.

Many New Yorkers began to abandon the old factions comprising the ruling class because they were obliged to choose between adhering to Congress, even if it meant rebellion and independence, and adhering to Britain, even if it meant submission to Parliamentary authority. This process gradually developed between the session of the First Continental Congress and the adoption of the Declaration of Independence. Its earliest stages can be seen in the last session of the New York Assembly, where Philip Schuyler and a minority fought the more conservative De Lanceys—a group which ultimately became loyalists. Here was a division of conservatives. The loyalists inclined to side with Britain, and the patriots made ready to join Congress. Some conservatives made their choice as soon as the resolutions of the First Congress were published. They were reluctant rebels. Philip Schuyler's advocacy of congressional procedure made him a "patriot," albeit a conservative one. When the assembly factions divided anew in 1775, the lines were those of the old parties struggling for local power. It is more than a coincidence that the privileged clique within the governing class sided with the imperial government, while those members of the same general class who had thirsted for a greater measure of influence now joined the radical movement, tempered it, and brought it under control as a means of establishing themselves in the seats of the old privileged coterie they ousted. The measure of Schuyler's conservative patriotism was indicated by his later interest in the New York Constitution of 1777 and his subsequent swing into Federalism; both revealed his convictions about who should rule at

[17] *Ibid.,* pp. 144, 147–148, 151, 155.

home once independence had been won. It is this general line of behavior, too, when joined with that of other partisans who were unable to realize ambitions within the colonial governing class, which suggests that the factional contests for power in the New York Assembly were more fundamental to the politics of the province than any great interest in "home rule"—a blessing the colonists already enjoyed in large measure.[18]

Before the last session of the colonial assembly opened, Philip Schuyler chose the course of action to pursue in the house. Just as the Continental Congress in large measure determined what New York's policy would be, just as the Association helped create loyalist and patriot groups, so they helped one man decide his personal conduct. It was no easy process, nor was it quickly done. On October 2 the colonel's observation that "The controversy between the mother Country and this begins to wear a dark & disagreeable aspect," was about as much as he could say, considering the lack of information from Philadelphia. "I fear," he wrote, "the result will be very serious. The Grand Congress Continue to Sit, but very little transpires as they have entered into Engagements of Secrecy." [19] But as the Congress formed and implemented the Association, Schuyler could better understand what had "transpired." Active loyalist opposition appeared in New York, and the question of enforcing the Association became the center of renewed struggles, for the conservative committee of fifty-one was composed largely of men opposed to the Association.[20]

William Smith, Jr., continued to provide Schuyler with the latest political gossip; the New York delegates had been converted to the sentiments of Congress notwithstanding their reluctance. Again the

[18] Stoddart, "Home Rule and the Development of the American Revolution New York, 1760–1775." Miss Stoddart's work nicely points up that "local factors" were behind the constitutional struggle between New York and Britain, and shows that New Yorkers really had "home rule." "Home rule" was no issue by April, 1775, because the colonists had won the right to tax themselves, to pass their own mutiny acts, to regulate Indian affairs, to print paper currency as legal tender, to provide for their own civil establishment, and to have duties on trade laid by Parliament paid into the provincial treasury. The secretary of state for the American Department was willing to let judges be appointed during good behavior and to permit jury trials in cases formerly under the jurisdiction of vice-admiralty courts. "Home rule" is not a satisfactory explanation of the Revolution in New York. The question of "who should rule at home" appears to have been a more vital issue. See especially pp. 3 n., 6, 158, 164–165, 174–177, 181, 183–184.

[19] Schuyler to Charles Gould (copies), Oct. 2, 1774. NYPL, Schuyler Papers Box 9.
[20] Becker, *Political Parties*, pp. 158–163.

provincial power struggle seemed evident. Smith suspected that the behavior of the delegates, especially Isaac Low and James Duane, might be due to their political ambitions to win office in the coming assembly elections. Smith surmised that the New York delegates aimed to win the support of merchants, some Episcopalians and all the dissenters as well as all of the "Liberty Boys." By this means they could "secure Places in the Assembly and laugh at the Discontented." Smith also reported that the committee of fifty-one was to be dissolved, and replaced by a new body which would enforce the Association. This was the more radical committee of sixty—congressional delegates, men approved by the "most active Liberty Boys." "With this hint," he told Schuyler, "you'l be able to predict what the Conduct of some old Politicians will be at the Session & will perceive that the Current will set all one Way for Liberty in both Houses unless Some Persons will throw Obstacles in the Way to blow up the Powder now concealed & draw certain Leaders into Day Light who must[,] for Fear of distant Wrath and to give the Project all the Wished for Extent of Success[,] be unknown." [21] Were the assembly factions to battle for the position of leadership of the radical elements outside the house lest their enthusiasm carry them all into uncharted dangers?

– 2 –

"COL. SCHUYLER AND CLINTON HOLD FORTH IN THE OPPOSITION"

AFTER MONTHS of radical agitation and jockeying for leadership out of doors, in January, 1775, interest again focused on the New York Assembly. It now had to endorse or reject the activities of the First Continental Congress and to decide about sending delegates to a second congress in May. No one could tell how the assembly would react, but its actions, as time proved, mirrored the general division of members into loyalist and patriot parties and also indicated how abiding were the partisan divisions which formed the basis for alignments on imperial disputes. Late in December, 1774, James Duane wrote that it was difficult to know the feelings of the assemblymen. Even the members in town seemed "either not to have formed decisive Sentiments or to act on the reserve till they try the pulses of their Breth-

[21] Smith to Schuyler, Nov. 22, 1774. NYPL, Schuyler Papers Box 24.

ren." But, said Duane, "The time swiftly approaches when they must declare themselves and take a conclusive part. . . ." [22] John Jay, another delegate to Congress, told Robert R. Livingston that "Provincial Politicks fluctuate. A Year may give them quite another turn. After the Assembly meets, I shall be able to give a better guess." [23] Encountered by questions of political principle, the assembly continued to divide along old factional lines. Partisanship persisted, as though it were too ingrained, too inflexibly determined to alter or to be altered by issues of wider import.

The session of January 10–April 3, 1775, indeed proved to be a "pulse feeling" exercise by which the factions made their decisions between support of the Continental Congress with all the concomitant dangers of resistance, and loyalty to the royal establishment and the empire. Philip Schuyler's role is not difficult to discern. He stood on the side of Congress, clearly an advocate of extralegal means of obtaining redress. His long identification with partisan opposition apparently determined his current posture. Indeed, as he was denied the position of advantage within the provincial establishment to which he aspired, he was not averse to the use of extralegal methods to force a greater place for himself and those of his fellows similarly denied the influence the De Lanceys would not share. The colonel's activities indicated that insofar as he favored certain modifications of expressing colonial grievances, he was a conservative. Both groups believed in the privileges and responsibilities of a ruling class. But the fact remains that the De Lanceys were more conservative than Schuyler, and their resistance even to his expressions of grievances, moderate as they were, helped drive him directly into the arms of the radicals and into rebellion. Once in their camp, he continued to labor for privilege and for the establishment of power in the hands of men of talent and position. His political temperament differed only in degree from that of the De Lanceys. The cleavage was encouraged by old partisan feuds. Events were to prove that there was greater difference between philosophic statements and phraseology on the one hand and ultimate choice of loyalty and of action on the other than there was between two varieties of conservative statement. And yet the conservatives in splitting, fell rather closely along old factional lines.

Schuyler was much occupied between September, 1774, and Febru-

22 Duane to Samuel Chase, Dec. 29, 1774. NYPL, Bancroft Transcripts: American, II.

23 Jay to Livingston, Jan. 1, 1775. NYHS, Robert R. Livingston Collection.

ary, 1775. He was ill, troubled with administering Bradstreet's affairs,[24] concerned for the management of his own estate, and contemplative of the Continental Congress and of the course of action New York must follow when the assembly met. On the latter issue the Albany Committee of Correspondence gave him some assistance. On November 23 the committee approved the proceedings of the Continental Congress, although the attendance at the meeting was very thin. But on December 10 with a few more members present, the committee again approved the proceedings. Early in January, before Schuyler left Albany for the assembly, the committee refused a third motion to confirm the approval it had given the Congress. Of the twelve members present, seven voted to instruct the colonel and Jacob Ten Eyck to persuade the assembly to approve the proceedings of the Congress. There was some local protest against the presumption of seven men who dared to speak for the whole county, especially as only twelve of a possible thirty-two members of the Albany committee attended at the time these instructions were voted.[25] But armed with the expression of sentiment, Schuyler went to New York City in mid-January, determined to follow the instructions.

At the outset of the session Lieutenant Governor Colden feared the assembly might approve of the work of the First Continental Congress. He vowed that if there was no majority to insure prudent measures, he would prorogue the house and hope that Parliament might have sufficient time to make a suitable response to the Congress. To Lord Dartmouth, the secretary of state, he wrote that unless the assembly met, an attempt might be made to convene a provincial congress. Toward the end of January he again wrote Dartmouth that he was much reassured about the assembly's loyalty.[26] But the house had not yet taken up any controversial issues when Colden made his premature report.

As a second Continental Congress was a foregone conclusion the New York Assembly's attitude toward it would pave the way for

24 Schuyler to Mrs. Butter and Miss Bradstreet, Feb. 1, 1775. NYPL, Schuyler Papers Box 9.

25 Rivington's *New-York Gazetteer*, Mar. 30, 1775. See also *Minutes of the Albany Committee of Correspondence, 1775–1778* (2 vols.; Albany, 1923–1925), I, iv–v, which says the Albany committee's first recorded meeting was Jan. 24, 1775. Cf. "Minutes of the Albany Committee of Correspondence, Aug. 13, 23, 30, 1774" in the Peter Van Schaack Papers, Columbiana, Columbia University.

26 Colden to the Secretary of State, Jan. 4, 1775. C.O. 5/1139:197–198. Colden to Dartmouth, Jan. 21, 1775. C.O. 5/1106:127. See also Becker, *Political Parties*, p. 175.

further action in dealing with Great Britain for a redress of grievances. Schuyler first helped define the assembly's position and then was caught up in the action that followed. His behavior in this last session of the house somewhat paralleled that of his first session; no radical, he believed in a firm assertion of rights, and this moderate but definite stand showed him both a conservative and a patriot. The present current seemed to sweep him toward the radical position and to independence. His essential conservatism was momentarily eclipsed. The seasons of partisan struggles for power merely conditioned this course of action.

On January 26 the assembly began to argue about the extralegal movement. This had been foreshadowed by its response to the governor's message. Colden had invited the house to examine colonial complaints with calmness, deliberation, and impartiality and urged it to use only constituted means of seeking redress, and to discountenance measures that might increase distresses. Schuyler's temper was revealed by a certain prolixity. He suggested that certain words be stricken from an address to the governor and replaced with a lengthier statement. Instead of saying the assembly would "with Calmness and Deliberation, pursue the most probable Means to obtain a Redress of our Grievances," Schuyler proposed to "consider and examine, with the utmost Calmness, Deliberation and Impartiality, the Complaints of our Constituents; and endeavour to obtain a cordial and permanent Reconciliation with our parent State, by pursuing the most probable Means to obtain a Redress of our Grievances." [27] The most probable means of redress! There was a good deal of leeway allowed in such a statement. Could the colonel have been protesting too much by his suggestion that partisanship threatened any consideration of grievances with "Calmness, Deliberation and Impartiality"? Schuyler's motion was lost; but he did not vote against the address, which gave every suggestion of the assembly's loyalty. On January 26, however, Holt's *New-York Journal* heralded the beginning of serious divisions in the assembly over the Continental Congress. The paper reported that "a Matter of high Importance to the Liberties of this Country, is to be agitated" and asked "Whether every Friend to this Country who is able, will not think it his Duty to attend?"

If moderate men like Schuyler had no great affection for the Continental Congress, they also feared the assembly might fall under the

[27] Assembly Journals, Jan. 13, 19, 26, 1775. C.O. 5/1201.

direction of demagogues if it repudiated the Congress. Therefore, the colonel endeavored to persuade the assembly to approve the Congress and the Association, to name delegates to a second Congress, and to formulate a statement of grievances. The provincial magnates might then hope to keep control of affairs in their own hands.

Schuyler's old friend Abraham Ten Broeck "surprized" the house by a motion to consider the proceedings of the Continental Congress, but one of the loyalists, Colonel Philipse, quickly asked if Ten Broeck's motion should even be put. The vote was narrow, but by 11 to 10 Schuyler's group failed to get the house even to consider Congress's proceedings.[28] The first step in winning approval of its extralegal proceedings and in securing delegates to attend the Second Congress failed. But the party lines were drawn. Lieutenant Governor Colden expected that "a Party . . . of very different Principles" in the house would "be continually endeavouring to do Mischief." The ten who voted to consider the measures of Congress were the whole strength of the non-loyalist group: Philip Schuyler, Nathaniel Woodhull, George Clinton, Pierre Van Cortlandt, Charles De Witt, Peter R. Livingston, Abraham Ten Broeck, William Nicoll,[29] Simon Boerum, and Zebulon Seaman. Colden believed that nine members who had not yet appeared would join the eleven loyalists, and thus insure against another surprise motion by the minority.[30] Five days later (on January 31) the house decided to set aside a day to consider the state of the colony and to prepare a humble, dutiful, and loyal, but firm petition to the king. James De Lancey then invited the house to prepare a memorial to the Lords and a remonstrance to Commons. A committee of three moderates, including Schuyler, and eight loyalists was named

[28] Assembly Journals, Jan. 26, 1775. C.O. 5/1201.

[29] Nicoll seems later to have gone over to the De Lancey loyalists, and John Thomas replaced him on the Schuyler side. Assembly Journals, Jan. 26, Feb. 16, 17, 21, 1775, and *passim*. C.O. 5/1201.

[30] Colden to Dartmouth, Feb. 1, 1775. C.O. 5/1106:131–133. The eleven loyalists were Jacob Walton, John Rapalje, James De Lancey, James Jauncey, Isaac Wilkins, Frederick Philipse, Christopher Billop, Leonard Van Kleeck, Daniel Kissam, Benjamin Seaman, and Crean Brush. The nine men whom Colden cited were actually only eight. In the 11 to 10 vote Speaker Cruger did not cast a ballot, though he was a De Lancey man. Jacob Mynderse, who was among the eight not voting on the "surprise" motion, was generally a Schuyler-Livingston man. The other six were Samuel Wells, Dirck Brinckerhoff, John De Noyellis (who died and was replaced by John Coe in Feb., 1775), Samuel Gale, Hendrick Frey, and Guy Johnson. Werner, *Civil List* (1884), p. 312. Cf. Assembly Journals, Jan. 26, 1775.

to prepare a statement of grievances. Until February 7, when the report was due, the house could get on with other business.

One of the measures passed by the assembly in 1775 was a bill to prevent electors in manors from casting votes for both manor representatives and the representatives of the city and county of Albany. This legislation revealed something of the political inclinations of the large landowners, who had been expected to be loyal to the Crown in times past but whose wealth and independence had inclined them to rely less and less upon the royal establishment. In accordance with the old instructions from the Albany corporation, Schuyler had presented this bill on January 18. The measure might well have threatened the moderate faction had it not been for their basic unity of interest and on the larger matters affecting the colony, for some of the moderates (Van Cortlandt, Livingston, Ten Broeck) were members from manors whose lords and freeholders opposed this kind of censure. Although the manor electors had, reportedly, never exercised a double vote, Lieutenant Governor Colden feared that if they did so, they would be able to determine any county election, and he vowed it was dangerous for one or two families to return so large a proportion of the assembly's members. The old belief that creating a large landed class would insure its support of the royal government was largely exploded, for Colden saw that the representatives of the manors in 1775 were opposed to the government and were supporting the Congress. He plainly thought it was time to curb them.[31]

February 7 came and went, but there was no action from the committee charged with formulating grievances. On February 16, Schuyler offered another issue on which to test the house: a motion to enter certain letters in the journals and to order their publication in the newspapers. The letters comprised the correspondence of the New York Committee of Correspondence with Edmund Burke and the Connecticut committee. But Schuyler's motion was rejected, 16 to 9. All of the members who sat on the New York Committee of Correspondence voted against it. The De Lanceys showed no inclination to broadcast the doings of a governing clique. On the following day still another attempt was made to have the assembly offer a gesture of approval to the Continental Congress. Nathaniel Woodhull proposed to thank New York's delegates to the First Congress for their faithful

[31] Assembly Journals, Jan. 18, Feb. 1, Mar. 10, 13, April 3, 1775. C.O. 5/1201. Colden to Dartmouth, April 4, 1775. C.O. 5/1106:316–317.

and judicious actions, but again the house refused, 15 to 9, and Schuyler's small core of supporters failed once more.

Day by day Schuyler's moderates endeavored to lead New York into a clearer position of approving the congressional program of petition and non-intercourse, and of firm protest and determined demands for redress. On February 21, Peter R. Livingston proposed that the assembly thank the merchants and inhabitants of New York for their "repeated, disinterested, public-spirited, and patriotic Conduct" in refusing importation of goods from Britain and in adhering to the Association. This was refused, 15 to 10. The Association, as Cadwallader Colden knew, was rigidly maintained, despite the strong loyal majority in the assembly. He was also aware that there were "mischievous" attempts afoot to obtain a provincial congress to name delegates to the Second Continental Congress.[32]

The house committee preparing a statement of New York grievances reported to the assembly on February 23, but the assembly postponed further action until March 1 and again until March 3. In the meantime, a discussion arose about the necessity of appointing delegates to the Second Continental Congress. The house was, of course, divided, and the debate was full. "Col. S[chu]y[le]r and Mr. C[linto]n, spoke several times in support of the motion, and were answered, with great clearness and precision my Mr. W[ilki]ns." And Crean Brush told the assembly that as it was the only legal and constitutional representative of the people, it would be a breach of trust to delegate that charge to another body.[33] It was evident that Philip Schuyler was not opposed to the Congress because it was an extralegal body; neither apparently did he believe that the Congress was revolutionary nor that the assembly was altogether representative of colonial sentiment toward grievances. His attitude toward Congress revealed both the principles he held about political machinery and the ambition he had always nourished for challenging the De Lanceys. But John Thomas' motion to take the sense of the house on naming delegates to Congress was rejected, 17 to 9,[34] and the partisan disagreement on principle suggested again how the factional divisions in New York politics were related to divergent views about the colony's place in the empire.

The house in committee of the whole began to consider New

---

[32] Colden to the Secretary of State, Mar. 1, 1775. C.O. 5/1139:221–223.

[33] Rivington's *New-York Gazetteer*, Mar. 2, 1775. See also Becker, *Political Parties*, p. 176 n.

[34] Assembly Journals, Feb. 23, 1775. C.O. 5/1201.

York's grievances on March 3. It is indeed curious that a colony which had acquiesced in the Declaratory Act, the reduced revenue acts, the Restraining Act and Mutiny Act, and the various government measures such as those of the vice-admiralty courts before and during the quiet years 1770–1773 should now turn to discuss them as grievances. It is remarkable that New York should now criticize Parliament's restriction on paper currency after having been given special permission to issue bills of credit, or that it should denounce the Restraining Act when in fact it had never been operative. It is also significant that the assembly should now decide the "coercive acts" leveled against a sister colony were New York's own grievances and that in its formal statements to the king and Parliament the house should disapprove the behavior of the Bay Colony while insisting that her punishment afforded dangerous precedents. All this is quite singular behavior. Could it be that New Yorkers and other colonists were seeking an issue? Or was this the resurgence of old discontents which in theory had never been fully resolved to the complete satisfaction of New Yorkers—irritants which lay dormant and which had never been totally eradicated? Earlier the Yorkers had shown no overt demonstration of anything but contentment within the empire, once Parliament had compromised its controls. They had tacitly admitted Parliamentary authority by voting supplies. Philip Schuyler himself helped pass appropriations for the royal establishment. They also submitted by implication to a greater power when they printed paper currency on the authority of an act of Parliament. They did not protest the Declaratory Act when it was passed, nor did they refuse to obey the law by which the vice-admiralty court at Halifax was given extended jurisdiction over all the colonies and by which prosecutors and informers could bring suit at their option rather than in local colonial courts.

But the fact that the colonists once agreed to *ad hoc* compromises need not necessarily suggest that they were ever fully contented, else why should they dredge up these old grievances that once were considered to be settled to the satisfaction both of the London ministry and of the province of New York? Nor does the fact that the imperial government repeatedly made expedient adjustments in its program suggest that it was wholly satisfied with a mere acceptance of Parliamentary sovereignty on the part of the colonists. Given a fresh set of crucial circumstances, each side could be expected to reassert what it held as fundamental principle: Parliament's sovereignty and the col-

onies' insistence on taxation only by local representation. Real difficulty arose over the difference between the philosophical acceptance
and the actual exercise of principles.

It is apparent that the assembly's formulation of its own set of
grievances which comprised the substance for its petition to the king
and addresses to Parliament was a tactic by the loyalists "to ignore
Congress altogether, and to take into their own hands the matter of
grievances." [35] Indeed, Schuyler's attempts to amend these expressions
of sentiment suggested that the minority wished to thwart the loyalists
as much as possible. The Reverend Doctor Samuel Seabury had invited
them to take this action rather than allow Congress or New England
or Virginia to bind New York. On the other hand, the conservatives or
moderates led by Schuyler, Livingston, and Ten Broeck wanted the
assembly to vote a formal assessment of the First Congress's work and
to elect delegates to the Second Congress. Thus far they had failed.
For all the obvious disagreement on principle, it must not be forgotten that the divisions fell along old party lines and that the dis-
unity suggested the prevalence of partisan power ambitions as much
as it did differences in sincere conviction and principle. When the
matter of grievances arose, Schuyler's followers found relatively little
on which to disagree with the De Lancey loyalists. In this the colonel
revealed himself still a cautious partisan. Yet Schuyler advocated even
stiffer phrasing in expressing the grievances than the De Lanceys
would allow. And in this the colonel suggested an inclination to
"patriotism" as much as his actions proved those of a partisan politician. Despite factional agreement, an essential division in the fight to
strengthen the official addresses to the king and Parliament was apparent.[36] It seemed that, even while agreeing, one faction could not

---

[35] Becker, *Political Parties*, p. 175.

[36] *Ibid.*, p. 177. Becker says the conservatives and loyalists contested some unimportant points and made slight modifications but that they were essentially agreed
insofar as the issue was one between the colonists and Great Britain. Although this
is true, a review of the votes and alterations may show that the divergence of the
two groups was rather more marked than Becker suggested and that this divergence
was designed for local partisan purposes. It was marked because the staunch loyalists
voted against declaring three of the grievances, while the moderates or conservatives
who became patriots passed one resolution of grievance with the help of those only a
little less devoted to the De Lancey variety of loyalism. On the resolutions of grievances the factions agreed on the first, second, fifth, sixth, seventh, eighth, ninth, tenth,
eleventh, and twelfth; they divided on the fourth, thirteenth, and fifteenth; on the
third Schuyler won stronger phraseology over the core of De Lancey opposition by a
vote of 14 to 11. Assembly Journals, Mar. 3, 1775. C.O. 5/1201. It is also possible that

tolerate the work of another faction or allow it to go unchallenged.

This essential division is apparent to the careful reader of the amendments that Philip Schuyler proposed to several of the fifteen resolves stating the grievances. There was a hint of divergence in the political philosophy as well. We may compare the work of the committee of the whole with the votes of the house to discover both the extent of agreement and disagreement on voicing grievances and formulating statements of the relationship of colony to empire.

The house was in complete accord in pronouncing both the Declaratory Act of 1766 and the 1764 Revenue Act as grievances. The former had declared Parliament's authority to bind the colonies in all cases whatsoever. The latter, moved as a grievance by Colonel Schuyler, was objectionable

so far as it imposes Duties for the Purpose of raising a Revenue in America,— extends the Admiralty Courts beyond their ancient Limits,—deprives his Majesty's American Subjects of Trial by Jury,—authorizes the Judges Certificates to indemnify the Prosecutor from Damages that he might otherwise be liable to,—and holds up an injurious Discrimination between the Subjects in Great-Britain and those in America.[37]

In the committee of the whole and in the house, James De Lancey stirred up more than a difference in opinion on mere words. He asked if the king and Parliament had a right to regulate the trade of the colonies and to lay duties on imports from a foreign country or colony that might interfere with the empire's products or manufactures. In the committee, Schuyler and George Clinton unsuccessfully voted to reject De Lancey's motion, and in the house they again failed to reject it by a vote of 15 to 10. They alone objected to De Lancey's resolution that the king and Parliament had a right to regulate the trade of the colonies and to tax foreign imports. Schuyler believed in Parliament's right to regulate trade, but objected to De Lancey. When Lieutenant Governor Colden reported to Governor Tryon on February 1 that the city, Staten Island, and other members were "firm on the right side," but that "Col. Schuyler and Clinton hold forth in the Opposition," [38] he recorded an accurate, albeit premature, assessment of the political currents.

they differed for the sake of differing and for the purpose of identifying themselves as parties for the benefit of their constituents in future elections.

[37] Assembly Journals, Mar. 3, 1775. C.O. 5/1201.

[38] Colden to Tryon, Feb. 1, 1775. Colls. N.Y. Hist. Soc. for 1877 (New York, 1878), X: Colden Papers, II, 391.

Schuyler proposed an addition to De Lancey's resolution about Parliamentary right of taxation. Parliament and the king had this right, he affirmed, *"Excluding every Idea of Taxation, internal or external, for the Purpose of raising a Revenue on the Subjects in America, without their Consent."* In the committee the De Lancey loyalists voted down this amendment seven to three, but Schuyler won its addition in the house by a vote of 14 to 11. A few of the De Lanceyites deserted their leader and thus helped stiffen this resolution.[39] Schuyler's objection to De Lancey's motion on the Parliamentary right to regulate trade, when taken with his amendment and views about Parliament's rightful functions, suggests not so much a real difference in substance or principle as a contrived divergence between partisan factions, one of which aimed at projecting itself into the popular mind as an identifiable political alternative to the De Lanceys.

The fourth resolve questioned an act (3 Geo. III c. 22 sec. 8) directing claimants of vessels to give certain sums as security. The committee voted seven to three that this was no grievance; Schuyler, Clinton, and Brinckerhoff thought it was, but the house showed a wider divergence of opinion when it voted 16 to 10 with the majority of the committee.

Eight other resolves were passed *nemine contradicente*. These declared a number of acts of Parliament grievances. Among them were: the concurrent jurisdiction given admiralty courts with common law courts; the prohibition of paper currency as legal tender within the colony; the duty on molasses, syrups, coffee, and pimentoes (1766); the Restraining Act; extension of the act of Henry VIII allowing trials of persons for treason in England; and the act of 1774 (14 Geo. III c. 88) imposing duties on certain imports to Quebec (whose boundaries were expanded in such a way) so, it was said, as to destroy New York's commerce with the Indians by limiting imports to the remote port of St. John on the Sorel River.

The last three resolves related to the "coercive acts," and here the assembly went quite beyond any limited concept of local grievances to complain on behalf of a neighbor.

The committee of the whole declared six to four that the act closing

39 Assembly Journals, Mar. 3, 1775. Cf. actions in the committee with those of the house. C.O. 5/1201 and C.O. 5/1220. Spaulding, *George Clinton*, p. 39, says the amendment to the De Lancey resolution was surprising except that even "reactionaries" may turn "ultra" in defense of their property interests. Spaulding has termed the assembly as dominated by "reactionaries."

the port of Boston was a grievance. The De Lancey minority of four grew to eleven in the house, but Schuyler's moderates with a few loyalist dissidents, 15 to 11, voted this a grievance. Three of the loyalists, however, agreed with Schuyler's group that the Boston Port Act was a grievance insofar, they said, as it affected New York's trade! The Massachusetts Impartial Administration of Justice Act was voted a grievance without disagreement both in the committee of the whole and on the floor of the house. It was a grievance because New York felt that it was a dangerous precedent which might be applied elsewhere. The final resolution protested against the Massachusetts Government Act. Once again a few less adamant loyalists joined Schuyler's moderates and agreed to declare it a grievance (16 to 10) because it might form a precedent to alter or take away charter rights contrary to the ordinary course of law.[40] Here, as in the Boston Port Act resolve, James De Lancey and three fellow partisans opposed the declaration of an injustice.

One scholar has said that "On the question of grievances the conservatives were practically in accord with the loyalists. They contested some unimportant points in the report, and succeeded in introducing some slight modifications; but the resolutions as adopted may be taken as representing the views of both factions in so far as the issue was one between the colonies and Great Britain." [41] Although this is correct, it does not present a complete picture. It ignores the distinction between the resolves first voted in the committee of the whole and then in the house on March 3 as compared with the resolves considered in the committee of the whole on March 8. It also does not give proper attention or weight to the differences, few as they were, between the De Lancey loyalists and the Schuyler conservatives as we have just seen from the proceedings of March 3. It does not reveal the assembly's factional divisions and partisan maneuvers nor does it explain how much factionalism determined the assembly's action. The point of internal and external taxation can hardly be called unimportant, and on the assembly declarations against the Boston Port Act and Massachusetts Government Act, the differences were significant enough to cause some of the less diehard De Lanceyites to join Schuyler's coterie in strengthening a protest that would not have been made at all had they voted strictly with their leaders. And the resolves

[40] Assembly Journals, Mar. 3, 1775. Portions of the day's transactions in C.O. 5/1201 and C.O. 5/1220. Cf. committee votes and the votes of the house.
[41] Becker, *Political Parties,* p. 177.

considered on March 8 again revealed a measure of divergence between Schuyler's conservatives and the loyalists and the manner in
which the former were tending, unconsciously or otherwise, toward a
more radical position by insisting on stiffening the language of protest. It is impossible to determine to what extent this tendency was
conditioned by the years of partisan antagonism, but it seems likely
that faction members also had their eyes on future elections, when
it would be convenient to offer their records as defenders of provincial
liberties to the voters for approval. The persistence of party divisions
suggests that the two factions were more or less automatically following well-established lines of action and an attitude toward one another
ingrained by long habit.

On March 8 the committee of the whole house considered five resolutions prepared by a committee composed largely of De Lancey loyalists. These resolutions were based on the grievances voted on March 3.
They agreed on three of them, but divided on two; the Schuyler
clique posed as advocates of a stronger definition of the position on
taxation. The votes for amending the two resolves were close: 14 to 13
on one and 14 to 12 on the other. The first resolve stated that the
colonies owed to the king the same allegiance as other Englishmen.
The fourth declared certain acts of Parliament to be subversive of
colonial rights—e.g., legislation (without representation) for revenue
to support civil government, extending jurisdiction of the admiralty
courts and providing that they share jurisdiction in cases hitherto
cognizable only in common law courts. The fifth declared jury trial in
all capital cases to be a birthright and that the transportation of residents for trial elsewhere was dangerous to the subjects' life and liberty.
There was no disagreement on these three.

But on the second and third resolves the Schuyler faction attempted
a stronger position. The second resolve declared New Yorkers owed
obedience to those acts of Parliament calculated for the general welfare of the whole empire and for the regulation of trade and commerce *not inconsistent* with the essential rights and liberties of all
Englishmen, at home or in the colonies. The Schuyler group proposed
to alter this by adding the words, "excluding every Idea of Taxation,
internal or external, for the Purpose of raising a Revenue on the Subject[s] in America, without their Consent." When the vote for insert-
ing the amendment was taken, the Schuyler forces lost by a vote of
14 to 13. The issue they were making was dealt with in the fourth

resolve; Schuyler's group appears to have been differing for the sake of differing—or rather offering a different phraseology as a means of identifying themselves as a faction distinct from the De Lanceys. The game, after all, was to appeal to the elements out of doors for support of a contested leadership. The anti-De Lancey forces again attempted to procure a stronger statement on taxation in the third resolve which declared the right of Englishmen to be free of taxes not laid by consent either given personally or through representatives in assembly. George Clinton moved to alter the simple statement that no taxes be imposed except by consent to one declaring that no taxes "of any Kind or Nature, or under any Denomination whatsoever" be imposed but by consent. But the De Lanceys prevented this by a vote of 14 to 12. Again Schuyler's forces lost their attempt to strengthen the language in such a way as actually would decrease the loyalist sentiment in the statement [42]—and as would give them credit and an identity distinct from their opponents.

The scholar who judged that the conservatives and loyalists "were practically in accord" on these resolutions of grievances was largely correct insofar as the two factions regarded colonial-British relations. But the partisan divergence is something else, for there were differences shown between March 3 and March 8; and the final vote by which the house passed the five resolutions on March 8 showed that the Schuyler conservatives were *not* in accord with their opponents and were not satisfied with the language which they had failed to alter. Perhaps they were agreed on substance, but it appears they sought a line to distinguish themselves from the De Lanceys for the benefit of their watchful constituents and for themselves in the elections to come. Twelve of them voted against the fourteen De Lancey loyalists who managed to pass the resolutions substantially as they had framed them.[43]

Having first considered grievances and then voted resolutions, the assembly turned to formulate a petition to the king, a memorial to the

[42] Assembly Journals, Mar. 8, 1775. C.O. 5/1220. The committee appointed to formulate a statement of grievances was named on Jan. 31 in response to Peter R. Livingston's suggestions to set aside a day to consider the state of the colony, to prepare a petition to the king, and in response to De Lancey's suggestion of a memorial to the Lords and a remonstrance to Commons as well.

[43] *Ibid.* Becker, *Political Parties*, p. 177, cites the Assembly Journals (Force, *American Archives*, Ser. 4, Vol. I, 1302, 1313, 1316, 1318) but he has not carefully differentiated between the resolves voted on March 3 and those voted on March 8.

Lords and a remonstrance to Commons.[44] The resolutions formed the basis for these addresses. On March 9 three committees were appointed to draw up the formal representations. Philip Schuyler was excluded from all three. It is not surprising that the De Lancey loyalists should do this after the colonel had so clearly demonstrated his desire for greater elaboration and stronger terminology. But they could not yet expect to escape his reach. Schuyler had his chance to offer amendments on the floor of the house when the papers were subjected to a careful scrutiny. Aside from the resolutions, there apparently was little to indicate that anyone contemplated independence, though they were replete with implications of it. Like the papers drawn to the king and Parliament, the resolutions on which the papers were based disavowed any such intention. But the protests and contentions about taxation and liberty suggested that Schuyler and his fellows in New York and elsewhere were *in deed* defining a position that was incompatible with the principle of Parliamentary supremacy. When principle no longer could be compromised by practical concessions, the strainings between colonists and imperial authorities grew stronger.

On March 16 the drafts of the papers to the king and Parliament were ready. Eight days later a committee of the whole house began to consider them. When the addresses came to the floor of the assembly, Schuyler and George Clinton took the draft of the memorial to the Lords to William Smith, Jr. They wanted Smith to draw up an amendment they had devised, but Smith "put them off on acct of [his] Station, & the Watch of the De Lanceys & advised them to [consult] Scott & Jay." Schuyler also showed Smith the petition to the king, but he accepted Smith's refusal of "any Agency" in opposing Parliament. It appears that General Thomas Gage was expecting Smith to aid in preventing New York's acceptance of congressional projects, and that Smith hoped to win a special advantage with Gage whom he expected to use as a source of information; he therefore could not even appear to countenance those who labored for acceptance of the Congress.[45]

44 Spaulding, *George Clinton*, p. 39, says after the assembly stated its grievances, *many* county members went home. This does not seem correct in light of the Assembly Journals which show 25 to 27 members voting on the grievances and 23 to 24 members voting on the addresses to the king and Parliament.

45 Sabine, *Smith Memoirs*, I, 214. See also Assembly Journals, Mar. 16, 24, 1775. C.O. 5/1201.

The addresses to the king and Parliament seemed to indicate that the loyalists who drafted them wished to ignore the statement Schuyler had won earlier, regarding the right of taxation. The statement had vowed Parliament's right to regulate trade and to lay import duties "Excluding every Idea of Taxation, internal or external, for the Purpose of raising a Revenue on the Subjects in America, without their Consent." [46] When the addresses were considered, Schuyler had a new opportunity to insert stronger language—language that in fact suggested his swing into the patriot current of resistance—a current that led to rebellion and independence.

Lieutenant Governor Colden, never above partisanship himself, reported that Schuyler and his cohorts "made a violent Opposition" to the addresses framed by the loyalists, and that they had "made it evident throughout the Sessions, that they wish'd to bring this Colony into all the dangerous & extravagant Schemes which Disgrace too many of the Sister Colonies." They had already "openly espoused the Cause of the last Congress" and striven "hard to have Delegates appointed by the House for that which is to be held in May." [47] Colden did not specify the historic partisanship, but his account suggests how the old factionalism was merging more and more into the debate about the empire, power, and rights.

In attempting to alter the language of the petition to the king, Schuyler not only showed himself a less conservative partisan than the De Lancey loyalists, but also suggested a fundamental opposition to Parliamentary supremacy. Thus it was that principle was combined with partisanship. The discussion of grievances, resolutions, and now the debate over the addresses to the king and Parliament reveal some of the colonel's thoughts about royal government and the imperial system. Protestations of loyalty and disavowals of independence could not alter the underlying tone of the language that he proposed. First he moved to strike out certain words acknowledging "Appearances which may be construed to our Disadvantage, and that several of the Measures pursued by the Colonies, are by no Means justifiable." The assembly would "disapprove and condemn" them and "intreat" the king as an "indulgent Father . . . to view them in the most favorable Light" without considering them more than "honest, though disorderly Struggles of Liberty, not the licentious Efforts of Independ-

[46] Assembly Journals, Mar. 3, 1775. C.O. 5/1201.

[47] Colden to Tryon, April 5, 1775. *Colls. N.Y. Hist. Soc. for 1877* (New York, 1878), X: Colden Papers, II, 398–399.

260 PHILIP SCHUYLER AND THE AMERICAN REVOLUTION

ance [sic]." Schuyler offered a substitute paragraph that began with
the suspicion that "Pains have been taken" to make the king think his
subjects "impatient of constitutional Government." Schuyler would
entreat George III to believe their "Commotions are but honest
Struggles for maintaining our constitutional Liberty, and not dictated
by a Desire of Independance [sic]." And, finally, his language offered
a thrust at the ministry, and indirectly at Parliament. "Could your
princely Virtues as easily as your Powers, have been delegated to your
Servants," he proposed to say, "we had not at this Time been reduced
to the disagreeable Necessity of disturbing your Repose, on an Occasion which we sincerely lament." Disagreeable necessity indeed!
By 15 to 8 the committee of the whole rejected these words.[48]

Next, Colonel Schuyler attempted an alteration that resisted both
the idea of colonial subordination by reason of weakness and the idea
that the colonists had submitted without complaint. He moved to
strike out words admitting the colonists had "hitherto been in a State
of Infancy, and till lately have submitted implicitly, and without re-
pining, to the Authority of the Parent State; they have now reached
the Period of Maturity, and think themselves intitled to their Birthright, an equal Participation of Freedom with their Fellow Subjects in
Britain." Schuyler offered instead to admit only that the colonists had
"in some Instances submitted to the Power exercised by the Parent
State." Here was no admission that the exercise of that power was
legitimate. Here was no acknowledgment that when New Yorkers had
submitted to Parliamentary authority implied in the imperial legislation that they had really accepted the doctrine of Parliamentary
sovereignty. But this suggested alteration also failed, 14 to 9.

What Schuyler then proposed was an even more specific denial of
Parliamentary sovereignty in terms of law. He would admit it was a
supremacy based only on expediency, and even then he conceived it
limited and applicable to the regulation of trade and not to taxation
for revenue. Strike out the words, he advised, by which New York
"cheerfully acknowledge[d]" its "Subordination to" Parliament as the
"grand Legislature of the Empire." Strike out the words, he said,
which proclaimed only a wish "to enjoy the Rights of Englishmen,
and to have that Share of Liberty and those Privileges secured to us
which we are intitled to, upon the Principles of our free and happy
Constitution." Instead, he suggested, let the colonies proclaim that

48 Assembly Journals, Mar. 24, 1775. C.O. 5/1201.

the bases of their rights were "the immutable Laws of Nature" first, and "the Principles of the English Constitution" second. Let them only acknowledge the "Incompetency of the Colony Legislatures to regulate the Trade of the Empire" and that "such a Power in that august Body . . . is founded in *Expediency,* and *confined* to the Regulation of our external Commerce." Schuyler proposed that Parliament might then exercise its power "in such a Manner as will leave to us unimpaired those Rights which we hold by the immutable Laws of Nature and the Principles of the English Constitution." The general colonial shift to an appeal to the natural law was implicit in these suggestions. Again, this was too much for the De Lancey loyalists, and they rejected the amendment, 15 to 8.[49]

At this point Schuyler's colleagues, Nathaniel Woodhull, Charles De Witt, and George Clinton, gave the colonel momentary relief from leading the minority's attack on the petition. Woodhull moved to strike out a statement that the colonists did not enjoy rights *because* of the Declaratory Act. These words were a mild remonstrance against Parliamentary power to bind the colonies in all cases whatsoever, but Woodhull suggested stronger ones—that the Declaratory Act indicated Parliament's *intention* to infringe the rights of the colonies. The motion failed, 15 to 9. Charles De Witt suggested an alteration to a mild declaration that the Quebec Act produced uneasiness in many New Yorkers. He proposed to say that the act was "a most alarming Grievance," and that it offered a form of government dangerous to all royal, free, and loyal Protestant colonies. His substitute failed by a vote of 15 to 8. George Clinton then proposed to alter notably the reference to the Boston Port Act and the Massachusetts Government Act. The petition stated that New York disapproved of the conduct of the Bay colonists, but that the acts offered a dangerous precedent of punishing subjects without trial. Clinton's proposal dropped all mention of disapproving the Bay Colony's conduct and declared only that the ministry's poor policy since 1763 had produced "great Warmth" and that the "coercive acts" were abhorrent because of their principles subversive of colonial rights, privileges, and property. The De Lancey loyalists refused this motion, 15 to 8.

One other attempt at alteration failed. Instead of summarizing by saying simply that the assembly had stated its grievances with respect due the best of kings and with freedom becoming to the representa-

[49] Assembly Journals, Mar. 24, 1775. C.O. 5/1201. Italics added.

tives of an old and loyal colony, Clinton suggested a statement that it dare not trouble the king with *other lesser* grievances. Here was the warning that the colonists had more than a few major matters about which they could complain and for which they expected redress. Schuyler's group lost this motion to amend as it had most of the others. His faction failed to prevent the committee of the whole or the house from passing the petition as the loyalists had drawn it.

On the afternoon of March 24 the committee of the whole reported its deliberation on the memorial to the Lords and the remonstrance to Commons. Schuyler's conservatives were successful in procuring some amendments to the memorial, but none for the remonstrance. Again the issue of Parliamentary supremacy was divisive. And because this principle was central to the question of loyalty to the empire or independence, it is important that we consider how the colonel endeavored to alter the expressions of the loyalist faction.

The memorial to the Lords stated that New Yorkers considered themselves as a "part of one great Empire, in which it is necessary there should be some supreme regulating Power." But it also said that while it acknowledged "the Existence of such Power, yet we conceive it by no Means comprehends a Right of binding us in all Cases whatsoever, because a Power of so unbounded an Extent would totally deprive us of Security, and reduce us to a State of the most abject servitude." These were menacing words, but Schuyler's substitute was more threatening. Although the factions showed a certain amount of agreement of expression, it appears that their divisions were dictated largely by the consideration of which party was to enjoy an ascendancy as reflected in the determination of the battle of words, and not by any serious cleavage about the fundamental structure of the political system. The colonel's statement allowed that New York was indeed "an inseparable Part of the British Empire," but that its citizens were "intimately interested in and bound by a Variety of Considerations" and that "public Expediency must, in some Cases, induce a Submission to the Exercise of a supreme Legislative Power." However, the exercise of this power ought "never to take Place but in Cases of absolute Necessity," and then only "where our own Legislature is incompetent, and with a View to the general Weal of the Empire in the Regulation of Commerce." Here were limits to Parliamentary sovereignty—limits which, if carried to their logical conclusion, would reduce Parliament's authority to a cipher and really deny its sovereignty altogether. Schuyler failed to win this substitute provision by a vote of 16 to 8.

The De Lanceyites did allow Schuyler to make one notable alteration, however. They deleted statements that the colonies were not contemplated "when the Forms of the British Constitution were established" and that it "was undoubtedly intended that the People should
have a Share in the Legislature"—a privilege they always "zealously
asserted" as affording "the highest security." They also struck out a
paragraph stating that the English Constitution did not make provision for the colonies and that neither the "Nature of the Colonies nor
their constitutional Dependance [sic] on the Mother Country" were
even mentioned in the Constitution or ancient law books. Also stricken
were the words that a "new Relation sprung up between the Parent
Kingdom, and then a new System of Government adapted to it . . .
ought to have been established." Schuyler's alternative statement was
then inserted. It proclaimed in more explicit terms the theme of local
representation. The colonies were not contemplated when the Constitution was established, and therefore when they were planted, the
colonists carried with them "all the Rights they were entitled to in the
Country from which they emigrated." Because they could no longer
share in the representation in Parliament, "they of Right claimed and
enjoyed a Legislature of their own, always acknowledging the King
or his Representative as one Branch thereof." This was a precious
right which alone afforded them "that Security which their Fellow
Subjects" at home enjoyed.

Here was another blow to the principles of virtual representation
and Parliamentary supremacy. The Yorkers were using the most advantageous argument possible. In challenging the reality of the Coronation Oath Act of 1689 and the whole tenor of the revolutionary settlement by which the royal suzerainty over the colonies was clearly transferred to the *King in Parliament,* they were adopting a static view of
the Constitution and really using the argument of natural law. The
loyalists would not, however, agree to an addition to a simple statement that the government could raise no money or make any law
binding on the subject in Britain without the concurrence of his representative. They rejected Schuyler's stronger phraseology that, because of the above-mentioned statement, the colonists "can never
acknowledge an authority in the British Parliament to bind us in all
Cases whatsoever." [50]

By some unknown means Colonel Schuyler managed to make several apparently minor alterations in the memorial to the Lords. Yet

[50] *Ibid.*

they carried weighty import. Instead of referring to the Restraining Act simply as "the Legislature of this Colony has been suspended" (which in fact it never was), Schuyler proposed to deny by implication Parliament's right to suspend the legislature with the words, "Acts have been passed *for the Purpose* of suspending the Legislature of this Colony." Actually, the words were accurate, but it appears that the loyalists either failed to detect the nuance, were weary of the fight and allowed the change to pass, or in agreeing to it proved they were not completely "loyal" after all. Another alteration passed *nemine contradicente:* to substitute for the statement, "The American Subject is rendered liable in some Instances by a new Statute, and in others by the Construction made of an old one," the words, "New and un-constitutional Acts have been passed, and Constructions made of an old one. . . ." There was a noticeable difference suggested, too, in changing the words, "It is with Reluctance we" address their Lord-ships to "We are extremely unhappy that *Occasion has been given us to*" send a memorial to the House of Lords.

There was one final assault made on the loyalists' draft of the memorial to the Lords on March 24. Again Schuyler aimed at stiffen-ing the language. He moved to strike out two paragraphs which (1) promised cheerful submission to "the constitutional Exercise of the supreme regulating Power . . . and to all Acts calculated for the gen-eral Weal of the Empire, and the due Regulation of [its] Trade and Commerce" and (2) which defined "this Power" to include taxing all imports to the colonies from foreign countries or plantations which might interfere with the products or manufactures of Britain or her colonies. But no taxes must be imposed on the colonies except by their consent, "given personally or by their lawful Representatives." Schuy-ler offered instead a statement that the colonists would "never repine at the Exercise of a Parliamentary Authority, to regulate Trade for the general Weal of the Empire," provided that power was *"solely employed"* in taxing imports from foreign countries that interfered with the empire's produce or manufactures and "provided that in the Mode, every Idea of Taxation for the Purpose of raising a Revenue in America, be excluded." This attempt at alteration again suggests less difference in substance than it does a proclivity for quibbling in traditional partisan fashion. In many respects the two parties were so much alike that they were obliged to create differences in order to maintain an identity and to bid for support from the electorate as well as the radical element threatening their leadership from outside the house. On this last attempt the colonel again failed. His amendment was rejected, 16 to 8. Nor could his adherents prevent the committee from reporting to the house and the passage of the memorial largely as the loyalists had drawn it.

The remonstrance to Commons passed the assembly without any endeavor by Schuyler to amend or alter it. George Clinton attempted several minor changes which indicated what was fast becoming the "conservative patriot" temper. Instead of objecting to the Quebec Act in matter-of-fact terms, Clinton wanted to substitute for the words "the Roman Catholic Religion" the phraseology, "A sanguinary Religion equally repugnant to the genuine Simplicity of Christianity, and the Maxims of Sound Philosophy." But this failed, as did his attempt to strike out any expression of "Disapprobation of the violent Measures that have been pursued in some of the Colonies, which can only tend to increase our Misfortunes, and to prevent our obtaining Redress." [51]

The remonstrance did, however, make one point which particularly challenged Parliamentary supremacy: the statement that the harmony, strength, prosperity, and happiness of the empire might be rendered permanent only by drawing the line between Parliament's authority and America's freedom on just, equitable, and constitutional grounds. How exactly this was to be done, or by whom, was not indicated. And yet the issue directly involved the question of sovereignty. If the colonists decided where the line was between their freedom and Parliamentary supremacy, they, not Parliament, were sovereign—and independent. No protestation of loyalty, no disavowal of "independency" could alter that. New Yorkers called for a restoration of "Rights which we enjoyed by General Consent, before the Close of the last War." [52] Yet the asssembly's addresses implied a much greater claim than this. And as for the attention to rights enjoyed before 1763, the colonists were drawing the line between principle and practice. Certainly Parliament had more than the simple right to regulate trade before 1763. If it had not always insisted on a vigorous *practice* of the principle, the principle still remained. Had the colonists merely acquiesced in it so long as its practical enforcement had not been at stake? Now the

[51] *Ibid.*

[52] The Representation and Remonstrance to Commons. Assembly Journals, Mar. 24, 1775. C.O. 5/1220.

assembly factions had agreed in the wish to be left untrammeled by imperial administration and in the desire for a measure of "home rule" which seemed to them only to mean freedom from imperial regulations. As we have seen in the maneuvers and as we shall see in the developments following the assembly's last session under royal auspices, the factions had still not agreed on who was to rule at home; they had quarreled about who could best formulate an expression of colonial grievances. Their divergence on framing resolutions and addresses also indicated that the minority believed it was voicing the province's true sentiments and that the majority was really not worthy of governing them.

On March 25 the assembly directed that its addresses to the king and Parliament be sent to the New York agent in London, together with the statement of grievances and the list of resolutions which formed the bases for the addresses. Both loyalists and conservatives might agree that they must now await the response of the home government, but men like Philip Schuyler did not believe this should prevent them from engaging in further action. Indeed, the following month, even before Lexington and Concord, Schuyler boldly joined the extralegal movement to send delegates to the Second Continental Congress. He was clearly disappointed that the assembly had not seen fit to do this, but he would not accept its decision as final. Nor did he act as if he were convinced that the extralegal movement was necessarily revolutionary.

After the assembly voted grievances, resolutions, and addresses it spent the last few days in less extraordinary business. But a matter of dealing with land rioters in Cumberland, Albany, and Charlotte counties proved the abiding partisan divisions of the house.[53]

53 The New Hampshire Grants people led by Ethan Allen, Seth Warner, and others were already raising a rebellion that was to merge with the War of Independence. It was a rebellion both against Yorker neighbors and those elements of the imperial system which thwarted the ambitions of frontier farmers. Despite his concern for good order and for the protection of the landlords' interests, Schuyler voted against making any provision allowing Cumberland County to suppress the squatters' rioting. His was largely a partisan stand. He failed, however, to prevent the grant of £1,000 to the government for the suppression of the Cumberland riots. But regarding the Albany and Charlotte county measure he was victorious in denying appropriations for dealing with land riots. The votes on both questions indicated the old polarity of leadership in the factions and showed how others might shift sides on certain occasions. Proof of the partisanship is given in Lieutenant Governor Colden's correspondence with General Thomas Gage. Schuyler and his cohorts, said Colden,

Before the assembly adjourned it made various preparations for the following session—a meeting that was never to be held. Schuyler was named to a committee overwhelmingly dominated by De Lancey men to consider means for relieving the province from debt without laying a general tax. The assembly passed a resolution that in future it would allow no account to the royal government for performing services for which the government had not made application in advance. The speaker was ordered to correspond with other assembly speakers in order to present to their houses New York's grievances, resolves, and addresses for approval. On April 3, having appointed a standing committee of correspondence composed of De Lancey loyalists (ten), except for George Clinton, Simon Boerum, and Zebulon Seaman, the assembly was adjourned to May 3. Significantly, it had not voted supplies for the king's troops. It never met again. Its factionalism persisted out of doors, however, as New Yorkers divided between loyalty to the king or to Congress, between concepts of popular and more radical systems, and mixed, conservative frames of government. The loyalist sentiment in the colony proved so strong that New York furnished more loyalist troops to His Majesty's cause than did any other

---

nearly carried their point on the Cumberland case by working on the "parsimonious dispositions" of the members. The rioters wanted to shut up the courts, "yet Mr. Schuyler and his Party have industriously propagated an Opinion . . . that the violent Proceedings in Cumberland County are solely owing to the uneasiness and distress the People are under from the Disputes subsisting about the Title of their Lands." Colden insisted this was false, as no grant made by New York clashed with New Hampshire's claims except in Hindsdale Township, and there the people were peaceful. Colden believed Schuyler wanted to see the "Government in the same state of Disorder and confusion that prevails elsewhere." But the trouble in Cumberland County does appear to have been caused by disputed land titles, and Schuyler was probably not as rabid as Colden wrote. The colonel suggested only that a committee be named to investigate the cause of the disorders in the northeastern parts of Albany County and in Charlotte County, and that it report the following session. Here again was evidence of his conservatism and his partisanship; certainly a man who anticipated a future session of the assembly foresaw no course of events that would interrupt established order. But again he was defeated by the De Lanceys. And the house managed to provide additional £50 rewards for the jailing of each of the riot leaders (including Ethan Allen and Seth Warner) who had committed "violent outrages" against the Charlotte County justices of the peace. Assembly Journals, Mar. 25–April 3, 1775. C.O. 5/1201 and C.O. 5/1220. See also Colden to Gage, April 2, 1775. Colls. N.Y. Hist. Soc. for 1877 (New York, 1878), X: Colden Papers, II, 407–409; Colden to the Secretary of State, April 5, 1775, C.O. 5/1139:233–235; Mark, Agrarian Conflicts, pp. 176–177, 189–191.

American province.[54] Assembly partisanship shifted to the field. Philip Schuyler's cousins and partisan rivals, the De Lanceys, recruited and led loyalist troops against the cause their kinsman embraced and defended as a major-general in the continental forces.

[54] Division of Archives and History, University of the State of New York, *The American Revolution in New York* (Albany, 1926), pp. 73, 217–218. Half of the population of New York was estimated to be loyalists; they furnished 8,500 militia and 15,000 regulars to the king's cause.

CHAPTER VIII

Regimentals of Rebellion

– 1 –

DEFENDERS, NOT AGGRESSORS

FROM THE DECADE of the 1760's, when committees began to act in an extralegal governmental capacity, the established government of New York was faced with a potentially dangerous rival. And as the gap between royal and revolutionary authority widened, the committee system grew to bridge it, easily developing from several groups functioning within the colony—the county boards of supervisors, the assembly's standing committees and special committee of correspondence, and the merchants' committees on trade.[1] These groups began to function as a government and were the bases for the New York Provincial Convention or Congress, and for the election of delegates to the Second Continental Congress. The failure of the assembly to name delegates to a Second Congress ultimately led to the formation of a revolutionary government in New York. When the colonists were denied the opportunity of sending representatives to Philadelphia through established methods and institutions, they gathered in extralegal meetings to name congressional delegates and to set up a provisional government. As Lieutenant Governor Colden noted: Philip Schuyler, Abraham Ten Broeck, and Peter R. Livingston "strove hard to have Delegates appointed by the House"; and when they failed, they went "home to get that done by the election of People which they could not effect in the House."[2] It is uncertain what Philip Schuyler's relations, if any, were with the extralegal movement before 1774. He may have sympathized, but was not actively connected with the Sons of Liberty.[3] Schuyler was a member of a committee of correspondence in Albany formed in the summer of 1774. The committee

---

[1] Flick, III, 213–216.

[2] Colden to Tryon, April 5, 1775. *Colls. N.Y. Hist. Soc. for 1877* (New York, 1878), X: Colden Papers, II, 398–399.

[3] Lossing, I, 215, 246. See also *The New-York Gazette, or Weekly Post-Boy*, Jan. 23, 1766, and *The New-York Mercury*, Jan. 27, 1766.

chose him a delegate to the First Continental Congress, but when he could not go because of illness, it then authorized the delegates of New York City to act in his stead. The Albany committee also gave Schuyler instructions to procure the assembly's approval of the actions of the First Continental Congress, but in this the colonel failed. Neither would the assembly name delegates to the Second Continental Congress. Thwarted by the ultra-conservative De Lanceys, Schuyler more and more accepted other methods and procedures to obtain what he was denied in the regular channels of established government.[4] The more the assembly split, the weaker grew its resistance to Parliamentary measures. Now as factionalism became more pronounced in a new imperial crisis, the assembly leadership proved ineffective, and a third power, the radicals without, seized the initiative. They forced the assembly factions to re-form outside the legislature.

As early as February 25, 1775, Philip Schuyler with his colleagues, Ten Broeck and Livingston, proposed that the Albany Committee of Correspondence elect delegates to the Second Continental Congress. On March 1 the Albany committee decided to call the district committees to meet on March 21 "with full Power to appoint Delegates." [5] The action was that of a people who had proposed political independence, but no such course of action was intended, if we may believe the provincial protestations of loyalty to the king's government. Conservatives like Schuyler believed that the Congress offered a legitimate means of expressing colonial grievances and of soliciting redress, and he was determined, as were others, to secure what he conceived to be the rights of Englishmen, not those of an independent people. The conservatives also feared that the assembly's withdrawal "from the extra-legal movement would tend to place control of Congress in more radical hands," and to prevent this they joined the movement to procure temperate delegates who would not act precipitously.[6]

The determination to win a redress of grievances proved stronger than any concern for preserving allegiance to the empire, however. It was so strong that expression was given to the sentiment even before the assembly adjourned and as soon as it was known that the house would not name delegates. The move to name delegates to

[4] Jacob Lansing, Jr., to Schuyler, Aug. 23, 1774. NYPL, Schuyler Papers Box 24. "Minutes of the Albany Committee of Correspondence, Aug. 13, 23, 30, 1774." Peter Van Schaack Papers, Columbiana, Columbia University.

[5] *Minutes of the Albany Committee of Correspondence, 1775–1778* (2 vols.; Albany, 1923–1925), I, 7. Hereafter cited as *Albany Committee Minutes.*

[6] Becker, *Political Parties*, p. 178.

Congress came before the assembly even approved the addresses to the king and Parliament. In New York City the committee of sixty, a more radical successor to the committee of fifty-one, called for a provincial convention, and on March 6 it held a mass meeting to obtain "authority" to nominate eleven deputies. The conservatives preferred to support this radical committee rather than to give any appearance of refusing to support the Congress. But the De Lancey loyalists would have little to do with it. On March 15, New York elected its delegates to the provincial convention, and the next day the committee of sixty called upon the counties to follow. Schuyler had long since invited his county to name delegates to the Second Continental Congress, but now Albany joined the movement for a provincial convention to name the delegates. Support of the convention and of the Second Congress was another "long step in the direction of revolution." [7] It meant markedly increased radical activity even for politically cautious men like Philip Schuyler.

Albany County responded not so much to the invitation of the New York Committee of Sixty as to the suggestion of its assembly representatives who had advised the election of delegates to Congress in February. The Albany Committee of Correspondence dutifully elected their own assemblyman together with those of Livingston and Rensselaer manors to the provincial convention. It did not name Jacob Ten Eyck who, although a county committeeman, had been much of a De Lancey follower in the assembly. On March 21, Schuyler, Ten Broeck, and Peter R. Livingston were joined by Abraham Yates, Jr., and Walter Livingston as delegates.[8]

On April 20, seventeen days after the assembly adjourned and but a day after British troops clashed with provincials at Lexington and Concord, the deputies of the New York Convention assembled at the Exchange, only a short distance south of the city hall where the assembly had prevented the election of delegates to the Second Congress. The De Lanceys or loyalists would not frustrate them now. The convention after organizing decided on a system of majority voting in which the city and county of New York could cast four votes, Albany three, and other counties two each.[9]

The next day it was unanimously resolved that the delegates to the

[7] *Ibid.,* pp. 182–186.

[8] *Albany Committee Minutes,* I, 9.

[9] *Journals of the Provincial Congress, Provincial Convention, Committee of Safety and Council of Safety of the State of New-York, 1775–1776–1777* (2 vols.; Albany, 1842), I, 1. Hereafter cited as *Journals of N.Y. Congress, Convention, Committee.*

First Continental Congress be named to the Second Congress as a mark of approval of their action; these were Isaac Low, James Duane, Philip Livingston, John Jay, John Alsop, Henry Wisner, William Floyd, and Simon Boerum. Five others were added to the list: Philip Schuyler, George Clinton, Lewis Morris, Robert R. Livingston, Jr., and Francis Lewis. The delegation was not basically radical nor was it loyalist; it reflected the lines of the old minority party in the assembly remarkably well—men who were largely conservative and certainly moderate, but who had been momentarily driven from their natural conservatism largely because of the De Lanceys. Full power was given to any five of them to meet with the Congress on May 10 "and to concert and determine upon such measures as shall be judged most effectual for the preservation and re-establishment of American rights and privileges, and for the restoration of harmony between Great Britain and the Colonies." The third day the convention approved the credentials for its delegates subscribed by the members. There were forty-one in all.[10]

Although the New York delegation to Philadelphia was not as satisfactory as radicals like Alexander MacDougal and John Lamb may have wished, and although its members were fundamentally conservative or moderate, "it represented a decided victory for radicalism. The conservative program was rapidly breaking down; and of the old members of the conservative faction, one part was becoming indistinguishable from the revolutionists, while the other was in part already identified with the loyalists." [11] It seemed that the anti–De Lancey faction had finally gained a measure of power, though it was quite outside the constitutional and legal framework of provincial politics—and something of a departure from their traditional conservatism. Thus Schuyler's disposition to work with established order was momentarily obscured by his participation in the revolutionary movement. It was a dangerous game, but for the moment the fruits of power were more easily shaken from the revolutionary than from the established tree of government.

As of the spring of 1775 the factional divisions among New Yorkers prompted a newspaper editor to propose new partisan labels. Before, both factions claimed to be Whigs. But now a distinction between them as Whigs and Tories was more meaningful. Rivington's *New-*

10 *Ibid.*, I, 4–5.
11 Becker, *Political Parties,* p. 192.

York Gazetteer (March 9, 1775) suggested that the modern Whig was characterized by his revengeful attitude toward the mother country— a fellow who "Endeavours to justify every irregularity in American politicks . . . destroys constitutional liberty in the colonies, and boldly supports Anarchy and licenciousness [*sic*], insurrections and rebellion." In contrast, the modern Tory "Is Desirious to support the laws of his country, and instead of revenge against the parent state, is anxious to heal the dispute on constitutional grounds, with that becoming decency, which is due to the crown, from all his Majesty's loyal, grateful, and affectionate subjects." The definitions offered an apt commentary on what had occurred in the assembly, and on what was happening after its adjournment.

The New York Convention of April 20–22 did not inaugurate a new government, but the very nature of its activities encouraged this. Within a week after the convention adjourned, the committee of correspondence, prompted by the news of Lexington and Concord, addressed a circular letter to the counties, asking that they elect delegates to a provincial congress which would act as an interim assembly. Here was another challenge to royal government—the forerunner of a state legislature. The call for this congress was justified by the distresses and alarms "occasioned by the sanguinary measures adopted by the British Ministry, (to enforce which the sword had been actually drawn against our brethren in . . . Massachusetts) threatening to involve this continent in all the horrors of a civil war, obliges us to call for the united aid and council [*sic*] of the Colony, at this dangerous crisis." The New York Congress was to assemble on May 22.[12]

By the time the New York Congress met, Philip Schuyler was in Philadelphia, embarked on projects that would lead him from the cabinet to the field. Politics pulled him into a different service, and for two years he was almost more dependent upon New York politics than he was able to bring them under his own influence. His political dealings were those of a general importuning various governmental units for military supplies and reinforcements. Had he not been called to a military command he doubtless would have remained in the Continental Congress or have sat in the provincial congress with many other civilian colleagues. Even his brief military career was to illustrate how much the Revolution was a struggle among those who aspired to control local affairs. The clashes over "home rule" seemed

---

[12] *Journals of N.Y. Congress, Convention, Committee*, I, 5.

moot points of dispute, for the colonies had a large measure of self-government. Their challenges to imperial administration were basically threats of independence, not cries for home rule, but threats to Parliamentary supremacy. They can scarcely be construed differently. Protestations of loyalty were not as substantive as the acts which accompanied them. And the consistent threat of localism and partisan politics seem to offer as great a clue to the colonial *malaise* as do the sporadic outbursts of opposition to imperial administrative measures and regulations.

The day following the convention's adjournment Schuyler set out from New York for Albany. He had heard the news from Lexington that reached the city following the close of the convention. By the end of the month he was at Saratoga. On April 29 the colonel met with a sub-committee of the Albany Committee of Correspondence. The group sent a circular letter to the county's district committees, suggesting that in view of the Massachusetts crisis, a "Committee of Safety, Protection and Correspondence" be appointed. This committee was to be empowered to transact all business aimed at the "welfare of the American Cause." Accordingly, a meeting was called for May 10.[13]

From his country seat Schuyler wrote John Cruger, speaker of the assembly and chairman of its committee of correspondence, who was about to embark for England. His letter reveals his own grim resignation to the prospects of civil war, but he said,

we have only left . . . the choice between such evils and slavery. For myself, I can say with Semprenius:

Heavens! can a Roman Senate long debate Which of the two to choose, slavery or death! No; let us arise at once, etc.

for we should be unworthy of our ancestors if we should tamely submit to an insolent and wicked ministry. . . .

Schuyler's temper about the assembly addresses was also evident; no longer did he propose to wait "supinely . . . for a gracious answer to a petition to the King, of which, as a member of the assembly who sent it, I am ashamed." Schuyler recognized the difficulties. He knew that many New Yorkers were loyal or timid, but "when the question is fairly put," as he believed it was by the Lexington-Concord inci-

13 *Albany Committee Minutes,* I, 14–15.

dent, he was sure the great majority of the people would choose to
"fight for right and freedom" rather than be "ruled by a military
despotism." For his own part, much as he favored his "domestic happiness and repose, and desire[d] to see [his] countrymen enjoying the
blessings flowing from undisturbed industry," he would rather see "all
these scattered to the winds for a time, and the sword of desolation
go over the land, than to recede one line from the just and righteous
position we have taken as freeborn subjects of Great Britain." The
colonel urged Cruger to use all his influence in England to convince
"the people and the rulers that we were never more determined to
contend for our rights than at this moment."

Schuyler did not consider Americans *"aggressors,* but *defenders."*
Nor did he believe the De Lancey-ridden assembly "truly represented
the feelings and wishes of our people . . . I have watched the course
of the political currents for many months with great anxiety," he said,
and for over a year have been "fully convinced that unless Great
Britain should be more just and wise than in times past, war was inevitable." War—not independence. Now that it had begun, Schuyler
would say in the spirit of Joshua the prophet that, caring not what
others might do, he and his house would serve their country.[14] Whatever may have been his practical reasons for resisting the power of
Parliament, and whatever weight the partisan politics he had played,
Schuyler justified the localism in idealistic terms and rationalized the
position to which he had been driven.

On Sunday, April 30, Colonel Schuyler attended divine services at
"the Flatts," part of the old family estate north of Albany. The congregation was so visibly moved by reports of Lexington that "The
preacher was listened to, with very little attention." Following the
service, the colonel was surrounded by tenants and local farmers who
looked to him as "the oracle of [the] neighborhood . . . His popularity was unbounded; his views upon all subjects were considered sound,
and his anticipations almost prophetic." Schuyler confirmed the news
of Lexington and told the people that he believed "an important crisis
had arrived which must sever us forever from the parent Country." [15]
If the narrator of this account was correct, Philip Schuyler was thinking of independence even before the Second Continental Congress
met! He may not have hoped for it, but he could not escape a certain

14 Schuyler to Cruger, April 29, 1775. Lossing, I, 307.

15 [John P. Becker], *The Sexagenary, or Reminiscences of the American Revolution*
(Albany, 1833), p. 21.

conviction that it would now come. Was he consciously, or otherwise, moving toward an espousal of independence? As early hostilities took on the color of a more determined, irreconcilable contest he was steadily drawn into a struggle that was not to be easily terminated by mere reconciliation with the mother country.

On May 1, Schuyler was again in Albany for a meeting of the committee of correspondence's sub-committee. There it was decided to hold a public meeting to determine on further action. The populace was to be asked if they wished to cooperate with others in opposing "the Ministerial Plan now prosecuting against us" and whether or not they would appoint a committee of safety empowered to take further action. The meeting was held that very day, and the questions favorably passed. Schuyler was not named to the new committee of safety. His impending duties elsewhere probably dictated his omission. Within a brief time the inhabitants of Albany began to arm and drill.[16]

At this crucial interval between the assembly's last session and the opening of the Second Continental Congress we may ask why Philip Schuyler became a patriot and not a loyalist—why he espoused the cause of Congress and then of armed rebellion and independence rather than Parliament and the empire. The framework of partisan politics in the assembly was responsible for much of his position. It was analogous to an observation made in 1780 about the two factions at the moment of crisis in 1775: "the Livingstons waited to see what side the De Lanceys would take, and when [they] . . . attached themselves to government, the Livingstons instantly joined the other party." [17] The philosophical justification of position was rationalized in far less practical terms, but even these are not completely hidden by the language of ideology. We have seen how the colonel complained both of the "wickedness" of the ministry and the ill representation of the province by the De Lancey–dominated assembly. The De Lanceys were more vividly associated with the royal establishment and the empire than the Livingstons. Schuyler also showed the same shift in argument that many of his fellow colonists did—a shift from opposing internal taxes and allowing external taxation for regulation to the denial of effective Parliamentary power even in regulating trade. If the powers of Parliament were to be as circumscribed as Schuyler proposed in the last assembly session, the "grand legisla-

---

16 *Albany Committee Minutes,* I, 16–18, 24.
17 Jones, *History of New York,* II, 560, citing the *Political Magazine,* April, 1780.

ture of the Empire" would not be sovereign at all. In December, 1768, the colonel had supported assembly resolves declaring against taxation without direct representation, but at that time he also voted against any declaration that the Restraining Act was an infringement of freedom. He could vote in this fashion perhaps because at the time the house believed that its resolve that the assembly had a right to correspond with neighboring colonies or any other of His Majesty's subjects implied a censure of the Restraining Act; there was no need for a further, particular, or offensive mention of it.[18] Yet for practical purposes the insistence upon direct representation implied a real challenge to Parliamentary supremacy.

The First Continental Congress may have been prepared to deny all Parliamentary authority, but in March, 1775, Schuyler's attempts to alter the New York Assembly's statements of grievances and resolutions indicated that he believed Parliament's power to tax, merely as a device for regulating commerce, might be admitted. He denied Parliament the right to lay any tax for raising a revenue and was willing to admit that its power was founded in expediency more than in right.[19] The colonel indicated in miniature the wider and more general shift to arguments of natural law. He argued that rights were based on the "immutable Laws of Nature" first, and the "Principles of the English Constitution" second.[20] His activities indicate that the revolutionary issue in New York was a matter of "home rule" insofar as that meant freedom from certain Parliamentary taxation. But they more clearly indicated that the issue concerned who was to rule at home. Schuyler's attempts to modify the addresses to the king and Parliament in March, 1775, suggest the former. His partisan battle with the loyalist De Lanceys which later merged with the "home rule" issue shows how wide the divisions were within the governing class—divisions of ambition as to which faction of the class was to rule, and whether government was to remain in the hands of one group of aristocrats or another, or be shared with a lesser breed.

John Adams once remarked that the object of the Revolution was "resistance to innovation and the unlimited claims of Parliament, and not any new form of government." Schuyler's behavior and expressions indicate the truth of this; yet the denial of all Parliamentary power except for the regulation of trade was an innovation. Appar-

18 Assembly Journals, Dec. 31, 1768. C.O. 5/1100:123–125.
19 Assembly Journals, Mar. 24, 1775. C.O. 5/1201.
20 Ibid. See also Becker, Political Parties, p. 17.

ently Schuyler believed Parliament itself was innovating, but perhaps he was more concerned that it was extending claims to power beyond reason. In April, 1769, when he moved that the assembly set aside a day to consider the state of the colony and spoke of *preserving* the union and *restoring* harmony, he gave no indication of dissatisfaction with the essential structure of government. Again in March, 1775, he spoke of *"maintaining* our constitutional Liberty" and complained that the king's regal powers but not his virtues had been so delegated to his ministers that the colonists were "reduced to the disagreeable necessity" of disturbing "the King's Repose" by petition.[21] Yet we have also seen how the assembly factions illustrated John Adams's observation on innovation. Innovation was a local matter, not merely a threat from afar. Were not interpretations of the residency law partisan innovations to exclude rivals from the same governing class? Were there not suggested innovations in the proposal to use secret balloting in place of the *viva voce* method of election polling? Was not the entire history of Schuyler's assembly career a testimonial to partisan adjustments to conditions within the established government? It is not easy to differentiate between factionalism and the debate on political principle or imperial theory because these issues were inextricably bound together, one conditioning the other, the latter largely revitalizing and agitating the former.

Both the De Lancey and Schuyler factions asserted colonial rights against Parliament, but Schuyler's proposed amendments to these assertions were generally sharper than the De Lanceys would allow. We can scarcely explain this in terms other than partisanship. The colonel's opposition to their resolves was a way of bidding for support against an opposition faction almost as much as it was an expression of grievances about the empire or "home rule." New York, the colonel conceded, was an inseparable part of the empire, but he also believed submission to Parliament's supreme legislative power was an expediency that was tolerable only "in cases of absolute necessity, and where our own Legislature is incompetent," and that he could "never acknowledge an authority . . . to bind us in all Cases whatsoever."

As a conservative, Schuyler joined the extralegal committee movement to control it, but in view of the refusal of the loyalist assembly to approve the Continental Congress, he also believed that the extralegal movement was a necessary and legitimate instrument to procure

21 Assembly Journals, April 8, 1769; Mar. 24, 1775. C.O. 5/1100 and C.O. 5/1201.

redress. His assembly record shows Schuyler's "patriotism" was a mark of his ambition. But it was also a mark of his despair—dismay at a situation produced by a ministry which he believed showed more concern for legal rights than for the wisdom and expediency of administrative measures—dismay, too, at the local factional arrangement. In August, 1775, with the advantage of some hindsight, Schuyler lamented that the "admirable Constitution . . . has of late been most Notoriously trampled upon & attempted to be overthrown by the Nefarious Manoeuvres of a Sanguinary Ministry, & their wretched Sycophantic Abbettors, both in great Britain & America." [22] This was telling evidence that the colonel, then a general, disliked both the ministry and the local faction in power—"Sycophantic Abbettors," as he called them. The latter were identified with the former, and in opposing one, he might resist the other. He became a patriot insofar as he was carried in the flood of opposition to the power of the De Lancey loyalists. But temperamentally aristocratic, he could not go the way of a George Clinton or Sam Adams. Once the stream of rebellion broke, Schuyler attempted to dam the more extreme forces which were allowed to rampage when he helped open the floodgates.

– 2 –

RAISING A MILITARY SPIRIT

PHILIP SCHUYLER was late in arriving at Philadelphia for the opening of the Second Continental Congress on May 10, 1775. On May 9 he left Albany, bearing a letter to the New York Committee of Correspondence from his own county committee, asking advice about provisioning Connecticut troops for an attack on Ticonderoga.[23] His stay in New York for further consultations delayed his departure. The martial spirit in the province had risen almost beyond description, so one newspaper reported. On May 8 the delegates from Massachusetts and Connecticut and six New York delegates were accompanied to the North River ferry by about five hundred men, including two hundred militia under arms. Four days later Schuyler and George Clinton followed the advance party to Philadelphia.[24]

22 Schuyler to Abraham C. Cuyler, Aug. 23, 1775. NYPL, Schuyler Papers: Letter Book 1775–1776, pp. 195–196.

23 Lossing, I, 315.

24 *The New-York Journal, or the General Advertiser,* May 11, 18, 1775. *The New-York Gazette, and the Weekly Mercury,* May 8, 15, 1775.

From the very outset Congress gave Schuyler a part in the United Colonies' military concerns—a role that developed into an active military career and later into an advisory position in Congress. His old friend and legal adviser, William Smith, Jr., warned him against military resistance and offered advice about the policy Congress should pursue. Smith hoped for an American parliament and a continued union with the empire. "For Heavens sake," he told the colonel, "don't flip so fair a Prospect of gaining what you run the greatest Risk of losing upon a Change of Men." Smith expected a change in the ministry, believing that the moment to win a concession was imminent. But even Lord North's conciliation plan of February seemed less influential at the moment than the military clashes in Massachusetts. The plan included Parliament's promise to "forbear" to lay any but regulatory taxes, provided the colonies laid their own taxes for defense and the support of civil government. If Lord Chatham became first minister, Schuyler could expect only that the colonies would be exempted from internal taxation. Smith advised Schuyler to contend for an explicit declaration of peace based on certain assurances that Britain might give: that no taxes be raised without local consent; religious matters be left to the assemblies; revenue from the trade regulation should pass into the colonial treasuries, and an American parliament be established to settle the imperial revenues and to levy quotas for each colony with power to force a defaulting colony to pay. "Why raise a military spirit," he asked, "that may furnish unmanageable adventurers on this Side of the water unfriendly to a Province in which you and I have something to lose." Unmanageable adventurers and something to lose indeed! Schuyler's espousal of armed rebellion was a grave risk which demanded as much of his idealism as it did a realistic consideration of ambition and personal well-being. He found that it required energy to prevent "adventurers" from entrenching themselves in power. "For God's sake be slow," Smith warned. "Guard against those who are interested in pushing Matters to Extremities for their personal safety or private Interest. There may be among you those who look for salvation from the Number of the obnoxious as well as for Elevation from a Change of the Ministry. Your Country wants nothing but a Change of Measures." 25

From Congress, Schuyler wrote Smith a letter on May 22 to which the latter's response indicated a certain relief. "You have made me

25 Smith to Schuyler, May 16, 1775. NYPL, Schuyler Papers Box 24.

easy," Smith wrote: "This is the Time for negotiating to advantage." [26]

Schuyler, however, had scarcely written his friend than he was named to a committee on ways and means of supplying the colonies with ammunition and military stores.[27] His further involvement in military resistance led to a break in his connections with Smith. Their friendship Smith held sacred; their aims were mutual, but they parted on the means of accomplishing them.[28] In June, Schuyler served on committees concerned with other military affairs—estimating necessary funds for the colonial effort, devising ways and means of introducing the manufacture of saltpeter to the colonies, and drafting the first rules for the government of the army. He also sat on a committee established to devise steps "for securing and preserving the friendship of the Indian Nations." [29] The problems of these committees became Schuyler's direct personal concerns throughout the two years during which he commanded the Northern Army.

Congress faced an important responsibility in selecting the chief military officers to lead the armed resistance. It was necessary to represent various sections of the country on the high command in such a way as to draw their support to the common cause. John Adams suggested Washington as commander in chief, not only because of his personal abilities and prestige, but also because Massachusetts men wanted to draw Virginians more securely within the rebel camp. Early in June the New York delegates had written their provincial congress, asking that it suggest a person to command the continental troops in New York.[30] Richard Montgomery who was to serve as Schuyler's brigadier general wrote to his brother-in-law, Robert R. Livingston, wondering about Schuyler's qualifications. "Phil Schuyler was mentioned to me by Mr [John Morin] Scot[t]," he said. "His consequence in the Province makes him a fit subject for an important trust—but has he *strong nerves*? I could wish to have that point well ascertained with respect to any man so employed." [31]

The New York Congress evidently considered that Schuyler's "con-

[26] Smith to Schuyler, June 1, 1775. NYPL, Schuyler Papers Box 24.

[27] Worthington Chauncey Ford, *et al.* (eds.), *Journals of the Continental Congress, 1774–1789* (34 vols.; Washington, 1904–1937), II, 67. Hereafter cited as *C.C. Journals.*

[28] Smith to Schuyler, July 28, 1778. NYPL, Index to the Schuyler Letters, II, 76.

[29] *C.C. Journals,* II, 80, 86, 90, 93.

[30] Peter Force, *American Archives:* Series Four (6 vols.; Washington, 1837–1846), II, 898. Hereafter cited as Force, Ser. 4.

[31] Montgomery to Livingston, June 3, 1775. NYPL, Bancroft Transcripts: Livingston Papers, I, 33.

sequence" merited the appointment and did not question his "nerves." Their unanimous nomination settled the matter, and on June 19, Congress made Philip Schuyler one of the four major-generals chosen, it was said, "to Sweeten and to keep up the spirit" in the province of New York.[32] The New York Congress cited the new general's courage, prudence, and readiness in the use of expedients, his "nice perception," sound judgment, extensive knowledge of the sciences and, "above all, a knowledge of mankind." The political hostageship of the appointment was unmistakable. It was the price of power no less than the position was an advancement over the place Schuyler occupied in the provincial hierarchy. A general, the New Yorkers said, must be gifted by "fortune" that "he may rather communicate lustre to his dignities than receive it; and that his country, in his property, his kindred and connections, may have sure pledges that he will faithfully perform the duties of his high office, and readily lay down his power when the general weal shall require it." [33] Here was a concise statement of prevailing notions about men of suitable caliber participating in government.

Schuyler was assigned to the Northern Department, comprising New York and Canada. Although he did not leave Philadelphia until June 23, the new general apparently did not attend Congress after his appointment on the nineteenth.[34] Presumably the work with which he was now entrusted diverted his attention to military planning. On the day before his election Schuyler had ridden into the country with Silas Deane of Connecticut to discuss "another bold stroke like the Ticonderoga affair." [35]

The general set out from Philadelphia for New York with Washington, Charles Lee, and Thomas Mifflin on June 23. The next day he invited the New York Congress to send a delegation to meet Washington and his party at Newark and to provide for a safe crossing of the river.[36] They were entertained at Leonard Lispenard's two miles out of the city after the militia, members of the provincial congress and other leaders had met them when they crossed the river from New

[32] Eliphalet Dyer to Joseph Trumbull, June 20, 1775. Edmund C. Burnett (ed.), *Letters of Members of the Continental Congress* (8 vols.; Washington, 1921–1936), I, 137. Hereafter cited as Burnett, *Letters.*

[33] *Journals of N.Y. Congress, Convention, Committee,* I, 33.

[34] Burnett, *Letters,* I, lvii.

[35] *Colls. N.Y. Hist. Soc. for 1886* (New York, 1887), XIX: Deane Papers, I, 61.

[36] *Journals of N.Y. Congress, Convention, Committee,* II, 10.

Jersey. On the afternoon of Sunday, June 25, the generals rode into New York City. That very evening Governor William Tryon returned from England, and many of the officials with the clergy and others who had greeted the rebels turned out to welcome Tryon [37]—an ironic twist, considering how the provincial congress was planning illegal action against constituted authority.

At New York, Schuyler was left with the instructions of the commander in chief to keep a sharp eye on Tryon and neither to delay the occupation of the northern posts nor to fail to observe Guy Johnson's dealings with the Indians lest they be incited against the colonists. Having conferred with Schuyler about the proposed invasion of Canada, the Indians, the loyalists, and the problems of supply, Washington departed from New York on June 26 for Cambridge.

Left with Washington's advice and confidence, Schuyler turned to the immediate work that lay before him. He was to spend two years laboring to collect adequate troops and supplies for an army. To this were added worries over insubordination and the vexations of ill health. What proved most galling of all were attacks made upon his character and conduct. In these respects his experiences proved to be not unlike those of Washington himself. The common cause and mutual difficulties forged a close bond between the two men. Even in temperament they were similar.

Schuyler remained in New York City for over a week, attending to the shipment of ammunition and other stores north to the bailiwick which had become a military department. His dealings with Governor Tryon were the motions of a man still agonizing between war and peace, rebellion and established authority. Yet his major-general's commission offered him a rationalization of his position: his duty was to repel every hostile invasion of American liberty and to defend it from assault.[38] The general lodged with William Smith, Jr., at his home on Broadway, opposite the house taken by Governor Tryon. One of his Tory contemporaries reported that Schuyler attempted to call on the governor to congratulate him upon his safe return and thus to pay Tryon the respect due a man to whom he and his father-in-law "were under great obligations" because of the settlement of previous land troubles. "But," wrote Thomas Jones, "can you conceive

[37] Sabine, *Smith Memoirs*, I, 228c.–228d. See also Jones, *History of New York*, I, 55–56.
[38] Schuyler's commission, dated June 19, 1775. NYSL.

it, gentle reader! he had the impudence to dress himself in the regi-
mentals of rebellion, go to the Governor's, and send in word that
'*General*' Schuyler would be glad to see him. The Governor, with his
usual spirit, returned for an answer, *that he knew no such man*. No
further attempts were ever after made for an interview." [39]

If Schuyler, indeed, made such an attempt to see the governor, he
did not wish to see Tryon again. On July 3, the general called in
William Smith, Jr., to reveal news that radical Isaac Sears, just returned from Philadelphia, "had divulged to him a Design . . . to
make a Prisoner" of the governor and to send him to Hartford. Schuyler protested and finally persuaded Sears and his cohorts "to drop the
Design as rash and unjustifiable, and what the Congress would not
countenance." Sears tried to pressure Schuyler by saying that other
delegates in Philadelphia had urged the kidnapping, but the general
insisted that he had Washington's written orders on the subject. When
Smith suggested that he inform Tryon of the plot, Schuyler "thought
it improper" and assured Smith that he would support the magistracy
"in all Cases, but where they opposed the Common Defense." Schuyler then had Smith draft an order "to make the Governor safe" when
the general should leave for Albany. Smith gave Schuyler the draft on
July 4, still much "imbarrassed" by the secret, but he decided not to
reveal it unless there were greater "Cause for Apprehension of Mischief." [40]

On July 3, Schuyler, accompanied by brigadier generals Richard
Montgomery and David Wooster, reviewed a battalion of city militia
in the presence of "a very respectable number" of New York's principal gentlemen and ladies.[41] Yet his reasons for such a rebellious display were conservative ones. In accordance with the order Smith
drafted for him, Schuyler wrote specific instructions to Wooster about
the purposes of armed resistance. "America has Recourse to Arms
merely for her Safety and Defence, and in resisting Oppression," he
said. "She will not oppress. She wages no War of Ambition Content
if she can only retain the fair Inheritance of English Law and English
Liberty . . . We are Soldiers ambitious only to aid in restoring the
violated Rights of Citizens—and these secured, We are to return instantly to the Business & Employments of Civil Life . . . All unnecessary Violence to the Person or Property of any of his Majesty's

39 Jones, *History of New York*, I, 58.
40 Sabine, *Smith Memoirs*, I, 232.
41 *The New-York Journal, or the General Advertiser*, July 6, 1775.

Subjects *must therefore most strictly be forbidden, and avoided.*" [42]

This cautious approach to revolution Schuyler reflected in a report to Congress later in the month when he revealed his predilection for property as well as liberty. "A Sett of People," he said, "calling themselves a Committee of War" had taken Colonel Philip Skene's forge and farm under the pretense of public service, but actually "to embezzle every Thing." Schuyler gave orders to restore Skene's property so "that no Disgrace may be brought on our Cause by such Lawless Proceeding." [43] He was still cast in the role of defender, not aggressor —still the conservative landlord for all his patriotic acts of rebellion.

Schuyler left New York in early July for his return to Albany. The remonstrance to the House of Commons which he had wanted to sharpen during the last assembly session was rejected, and Schuyler was pleased that this had "the good Effect to make those in [New York] City hearty in the Cause of America, whose Sentiments tho' friendly differed as to the Mode of procuring Redress." [44] In Albany he was also cheered by the warm reception given by his neighbors on July 9. He was received at his landing by members of the general committee of the city and county, the Albany city troop of horse, and an Association company which escorted him to city hall for an address. Dr. Samuel Stringer, his old physician, reminded the general that freedom had raised him "to a state of opulence and envy" and while the company deplored the necessity of his appointment, yet it was pleased by the prospect of the general's "unremitted exertion" of "knowledge, prudence, and experience, for the restoration of harmony and peace upon constitutional principles. . . ." Schuyler again insisted that they were to fight only to restore violated rights, and he volunteered to return his sword to its scabbard whenever reconciliation or his constituents directed. Following his "polite answer," the company enjoyed an elegant entertainment at the King's Arm Tavern.[45] The general hoped the ministry might "be induced to give up their odious Claims and pursue Measures tending to a Reconciliation

[42] Schuyler to Wooster, July 3, 1775. NYPL, Schuyler Papers: Letter Book 1775–1776, p. 24. Cf. Sabine, *Smith Memoirs,* I, 232–233.

[43] Schuyler to the President of Congress, July 21, 1775. NYPL, Schuyler Papers: Letter Book 1775–1776, p. 52.

[44] Schuyler to the President of Congress, July 2, 1775. NYPL, Schuyler Papers: Letter Book 1775–1776, pp. 17–18.

[45] Rivington's *New-York Gazetteer,* Aug. 3, 1775. Cf. *Albany Committee Minutes,* I, 127, 128, 134.

instead of the Nefarious and hostile Ones which they had adopted."
As the weeks passed into months he began to complain of a vexed
spirit, ill health, anxiety about supplies, desertions, the scandalous
want of subordination, and ultimately about being prevented from
reaping the laurels for which he labored. "If Job had been a General in
my Situation," he moaned, "his Memory had not been so famous for
Patience. But the Glorious End we have in View and which I have a
Confidential hope will be attained will Attone for all." [46]

– 3 –

WAR AND POLITICS

As LONG AS Philip Schuyler served as major-general in command of
the Northern Department, his chief political connections lay with the
Continental Congress and the New York Provincial Congress. As a
military commander, he experienced great difficulty procuring adequate troops and supplies from both bodies; his relations with them
were generally less political than logistical, and certainly less partisan
on the whole than were his connections as a civilian politician with
a civilian assembly. And yet at times the distinctly political, the clearly
partisan element, quite eclipsed the military aspects of his task. He was
responsible primarily to the Continental Congress, yet he was obliged
to conduct business through George Washington and with the New
York government. His importunities smacked of political wheedling.
Washington he respected, and for his chief's sake Schuyler wished to
encourage a proper system of subordination. But the New Yorker's
reports to Congress and its unhesitating penchant for giving orders
and complicating military appointments did not exactly simplify
Schuyler's problems or his administrative procedures. Moreover,
Schuyler could rely on Congress only to endorse his appeals to the
states, even his own state, for it had no coercive power to levy troops
or force monetary contributions.[47]

Schuyler spent the remainder of 1775 preparing an invasion of
Canada. When the Continental Congress adjourned in August, he was
obliged to direct more of his pleas for support to other public bodies

[46] Schuyler to Governor Trumbull, July 31, 1775; Schuyler to the President of
Congress, Sept. 25, 1775. NYPL, Schuyler Papers: Letter Book 1775–1776, pp. 79–80,
140–141.

[47] For a study of Schuyler's relations with civilian bodies see my "Philip Schuyler
and the Continental Congress, 1775–1777" (M.A. thesis, University of Nebraska, 1956).

which might lend immediate assistance. And for the period of his command, his largest correspondence was with Congress, the New York Convention, various New York committees, and with the Connecticut officials. The Canadian expedition was delayed until supplies and transportation were collected. The general labored vigorously to resolve these difficulties of preparation. He also solicited the prayers of Dominie Westerloo and the Albany Dutch Reformed Church for the success of the Continental Army.[48] In December the attack on Canada failed, and Schuyler's chief lieutenant, Richard Montgomery, fell before Quebec while the general, too ill to remain in the field, labored from his sickbed to keep his army together and properly supplied.

The old shortages, the old demands, and the frequent failures to meet the army's needs continued in 1776. Much of the failure appears to have been due to the absence of a central authority for collecting and dispensing supplies more systematically and regularly than could the states or even the relatively unorganized quartermaster and commissary departments.[49] Schuyler was obliged to rely heavily upon local government bodies and officials, which like Congress, were not always ready or able to supply him regularly or systematically. His relation to the New York Provincial Congress was dictated largely by supply demands and the execution of military security.[50]

When the Continental Congress finally responded to Schuyler's request for political assistance and in February, 1776, named a committee to visit him in preparation for the spring campaign against Canada, the committee was given broad instructions to assist in the new campaign on Canada.[51] The committeemen were to visit Quebec and use political persuasion to procure the support of the Canadians for the American cause. When the army then retreated from Canada in the face of strong British forces, Schuyler clashed with Horatio Gates, whom Congress had sent to command the troops in Canada. Schuyler denied Gates' jurisdiction because there was then no army *in*

48 Kenney, "The Albany Dutch: Loyalists and Patriots," p. 343.
49 Edmund Cody Burnett, *The Continental Congress* (New York, 1941), pp. 99, 273, 310.
50 *Journals of N.Y. Congress, Convention, Committee*, I, 59, 60, 62–67, 77, 79–80, 94–97, 103, 106–109, 111–113, 125, 131, 154, 167–168, 178, 185, 192, 194, 200, 211, 245, 254, 256, 265, 276, 286, 293–294, 315–316, 319, 328, 334, 347–348, 351, 357, 364, 418, 453.
51 *C.C. Journals*, IV, 151–152, 192, 197–198, 213, 215–218.

Canada, and after a brief jurisdictional altercation Gates accepted a subordinate position.[52]

The subsequent reverses in October, 1776, when Benedict Arnold's naval force was defeated on Lake Champlain, prompted fresh political outbursts against Schuyler—questions of his competency and even his loyalty—and encouraged partisans to plot his removal. Schuyler's army was spared further danger when the British withdrew from Lake Champlain for the winter. But malicious partisan gossip and maneuvers damaged the general's reputation and raised his ire. Suspicions of his loyalty to the colonial cause seem particularly preposterous, because he persevered in his labors and made personal sacrifices in the war effort, contributing his private means to the patriot cause. Gestures such as he made in July, following the New York Convention's approval of the Declaration of Independence, when the general dutifully ordered the document read to the troops, do not indicate disloyalty, however much he wished for peace and reconciliation with Britain.

Schuyler decided he must have a personal hearing from Congress as early as the summer of 1776. But the press of military affairs prevented his trip to Philadelphia until March, 1777. No direct charges had been leveled against him, but there were sly insinuations that he was making an enormous fortune at the public expense and that he had converted specie for the Canadian expedition to his own private purposes. Insinuations were also made which led him to request Congress to inquire how far the miscarriages in Canada could be imputed to his direction of the army.[53] Schuyler offered to resign his command in September, 1776, but Congress refused, and the New York Convention also insisted that he remain at his post. The provincial convention and the delegates it sent to Philadelphia were his main defenders. They, together with the Albany committee, feared that no one as capable could be found to replace him. The New York Convention quickly voted a statement of confidence; they passed resolutions citing his fidelity, skill, and assiduity. They promised to give him an inquiry that would put an end to the calumny. Indeed, because the New York Convention had recommended him for the command, they could not admit charges against him without bringing censure on themselves. The convention and its delegates to Con-

52 C.C. Journals, V, 448–449, 526. Lossing, II, 93. Force, Ser. 5, I, 20, 232, 394, 396, 454, 511, 629, 693, 747, etc.

53 Burnett, Letters, II, 357–358. Force, Ser. 5, I, 983.

gress indicated by their labors on his behalf that Philip Schuyler was not a prophet without honor in his own country. Indeed, one of the major tasks the New York delegates in Congress had was the defense of their general! [54]

The New York Convention did not hesitate to offer Schuyler advice regarding preparations for the 1777 campaign. Before setting out for Philadelphia and a personal visit with Congress, he called on the convention for more assistance. The results were fair. He could not get artillery to defend Ticonderoga or to arm the vessels on Lake George, but he was promised a $25,000 loan. He recommended that a law be passed, allowing the deputy quarter-master general and deputy commissary general to seize foodstuffs and lumber from monopolizers and hoarders and to pay the usual price, or better yet, a price the convention might determine. The committee of safety, executive agency of the convention, first replied that the way to combat the monopoly problem was to lay taxes and provide judicial procedure; they feared that price-setting and military seizures would discourage trade. Not until March did the New York Committee of Safety, which sat between sessions of the convention, direct chairmen of local committees of safety to seize foodstuffs from monopolizing middlemen upon application of the quarter-master or commissary generals.[55]

The New York Convention was even more successful in managing Schuyler's vindication in Congress and in restoring him to a command in which he had been temporarily replaced by Horatio Gates from March to June, 1777. It had interceded on his behalf in September, 1776, by suggesting that Congress not accept his resignation and that it give him the inquiry he requested as a means of clearing his reputation. Unless Congress did this, the New York body threatened it would make an inquiry itself as a means of vindicating its recommendation of the general for an appointment in 1775. Congress refused the resignation, but delayed any inquiry until Schuyler should have an opportunity to visit Philadelphia. Meantime, the general busied himself with preparations for the next campaign.[56] The matter of his resignation was held in abeyance until the general set out for Philadelphia in late March, 1777.

[54] Flick, III, 301–302. *Journals of N.Y. Congress, Convention, Committee*, I, 622–623, 635, 656–657.

[55] NYPL, Schuyler Papers: Letter Book 1776–1778, pp. 43, 47–48, 62. See also *Journals of N.Y. Congress, Convention, Committee*, I, 792–793, 819, 864.

[56] Force, Ser. 5, II, 709; III, 1495–1497.

Although he held a high military position, Schuyler had remained an official delegate to the Congress since his selection in April, 1775. His military duties had merely made attendance impossible after June, 1775, but now he was to return to the body which had sent him on his mission of war. Schuyler did not trust to a sudden confrontation of Congress without preparation. On March 17 he wrote Robert R. Livingston, wishing that he, John Jay, and James Duane could be in Philadelphia to help in the defense. If these men could not be spared, he hoped the New York Convention would name William Duer and Gouverneur Morris as delegates. The convention obliged, and on March 29 it named William Duer a delegate to work in his behalf.[57] On May 13, 1777, after his arrival at Congress, the New York Convention renewed the general's power by reappointing him together with Duer, Jay, Duane, and Morris as delegates, and this served to remind Congress that he had the full confidence of his colleagues at home.[58] Schuyler had a dedicated set of partisans to work in his behalf. Philip Livingston and James Duane were especially strong friends, and they exerted every effort to restore his injured reputation and reinstate him in the command which Congress had given to Horatio Gates in March.

Duane and Livingston were first obliged to become acquainted with new members in Congress in order to "undeceive them." They procured a committee to inquire into Schuyler's conduct "at large." When that went on "heavily," they struck upon a more direct course—that of re-examining his public accounts. The Treasury Board cleared him of suspicions of peculation, and many members finally acknowledged they had been deceived about the general's conduct and character. Congress then passed a memorial exonerating him, and finally, the New Yorkers persuaded Congress to reinstate Schuyler in command of the Northern Department. Livingston and Duane could report to the New York Convention that "every point" was "adjusted entirely" to Schuyler's and "our Satisfaction. This Business with which more than the *Reputation* of our State was so closely connected re-

[57] Schuyler to Robert R. Livingston, Mar. 17, 1777. NYHS, Robert R. Livingston Collection. See also Werner, *Civil List* (1888), p. 116.

[58] Werner, *Civil List* (1888), p. 116. See also *Journals of N.Y. Congress, Convention, Committee*, I, 931. On Feb. 5, 1777, the Albany Committee of Correspondence instructed the deputies of Albany County to use their influence in the provincial congress to have Schuyler named a delegate to the Continental Congress. *Albany Committee Minutes*, I, 675.

quired address and great attention. . . ." [59] William Duer, another delegate and one of the general's friends, vowed Schuyler's exoneration and reinstatement proved a "Difficult Card to play" because Gates had so cleverly "insinuated" himself into the "good Graces of even the honest Part of the House, and the Unkindness to poisin [sic] the Minds of most with Prejudices against Genl. Schuyler which operated so strongly that nothing but Time, and great Temper and address could have dispelled the Mist of Error which had clouded the Eyes even of those who were Friends to ye great Cause, and to the State of New York." The delegates of New Hampshire, Massachusetts, and Connecticut had voted against Schuyler's reinstatement. Georgia's and New Jersey's were divided, and Delaware and Rhode Island were not represented.[60] The issue of maintaining an able man in office, of countering political schemes to replace him, and of insuring the continuance in power of an influential leader of New York's governing class had been resolved, on the whole, successfully. Thus, the connection of war and politics for Philip Schuyler.

[59] Philip Livingston and James Duane to the New York Convention, May 23, 1777. NYHS, Duane Papers. See also *Journals of N.Y. Congress, Convention, Committee,* I, 941, 951–952; *C.C. Journals,* VII, 336.

[60] Duer to Robert R. Livingston, Jr., May 28, 1777. NYHS, Robert R. Livingston Collection.

CHAPTER IX

A General and Wartime Politics in New York 1775—1777

—1—

"INDEPENDENCE & HAPPINESS ARE NOT SYNONYMOUS"

BEFORE MEN like Philip Schuyler could hope to establish a government for New York in which they might be assured a greater role in the direction of affairs, a military struggle claimed their immediate attention. From a delegate to the Second Continental Congress Schuyler moved into the field as major-general in command of the Northern Department. Even in the War of Independence Schuyler was not entirely free from politics. His relations with New York political bodies as well as with the Continental Congress embroiled him in new partisan struggles. He was chosen a major-general because it was necessary "to Sweeten and to keep up the spirit" of New York.[1] Yet the military reverses and delays, combined with his forced absence from the field due to periodic illness, subjected Schuyler to attacks from partisan congressmen, largely Yankees, who questioned his abilities and even his loyalty. The New York Provincial Convention and the delegates it sent to Congress were his main defenders. The latter learned that one of their major tasks in Congress was the defense of their general from such attacks. In the spring of 1777 they managed to vindicate Schuyler after he had been charged with misusing military funds and blamed for miscarriages in the assault on Canada. Schuyler himself returned to Congress in April, 1777, to force the vindication. And although he intended to resign his commission, he returned to his post in June.

The general's military difficulties were further compounded by a political defeat in June when New York held its first state elections. Thus, 1777 was a nadir year for Philip Schuyler. His political career

[1] Eliphalet Dyer to Joseph Trumbull, June 20, 1775. Burnett, *Letters*, I, 137.

had been building to a peak—not without frustrations and delays, but nonetheless in a gradual ascent. And from the eminence of a politician turned soldier he was cast down from fame and impending military success to momentary failure, notoriety, and odium. It was at this point that his fortunes in the struggle with a newly emerging radical element turned decidedly for the worse.

The movement toward independence and the establishment of a state government in New York was in part a continuation of the colonial struggle between factions, between two sets of partisans. But by 1776–1777 the contest was more than one between court and country, between De Lanceys and Livingstons. It was now a struggle between conservatives and radicals. Though the radicals had won substantial victories since the beginning of the resistance, they had won "because a considerable group of the old conservative faction," including Philip Schuyler, "was always prepared in the end to come over to the radical position rather than withdraw altogether from the extralegal movement." [2] Once revolution was assured, however, the less radical patriots proceeded to arrange checks and controls to deal with their more liberal brethren. During the last days of royal government the issue was between two elements of a single class. With the war it developed into a struggle between a segment of the old governing class and the less privileged element of provincial society. Some of the latter had been on the fringe of privilege, and others had come from the "lower orders." The question of who was to rule at home remained a vital one, and, as we shall see, Schuyler even as a general became involved again in the controversy—a controversy resolved by a curious "compromise"—a conservative victory in the promulgation of a constitution for the new state, but a moderate defeat for conservatives in the first gubernatorial elections.

Before 1776, New York generally showed no desire for total independence. Yet there was a positive, rather unconscious movement toward virtual independence implied in the whole extralegal procedure of committees and congresses.[3] Philip Schuyler himself mirrored the sentiment. In July and again in November, 1775, after the rebellion had gone quite beyond the limits of mere protest, Schuyler wrote Governor John Trumbull of Connecticut of his hopes that the ministry "may be induced to give up their odious claims, and pursue measures tending to a reconciliation, instead of the nefarious and

2 Becker, *Political Parties,* p. 195.
3 Flick, III, 273–274.

hostile ones they had adopted." In the second letter he voiced the desire of a conservative as well as of a dismayed general. "May Heaven still prove propitious," he said, "that a speedy termination may be put to this afflicting controversy, and Britons and Americans once more regard each other with the fond tenderness of a parent and child, and jointly establish an empire on such a solid basis, that no power on earth may be able to destroy it, and that shall last until the omnipotent Being is pleased to blot out all the empires of the earth." [4]

But in January, 1776, Schuyler began to shift his views and to show new resolution. Having devoted himself to the country's service, he said, he was firmly resolved to sink or swim with it "unanxious how I quit the stage of life, provided that I leave to my posterity the happy reflection that their ancestor was an honest American." By late March he no longer expected the British to cease their plans (though they had withdrawn from Boston), though they would bring only ruin which, he said, "must inevitably happen whenever we are driven to the necessity of declaring ourselves an Independent State." The general's reference to one state also indicated that he was not parochial in his outlook or vision. The sentiment for independence grew steadily during the early months of 1776, even among men of Schuyler's temperament—men who earlier would have been content with reconciliation. Yet the general was learning, as his old friend William Smith, Jr., later told him, that "Independence & happiness are not Synonymous." [5]

Schuyler was not a member of any of the provincial congresses, the fourth of which on July 9, 1776, approved the Declaration of Independence. But he had political connections with the government, and no little influence with its members. The strength of this influence was based on a common interest shared by the men who had won a large measure of power in directing the forces of independence. Once separation was proclaimed, New York followed the advice of Congress and devised a new state government. The provincial congress which met from July 9, 1776, to May 13, 1777, framed and promulgated New York's first constitution and conducted the first state elections in June, 1777. It arrogated the work of a constitutional convention and

4 Schuyler to Trumbull, July 31, Nov. 18, 1775. Force, Ser. 4, II, 1762; III, 1603–1604.

5 Schuyler to Washington, Jan. 5, 1776. Force, Ser. 4, IV, 580; Schuyler to Trumbull, Mar. 27, 1776. *Ibid.*, V, 519. See also William Smith, Jr., to Schuyler, July 28, 1778. NYPL, Schuyler Papers: Index to Schuyler Letters, II.

selected some of the new state officials before the gubernatorial and legislative elections.

The gradual movement toward independence and the establishment of new state government was based on a rejection of British conduct. Early in 1775, Parliament adopted Lord North's plan by which Parliament would simply "forbear" laying any but regulatory taxes on the colonies whose assemblies raised money to support the civil and military establishment. Notwithstanding North's concession to this demand of New York and her sister colonies, his conciliatory scheme was not accepted, perhaps because there was no body to which it might be effectively presented. The news of Lexington and Concord apparently stirred local tempers against its reception. Moreover, the British government had not received New York's addresses to the king and Parliament satisfactorily as far as the province was concerned. And the heats of military action proved more overwhelming than the interest in working out a plan for reconciliation short of warfare. New York followed successively the leadership of the provincial and continental congresses which guided her step by step toward complete separation and the establishment of a new government. Philip Schuyler was active among those who participated in this process.

The "moderate-radical combination" that led New York into revolution did not last long. Having won substantial political control, the moderates, once a part of the ruling class in the assembly and a faction with its own peculiar identity, began to exclude their more radical brethren from the direction of affairs when the New York Congress began plans for a permanent frame of government in 1776. If the moderates had abandoned the empire, they did not look favorably upon the possibility of losing power to the radicals.[6] Events had driven some conservatives forward on the road to revolution. They did not propose to permit the radicals to drive them too far.

In April, 1776, new elections for the provincial congress saw the "reappearance of earlier party distinctions" of conservatives and moderates. Conservatives aimed at preventing the government of New York from making "rash democratic experiments,—to keep it, in fact, 'as near the old form of government' as possible." [7]

The formation of New York's constitution illustrated to what extent the Revolutionary issue in New York had been a question of

[6] Becker, *Political Parties,* pp. 206–209.
[7] *Ibid.,* pp. 256–257, 259–260, 267, 269, 272.

who was to rule at home; it was not a matter of one class challenging another for the privilege, but of one element of a class struggling with its peers. The same was true in the new governing class that appeared —the revolutionists, who fell into conservative and radical camps within a single broad and ideological position. On August 1, 1776, the fourth provincial congress named a committee to draw a plan for government. The composition of the committee was predominantly conservative, and because of wartime exigencies, the members did not complete their work until March, 1777.[8]

Philip Schuyler could rest easily, knowing that New York's government would be soundly drawn. In June, 1776, he advised some Charlotte County citizens that he was not averse to the choice of William Duer as representative to the fourth New York Congress. Duer was politically solid, and the general knew that when the framing of the government took place, it would be wise and "incumbent" on all New Yorkers to "depute the most sensible" men "on so great an occasion." [9] Sensible men were of course conservatives. Duer was one of them; he was also named to the committee which drafted the constitution.

The general himself could not join the committee's deliberations on a frame of government for New York. He was not a member of the provincial congress, and he was obliged to discharge military responsibilities. He did, however, show interest, offer support, and answer requests for advice. His old friend William Smith, Jr., asked him whether or not as a great landholder his interest in fashioning a new government should not call him from the field to the cabinet.[10] But Schuyler did not desert his military post. In October, 1776, Robert R. Livingston, who was a member of the drafting committee, reminded Schuyler that he had promised to write his views about the constitution and urged that the general do so as soon as possible.[11] Leonard Gansvoort, also a provincial congressman, submitted drafts of the proposed constitution to him and then had to call on Schuyler to return the papers, "together with your Observations." [12] Whatever the general's counsels to committee members and to others were, we can be

8 Flick, IV, 153–155.

9 Schuyler to Rev. Dr. Clark, et al., June 18, 1776. NYPL, Schuyler Papers: Letter Book 1776, p. 190.

10 Smith to Schuyler, Aug. 17, 1776. NYPL, Schuyler Papers: Index to Schuyler Letters, II.

11 Robert R. Livingston to Schuyler, Oct. 2, 1776. NYPL, Schuyler Papers Box 31.

12 Gansvoort to Schuyler, Nov. 17, 1776. NYPL, Schuyler Papers Box 31.

sure that he played some role in forming the government, notwith-standing his avowal in 1777 that "it is out of my Sphere to enter into any political Disquisitions." [13] On December 6, 1776, he wrote the committee chairman, Robert Yates, to thank him for the promise to send a copy of the constitution when it was completed. "I am very apprehensive," he confided, "that much Evil will arise if a Govern-ment is not soon established for this State. The longer it is delayed the more difficult it will be to bring the unprincipled and licentious to a proper Sense of their Duty and we have too many such amongst us." [14] It was clear what Schuyler expected of the new government.

The New York constitution presented to the congress was a dis-tinctively conservative frame of government. It mirrored the attitude of persons who tended to support the existing outlines of mixed gov-ernment, of social relationships in opposition to too much modifica-tion. The characteristics of conservatism in 1777 can be read from the document as much as they may be implied from the aristocratic be-havior and expressions of the men who fashioned and implemented it—men who believed in privilege, responsibility, and mixed govern-ment. The oligarchs of the day may appear more reprehensible than they in fact were, largely because they spoke in terms of liberty and property instead of democracy and equality.

The constitution provided a bicameral legislature. The governor's power was curbed by a council composed of four senators who shared in the appointive power. A council of revision composed of the gov-ernor, chancellor, and supreme court judges had the power of veto —not the governor alone. Unless each house approved a bill by a two-thirds vote, the council was obliged to pass on all legislation. Thus, it also restricted the power of the legislature, and gave judges a de-cidedly political function. The elector's qualification to vote for as-semblymen was a £20 freehold or a forty shilling leasehold (equal to $5), provided the taxes on such property were not in arrears. Freemen of the cities of New York and Albany continued to hold the right to vote. In this way New York retained much of the flavor of her colonial establishment.[15]

[13] Schuyler to Israel Pemberton, May 22, 1777. NYPL, Schuyler Papers: Letter Book 1776–1778, pp. 140–141.

[14] Schuyler to Yates, Dec. 6, 1776. NYPL, Schuyler Papers: Letter Book 1776–1778, p. 14.

[15] See the charters of Albany and New York City (1686) and the election laws of 1699 and 1701 in State of New York, *The Colonial Laws of New York*, I, 192–193, 210, 405–408, 453. E. Wilder Spaulding, *New York in the Critical Period, 1783–1789*

Men qualified to vote for an assemblyman were also entitled to hold his office. To qualify to vote for senators, the governor, and lieutenant governor, New Yorkers were obliged to own a freehold worth £100 clear of all encumbrances. According to one observer, the dual suffrage qualification was due "to the colonial aristocracy . . . whose allegiance to the Revolution would have been jeopardized if an overly democratic government had been established." Without residence and property tests, Tories, Hessians, and other undesirables would have made it more difficult for "safe and sound Whigs to be elected." [16]

Other provisions indicated how the government was kept as close to old outlines as possible. The governor, lieutenant governor, and senators themselves had to be £100 freeholders. Sheriffs and coroners were to be appointed anually. Town clerks, supervisors, assessors, constables, and collectors were elected locally, while the legislature was to provide for the election of loan officers, county treasurers, and clerks. The colonial court structure was retained: a supreme court, chancery, admiralty, county and probate courts; but a court of impeachment was added. The assembly was to be chosen annually—seventy members apportioned according to population. The senate of twenty-four members from four great districts was elected for four-year terms, while the executive served for three years.[17] There was no radical departure from old institutions.

On April 20, 1777, the new constitution was proclaimed at Kingston without a popular referendum. A powerful democratic element in the congress had allowed the conservatives to promulgate their system largely because of its preoccupation with the military struggle.[18] But more than that, the conservatives had managed the radical Revolution in such a way as to rid New York of Parliament without depriving it

---

(New York, 1932), pp. 84–101, has a good, brief survey of politics and the constitution of 1777, except that he errs in including Schuyler as a member of the convention which formulated the constitution. Cf. Werner, *Civil List* (1884), pp. 312–314. That the constitution was the work of conservatives it need only be pointed out that Robert R. Livingston proposed the council of revision, and that John Jay suggested the council of appointment.

[16] Williamson, *American Suffrage From Property to Democracy, 1760–1860*, pp. 197–198.

[17] Flick, IV, 157–163. See also Dangerfield, *Livingston*, pp. 88–92, and Alden Chester (ed.), *Legal and Judicial History of New York* (3 vols.; New York, 1911), II, 27–30.

[18] Flick, IV, 165.

of a system of privilege. They persuaded the revolutionaries, "captivated" them "by the magic of a history" which they detested only in part. The colonial landlords may have robbed their tenants, but "they had also resisted Parliament: if they had lived by privilege, they had fought prerogative." And "the Constitution was compact, well-written, fertile in compromise, and apparently not in conflict with accepted theory—or in conflict only to the point where it dissatisfied but did not actually outrage radical opinion." [19]

Before adjourning, the congress named a council of safety to govern until the new government should be installed, and it was this council which ordered the county sheriffs to conduct the polling in June for governor, lieutenant governor, and the legislature. The congress provided other state officials: John Jay as chief justice, Robert R. Livingston as chancellor, John Sloss Hobart and Robert Yates as judges, and Egbert Benson, attorney general. The first council of appointment confirmed these men in office.

On April 25, Robert Benson sent Philip Schuyler and the other New York delegates in the Continental Congress a copy of the new constitution under which the general was to live out his days.[20] Schuyler's friends and men of common interest had devised a satisfactory system, despite its somewhat liberal innovations, replete with the conservatism so agreeable to his composure. He was to share in its semi-oligarchic arrangements as a state senator and as a member of the council of appointment, thus empowered to check the executive which he had been unable to do as freely in colonial days. The council of appointment proved to be the means of one of the most powerful political combinations ever formed in the state of New York. The maintenance of English common and statute law, as well as old colonial statutes, was another provision far from original or from innovation. The land system remained intact. There was no bill of rights. Yet had Schuyler been elected governor in June, 1777, he might have viewed the checks upon executive power with something less than equanimity; though New York conservatives who remembered their colonial past did not exactly favor a strong executive, Schuyler possessed a temperament that inclined him to favor the strong central government that is usually associated with executive power. His ex-

[19] Dangerfield, *Livingston*, pp. 92–93.
[20] Benson to Schuyler, *et al.*, April 25, 1777. NYPL, Bancroft Transcripts: Schuyler Letters, 173.

periences during the war and the Confederation eventually convinced him that if New York did not require centralized authority, the United Colonies become independent states needed it desperately.

– 2 –

"THE SPIRIT OF ELECTIONEERING"

THE NEW YORK elections of June, 1777, were remarkably quiet. There was nothing approximating the furor of two elections that Philip Schuyler witnessed in 1768 and 1769. The wartime emergencies diverted attention elsewhere, and many people appeared apathetic. No parties existed as we know them today, and there were no public nominations nor widely organized and executed campaigns. Indeed, the very concept of "party" was deplored, and as in the colonial regime candidates were presented by semi-private combinations of men who persuaded their fellows to stand for election and then quietly corresponded and conversed on their behalf.

General Schuyler emerged as a candidate for governor by a process of elimination. He had not been active in local politics for the past two years. His main connections with New York's congress and committees of safety were those of an importunate commander seeking supplies and arms, enforcing military security on civilians and relaying information of troop operations.[21]

The conservatives were so certain of themselves that John Jay, popular as he was, did not wish to be governor; he was satisfied with being chief justice, although his popularity might have been a better asset for assuring victory in the gubernatorial race. Philip Livingston was eliminated because there were objections to "having two brother Governors." William Livingston was soon to be governor of New Jersey. And Philip Livingston's candidacy might lose votes to John Morin Scott, especially in areas, such as Dutchess County, where the

21 Journals of N.Y. Congress, Convention, Committee, II, 11–15, 20, 43, 76, 114, 121, 123–124, 131, 134, 154, 170, 190, 194, 196, 208–209, 231, 251, 253, 265, 268, 314, 316, 336, 339, 344, 348, 349, 357, 360, 377, 394, 404, 462, 469, 501, 505, 507, 511, 514–516. See also NYPL, Schuyler Papers: Letter Books 1775–1776, 1776, 1776–1778, which give no evidence that Schuyler's activities were very political aside from military involvements. The original papers for these letter books, together with transcripts and copies of other correspondence relating to his military command, are to be found in National Archives Microfilm Publications: Microcopy No. 247, "Papers of the Continental Congress, 1774–1789" (The National Archives and Records Service, General Services Administration; Washington, 1959), Item 63 (Roll 77), Item 153 (Rolls 172–173), Item 154 (Roll 174), Item 166 (Roll 183), and Item 170 (Roll 189).

Livingston interest was decidedly unpopular. The tale that the Livingston family and their allies decided to support George Clinton at the advice of their matriarch, Margaret Beekman Livingston, has no basis in fact, for the conservatives' best hopes fell on Schuyler. They were willing, however, to back Clinton for lieutenant governor as a recognition of his popularity and of his contribution to the war.[22] He had been a colleague of General Schuyler in the last colonial assembly. John Morin Scott, a favorite of the radicals, and quite unacceptable to the conservatives in every respect, was the third leading candidate.

Philip Schuyler's attitudes toward the war and independence smacked of ambivalence before he became involved in the political campaign of 1777. Curiously, his weariness with the war led him to express sentiments fit only for the ears of close friends. Early in January, 1777, enroute to Fishkill, Schuyler stopped to visit with William Smith, Jr. There the general declared "agt. the Disunion of the Empire," and Smith wrote that he spoke "in Despair of the Abilities of the Colonies and with Disgust at the Conduct of their Leaders." According to Smith, Schuyler was much disheartened by the lack of arms and supplies, and wished "Negotiations were opened for Peace." The general even went so far as to suggest that the New York Convention urge the Continental Congress to make overtures for peace, for the province "might as safely submit to the British Power at once as treat seperately—but as a Colony she might suggest her advice." When Schuyler revisited Smith on January 20 after his meeting with the New York Convention, the general lamented his inability to make any "Impression on the Convention," and confided that he doubted the possibility of raising an army "upon the Scheme of Independency." The convention would not accept his resignation, but he believed that if he refused to act, he would be made a prisoner. Schuyler's despair was clearly one of a beleaguered general, for he was convinced the colonies were exhausted and that nothing could save them from a British invasion expected during the summer except French assistance. He had even refused an offer by the convention to grant him dictatorial powers similar to those given to Washington in December by the Continental Congress.[23]

22 Dangerfield, *Livingston*, pp. 94–95. See also Spaulding, *George Clinton*, p. 91.

23 Sabine, *Smith Memoirs*, II, 62–63, 70. Schuyler's letter to John Hancock, Jan. 25, 1777, reveals his fears that the "incompetency" of the Ticonderoga garrison would lead to its downfall, and when the British seized it, he believed, "the Consequences will inevitably be the Loss of this State and probably draw with it that of the Eastern

After this moment of dejection Schuyler rode back to his command to do what he could to raise troops and prepare for the invasion from the north. Nor was he uninterested in the political developments regarding the new government to be inaugurated in New York. Again on March 2, when Schuyler once more called on Smith, the general seemed less disheartened, and his old friend "found him less confidential." Schuyler seemed more hopeful of French assistance, but said when he visited Congress later, he would urge it to "open a Treaty & bargain away the Bubble of Independency for British Liberty well secured." When Smith pointed out that New York's "Success in a Seperation would be the Ruin of this Colony," unless New Englanders would give up their claims to New York lands and when he reminded Schuyler of the "sinking" of their personal estates because of paper currency, the general "grew warm and serious, and said he would insist at the Congress . . . that this Province should not go an Inch farther without a Disclaimer. . . ." Still, Schuyler "had Confidence that a respectable Army would be formed, and . . . would succeed. That there would be then a perfect Union in America, & all Men weaned from their British Attachments." [24]

After his visit to Congress that spring, Schuyler returned, his spirits raised, to command the Northern Department. Indeed, William Smith, Jr., at whose breakfast board the general sat on June 3, said Schuyler talked "with great Confidence in the Success of the American Opposition." Now there were no thoughts of peace overtures with the British. "The Congress durst not make any for Fear of France," and though he acknowledged the colonies "were on the Point of Ruin . . . thought GB would fall first." [25] Perhaps the general was emboldened, too, by his chances for being chosen governor of New York.

Even before New York was presented with a constitution or before he became a candidate, Schuyler was occupied with the imminent election. In February, 1777, two months before setting out for Philadelphia, he wrote John Jay about the candidates for state office. Abraham Yates, he had heard, was to be nominated for lieutenant governor.[26] William Duer, one of Schuyler's political allies, shared with

ones, and bring on the Subversion of American Liberty." "Papers of the Continental Congress," Microcopy No. 247, Roll 173, vol. III, p. 46. See also his other letters to Hancock, Jan. 7, 13, 1777, pp. 28, 35–37, which indicate his importunities to the New York Convention and tell of the depreciation of currency and credit.

[24] Sabine, *Smith Memoirs*, II, 86–87. See also p. 83.
[25] *Ibid.*, p. 150.
[26] Schuyler to Jay, Feb. 1, 1777. Jay Collection, Columbia University.

Jay his confidence in the new constitution, but he was "not without . . . Fears concerning the Choice which will be made of those
who are to Set the Machine in Motion. Our all Depends on it," he
said. Schuyler, knowing Duer's predilections, communicated them to
Jay, thus seconding Duer's fears. Duer noticed that in other states a
"Want of proper Power being vested in the Executive" or "the Contention of Parties" had resulted in much disaffection and "unhappy
languor." New York's government, he hoped, might "continue to act
with that Spirit, Integrity, and Wisdom wh[ich] animated the Councils of the old!" Only a proper choice of chief executive would insure
this. Schuyler may well have remembered William Smith, Jr.'s, admo-
nition in 1775 that it was important that "unmanageable adventurers"
not be given an opportunity to establish themselves in power.[27]

The New York Council of Safety agreed with John Jay in supporting Schuyler's candidacy for governor. The council had not only been
left with the task of conducting the elections; it seemed the conservatives had also left it with a freedom to select the candidates. Moreover, the officials already named by the provincial congress, men like
Jay and Livingston, proceeded to use patronage at their disposal to
encourage the support of Schuyler. The council issued a statement of
program which they urged the people to ratify—the election of Schuyler, and of George Clinton as lieutenant governor. As the general had
met with them at Kingston enroute to his command in which Congress
had reinstated him, the council knew Schuyler would accept the office.
They believed he would have many votes in the upper counties. "Let
us not loose [sic] our Credit," they said, "in committing the Government . . . to men inadequate to the Task. . . . Let us endeavour to
be as unanimous as possible. Interest is making for others; But we
hope Care will be taken to frustrate the Ambitious Views of those
who have neither Stabillity [sic], uniformity or Sobriety to recommend
them." The council felt that both Schuyler and Clinton were "respectable Abroad," and "their Abilities unquestionable." [28] But Clinton seems not to have been overly concerned about unanimity or uniformity, and he did nothing to discourage his own candidacy for the
governorship.

Schuyler seems to have done relatively little in his own behalf to

[27] Duer to Jay, May 28, 1777. Jay Collection, Columbia University. See also William
Smith, Jr., to Schuyler, May 16, 1775. NYPL, Schuyler Papers Box 24.
[28] "A State of the Committee of Safety" by John Jay, Charles De Witt, Zepheniah
Platt, Matthew Cantine, and Christopher Tappen, June 2, 1777. *Public Papers of
George Clinton, First Governor of New York, 1777–1795, 1801–1804* (10 vols.; Albany,

win the governorship. George Clinton did not campaign either. The general was preoccupied with renewed preparations against Burgoyne's invasion, and even Clinton's military duties kept him from open politicking. But Schuyler was interested in the election, and he told Chief Justice Jay that his return to Albany had "given almost universal Satisfaction to my Countrymen"—a favorable omen for the election. A number of his fellow citizens had also spoken to Schuyler "on the Subject," and the chief justice had mentioned the general's candidacy at Kingston.[29] Still, people at Albany also spoke favorably of Jay for the governor's chair. Peter W. Yates wrote him to ask how election matters stood in the lower counties. As both Jay and Schuyler were mentioned favorably in Albany, Yates suggested that the chief justice offer a few lines in order that the electors at Albany might know how to conduct themselves.[30]

When Jay heard his friends at Albany intended to vote for him as governor, he quickly replied that he would prefer the bench, especially as he desired as much unanimity on the election as possible. "When I consider how well General Schuyler is qualified for that important office," he told them, "I think he ought in justice to the public to be preferred to Your most obt. humbl. Servt." [31] The very day Jay wrote this letter to John Ten Broeck of Albany, the Albany Committee of Correspondence "agreed to hold up" Schuyler for governor and Abraham Ten Broeck for lieutenant governor.[32]

Schuyler had his own observations about the elections. He wrote his brother delegates in the Continental Congress that he had hoped "the Good People of this State would not have differed in Opinion on the Appointment of the first Magistrate." But Philip Livingston, Jay, Scott, and himself were mentioned for the office, and Clinton, Duane, Abraham Ten Broeck, and a Mr. Snyder were considered for the lieutenant governorship. Schuyler was obviously worried about the proliferation of candidates; "Mr. Scott I am informed has been as-

---

1899–1914), I, 855–856. For examples of Jay's and Livingston's politicking for Schuyler see Sabine, *Smith Memoirs*, II, 157, 160, 163, 165. Jay offered Richard Morris a clerkship of the supreme court. Livingston was accused of offering chancery posts to influence the elections. Schuyler termed the committee of safety a council, which explains the usage here.

[29] Schuyler to Jay, June 4, 1777. Jay Collection, Columbia University.

[30] Yates to Jay, June 5, 1777. Jay Collection, Columbia University.

[31] Jay to John Ten Broeck, June 6, 1777. NYPL, Bancroft Transcripts: Schuyler Letters 1776–1788, p. 189.

[32] *Albany Committee Minutes*, I, 787.

siduously employed by himself and his Agents in making Interest to be elected." Two tickets were circulating in Albany County: one named Philip Livingston and Abraham Ten Broeck, and the second, Schuyler and James Duane. "I hope," he wrote, "the first & last will have a great Majority of Voices." [33] Whatever the general's "hopes" were for the governorship, he had, as Robert R. Livingston said, "consented to take it upon him," and Livingston was "in great hopes that he will be elected." Indeed, a defeat would be a blow to the Livingston interest in controlling the Revolution. The Livingstons did not adhere to their preference when John Morin Scott blew "up a flame about the impropriety" of Philip Livingston's election in view of his brother William's election to the New Jersey executive. This, Robert R. said, "unaccountably opperating very strongly with some other party matters, made it absolutely necessary . . . our battery" be swung from support of Philip Livingston's candidacy. They preferred Schuyler rather than "see our government drowned in a bowl of grog." [34] Scott was a notorious tippler.

Despite the appearances of a quiet campaign, conducted in the face of a threatened British invasion and despite lack of information extant, the electioneering must have been spirited for those who were vitally interested. On June 19, William Duer, writing to Schuyler, expressed sorrow that "the Spirit of Electioneering has gone forth in our State." He dreaded the consequences—"that Sourness of Mind which is the natural Result of contested Elections"—and feared the new government would not be as vigorous as the old convention and committee system. But perhaps the complaint was leveled less at the framework than at the composition. John Morin Scott was railing at "an *Aristocratic Faction* which he pretends has form'd and Organized the new Government," and Duer expected him to "make use of every Act however gross or wicked which he thinks will serve to make himself popular." [35] James Duane also deplored the party spirit, and bewailed Scott's responsibility for frequently causing "civil discord." Scott

[33] Schuyler to Philip Livingston, James Duane, William Duer, June 9, 1777. NYPL, Schuyler Papers: Letter Book 1776–1778, p. 157.

[34] Robert R. Livingston to Duer, June 12, 1777. NYHS, Robert R. Livingston Collection. For other evidence of how the conservatives hoped to control the government structure see Staughton Lynd, "Who Should Rule at Home? Dutchess County, New York, in the American Revolution," *The William and Mary Quarterly: Third Series*, XVIII (July, 1961), 330–359.

[35] Duer to Schuyler, June 19, 1777. NYPL, Schuyler Papers Box 33.

blamed Duane, Philip Livingston, and Duer for his failure to win a position on the bench, and accused them of concerting with Robert R. Livingston, Jay, and Gouverneur Morris to create factional and family interests. His cries appeared to be those of a man excluded from an influence which a privileged few had affected. It appeared that Schuyler's faction had at long last won the advantage. It was a faction whose antecedents ran back to an earlier party denied its ambitions in the colonial assembly. James Duane, however, insisted that he had not wanted to appoint state officials or to institute government until *after* the election, and if this assertion was not made too late to be used advantageously, he would invite Schuyler to pass word of it about so as to oppose the spirit of faction and party.[36]

On June 20, Jay informed Schuyler that the elections in the middle districts were going so favorably that he hoped soon to be able to address the general as "Your Excellency." Jay thought that Clinton's candidacy for both governor and lieutenant governor, when compounded with Scott's drawing votes from him, might mean Clinton would get neither office, and Schuyler would be elected.[37] As it happened, Clinton won both the posts!

In the midst of the June elections Schuyler was troubled by military problems and domestic difficulties. They were all a part of the nadir into which his reputation was sinking—sinking to the point where he could be dismissed from his military command and replaced by a partisan rival. When he returned to take charge of the Northern Department, following his reinstatement by the Continental Congress, he discovered that General Gates had done very little in his absence to make ready the defenses against an expected British invasion from Canada. When Gates returned to Congress, he audaciously recited his own merits, caused so much commotion that he was ordered off the floor, and was instructed thereafter to present any information or memorials he might offer in writing. Gates was jockeying to be reinstated in the Northern Department because he thought Schuyler would be elected governor of New York and would, consequently, resign his command.[38] Gates won an advantage when Schuyler was

---

[36] Duane to Schuyler, June 19, 1777. NYPL, Schuyler Papers Box 33, or in Burnett, *Letters,* II, 382–383.

[37] Flick, IV, 169.

[38] Lossing, II, 183–186. See also James Duane to Schuyler, June 19, 1777. NYPL, Schuyler Papers Box 33.

blamed for the fall of Ticonderoga and Congress decided Schuyler must step down.

Because of military problems and domestic difficulties Schuyler found little time to spend on the political campaign. Meantime, miscreants tried to fire his house at Saratoga. Happily, the blaze was discovered soon enough to be extinguished before more than part of a wall had burned.[39] But it was saved only to be put to the torch by order of General Burgoyne in October.

As for purely domestic difficulties, Schuyler's eldest daughter, Angelica, ran off with a fellow about whom the general and his lady knew very little—John Barker Church, alias John Carter, an English entrepreneur and later a member of Parliament. They strenuously objected to the marriage after Schuyler had evidently refused Church's request for his daughter's hand. So violent were the Schuylers' reactions to the elopement that Angelica and her husband had great difficulty, even with the help of her grandparents, the John Van Rensselaers, in winning a reconciliation, or as Church put it, "to make Peace."

The Schuylers were famous for their hospitality and generosity, but they were also "capable of projecting upon situations or persons they conceived to be beneath them" as Church experienced, "a freezing pride of place." [40] At first the Schuylers refused to answer the letter sent by the couple from the Rensselaer estate at Green Bush. Mrs. Rensselaer asked Schuyler to send for his daughter. Schuyler insisted that her duty should bring her home without sending. When the Rensselaers finally called on Schuyler to intercede, "the General scarcely spoke a dozen Words. . . . Mrs. S was in a most violent Passion and said all that Rage & Resentment could inspire"; she was a mother deprived of marrying off her eldest daughter in proper style. Schuyler, however, calmed his wife when her father exercised his paternal privilege of remonstrance. The old man insisted that Church was a suitable husband. A very cool exchange of notes followed and when at last Angelica and Church entered the Schuyler parlor, the general succumbed to their importunities for forgiveness.

Schuyler did not easily forgive his daughter and new son-in-law. The old pride was still dominant. If Church was to be his son, Schuy-

---

[39] Schuyler to the President of Congress, June 25, 1777; Schuyler to the New York Council of Safety, June 26, 1777. NYPL, Schuyler Papers: Letter Book 1776–1778, pp. 182, 289.

[40] Dangerfield, *Livingston*, pp. 29–30.

ler vowed "he should take the Freedom of giving me his Advice," Church reported, "when he thought I stood in need of it with the Candour of a Parent." Church promised always to pay due deference to such advice. Yet all was not well. Angelica remained "much distressed" at her parents' continued coolness—behavior that Church thought proved the Schuylers' reconciliation "only proceeds from the Fear of disobliging Mr. R[ensselaer]." [41]

Schuyler was much less distressed once he knew more about his son-in-law's origins and capabilities. But in June and July the general could only react to the unpleasantries as a part of a great decline in his personal and public affairs. The elopement incident indicated one of his grave political handicaps—pride and a patronizing air—which was a serious liability in a world of emerging popular government, not to mention the immediate gubernatorial election.

By the end of June the polling had been completed. There may have been no stump speeches, no campaign nor parties, but the correspondence and private maneuvering must have been considerable. When Schuyler heard that Clinton had received "a Majority of votes for the Chair," he told John Jay that if this were true, Clinton had "played his Cards better than was Expected." Schuyler, it seems, made no great effort to win the game; perhaps he trusted his friends could manage his election as well as they had the framing of the state constitution. Even as he wrote he was much concerned about Ticonderoga and the state of defense against the British march southward. He suggested to the council of safety that they go up to Albany to "Inspire the people with Confidence." [42]

"It was, perhaps, a little optimistic to hope that the torrent would sweep such a personage as Philip Schuyler into the governorship." Quick to resent a slight or familiarity, appearing always unbendingly proud, he was noted for manners that led suspicious people to think him a loyalist.[43] This then was another measure of his conservatism. Perhaps he was too forbidding a patrician to win such a broadly popular election. Capable, honest, and virtuous, he nevertheless inspired little confidence or affection except within a narrow circle of friends or neighbors who knew the man's entire character. And the power of Schuyler's coterie could not as easily manage the polls as they had so

[41] John Carter to Walter Livingston, July 3, 1777. NYHS, Robert R. Livingston Collection.

[42] Schuyler to Jay, June 30, 1777. Jay Collection, Columbia University.

[43] Dangerfield, *Livingston*, p. 94.

facilely won a constitution. The electorate refused to be directed. Yet if it had not been for the soldiers' votes, or the plurality of candidates, George Clinton may not have defeated his old assembly colleague. Both men were in the field during the election. Clinton had an appeal to many voters who were something less than aristocrats, though he also had the support of some lesser landlords in Ulster County and the popular leaders of Dutchess County who, though not poor farmers but entrepreneurs, still chose to swim with the popular current. Clinton also benefited from antagonism against the Livingston interest with which Schuyler was identified.

Because of the fragmentary and limited remains of the election returns and other evidence extant, it cannot be determined exactly how many people voted or how all sections of the state cast their ballots. Returns from Albany, Cumberland, Dutchess, Tryon, Ulster, and Westchester counties divided the vote as follows:

Schuyler	1,012
Clinton	865
Scott	386
Jay	367
R. R. Livingston	7
Philip Livingston	5

But the votes from Orange County and the southern areas were enough to throw the election to Clinton.[44]

As for Ulster and Dutchess counties, it is apparent that Schuyler failed to win because of his longstanding connection with the Livingstons. On June 3, Schuyler had told his old friend William Smith, Jr., that Dutchess and Ulster were "jealous of the Livingstons" who already had seized "all the valuable Places," but the general "said vauntingly They may chuse who they will I will command them all." Evidently he was convinced that he could be elected. But later Smith judged that "the People of Dutchess and Ulster were perswaded in chusing a Govr. to name no Livingston nor any in Connection with that Family & hence Clinton was preferred to Jay & Schuyler." [45]

Aside from this kind of explanation, the most decisive factor was probably the soldier vote, and with the ballots from Orange County, Clinton reaped 963 more votes while Schuyler won only 187, thus

[44] Werner, *Civil List* (1884), p. 156.
[45] Sabine, *Smith Memoirs*, II, 151, 326.

shifting the latter's balance from 1,012 to 1,199 and Clinton's from 865 to 1,828. This large number suggests a separate count of the soldier vote. Clinton was elected both governor and lieutenant governor. Only one of six counties for which the returns exist did not give Clinton the lead either for governor or lieutenant governor, and that was Albany, Schuyler's own particular bailiwick.[46]

At the conclusion of the election Schuyler might well wish "that the organization of the government had been left to a future day." He was "deeply Chagrined at the intemperance of some people . . . who having wished for offices which it would be improper they should hold, and since they are not likely to obtain them, become noisy and troublesome." Schuyler meant John Morin Scott, who had "left no art untried to procure the chair of Government. . . ." With proper politeness the general told William Duer, "Happily for me not above one half of the people of [Albany] County gave in their ballots otherwise that burthen would have fallen on me." But Schuyler believed that regardless of who headed the government, "we shall never equal the vigor of Conventions & Committees, the reason is too evident to dwell upon." Although he wished the organization of the government had been postponed, once it was done he vowed "we must now as good citizens strenuously exert ourselves to counteract the wicked, the weak, & the disappointed, and I trust that we shall be able to succeed and support the friends of the country in office against their malignant opponents." [47]

The general had mixed feelings about George Clinton. He hoped the new governor would not cause any divisions among the "friends of America" now that he had the executive chair. There was danger that partisanship and factions would weaken the American cause. "Altho his family & Connections do not Intitle him to so distinguished a predominance," proud Schuyler naively said, "Yet he is virtuous and loves his Country, has abilities and is brave, and [I] hope he will Experience from Every patriot what I am resolved he shall have from me, Support Countenance & Comfort." [48] Who should know Clinton's qualifications better than a man who had worked with him since their days in the colonial assembly? Schuyler offered Clinton his congratulations on August 4, and assured him that he would "embrace every

---

[46] Spaulding, *George Clinton*, pp. 91–92. See also Flick, IV, 169–170.

[47] Schuyler to Duer, July 3, 1777. NYPL, Bancroft Transcripts: Schuyler Letters 1776–1788, pp. 251–252.

[48] Schuyler to Jay, July 14, 1777. Jay Collection, Columbia University.

opportunity to make you sit as easy in the Chair of Government as the Times will admit." [49] The two old friends who had shared an opposition to the De Lanceys in assembly days had, however, come to a parting of the way. Within a decade their politics differed sharply. The election marked the first decisive fragmentation of the Whig coalition in New York. And Schuyler, together with Robert R. Livingston, James Duane, John Jay, William Duer, and Gouverneur Morris, began a powerful, coordinated campaign to strengthen and then to capture the national government.[50]

Clinton's election was a great disappointment—even a humiliation—to the conservative governing class. And they did not look kindly upon parvenus. The aristocrats did not really welcome the new governor, but "times were such that they were soon glad to make the best of him." One of them, Gouverneur Morris, said, "We are all hellishly frightened, but . . . we shall get our spirits again. . . . We fought gloriously below. . . . We shall beat them soon. We should soon do so if we had as good officers as our Governor." [51] Their only choice now was to resolve to get along as best they could with Clinton, and to comfort themselves that the judiciary and legal offices were in the proper hands, and that with management, both the senate and assembly might also fall under their sway. The elections may have been a reversal to the conservatives, but their position of influence and prestige, and the state constitution comprised their certain hope. For the moment their victory evidenced in the promulgation of the constitution had run its course. After a decade Clinton lost his grip on the state, and the conservative tide again ran strongly, this time carrying Philip Schuyler and his fellows into Federalist partisanship and statesmanship. The members and heirs of the faction in the colonial assembly at long last won a place of advantage for themselves.

[49] Schuyler to Clinton, Aug. 4, 1777. NYPL, Schuyler Papers: Letter Book 1776–1778, p. 312.

[50] Lynd, "Who Should Rule at Home? Dutchess County, New York, in the American Revolution," p. 343.

[51] Dangerfield, *Livingston* p. 96.

APPENDIX A

Genealogical Chart

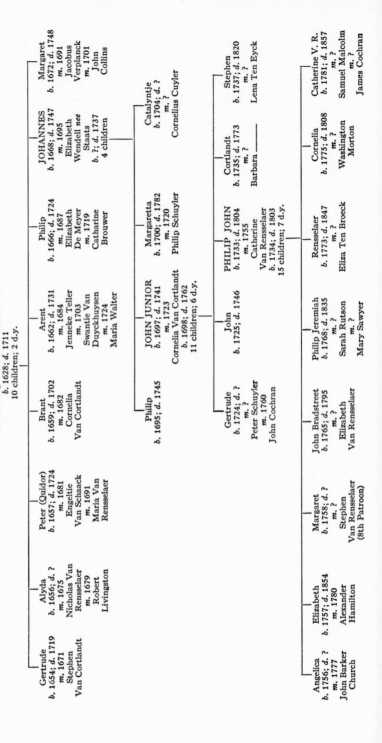

APPENDIX B

Schuyler Family Landholdings

LANDHOLDING was of the greatest importance in the American colonies, and especially in New York, where the proprietary and royal regimes were particularly kind to the great landlords. Land was the principal form of investment and speculation. Owners of large estates, whether as manor lords or otherwise, possessed certain privileges and influence because of their real property. Up to the Revolution provincial politics were largely in the hands of this landed aristocracy—or perhaps better, the landed squirearchy. Land determined in large measure a man's social position, the weight of his political influence, and even the franchise. How he administered his holdings of course determined his wealth. The intermarriage of the principal families was an additional factor in determining the extent of a man's enjoyment of economic advantages and political interests.

Details of early land acquisitions in New York are often difficult to determine. The Schuyler family holdings have been mentioned in a general fashion by monographists and "survey" historians. But a more specific outline of their property holdings may prove valuable to a better understanding of Philip Schuyler's position, as they certainly do to the reader interested in particulars.

A study of the holdings of the entire Schuyler family would be monumental, for the clan was a numerous one and their acquisitions extensive. However, a review of the acquisitions of General Schuyler's father, grandfather, and great-grandfather will further clarify the story told in Chapter I.

Philip Schuyler (1628–1683), the founder of the family in America, laid the sub-structure of the Schuylers' position by beginning to accumulate the substance of the family interest. In May, 1664, he and Goosen Gerretse (Van Schaack) petitioned the Director General and Council of New Netherland for permission to buy the major part of a tract called the "Half Moon" above Rensselaerwyck on the Mohawk River. The matter was deferred until the spring of 1665, when Schuyler petitioned Governor Richard Nicolls under the new regime for a license to purchase the land from the Indians. The governor granted the request, and in October a patent was issued. No quitrent was provided.[1] Although no acres were stipulated, and as it is difficult to ascertain even

---

[1] Schuyler, *Colonial New York*, I, 151–152. Cf. C.O. 5/1134:1, "Abstracts of New York Land Grants, 1666–1764." In July, 1681, Schuyler sold his half interest in the Half Moon tract to Van Schaack's widow. Thus the tract did not form any part of his holdings that passed to successive generations of Schuylers, but it doubtless con-

the approximate extent of the property from existing records, it is likely that
Philip the Founder's lands can be counted in the hundreds rather than the
thousands of acres. His sons did considerably better in expanding the family
holdings.

In 1667, Schuyler added other small pieces to his possessions, this time several
houses and lots in New York City east of "the Great Broadway," about seventy
acres in the village of Esopus, additions to his house lots in Albany, and a plot
of ground with a parcel of woodland near Albany.[2] The irregular measurement
of the latter (105 rods long, 50 rods on the south, and 36 rods on the north)
was not an unusual description for tracts at the time.

Philip the Founder's acquisitions apparently were purchases, like that of the
farm called "the Flatts" a few miles north of Albany. In June, 1672, he paid
Jeremias Van Rensselaer 5,000 guilders for this land, but he was also bound to
pay an annual rent of twenty bushels of wheat and merchantable corn and
"two coppel off henns," for the tract lay within the patroon's territory.[3]
What he accumulated was indeed minor as compared to the enormous land
grants made after his death when his eldest son, Peter, and six others acquired
the Saratoga Patent (1684) estimated at over 168,000 acres, a tract stretching
twenty-two miles north and south along the Hudson and twelve miles wide.[4]
Yet it was a beginning.

Philip and Margaretta Schuyler made a mutual will, giving the survivor the
benefit of their entire estate for life. Thereafter it was to be divided equally
among eight surviving children. Primogeniture applied only to the estates of
persons who died intestate. Even when the eldest son acquired "the Flatts,"
he was obliged to pay the sum of £600 into the estate, which was in turn
equally divided among all the heirs.[5]

Captain Johannes Schuyler (1668–1747), the sixth and youngest son of Philip

---

tributed to the family substance. The Half Moon Patent was a peninsula north of
the junction of the Mohawk and Hudson Rivers. See "A Chronographical Map of
the Province of New York," in *Doc. Hist. N.Y.,* I. The tracing of its boundaries in
"Abstracts of New York Land Grants, 1666–1764," *supra,* is fairly typical of the
vague manner in which land was then described: "A Certain tract of Land called
Mathahenaack lying to the North of the fourth Spring beyond and above the Colony
of Renslaerswick near Albany being the foremost of a parcel of land called the half
Moon, otherwise by the Mahikanden Nacktenack, stretching along the River
Northwd. from the said Spring to a Creek proceeding out of a great Meadow lying
West of the said River, and so forth, into the Woods unto the Maguas Hill."

[2] C.O. 5/1134:2, 3, 5, 14.

[3] Schuyler, *Colonial New York,* I, 157–158.

[4] Ibid., II, 96; C.O. 5/1134:35.

[5] Schuyler, *Colonial New York,* I, 159, 162–166. See also Berthold Fernow (comp.
& ed.), *Calendar of Wills on File and Recorded in the Offices of the Clerk of the
Court of Appeals, of the County Clerk of Albany, and of the Secretary of State*
(New York, 1896), p. 336.

the Founder, acquired a portion of the Saratoga Patent which formed the nucleus of the estate that eventually passed to the hands of his illustrious grandson, Major-General Philip Schuyler (1733–1804). Although Johannes' marriage to Elizabeth Staats, the widow of Johannes Wendell, did not entitle him to this part of the Saratoga grant in which her former husband had been a holder, Johannes Schuyler bought the tract from Wendell's son in 1702. And by a confirmation of the Saratoga Patent (1684) made in 1708, the royal government acknowledged that Wendell's share in the land had passed into Schuyler's hands.[6] The confirmation had evidently been necessary because of the changes in the original patentees.

Although Johannes Schuyler's major acquisition was Wendell's one-seventh share in the Saratoga Patent, he began his accumulations more modestly. In December, 1695, the year of his marriage, he bought about 180 acres of his brother Peter's share in the tract. From these rather humble beginnings his holdings grew immensely. Wendell's one-seventh share at Saratoga which Schuyler bought was almost thirty-eight square miles, or about 24,000 acres. His brother Peter also held a one-seventh share, and the two Schuylers thus formed from the Saratoga Patent the nucleus of all the other speculative holdings they managed to acquire by buying additions from other patentees and their heirs in the same tract.[7] Johannes Schuyler's tract lay along the west side of the Hudson River; its northern boundary was the Fish Kill, the outlet of Saratoga Lake. This was to pass to his grandson, Philip Schuyler the general, by inheritance.

Some of Johannes Schuyler's acquisitions were arranged in partnership with other petitioners for land. In November, 1714, he and four partners (Myndert Schuyler, Peter Van Brugh Livingston, Robert Livingston, and Henry Wildman) purchased from Governor Robert Hunter a patent to 10,000 acres. The terms were a quitrent of 2s. 6d. per one hundred acres, and the tract known as Huntersfield was more regularly surveyed by degrees and rods with mention of natural landmarks thrown in for supplementary information.[8] By this time land grants were limited to about two thousand acres per patentee; hence the practice was for partners to combine to acquire a more manageable tract for purposes of survey and partition—and sometimes for purposes of allowing one partner to procure the shares of his fellows after the patent had passed. The Huntersfield patent, also known as the Schoharie or Schuyler patent, brought Johannes 2,000 acres more at the juncture of Schoharie Creek and the Mohawk River—unless he disposed of it or added to it by receiving the others' shares.

[6] Certified copies of land grants. NYPL, Schuyler Papers Box 16. See also Schuyler, *Colonial New York*, II, 99.

[7] *Ibid.*, pp. 99, 101. For a résumé of how parts of the Saratoga Patent passed from one hand to another see pp. 95–107. General Philip Schuyler also bought some of the Livingston holdings in the Saratoga tract; see Chapter II.

[8] C.O. 5/1134:55.

Four years later he acquired 1,696 acres at Canistigione, east of Schenectady and north of the Mohawk, this time without the assistance of partners.[9] The usual 2s. 6d. quitrent terms were stipulated.

When his brother Peter, as senior member of the governor's council, was acting-governor, Johannes and "Cornelius Son, Gerrard Schuyler" received a tract of 3,292 acres in Ulster County for the usual quitrent. The land was described only as "being in the County of Ulster beginning at the NE Corner Tree of the Land lately laid out for Phineas Mcintosh and Runs thence NE 112 Chains to a large White oak Tree marked on 4 sides with 3 Notches from thence &ca Containing 3,292 Acres." [10]

Close upon this came another of Johannes' petitions with five partners (Oliver Schuyler, David Provost, Philip Cortlandt, John Cruger, Jacobus Kipp) for a warrant to survey 7,000 acres in the vicinity of "Quasaiek Brook." The request was granted, and again he benefited from the hand of his brother, then the acting-governor of the province.[11]

Two other governors authorized land patents for Johannes Schuyler and his partners. On March 18, 1722, Governor William Burnet designated "Six tracts of Land being for Each [of six petitioners: Schuyler, Francis Harrison, John Spratt, Abraham Wendell, Lewis Morris, Jr., and John Haskall]." Each petitioner received 2,000 acres. Schuyler's tract lay along the "Maquas" or Mohawk River.[12] Governor George Clarke made two other grants to Johannes Schuyler. One was in partnership with Joachim Bradt. This last major acquisition was for land on both banks of Tomlenack Creek, east of the upper reaches of the Hudson. In May, 1730, Schuyler and Bradt procured a deed from the Indians for 2,000 acres, after petitioning for a license to buy twice that amount. Following the petition for a patent (July, 1730), Surveyor General Cadwallader Colden laid out their lands in November, 1731. In May, 1735, a warrant for the patent was finally issued. Two years later, after Bradt died, Schuyler was evidently obliged to procure an alteration in the patent in order that Bradt's widow might share in the acquisition. Governor Clarke confirmed the earlier grant on July 29, 1737.[13]

Johannes Schuyler made what appears to be his last land operation when in October, 1741, Governor Clarke conferred title to Mase Island to him—an eleven-acre island in the Hudson about seventeen miles above Albany.[14]

[9] C.O. 5/1134:56. Cf. *Calendar of N.Y. Colonial MSS indorsed Land Papers*, p. 122.

[10] C.O. 5/1134:51. (Mar. 17, 1719/20)

[11] C.O. 5/1134:53. The petition and warrant for survey are dated Nov. 26, 1719. The patent is dated Oct. 17, 1720. Cf. *Calendar of N.Y. Colonial MSS indorsed Land Papers*, p. 133.

[12] C.O. 5/1134:61.

[13] *Calendar of N.Y. Colonial MSS indorsed Land Papers*, pp. 193–194, 202, 217, 221, 229–230. C.O. 5/1134:76.

[14] C.O. 5/1134:87. Cf. *Calendar of N.Y. Colonial MSS indorsed Land Papers*, p. 244.

Not all of Johannes Schuyler's requests for land were fulfilled. In 1710 he and Robert Livingston, Jr., petitioned for 800 acres east of the Hudson, territory granted earlier to Godveredus Dalleus. The petition seems to have been denied; no evidence exists of a grant, nor for one for 2,000 acres Schuyler requested in 1714, nor a third for an undesignated amount on Wood Creek in 1733.[15] Still, he had done well. He had collected about 24,000 acres of the Saratoga Patent,[16] 2,000 acres in the Schoharie valley, 1,696 acres east of Schenectady (Canistigione), 1,000 acres along Tomlenack Creek east of the Hudson, not to mention 2,000 acres north of the "Maquas River," over 1,000 acres on "Quasaiek Brook," and over 1,000 acres in Ulster County.[17]

Johannes Schuyler survived all his brothers, his wife, and his sons Philip and John, Jr. What better testimonial to his hardiness and a vigorous life! When he died in February, 1747, he had provided an equitable division of his estate, although the eldest son was to receive rather more than the others in accordance with the spirit of the English family settlement. However, by then his eldest son was dead and had left no issue; hence the estate passed to his daughters and the heirs of the younger son, John, Jr.

To Philip, his eldest son, Johannes Schuyler left the "farm" at Saratoga with all his Negroes (unspecified as to number) and a half interest in the sawmill. The right to grind free of charge was reserved to the children of Philip's brother, John, Jr., but a gristmill was likewise given to Philip. Johannes' two daughters were each to receive £475 current New York money (plus £50 to each to be paid by their brother Philip), and Margaretta fell heir to the Albany house. His sister, Catalyntje, was to have it on Margaretta's death. Other personal effects were divided among his two surviving daughters, a step-daughter, and the heirs of his youngest son.

To the children of his younger son, John, Jr., old Johannes Schuyler gave a one-fourth interest in one half of his Saratoga lands. One half was given to the elder son, and the other half was to be divided in four parts to be shared by the two daughters, the elder son, and the heirs of John, Jr.[18]

In spite of the fact that Johannes Schuyler altered his will after the death of his only surviving son, he did not make any substantial changes, much less an

15 *Ibid.*, pp. 98, 109, 208, 213.

16 Schuyler, *Colonial New York*, II, 241, says it was 18,000 acres, but a closer look at the extent of the Saratoga Patent (22 miles long and 12 miles wide) suggests that a one-seventh share was closer to 24,000 acres. The discrepancy in the figures might be due to the fact that the 18,000 acres were surveyed and divided parcels, while the 24,000 figure included both the divided and undivided portions of the patent. However, the patent may have been so irregular in width that the fair uniformity of a 22 mile by 12 mile tract did not, in fact, exist.

17 There is no mention of the 1,000 acres in Ulster County by Schuyler, *Colonial New York*, II, 240, and Schuyler may have sold this tract before his death.

18 An attested copy of Johannes Schuyler's will, signed Feb. 25, 1741/42, and codicil dated Feb. 25, 1746/47. NYHS, Misc. MSS: Schuyler.

adjustment of the half part of the Saratoga lands which were to go to this son. And his share (one-seventh) of the Saratoga Patent remained intact except for the farms he had given his two sons.[19] The estate must then have been divided in equal shares among the two daughters and the heirs of John Schuyler, Jr.—in accordance with the other provisions of the will—for the elder son (Philip, 1695–1745) left neither wife nor children.

Major-General Philip Schuyler's (1733–1804) grandfather (Johannes) appears to have been the most energetic and successful of the line, for neither the general's great-grandfather (Philip the Founder) nor his father (John, Jr.) quite matched the vigor of Johannes. John Schuyler, Jr., left a relatively small estate, and as his father outlived him, he received no patrimony which he might in turn pass on to his children or use as the basis for larger acquisitions of his own. He did manage to acquire some land, however. Late in 1722 he began his own accumulations when he bought a one-fourteenth portion of the Saratoga Patent east of the Hudson and south of the Batten Kill for £200. But this proved no permanent gain. The parcel was sold back to a Livingston.[20]

Early in December, 1737, John Schuyler, Jr., joined several other men to petition for a grant of 6,000 acres east of the Hudson above Saratoga, but what happened to this request is uncertain. In July the following year a warrant and certificate were issued for a patent for 12,000 acres east of the Hudson in the same vicinity.[21] And in June, 1739, Governor Clarke made a grant of 1,900 acres to Schuyler "North . . . of the Maquase River about 48 miles above Schenectady. . . ." This he obtained in a cooperative venture with Arent Bradt, Jacob Glen, Lendert Helmer, and a Philip Schuyler who was probably his brother.[22] The terms were the customary quitrent of 2s. 6d. per hundred acres.

Finally, in July, 1740, the year before John Schuyler, Jr., died, Governor Clarke granted 12,000 acres to six patentees; Schuyler was included with a 2,000-acre share,[23] subject to regular quitrents. The tract lay east of the Hudson above Saratoga. Thus, unless he purchased the interests of fellow patentees or sold his own after the grants were passed, John Schuyler, Jr.'s, total minimal holdings of about 6,000 acres were considerably more modest than his father's which probably amounted to about 32,000 acres. But his life cut short, it can

19 *Ibid.* See also Schuyler, *Colonial New York*, II, 240. An abstract of Johannes Schuyler's will is also printed in *Colls. N.Y. Hist. Soc. for 1895* (New York, 1896), XXVIII: Abstracts of Wills, IV, 134–135. The elder son of Johannes Schuyler (Philip Schuyler), who was the general's uncle, willed half of his real and personal estate to his two nephews, the general and his brother, John. P. 136.

20 Schuyler, *Colonial New York*, II, 103.

21 *Calendar of N.Y. Colonial MSS indorsed Land Papers*, pp. 232, 234. That the patent was issued see *Colls. N.Y. Hist. Soc. for 1923* (New York, 1923), LVI: Colden Papers, VII, 372.

22 C.O. 5/1134:83. See also Schuyler, *Colonial New York*, II, 247.

23 C.O. 5/1134:79.

only be conjectured what more he might have accumulated or accomplished had he lived.

John Schuyler, Jr.'s, widow, Cornelia Van Cortlandt, managed an acquisition of her own for the family. In 1742 she joined Edward Collins, Arent Stephens, and Henry Holland to request land of Lieutenant Governor Clarke. On July 16, Clarke issued her a patent to 1,300 acres east of the upper reaches of the Hudson, near Fort Miller, with the usual quitrent stipulations.[24] Moreover, she added to the Schuyler fortunes by her inheritance from her father. A cousin as well as wife to John Schuyler, Jr., Cornelia was an heiress of the Van Cortlandt Manor estate in which she shared as one of eleven children. There appears to be no record of a dowry, but by her inheritance the Schuyler holdings must have been increased handsomely, for her father's manor alone contained over 86,000 acres, and there were other lands, houses, and personal property as well.[25] Cornelia demonstrated that a woman's and a mother's role was not altogether a submissive or limited one in colonial New York. By law a subordinate, but in actuality very much an equal with her husband, she efficiently managed her husband's affairs after his early death, and as has been noted even added to his estate for their children.[26]

On October 28, 1741, John Schuyler, Jr., dictated his last will and testament. It was the gesture of a dying man. His widow was to have the care and use of all his property, including the lands she inherited from her father. By giving £30 to his eldest son, John, he extinguished any claims he might otherwise have had under the law. By English law the intestate death of the father meant the eldest son received the real property, the widow's dower right, and the right of thirds, so the younger sons and daughters received little, if anything.[27] However, the Schuylers, not unlike many of their contemporaries, permitted no operation of the law of primogeniture. They were careful to leave wills, just as John, Jr., had done on his very deathbed. According to Schuyler's will, all lands and estates bequeathed to his wife by her father were

---

[24] C.O. 5/1134:88. Cf. *Calendar of N.Y. Colonial MSS indorsed Land Papers,* p. 246.

[25] Schuyler, *Colonial New York,* I, 198–203; II, 248. Cornelia's mother was Gertrude Schuyler (1654–1719), a daughter of Philip Schuyler the Founder, who married Stephen Van Cortlandt. Gertrude was thus the sister of Johannes Schuyler and the aunt of John Schuyler, Jr. Stephen Van Cortlandt's will is in *Colls. N.Y. Hist. Soc. for 1892* (New York, 1893), XXV: Abstracts of Wills, I, 98. The major portion of his estate seems to have been devised to his eldest son, but all the children shared in it. Cornelia's share in Van Cortlandt Manor consisted of at least thirteen farms (announcement of a sale, Nov. 20–21, [1766] NYPL, Schuyler Papers Box 19) of which ten were advertised for sale in *The New-York Journal, or General Advertiser* (John Holt), April 14, 1768. These ten farms totaled 2,175 acres. Mark, *Agrarian Conflicts,* pp. 69–70, says Van Cortlandt's will provided an equal division of the estate among eleven children.

[26] Ironside, *op. cit.,* p. 36.

[27] *Ibid.,* p. 73.

to be left in her hands, together with the Schuyler house and lot in Albany next door to old Johannes Schuyler's dwelling at the corner of Pearl and State streets. Cornelia was to use all the real and personal estate for the advancement and education of the children who were to share the entire estate after their mother's death.[28] John Schuyler, Jr., could not leave a share of his father's estate to his children because the old man lived on. But their grandfather's property passed to them by right of their father's share or interest in it.[29]

A review of the various acquisitions of land by Philip Schuyler's father and mother, his grandfather, and great-grandfather who founded the family in America thus indicates that a great share of the holdings was accumulated by grants from the royal government of New York. Part of their vast domain was, however, the result of private exchange between landlords. Major-General Philip Schuyler followed the practice of his acquisitive forebears, but his activities indicate a heavier reliance upon private purchase and inheritance than upon the largesse of the colonial authorities. And they outreached even his successful grandfather's accomplishments.

[28] *Colls. N.Y. Hist. Soc. for 1894* (New York, 1895), XXVII: Abstracts of Wills, III, 387.

[29] NYPL, Schuyler Papers Box 21. A list of divisions of John Schuyler, Jr.'s, Saratoga lands, Jan. 6, 1763, shows his children's portions of the Saratoga Patent. The share was over 6,500 acres in surveyed lands, but there were unsurveyed lands which were not finally distributed until 1769. See Box 22, a field book dated Aug. 17, 1769, showing the lots surveyed of the remainder of the undivided lands of the Saratoga Patent. These totaled about 7,600 acres.

APPENDIX C

Outline of New York Real Property Law and Electoral Rights

An OUTLINE of the existing law of real property and of electoral rights at the time Philip Schuyler became active in provincial politics affords a better appreciation of the structure of the politics, economy, and society of colonial New York as well as the role Schuyler himself played in the province. It has been popularly assumed that the electorate in New York, not to mention other provinces, was so proscriptive and that politics and society were so aristocratic as to prevent much popular participation in government. Therefore, a review of the bases of the franchise in law is appropriate on two counts: to discover what Schuyler's practices as a landlord meant in terms of voters; to understand that if the political aristocracy enjoyed a position of leadership, it was perhaps not so much because the "lesser orders" lacked political privilege as that many people did not always exercise the opportunities to which they were entitled. There is a vast difference between having the vote and exercising it. And even if political activity was in effect widely limited, there is danger in oversimplifying the condition.

It is true that the landed magnates "directed the colony and found it easy to dictate nominations and control elections, because a great proportion of the electorate lived on manors and large estates." And "it was natural to expect tenants to follow the lead of their landlords. . . ." [1] But a survey of real property and electoral laws in the province points up two facts which ought not to be minimized: one, that the people living on manors and large estates were a considerable part of the electorate; two, that although the landlords were leaders, they did not always manage to have their way. Mention has been made in Chapter III of Judge Robert R. Livingston losing his assembly seat in 1768 because of the opposition of the voters of Dutchess County to his treatment of the tenants' cause during the "Great Rebellion." This was of course rather exceptional inasmuch as rural communities generally showed a marked indifference to politics or went along with their landlords. But there were other incidents that demonstrated that the sway of the landed magnates was not always an absolute one. A survey of tenure conditions also suggests why it was not.

New York real property law from 1664 to the Revolution was basically

[1] Flick, II, 381.

English law. By the early eighteenth century this law in the province of New York had become uniform; even the modifications of it by local statute and usage were not very great.[2] Therefore an examination of English real property law is essential for a proper understanding of property usage and the franchise connected with it.

Basic to the English land system was the relation between the lord and tenant. This relationship is known as tenure, and the tenant received an estate which he held by one of several tenures: free and servile.[3] Because according to an act of 12 Charles II, c. 24 (confirming a 1645 statute of Parliament) and to the Duke of York's patent from Charles II, free and common socage tenure was established in New York,[4] it will be necessary only to examine the combination of free and common socage varieties of tenure.

Socage [5] could be held in varying estates ranging from an estate for life to one in fee simple. In general, socage holders did not perform labor as a condition of their grant. In England labor services were limited to copyholds. Legally the copyhold did not apply in New York because all tenure, even that of the manors in which copyholds were otherwise provided, was made in terms of free and common socage.[6] But New York landlords enjoyed the advantages of the copyhold system when they conveyed lands with perpetual rents reserved and riding services stipulated.

Anyone who held land in free socage was a freeholder. Any person who held land for a specified term of years was no freeholder, and could not, for example, vote for knights of the shire as members of Parliament. "A freeholder must hold land at least for the life of himself or of some other person." And it was a clear dictum that "He who holds for a fixed term of years however long, a thousand years or more, is no freeholder." [7] It was also characteristic of a freehold that the holder was permitted to alienate his land freely

[2] Robert Ludlow Fowler, *History of the Law of Real Property in New York* (New York, 1895), pp. 51, 54–61. Hereafter cited as Fowler.

[3] Harry A. Bigelow, *Introduction to the Law of Real Property: Rights in Land* (St. Paul, 1919), p. 3. For a discussion of the other free estates—military and frankalmoyn tenure—see pp. 4–7, 10. Since these did not apply in New York, only socage is discussed.

[4] *Ibid.*, p. 16; Fowler, p. 14; Kenelm Edward Digby, *An Introduction to the History of the Law of Real Property* (5th edition; London, 1897), pp. 395–396. Hereafter cited as Digby.

[5] F. W. Maitland, *The Constitutional History of England* (Cambridge, 1955), p. 31. Hereafter cited as Maitland. See also Bigelow, p. 8, and Digby, pp. 45 n., 46.

[6] Maitland, p. 35; Fowler, p. 32. It may be noted that under some of Philip Schuyler's leases to tenants, the plowing service (labor) was replaced by a provision for so many days "riding." See for examples, NYPL, Schuyler Papers: Account Book, 1769–1805, pp. 61, 115.

[7] Maitland, p. 36.

where he enjoyed a fee simple.[8] A fee simple was one of four varieties of freehold—the others being: fee tail, other qualified fees, and the life estate.[9]

Under a fee simple the freeholder enjoyed the right to do as he saw fit with his estate. He was entitled to be protected in his privileges up to the limits of what was socially unjustifiable, and he had complete freedom to do as he pleased, subject only to the law—and on death to pass his estate to his heirs so long as any were in existence.[10] Further, "The socage tenant was for all practical purposes the owner of the soil, and fealty to the Crown soon lapsed into a mere natural allegiance of the subject." [11]

Every landholder in New York with an estate granted by the Duke of York was a tenant. The freeholder was, then, a tenant holding an estate in lands worthy of a freeman, and this meant the estate could not be one for less than life. Even the manors were "freehold manors, not feudal manors" because in creating them the Duke of York's patents (and subsequently the king's) had to confer free and common socage tenure.[12] A manor lord could grant a fee simple to a tenant, but reserve rent "forever" as a valid rent charge. Such rent was not always the sign of an estate "for years," or "at will," or "by sufferance." And reserving a perpetual rent on an estate in fee was very common before and after 1776. It was a singular departure from the English law that conveyances in fee were frequently termed "leases," "durable leases," or "leases

8 Fowler, pp. 26–27; Bigelow, p. 13. The statute *Quia Emptores* (1290), 18 Edward I, c. 1, permitted this.

9 Bigelow, p. 19.

10 Digby, p. 270; Bigelow, p. 20. A fee tail provided specified limitations as to the disposal of the estate and stipulated how, under certain conditions, it might revert to the grantor or his heirs. A fee conditional referred to an estate granted on condition that the holder have heirs to his body. Life estates were the most limited of freeholds. They were of two kinds: estates created by an act of a party, and those created by the operation of the law. Estates created by an act of a party were made in one of two forms: for the life of the tenant or for the life of some third person(s). Estates created by the operation of the law were of three categories: curtesy, dower, and tenant in special tail. The curtesy estate applied when a man married a wife seised of an estate of inheritance, had issue by her which was (were) capable of inheriting her estate, and thus by curtesy was able to hold his wife's land for life. The dower estate applied when the husband seised of an estate of inheritance died. His wife then had a one-third part of all lands and tenements of which he was seised in fee (i.e., inheritable) during the coverture to hold for her lifetime. The tenant in special tail with the possibility of issue extinct was very rare. This applied when A granted land to B and the heirs of his body by his wife C. But if C died without issue, the estate ended with the life of B. Bigelow, pp. 22–23, 26–30.

11 Fowler, p. 27; Digby, p. 236, says after the act 12 Charles II, c. 24, the relation between a freeholder and his lord fell into abeyance, and the freeholder for all practical purposes became the owner of the soil.

12 Fowler, pp. 28–29; Digby, p. 48.

in fee." Such designations were misnomers in the law.[13] Conveyancing in colonial New York had its own peculiar terminology. "Documents were sometimes labelled leases which today would be called deeds granting freehold estates of inheritance." [14] Likewise, the great landed magnates, though not lords of manors under the law, could also make such arrangements with their tenants. Once a manor lord granted land in fee simple without reserving suit and service, he could not claim the lands as part of the manor, although the tenant's rents and dues remained. "In this way the grantee of the lands was often enfranchised or rendered free of the spirit and custom of the manor." [15]

When the Crown granted land in New York, the tenure was in fee simple, but rents were reserved in the form of quitrents. Crown patents had no provision for a distress, re-entry, or forfeiture on the failure of tenants to discharge their quitrents however, and there appears to have been no adjudged case in New York, determining that the Crown grants in fee simple reserving a quitrent were to be construed as creating an estate upon condition.[16]

Certainly, the landed magnates of New York such as Philip Schuyler were freeholders, but it is also clear that some of their tenants were likewise freeholders because they held their lands on terms of one to three lives. Estates for life or for the lives of two or three persons were but the most limited kind of freehold, but freeholds they were. And this was true although many holders of leases fell under the category of non-freeholders.

Non-freehold estates (or leaseholds) fell into four categories: an estate for years, from year to year, at will, and at sufferance.[17] Certain rules governed the leasehold interests. Possession of the land was in the tenant. The landlord reserved the rent. "Distress was provided as a rent collection procedure." The tenant was forbidden to waste the property, and the "term could be by will, sufferance, year to year, a term of years, or for life or lives." [18] However, it must be noted that a leasehold for life or lives partook of the nature of a freehold, and, as will be indicated, placed the lessee in the position of exercising the franchise as a freeholder.

A lease made for years specified the number of years the lessee could hold the estate (generally three to twenty-one), and gave him a right "in the nature of a contract right against the lessor" rather than one in "the nature of a

13 Fowler, p. 118.
14 Mark, *Agrarian Conflicts*, p. 63. Mark further states that "There were other freeholds that were usually fee tails, where an estate was conveyed to a grantee and then to all or specified heirs of his body; or life estates, where the term was usually limited by the span of two or three lives in being. The non-freehold estates were leaseholds for some determinable period, usually of years." Pp. 63–64.
15 Fowler, p. 31. See also Mark, *Agrarian Conflicts*, p. 64.
16 Fowler, pp. 39, 41.
17 Bigelow, p. 19.
18 Harris, *Origin of the Land Tenure System in the United States*, pp. 404–405.

property right in the land." In tenancy from year to year, either the lessee or lessor could terminate the indenture by giving the other a half year's notice. Under a tenancy at will, A leased to B to hold at the will of A; A might terminate the lease at any time, and B enjoyed a reasonable time to remove his property and the right to the annual crops then growing. Tenancy at sufferance was not, strictly speaking, a tenancy. The lessee whose estate had terminated still remained in possession of the land and could not be charged with trespassing because his entry had been lawful. The tenant's retention of possession then might be express or implied, but it remained unlawful, and to call him a tenant is a misnomer. But the landlord might "at any time turn him into a tenant by treating him as such." [19]

It may be observed that Philip Schuyler as a landlord generally used one of two forms of grant for his tenants: estates for one to three lives and estates for years, the first of which gave the grantee the franchise; the second did not. Although leases for years were most commonly used, on large estates colonial landlords frequently used leases for life or three lives because they could avoid the trouble of frequent changes and could encourage the lessee to develop the land by giving him time whereby he might recompense himself for improving another person's property.[20] Moreover, it is very likely that men like Philip Schuyler could have used such conveyances not only to create an impression that the estate would last longer, but also to create votes which they then might influence.

Closely linked with New York real property law were the qualifications for the suffrage. But patroonships, manors, and large estates did not completely dominate the economic, social, and political life of the province because of "strong and numerous groups of small freeholders." [21] For purposes of assembly elections, it is apparent that certain leaseholders were qualified for the suffrage.

New York operated within a general framework or spirit of English law, and in turn its electoral statutes modified this framework. The county franchise in New York (i.e., the election of assemblymen) corresponded to England's. In England an elector had to be possessed of a forty shilling freehold.[22] A freeholder was required to hold his land for his lifetime or the life of some other person, and he who held for a fixed term of years was deemed no freeholder. Therefore, because leaseholds were made in terms of the life of some

[19] Bigelow, pp. 31–32; Digby, pp. 244–245.
[20] Harris, *Origin of the Land Tenure System in the United States*, pp. 341–342.
[21] *Ibid.*, p. 97.
[22] Maitland, pp. 87, 173. The act 8 Henry VI, c. 7 (1430), which regulated the franchise for four centuries, stipulated that electors must reside in the county in which they exercised the franchise, and that they must have a freehold worth forty shillings per year above all charges. Copyholders and leaseholders then had no vote no matter how valuable their lands might be.

person "some leaseholders were deemed freeholders in English law." A statute
of 1540 conferred on certain landowners the right to make leases for the life
of the lessee and the lives of other persons named in the lease. "Such tenancies
were deemed freeholds. The leaseholder was qualified to vote in parliamentary
elections if the annual income from his holding reached 40 shillings." Black-
stone referred to these leases as freeholds and designated them as forms of
real property. But leases for certain years, even a thousand, were not so defined.[23] This same arrangement apparently prevailed in New York. An examination of the legal provisions for provincial elections provides some revealing
information about opportunities for the franchise in New York.

The first bill for regulating elections of New York Assembly representatives
was passed on May 16, 1699. The occasion for this legislation was explained by
the statute; recent tumults and deceptions had deprived the subjects of their
birthright to choose representatives. The law stipulated that the elector must
reside in the district in order to vote for its representative. This was in keeping
with the English statute of 1430. Second, the elector must have land or tenements improved to the value of £40 "in free hold free from all Incumbrances
& have possessed ye Same three months before ye test of ye said writ. . . ."
A representative was also obliged to dwell and reside within his particular
constituency—city, county, or manor. The sheriff certified who received a
majority of the votes from the qualified electors, and was empowered to
examine on oath every voter as to his qualifications. Constables assisted the
sheriff in notifying the people of the election. Polling records were to contain
the name of each elector, his place of residence and freehold, and the person
for whom he voted. And each candidate was entitled to an inspector at the
polls to challenge an elector's qualifications to vote. Sheriffs were forbidden
to adjourn the poll to another place without the consent of the candidates. No
person under twenty-one could vote or be elected an assemblyman. The freemen of New York City and Albany might vote in their corporations, provided
they *were* freemen and had actually established residence there for three
months before the writ of election. Although this act was repealed on November 27, 1702, another had taken its place by way of supplementation.[24]

The franchise for freemen of New York City and Albany was provided by
Governor Dongan's charters to these two corporations in 1686. The New York
charter empowered the mayor, recorder, and aldermen, or the mayor and any
three or more aldermen to create freemen. There were two qualifications for
a freeman: one, that he be a natural-born subject of the king, or naturalized
by an act of the assembly, or that he have letters of denization from the lieu-

[23] Williamson, *American Suffrage From Property to Democracy, 1760–1860*, p. 7.
[24] New York (state), *The Colonial Laws of New York From the Year 1664 to the
Revolution* (5 vols.; Albany, 1894), I, 405–408, 523–524. Hereafter cited as *Colonial
Laws N.Y.* In examining these volumes the author has been obliged to refer to an
1896 printing of Vol. I.

tenant governor or the commander in chief; two, that "all Persons to be made free . . . shall and Doe pay . . . such Sume & Sumes of Mony [sic] as heretofore hath been used and Accustomed to be paid and Received on their being Admitted ffreemen [sic] . . ." provided that no fee be more than £5. The charter for Albany contained the same naturalization requirement, but provided a lesser fee as well as fees of different amounts for the varying economic status of the candidate. A merchant was to pay not more than £3 12s. and a craftsman or tradesman not more than £1 16s.[25]

A second act "for the more regular proceedings in . . . Elections" was deemed necessary in 1701, avowedly because there had been much fraudulent and deceitful activity in spite of the 1699 law. First of all, this new statute provided a religious qualification for officeholding as well as for the franchise; it required papists to swear a special oath of allegiance. Secondly, because doubts had arisen about whether the vote should be allowed to a person having an estate of freehold in possession for his life or the life of his wife, it was stipulated that all persons not otherwise excepted by the act, "haveing [sic] in his or their possession an Estate of ffreehold [sic], during his Life, or for and dureing [sic] the Life of his Wife, to the Value or quantity in the above recited Act Expressed [i.e., the 1699 law establishing the £40 freehold], shall be and is hereby qualified to . . . Vote . . . for Representatives . . . Provided he be further Qualified, as in the aforesaid Act. . . ." Nor was a mortgage of lands to "debar the party . . . from the giveing [sic] of his Vote, provided he be in possession thereof, or receive the Incomes of the Same." [26]

Under practices of landlord-freeholders "leasing" their property, the life estate was the most restricted form of freehold.[27] Freeholders such as Philip Schuyler who leased a tenant an estate for life or three lives in effect enabled that tenant to qualify under the election law as a freeholder because the tenant then held "an Estate of ffreehold [sic], during his Life." Such a tenant could then qualify, if his holding was valued at £40. Most of Philip Schuyler's "conveyances were freehold grants for a term of three lives, although there were a few fees simple with reservations of perpetual rent, and long and short term leases." [28]

Something further might also be said about the manors where it is apparent that tenants, though not freeholders, enjoyed a measure of self-government by means of local elections. Those who had life estates of course qualified for the county franchise. And according to several acts passed in 1756, 1768, and 1769,

[25] *Colonial Laws N.Y.*, I, 192–193, 210.

[26] *Ibid.*, p. 453.

[27] Mark, *Agrarian Conflicts*, p. 61. "Documents were sometimes labelled leases which today would be called deeds granting freehold estates of inheritance." P. 63. "The non-freehold estates were leaseholds *for some determinable period,* usually of years." Pp. 63–64. Italics added.

[28] *Ibid.*, p. 72. See the indentures in NYPL, Schuyler Papers Boxes 16, 21, 22.

the inhabitants as well as freeholders of Cortlandt, Livingston, and Rensselaer manors were empowered to elect annually various manor officials: constables, overseers of the highways, assessors, supervisors, treasurers, fence-viewers, clerks, and poundmasters.[29] These statutes appear to have confirmed a practice already recognized, for they provided authority for these people to choose *additional* officials in order to meet the needs for more government.

Another election law further elaborated the suffrage provisions of the provincial political system. An act was passed on May 20, 1769, explaining and amending the election law of 1699. The 1769 act dealt primarily with residence requirements. All persons whatever, having and holding freehold estates (in lands and tenements worth £40) in cities, towns, counties, boroughs, and manors, were declared qualified to vote for their respective representatives, although such electors might not be in actual residence in their particular constituency, and provided that they were otherwise qualified by law to vote. A person chosen to be a representative was required to have his usual place of abode in the district from which he was elected at least six months before the test of the writ of summons. Likewise, he was required to have a sufficient freehold (free of all encumbrances) for a like period in the constituency from which he was chosen. This was deemed necessary if an assemblyman was to be familiar with the circumstances, needs, and wishes of his constituency. The residence requirement for freemen of the cities of New York and Albany to vote was three months before the test of the writ of summons. But persons who held estates by descent or devise were exempted from the requirement. Every elector might also be required by an assembly candidate to take an oath. The oath included a statement that the elector was a £40 freeholder of a particular county, that he did not hold the property as a trustee, that he possessed the same for three months before the test of the writ unless the freehold was held by descent or devise, that he had not been polled earlier at the election, and that he had not "procured this Freehold to gain your Voice particularly for this Election, so help you God." [30]

In summary, it can be said that local elections, unless otherwise provided by city or borough charters, were confined to freeholders. In New York and Albany the suffrage was exercised by £40 freeholders and persons made freemen, so that non-freeholders could vote and enjoy the privilege of engaging in certain mercantile pursuits. But as has been noted, holders of leases for life fell under the designation of freeholders.

Tenants on the manors and large estates comprised a large portion of the electorate because they could qualify as freeholders—possessors of life estates.[31] It is estimated that assembly electors in about 1771 comprised a little more than half the adult males of the province. A sampling for 1779 shows higher

[29] *Colonial Laws N.Y.*, IV, 85–86, 1056, 1065–1067, 1116–1117.
[30] *Ibid.*, pp. 1094–1096.
[31] Mark, *Agrarian Conflicts*, p. 95.

figures. Among adult male residents and in some cases among all male taxables, 50 to 80 per cent were freeholders. In New York "there were more leaseholds which qualified as freeholds . . . than existed anywhere else, except perhaps in Virginia." The weight of historical opinion favors the belief that, except for Westchester County, "the overwhelming majority of leaseholds would qualify as freeholds." This was certainly true of lands leased by James Duane, Lieutenant Governor George Clarke, and the Philipse family. Virtually all leases on Rensselaer Manor qualified as freeholds.[32] Lieutenant Governor Colden opined in 1775 that freeholders on the manors of Livingston and Rensselaerwyck were numerous enough to control Albany County elections. Most inhabitants on Heathcote's Scarsdale Manor (Manhattan Island) held land on long leases and some owned farms of 50 acres or more outright.[33] At least 201 adult males who were tenants resided on Philip Schuyler's Saratoga estate right after the Revolution, and of these 141 would be deemed freeholders and the rest holders of leases for specified terms of years.[34]

Property qualifications for the franchise, and the manors, which in effect were pocket boroughs, added substantially to the dominance of New York landlords. But it is not likely that the extent of the franchise was as limited as once was supposed, nor that the landlords were unbeatable in every instance.[35] It can be said that their political aims were perhaps best served by the absence of a secret ballot, the distance the voter often had to travel to the polls, a widespread indifference among qualified electors, and by colonials ignorant of their own opportunities.[36]

[32] Williamson, *American Suffrage*, pp. 27–28. See also Milton M. Klein, "Democracy and Politics in Colonial New York." Klein's studies suggest that from 50 to 75 per cent of New York's free adult males had the vote. He estimates that virtually all white adult males in New York City and probably Albany, and 65 per cent of such males in rural counties had the vote.

[33] Flick, II, 383.

[34] Williamson, *American Suffrage*, pp. 27–28. Cf. NYPL, Schuyler Papers Boxes 20, 21, 22.

[35] Becker, *Political Parties*, pp. 10–11. Cf. Mark, *Agrarian Conflicts*, p. 95; Klein, "Democracy and Politics in Colonial New York," and Williamson, *American Suffrage*.

[36] Despite the lack of overwhelming evidence of this ignorance, the condition is suggested by the circumstances of the contested elections of 1768 when certain men's votes were questioned, and they themselves seemed uncertain about their qualifications. See Chapter IV, "The Initiation to Assembly Politics."

Bibliography

MANUSCRIPTS

Albany Institute of History and Art, Albany, New York.
  Assessment Roll of the Real and Personal Estates in the First Ward of the City of Albany . . . [September 5, 1799].
  A Census of the Inhabitants in the County of Albany . . . April 6, 1801.
  Miscellaneous Schuyler Papers
British Museum, London: Additional Manuscripts.
  Auckland Papers
  The Digby Diary
  Haldimand Papers
  Newcastle Papers
  Stevens Transcripts
British General Post Office Headquarters: London.
  Commission Book, 1759–1854
British Public Record Office: London.
  Audit Office Papers
  Colonial Office Papers
  State Papers
  Treasury Papers
  War Office Papers
Columbia University Libraries.
  John Jay Papers, Butler Library
  Gouverneur Morris Papers, Butler Library
  Peter Van Schaack Papers, Columbiana
National Archives Microfilm Publications: Microcopy No. 247, "Papers of the Continental Congress, 1774–1789" (The National Archives and Records Service, General Services Administration. Washington, 1959).
  Item 63 (Roll 77) Letters and Papers relating to Charges against Gen. J. Sullivan & Dr. J. Morgan, & to British advances in the Mohawk Valley, 1776–1779.
  Item 153 (Rolls 172–173) Letters from Maj. Gen. Philip Schuyler, 1775–1785.
  Item 154 (Roll 174) Letters from General Gates, 1775–1782.

Item 166 (Roll 183) Letters & Papers relating to Canadian Affairs—Sullivan's Expedition & Northern Indians, 1775–1779.
Item 170 (Roll 189) Transcript of Letters from Maj. Gen. Philip Schuyler, 1775–1781.
New-York Historical Society.
  De Lancey Papers
  James Duane Papers
  William Duer Papers
  John W. Francis, "Old New York" (New York, 1865). Bound volumes of manuscripts.
  Robert R. Livingston Collection
  Alexander MacDougal Papers
  Miscellaneous Manuscripts: Nicholas Bayard; Grove Bend; Bradstreet; George Clinton; Schuyler.
New York Public Library.
  Bancroft Collections (Transcripts)
  Bleecker Papers
  Chalmers Manuscripts
  Emmett Collection
  Schuyler Papers
New York State Library (Albany, New York).
  Miscellaneous Schuyler Papers
  Elkanah Watson Papers
William L. Clements Library, the University of Michigan.
  Gage Papers
  Germain Papers
  Miscellaneous Manuscripts

GOVERNMENT PUBLICATIONS: FEDERAL

Force, Peter (ed.), *American Archives,* Fourth Series (6 vols.; Washington: M. St. Clair Clarke & Peter Force, 1837–1846), and Fifth Series (3 vols.; Washington: M. St. Clair Clarke & Peter Force, 1848–1853).
Ford, Worthington C., *et al.*, (eds.), *The Journals of the Continental Congress, 1774–1789* (34 vols.; Washington: Government Printing Office, 1904–1937).
Wold, Ansel (comp.), *Biographical Dictionary of the American Congress, 1774–1927* (Washington: Government Printing Office, 1928).

GOVERNMENT PUBLICATIONS: STATE

Calendar of Historical Manuscripts relating to the War of the Revolution in the office of the Secretary of State (Albany: Weed, Parsons & Co., 1864).
Calendar of New York Colonial Manuscripts indorsed Land Papers; in the office of the Secretary of State of New York, 1643–1803 (Albany: Weed, Parsons & Co., 1864).

Catalogue of Maps and Surveys, in the Offices of the Secretary of State, State Engineer and Surveyor, and Comptroller, and the New York State Library (Rev. ed.; Albany: Charles Van Benthuysen, 1859).

Day, Richard E. (comp.), *Calendar of the Sir William Johnson Manuscripts in the New York State Library* (Albany: University of the State of New York, 1909).

Division of Archives and History, University of the State of New York, *Minutes of the Albany Committee of Correspondence* (2 vols.; Albany: J. B. Lyon Co., 1923–1925).

Documents of the Assembly of the State of New York (Vols. XXIX, XXXII; Albany: J. B. Lyon Co. & The Argus Co., 1918, 1912).

Hastings, Hugh (supervisor of publication), *Ecclesiastical Records: State of New York* (6 vols.; Albany: J. B. Lyon Co., 1901–1905).

Journal of the Legislative Council of the Colony of New York, 1691–1775 (2 vols.; Albany: Weed, Parsons & Co., 1861).

Journals of the Provincial Congress, Provincial Convention, Committee of Safety and Council of Safety of the State of New York, 1775–1776–1777 (2 vols.; Albany: Thurlow Weed, 1842).

Journals of the Votes and Proceedings of the General Assembly of the Colony of New York (May 27—June 6, 1767; Nov. 17, 1767—Feb. 6, 1768; Oct. 27, 1768—Jan. 2, 1769; April 4, 1769—May 20, 1769; Nov. 21, 1769—Jan. 27, 1770; Dec. 11, 1770—Mar. 4, 1771; Jan. 7, 1772—Mar. 24, 1772; Jan. 5, 1773—Mar. 8, 1773; Jan. 6, 1774—Mar. 19, 1774; Jan. 10, 1775—April 3, 1775). William Weyman and Hugh Gaine, printers.

Lincoln, Charles Z. (ed.), *State of New York: Messages from the Governors* (11 vols.; Albany: J. B. Lyon Co., 1909).

Names of Persons for whom Marriage Licenses were issued by the Secretary of the Province of New York Previous to 1784 (Albany: Weed, Parsons & Co., 1860).

New York State Historian Annual Report: Colonial Series (2 vols.; New York: Wynkoop, Hallenbeck, Crawford Co., 1896–1898).

New York State Library Bulletin 58: "Calendar of New York Council Minutes, 1668–1783" (Albany: University of the State of New York, 1902).

O'Callaghan, E. B. (ed.), *Calendar of Historical Manuscripts in the Office of the Secretary of State, Albany, N.Y.* (2 parts; Albany: Weed, Parsons & Co., 1865–1866).

—— (abstractor), *Calendar of New York Colonial Commissions, 1680–1770* (New York: The New-York Historical Society, 1929).

—— (ed.), *The Documentary History of the State of New York* (4 vols.; Albany, 1849–1851).

O'Callaghan, Edmund B. and Berthold Fernow (eds.), *Documents Relative to the Colonial History of the State of New York* (15 vols.; Albany: Weed, Parsons & Co., 1853–1887).

Report of the Regents' Boundary Commission upon the New York and Pennsylvania Boundary (Albany: Weed, Parsons & Co., 1886).

Report of the Regents of the University on the Boundaries of the State of New York (Vol. II; Albany: The Argus Co., 1884).

The Colonial Laws of New York From the Year 1664 to the Revolution (5 vols.; Albany: J. B. Lyon Co., 1894).

NEWSPAPERS

The New-York Gazette (W. Weyman)
The New-York Gazette, and the Weekly Mercury
The New-York Gazette, or Weekly Post-Boy
The New-York Journal, or the General Advertiser (John Holt)
The New-York Mercury
Rivington's *New-York Gazetteer*

BROADSIDES

"Philanthropos—A Few Observations on the Conduct of the General Assembly of New-York, for some years past, addressed to the Freemen and Freeholders of the City and Province" (New York: February 9, 1768: NYPL. Printed but not published).

"Reasons For the present glorious combination of the dissenters in this city, against the further encroachments and strategems of the episcopalians, from a brief recollection of what the latter have already done, to exalt their own party on the ruins of every other religious persuasion amongst us" [1769] (NYPL).

"The Case of the Manor of Livingston and the Conduct of the Honourable House of Assembly, towards it, considered" [1769] (NYPL).

"The Watchman No. 5." A supplementary broadside to Holt's *New-York Journal,* printed April 21, 1770 (NYPL).

MEMOIRS AND WRITINGS OF PUBLIC MEN

Burnett, Edmund C. (ed.), *Letters of Members of the Continental Congress* (8 vols.; Washington: The Carnegie Institution of Washington, 1921–1936).

Carter, Clarence Edwin (comp. & ed.), *The Correspondence of General Thomas Gage* (2 vols.; New Haven: Yale University Press, 1931–1933).

Cushing, Harry Alonzo (ed.), *The Writings of Samuel Adams* (4 vols.; New York: G. P. Putnam's Sons, 1904–1908).

De Chastellux, Marquis, *Travels in North-America in the Years 1780, 1781, and 1782* (2 vols.; London, 1787).

———, *Voyages De M. Le Marquis De Chastellux Dans L'Amerique Septentrionale Dans les années 1780, 1781 & 1782* (2 vols.; Paris, 1786).

De Riedesel, Madame, *Letters and Memoirs Relating to the War of American Independence and the Capture of the German Troops at Saratoga* (English translation; New York: G. & C. Carvill, 1827).

Division of Archives and History, University of the State of New York, *The Papers of Sir William Johnson* (12 vols.; Albany: University of the State of New York, 1921–1957).

Fitzpatrick, John C. (ed.), *The Diaries of George Washington* (4 vols.; Boston and New York: Houghton Mifflin Co., 1925).

———, *The Writings of George Washington, 1745–1799* (37 vols.; Washington: Government Printing Office, 1931–1940).

Hoffman, Ross J. S., *Edmund Burke, New York Agent with his letters to the New York Assembly and intimate correspondence with Charles O'Hara, 1761–1776* (Philadelphia: The American Philosophical Society, 1956).

Johnston, Henry P. (ed.), *The Correspondence and Public Papers of John Jay* (4 vols.; New York: G. P. Putnam's Sons, 1890–1893).

Kent, William (ed.), *Memoirs and Letters of James Kent* (Boston: Little, Brown & Co., 1898).

Sabine, William H. W. (ed.), *Historical Memoirs from 16 March 1763 to 9 July 1776 of William Smith* (New York: Colburn & Tegg, 1956).

———, *Historical Memoirs from 12 July 1776 to 25 July 1778 of William Smith* (New York: Colburn & Tegg, 1958).

Stone, William L. (trans.), *Memoirs, and Letters and Journals, of Major General Riedesel during his Residence in America* (3 vols.; Albany: J. Munsell, 1868).

Watson, Winslow C. (ed.), *Men and Times of the Revolution or Memoirs of Elkanah Watson* (2nd ed.; New York: Dana & Co., 1856).

OTHER PRIMARY SOURCES

Baxter, Katharine Schuyler, *A Godchild of Washington* (New York: F. Tennyson Neely, 1897).

[Becker, John P.], *The Sexagenary, or Reminiscences of the American Revolution* (Albany: W. C. Little & O. Steele, 1833).

Benson, Adolph B. (ed.), *Peter Kalm's Travels In North America* (2nd ed., 2 vols.; Albany: Wilson-Erickson Inc., 1937).

Bonney, Mrs. Catharina V. R. (comp.), *A Legacy of Historical Gleanings* (2nd ed., 2 vols.; Albany: J. Munsell, 1875).

[Bradstreet, John], *An Impartial Account of Lieut. Col. Bradstreet's Expedition to Fort Frontenac* (Toronto: Rous & Mann Ltd., 1940).

Collections of the New-York Historical Society (38 vols.; New York: The New-York Historical Society, 1868–1906).

Grant, Anne, *Memoirs of An American Lady* (2 vols.; New York: Dodd, Mead & Co., 1901).

Grant, W. L., and James Munro (eds.), *Acts of the Privy Council of England:*

Colonial Series (6 vols.; London: Anthony Brothers Ltd., The Hereford Times Co., Ltd., 1908–1912).

Greene, Evarts B., and Virginia D. Harrington, *American Population Before the Federal Census of 1790* (New York: Columbia University Press, 1932).

Meriwether, Coyler (ed.), *Publications of the Southern Historical Association* (Vols. VII, VIII; Washington, 1903–1904).

Moore, Frank (comp.), *The Diary of the Revolution, 1775–1781* (Hartford: J. B. Burr Publishing Co., 1876).

Munsell, Joel, *Collections on the History of Albany from its Discovery to the Present Time* (4 vols.; Albany: J. Munsell, 1865–1871).

——, *The Annals of Albany* (10 vols.; Albany: J. Munsell, 1850–1859).

Schuyler, Philip, Letters of 1776, 1777, 1779 in *Proceedings of the New Jersey Historical Society*, LXII (April, 1944).

Sparks, Jared (ed.), *Correspondence of the American Revolution* (4 vols.; Boston: Little, Brown & Co., 1853).

The Parliamentary Register; or, History of the Proceedings and Debates of the House of Commons (17 vols.; London: J. Walker, R. Lea and J. Nunn, 1802).

Werner, Edgar A., *Civil List and Constitutional History of the State of New York* (Albany: Weed, Parsons & Co., 1884 and 1888).

GENERAL HISTORIES

Alden, John Richard, *The American Revolution, 1775–1783* (New York: Harper & Brothers, 1954).

Alexander, De Alva Stanwood, *A Political History of the State of New York* (3 vols.; New York: Henry Holt & Co., 1906–1909).

Ellis, David M., James A. Frost, Harold C. Syrett, and Harry J. Carman, *A Short History of New York State* (Ithaca: Cornell University Press, 1957).

Fiske, John, *The American Revolution* (2 vols.; Boston: Houghton, Mifflin & Co., 1891).

Flick, Alexander (ed.), *History of the State of New York* (10 vols.; New York: Columbia University Press, 1933–1937).

Gipson, Lawrence Henry, *The British Empire Before the American Revolution: Provincial Characteristics and Sectional Tendencies in the Era Preceding the American Crisis* (10 vols.; Caldwell, Idaho: The Caxton Printers, Ltd.; New York: A. A. Knopf, 1936–1961).

——, *The Coming of the Revolution, 1763–1775* (London: Hamish Hamilton, 1954).

Jones, Thomas, *History of New York During the Revolutionary War*, ed. Edward Floyd De Lancey (2 vols.; New York: Trow's Printing & Bookbinding Co., 1879).

Maitland, F. W., *The Constitutional History of England* (Cambridge: Cambridge University Press, 1955).

338   BIBLIOGRAPHY

Trevelyan, George Otto, *The American Revolution* (new ed., 3 vols.; New York: Longmans, Green & Co., 1905–1908).
Ward, Christopher, *The War of the Revolution,* ed. John Richard Alden (2 vols.; New York: Macmillan Co., 1952).
Wright, Esmond, *Fabric of Freedom, 1763–1800* (New York: Hill & Wang, Inc., 1961).

BIOGRAPHIES AND SPECIAL MONOGRAPHS

Abbott, Wilbur C., *New York in the American Revolution* (New York: Charles Scribner's Sons, 1929).
Adams, Randolph G., *Political Ideas of the American Revolution* (3rd ed.; New York: Barnes and Noble, Inc., 1958).
Alden, John Richard, *General Charles Lee, Traitor or Patriot?* (Baton Rouge: Louisiana State University Press, 1951).
———, *General Gage in America* (Baton Rouge: Louisiana State University Press, 1948).
Alexander, Edward P., *A Revolutionary Conservative: James Duane of New York* (New York: Columbia University Press, 1938).
Barck, Oscar Theodore, Jr., *New York City During the War For Independence* (New York: Columbia University Press, 1931).
Beach, Allen C., *The Centennial Celebration of the State of New York* (Albany: Weed, Parsons & Co., 1879).
Becker, Carl Lotus, *The History of Political Parties in the Province of New York, 1760–1776* (Madison: University of Wisconsin Press, 1960).
Benton, R. C., *The Vermont Settlers and the New York Land Speculators* (Minneapolis: Housekeeper Press, 1894).
Bigelow, Harry A., *Introduction to the Law of Real Property: Rights in Land* (St. Paul, Minnesota: West Publishing Co., 1919).
Bond, Beverley W., Jr., *The Quit-Rent System in the American Colonies* (New Haven: Yale University Press, 1919).
Bond, Richmond P., *Queen Anne's American Kings* (Oxford: Clarendon Press, 1952).
Burnett, Edmund Cody, *The Continental Congress* (New York: Macmillan Co., 1941).
Burns, John F., *Controversies Between Royal Governors and Their Assemblies in the North American Colonies* (Boston: Wright & Potter Printing Co., 1923).
Chester, Alden (ed.), *Legal and Judicial History of New York* (3 vols.; New York: The National Americana Society, 1911).
Cochran, Thomas C., *New York in the Confederation* (Philadelphia: University of Pennsylvania Press, 1932).
Dangerfield, George, *Chancellor Robert R. Livingston of New York, 1746–1813* (New York: Harcourt, Brace & World Co., 1960).

Digby, Kenelm Edward, *An Introduction to the History of the Law of Real Property* (5th ed.; London: Clarendon Press, 1897).

Dillon, Dorothy Rita, *The New York Triumvirate* (New York: Columbia University Press, 1949).

Division of Archives and History, University of the State of New York, *The American Revolution in New York* (Albany: University of the State of New York, 1926).

East, Robert A., *Business Enterprise in the American Revolutionary Era* (New York: Columbia University Press, 1938).

Einstein, Lewis, *Divided Loyalties* (New York: Houghton Mifflin Co., 1933).

Ellis, David Maldwyn, *Landlords and Farmers in the Hudson-Mohawk Region, 1790–1850* (Ithaca: Cornell University Press, 1946).

Ford, Henry Jones, *Alexander Hamilton* (New York: Charles Scribner's Sons, 1920).

Fowler, Robert Ludlow, *History of the Law of Real Property in New York* (New York: Baker, Voorhis & Co., 1895).

Fox, Dixon Ryon, *Caleb Heathcote* (New York: Charles Scribner's Sons, 1926).

———, *The Decline of Aristocracy in the Politics of New York* (New York: Longmans, Green & Co., 1919).

———, *Yankees and Yorkers* (New York: New York University Press, 1940).

Hamilton, Allan McLane, *The Intimate Life of Alexander Hamilton* (New York: Charles Scribner's Sons, 1910).

Hamilton, John C., *The Life of Alexander Hamilton* (2 vols.; New York: Halsted & Voorhis, D. Appleton & Co., 1834–1840).

Hammond, Jabez D., *The History of Political Parties in the State of New York from the Ratification of the Federal Constitution to December, 1840* (2 vols.; Albany: C. Van Benthuysen, 1842).

Harrington, Virginia D., *The New York Merchant on the Eve of the Revolution* (New York: Columbia University Press, 1935).

Harris, Marshall, *Origin of the Land Tenure System in the United States* (Ames, Iowa: Iowa State University Press, 1953).

Hickcox, John H., *A History of the Bills of Credit or Paper Money Issued by New York, From 1709 to 1789* (Albany: J. H. Hickcox & Co., 1866).

Higgins, Ruth L., *Expansion in New York,* The Ohio State University Studies No. 14 (Columbus: Ohio State University, 1931).

Howell, George R., and Jonathan Tenney (eds.), *Bi-Centennial History of Albany: History of the County of Albany, N.Y., From 1609 to 1886* (New York: W. W. Munsell & Co., 1886).

Humphreys, Mary Gay, *Catherine Schuyler* (New York: Charles Scribner's Sons, 1897).

Ironside, Charles Edward, *The Family in Colonial New York* (New York: Columbia University, 1942).

Jameson, John Franklin, *The American Revolution Considered as a Social Movement* (Gloucester, Mass.: Peter Smith, 1926).

Jay, William, *The Life of John Jay* (2 vols.; New York: J. & J. Harper, 1833).

Knollenberg, Bernard, *Washington and the Revolution* (New York: Macmillan Co., 1940).

Labaree, Leonard Woods, *Conservatism in Early American History* (Ithaca: Cornell University Press, 1959).

Leonard, Lewis A., *Life of Charles Carroll of Carrollton* (New York: Moffat, Yard & Co., 1918).

Lilly, Edward P., *The Colonial Agents of New York and New Jersey* (Washington: Catholic University of America, 1936).

Livingston, Edwin Brockholst, *The Livingstons of Livingston Manor* (New York: Knickerbocker Press, 1910).

Lossing, Benson J., *History of American Industries and Arts* (Philadelphia: Porter & Coates, 1876).

——, *The Life and Times of Philip Schuyler* (2 vols.; New York: Sheldon & Co., 1872).

MacMillan, Margaret Burnham, *The War Governors in the American Revolution* (New York: Columbia University Press, 1943).

Mark, Irving, *Agrarian Conflicts in Colonial New York, 1711–1775* (New York: Columbia University Press, 1940).

McKee, Samuel, Jr., *Labor in Colonial New York, 1664–1776* (New York: Columbia University Press, 1935).

Miller, John C., *Origins of the American Revolution* (Boston: Little, Brown & Co., 1943).

——, *Triumph of Freedom* (Boston: Little, Brown & Co., 1948).

Mitchell, Broadus, *Alexander Hamilton: Youth to Maturity, 1755–1788* (New York: Macmillan Co., 1957).

Namier, L. B., *England in the Age of the American Revolution* (London & New York: Macmillan & Co., Ltd., and St. Martin's Press, Inc., 1930).

——, *The Structure of Politics at the Accession of George III* (2 vols.; London: Macmillan & Co., Ltd., 1929).

Pargellis, Stanley McCrory, *Lord Loudoun in North America* (New Haven: Yale University Press, 1933).

Pell, John, *Ethan Allen* (London: Constable & Co., Ltd., 1930).

Pound, Arthur, *Native Stock* (New York: Macmillan Co., 1931).

Ritcheson, Charles R., *British Politics and the American Revolution* (Norman, Okla.: University of Oklahoma Press, 1954).

Rossman, Kenneth R., *Thomas Mifflin and the Politics of the American Revolution* (Chapel Hill: University of North Carolina Press, 1952).

Schachner, Nathan, *Alexander Hamilton* (New York: D. Appleton-Century Co., Inc., 1946).

——, *The Founding Fathers* (New York: G. P. Putnam's Sons, 1954).

Schuyler, George W., *Colonial New York: Philip Schuyler and His Family* (2 vols.; New York: Charles Scribner's Sons, 1885).

Scott, Kenneth, *Counterfeiting in Colonial America* (New York: Oxford University Press, 1957).

Sosin, Jack M., *Whitehall and the Wilderness* (Lincoln, Nebr.: University of Nebraska Press, 1961).

Sparks, Jared, *The Life of Gouverneur Morris* (3 vols.; Boston: Gray & Bowen, 1832).

Spaulding, E. Wilder, *His Excellency George Clinton: Critic of the Constitution* (New York: Macmillan Co., 1938).

———, *New York in the Critical Period, 1783–1789* (New York: Columbia University Press, 1932).

Story, D. A., *The De Lanceys* (Halifax: Thomas Nelson & Sons, Ltd., 1931).

Tuckerman, Bayard, *Life of General Philip Schuyler, 1733–1804* (New York: Dodd, Mead & Co., 1903).

Ubbelohde, Carl, *The Vice-Admiralty Courts and the American Revolution* (Chapel Hill: University of North Carolina Press, 1960).

Umbreit, Kenneth, *Founding Fathers* (New York: Harper & Brothers, 1941).

Van Doren, Carl, *Benjamin Franklin* (New York: The Viking Press, 1938).

———, *Secret History of the American Revolution* (New York: The Viking Press, 1941).

Van Schaack, Henry C., *The Life of Peter Van Schaack, LL.D.* (New York: D. Appleton & Co., 1842).

Ver Steeg, Clarence L., *Robert Morris: Revolutionary Financier* (Philadelphia: University of Pennsylvania Press, 1954).

Vrooman, John J., *Forts and Firesides of the Mohawk Country New York* (Philadelphia: E. E. Brownell, 1943).

Weise, Arthur J., *The History of the City of Albany, New York* (Albany: E. H. Bender, 1884).

Wilbur, James Benjamin, *Ira Allen Founder of Vermont, 1751–1814* (2 vols.; Boston: Houghton Mifflin Co., 1928).

Williamson, Chilton, *American Suffrage From Property to Democracy, 1760–1860* (Princeton: Princeton University Press, 1960).

Wright, Louis B., *The Cultural Life of the American Colonies, 1607–1763* (London: Hamish Hamilton, Ltd., 1957).

ARTICLES AND ESSAYS IN PERIODICALS, ANNUALS,
AND PUBLICATIONS OF LEARNED SOCIETIES

Becker, Carl Lotus, "Nominations in Colonial New York," *American Historical Review,* VI (Jan., 1901).

———, "The Growth of Revolutionary Parties and Methods in New York Province, 1765–1774," *American Historical Review,* VII (Oct., 1901).

Champagne, Roger, "New York and the Intolerable Acts, 1774," *The New-York Historical Society Quarterly*, XLV (April, 1961).

Comstock, Helen, "The Schuyler Mansion, Albany, New York," *The Connoisseur Year Book, 1952* (London, 1952).

Delafield, John Ross, "An Armory of American Families of Dutch Descent," *New York Genealogical and Biographical Record*, LXIX (Jan., 1938).

Edwards, George William, "New York City Politics Before the American Revolution," *Political Science Quarterly*, XXVI (Dec., 1921).

Ekirch, Arthur A., Jr., "Thomas Eddy and the Beginnings of Prison Reform in New York," *New York History*, XXIV (July, 1943).

Elkins, Stanley, and Eric McKitrick, "The Founding Fathers: Young Men of the Revolution," *Political Science Quarterly*, LXXVI (June, 1961).

Ellis, David Maldwyn, "Albany and Troy—Commercial Rivals," *New York History*, XXIV (Oct., 1943).

Flick, Hugh M., "The Council of Appointment in New York State," *New York History*, XV (July, 1934).

Goebel, Julius L., Jr., "Some Legal and Political Aspects of the Manors in New York," Publication No. 18 of the Order of Colonial Lords of Manors in America (Baltimore, 1928).

Gregg, C. E., "General Philip Schuyler and the Schuyler Mansion," *The Dutch Settlers Society of Albany Yearbook*, XXV–XXVI (Albany, 1949–1951).

Kenney, Alice P., "The Albany Dutch: Loyalists and Patriots," *New York History*, XLII (Oct., 1961).

Kenyon, Cecelia M., "Republicanism and Radicalism in the American Revolution: An Old-Fashioned Interpretation," *The William and Mary Quarterly:* Third Series, XIX (April, 1962).

Klein, Milton M., "Democracy and Politics in Colonial New York," *New York History*, XL (July, 1959).

——, "Prelude to Revolution in New York: Jury Trials and Judicial Tenure," *The William and Mary Quarterly:* Third Series, XVII (Oct., 1960).

——, "The Rise of the New York Bar: The Legal Career of William Livingston," *The William and Mary Quarterly:* Third Series, XV (July, 1958).

Lynd, Staughton, "Who Should Rule at Home? Dutchess County, New York, in the American Revolution," *The William and Mary Quarterly:* Third Series, XVIII (July, 1961).

Mather, Frederic G., "The Schuyler House at Albany," *Magazine of American History*, XII (New York, 1884).

McAnear, Beverly, "The Albany Stamp Act Riots," *The William and Mary Quarterly:* Third Series, IV (Oct., 1947).

Morris, Richard B., "Class Struggle and the American Revolution," *The William and Mary Quarterly:* Third Series, XIX (Jan., 1962).

——, "Primogeniture and Entailed Estates in America," *Columbia Law Review*, XXVII (1927).

Naylor, Rex Maurice, "The Royal Prerogative in New York, 1691–1775," *The Quarterly Journal of the New York State Historical Association,* V (July, 1924).

Sachs, William S., "Agricultural Conditions in the Northern Colonies Before the Revolution," *Journal of Economic History,* XIII (Summer, 1953).

Schuyler, Montgomery, "The Patroons and Lords of Manors of the Hudson," Publication No. 23 of the Order of Colonial Lords of Manors in America (New York, 1932).

———, "The Schuyler Family," Publication No. 16 of the Order of Colonial Lords of Manors in America (New York, 1926).

Schuyler, Robert Livingston, "Philip Schuyler," *New York History,* XVIII (April, 1937).

The Order of Colonial Lords of Manors in America Year Book No. 27 (New York, 1911–1936).

Tolles, Frederick B., "The American Revolution Considered as a Social Movement: A Re-evaluation," *American Historical Review,* LX (Oct., 1954).

Van Tyne, C. H., "Review of Tuckerman's Life of General Philip Schuyler," *American Historical Review,* X (Oct., 1904).

Varga, Nicholas, "Robert Charles: New York Agent, 1748–1770," *The William and Mary Quarterly:* Third Series, XVIII (April, 1961).

———, "The New York Restraining Act: Its Passage and Some Effects, 1766–1768," *New York History,* XXXVII (July, 1956).

Williamson, Chilton, "New York's Impact on the Canadian Economy," *New York History,* XXIV (Jan., 1943).

MISCELLANEOUS

Albany's Tercentenary, 1624–1924 (Albany, 1924). A souvenir booklet.

Champagne, Roger James, "The Sons of Liberty and the Aristocracy in New York Politics, 1765–1790" (Ph.D. dissertation, the University of Wisconsin, 1960).

Cunningham, Anna K., *Schuyler Mansion a Critical Catalogue of the Furnishings & Decorations* (Albany: New York State Education Department, 1955).

Eberlein, Harold Donaldson, *The Manors and Historic Homes of the Hudson Valley* (Philadelphia: J. B. Lippincott Co., 1924).

Gerlach, Don R., "Philip Schuyler and the Continental Congress, 1775–1777" (M.A. thesis, University of Nebraska, 1956).

Giuseppi, Montagu S., *A Guide to the Manuscripts preserved in the Public Record Office* (2 vols.; London: Sir Joseph Causton & Sons, Ltd., 1923–1924).

Hamm, Margherita Arlina, *Famous Families of New York* (2 vols.; New York: G. P. Putnam's Sons, 1901).

Hatfield, Laura Adella, "The Frontier Policy of New York to 1776" (M.A. thesis, University of Chicago, 1916).

Howell, George Rogers, "The Origin and Meaning of English and Dutch Surnames of New York State Families (pamphlet: address to the Albany Institute, May 15, 1894).

Kent, James, "An Anniversary Discourse Delivered Before the New-York Historical Society, December 6, 1828" (New York: G. & C. Carvill, 1829).

Krout, John A., "Philip Schuyler," *Dictionary of American Biography*, ed. Allen Johnson, *et al.*, (20 vols.; New York: Charles Scribner's Sons, 1943), XVI, 477–480.

Lossing, Benson J., *The Pictorial Field-Book of the Revolution* (2 vols.; New York: Harper and Brothers, 1860).

Mason, Bernard, "Organization of the Revolutionary Movement in New York State, 1775–1777" (Ph.D. dissertation, Columbia University, 1958).

Mosca, Gaetano, *The Ruling Class*, ed. Arthur Livingston; trans. Hannah D. Kahn (New York: McGraw-Hill Book Co., Inc., 1939).

Munsell, Joel, "The Schuyler Family" (privately printed, 1874).

Proctor, L. B., "Historical Memories of the Old Schuyler Mansion" [Albany, 1888], pamphlet.

Reynolds, Cuyler (ed.), *Hudson-Mohawk Genealogical and Family Memoirs* (4 vols.; New York: Lewis Historical Publishing Co., 1911).

Schuyler, George L., *Correspondence and Remarks upon Bancroft's History of the Northern Campaign of 1777, and the Character of Major-Gen. Philip Schuyler* (New York: David G. Francis, 1867).

Schuyler, Georgina, "The Schuyler Mansion at Albany: Residence of Major-General Philip Schuyler, 1762–1804" (New York: De Vinne Press, 1911), pamphlet.

Stoddart, Jessie, "Home Rule and the Development of the American Revolution New York, 1760–1775" (M.A. thesis, University of Nebraska, 1961).

Williams, Sherman, *New York's Part in History* (New York: D. Appleton & Co., 1915).

Acknowledgments

My study of Philip Schuyler and the American Revolution began when I commenced graduate training in history in the autumn of 1954. From that day to this I have enjoyed the assistance and encouragement of several accomplished teachers and scholars. To Professor John Richard Alden I owe the inception of my interest in Philip Schuyler as well as the earliest direction of my research. Professor Aubrey C. Land ably guided my first written efforts and also has been most helpful in putting the book into its final form. Dr. Jack M. Sosin afforded the last major supervision of my doctoral dissertation entitled, "Philip Schuyler: The Origins of a Conservative Patriot, 1733-1777, A Study in Provincial Politics and the American Revolution in New York" (from whence this book sprang). I am particularly grateful for his critical but solicitous guidance. Not only did he steer me around pitfalls, force me to rethink interpretations and to sharpen my perceptiveness, but to him I am deeply indebted for the encouragement that only a good adviser can offer. Professors E. David Cronon, Robert Forster, and James C. Olson kindly offered corrections and suggestions. Professor Glenn W. Gray provided special assistance for Appendix C. And George Dangerfield graciously furnished some particularly good suggestions; I am grateful for his encouragement.

My thanks are likewise due the University of Nebraska for providing funds for microfilming, scholarships, and fellowships which enabled me to complete this study with a minimum of interruption. A Fulbright Scholarship offered me the invaluable experience of dipping into British archives and of imbibing the spirit of English history so helpful for an appreciation of colonial America.

The courteous service of librarians, archivists, and others, in this country and in England, is also worthy of acknowledgment. Mr. Robert W. Hill, Keeper of the Manuscripts, and his assistant, Miss Jean McNiece, of the New York Public Library, Mr. Wilmer R. Leech and Mr. Arthur J. Breton of the New-York Historical Society, Miss Juliet Wolohan, Senior Librarian of the New York State Library Manuscripts and History Section, Dr. Albert B. Corey, New York State Historian, Mr. Norman Rice, Curator of the Albany Institute of History and Art, and Mr. William Campbell, custodian of the Schuyler mansion, facilitated my researches and greatly added to the enjoyment of my labors.

Whatever merits are found in these pages are in no small measure due to the contributions of others. The errors are my own. It is perhaps fitting that the author indicate his reluctance to offer any final word on Philip Schuyler's life to 1777. Indeed, should this small contribution require any corrections because of his misjudgments, he trusts it shall have nonetheless furthered the development of Clio's cult and fostered a better understanding of the nature of eighteenth-century American politics and the role that individuals played in the origins of the republic.

The following publishers, libraries, and copyright owners have kindly granted permission to make quotations from the sources indicated in the bibliography: Cambridge University Press; the Carnegie Institution of Washington; Colburn and Tegg of New York; Columbia University Libraries; Columbia University Press; Harper and Brothers; Harcourt, Brace and World, Inc.; Hill and Wang, Inc.; Iowa State University Press; Louisiana State University Press; Macmillan and Company, Ltd., London; McGraw-Hill Book Company, Inc.; Mr. Arthur Pound; *New York History* magazine; Professor Ross J. S. Hoffman; Princeton University Press; St. Martin's Press, Inc., of New York; the American Philosophical Society; the Institute of Early American History and Culture; Macmillan Company of New York; the New-York Historical Society; the New York Public Library; the New York State Library; the Regents of the University of Wisconsin and the University of Wisconsin Press; the University of the State of New York; West Publishing Company of St. Paul, Minnesota; and the William L. Clements Library of the University of Michigan.

Index